SELECTED NONFICTION, 1962–2007

SELECTED NONFICTION, 1962–2007

J. G. BALLARD

EDITED BY MARK BLACKLOCK

FOREWORD BY TOM MCCARTHY

THE MIT PRESS   CAMBRIDGE, MASSACHUSETTS   LONDON, ENGLAND

This book was set in ITC Stone and Avenir by New Best-set Typesetters Ltd. Printed and bound in the United States of America.

Library of Congress Cataloging-in-Publication Data is available.

ISBN: 978-0-262-04832-3

10 9 8 7 6 5 4 3 2 1

CONTENTS

FOREWORD

Putting Ballard on a Master's course list, as I've done a couple of times, provokes a reaction that's both funny and illuminating. Asked to read *Crash* or *The Atrocity Exhibition*, the more vociferous students invariably express their revulsion for both, while the more reflective ones voice their frustration that, although the ideas might be compelling, the prose "isn't good." This is especially the case with students who've been exposed to creative writing classes: they complain that the books are so full of repetition they become machinic or monotonous; also that they lack solid, integrated characters with whom they can identify, instead endlessly breaking open any given plot or *mise-en-scène* to other external or even unconnected scenes, contexts, and histories, resulting in a kind of schizoid narrative space that's full of everyone and no one.

This second group, of course, is absolutely right in its analysis; what's funny (and, if I can teach them anything, reversible) about their judgment is that it is these very elements (repetition, machinism, schizoid hypermnesia) that make Ballard's work so brilliant. Not only are his rhythmic cycles in which phrases and images return in orders and arrangements that mutate and reconfigure themselves as though following some algorithm that remains beyond our grasp, at once incantatory, hallucinatory, and the very model and essence of poetry; they also, mirroring the way that information, advertising, propaganda, public (and private) dialogue, and even consciousness itself run in reiterative loops and circuits, constitute a realism far exceeding that of the misnamed literary genre. If his personae are split, multiplied, dispersed, this is because they are true subjects of a networked and fragmented hypermodernity—ones for whom identification, if it is to amount to anything more than a consoling fiction, must come through man's recognition of himself (as Georges Bataille put it) not in the degrading chains of logic but instead, with rage and ecstatic torment, in the virulence of his own phantasms.

While Ballard's more outwardly conventional books may give us solider, more stable realities, what these realities often present—in, for example, *Empire of the Sun*, digestible enough for a blockbuster Spielberg adaptation—is a child (or childlike figure) frolicking against a backdrop provided by the destruction of an older order of reality the world previously took for granted. It's a cipher for his oeuvre as a whole: endlessly playing among the ruins, reassembling the broken or "found" pieces (styles, genres, codes, histories) with a passion rendered all the more intense and focused by the knowledge that it's all—culture, the social order, the beliefs that underpin civilization—*constructed*, and can just as easily be unconstructed, reverse-engineered back down to the barbaric shards from which it was cobbled together in the first place. To put it in Dorothean: in every context and at every level, Ballard's gaze is fixed, fixated, on the man behind the curtain, not the wizard.

Ballard's novels are radical in the true sense, in that they reach back to and reanimate the novel's very roots. The presence of *Robinson Crusoe* in *Concrete Island* is glaring, as (I'd say) is that in *Crash* of *Tristram Shandy*, with its fascination with speeding mechanized land-yachts and the springs of broken carriages, with the geometry of ramparts, trenches, culverts, all superimposed on Uncle Toby's genital mutilation, his obsession with restaging assorted topologies of conflict. Or, for that matter, *Don Quixote*, with its hero's obsessive reenactments on the public highways of iconic moments from popular entertainment, the triumphs and tragedies of those late-medieval movie stars, knights-errant. And doesn't the same propensity for modulating and monotonously lullabying list-making run through Joyce, the Sinbad the Sailors and Tinbad the Tailers and Jinbad the Jailors parading through Bloom's mind as he drifts into sleep? Doesn't the same techno-apocalyptic imaginary characterize Conrad's bomb-carrying Professor, whose "thoughts caressed the images of ruin and destruction"? We could drag the literary cursor forward, through Ingeborg Bachmann, William Burroughs, Kathy Acker—or, indeed, all the way back to Homer and Aeschylus, to wheel-mounted wooden horses, flashing beacons, falling towers.

Ballard's intelligence (and I use that term in its dual sense of intellectual capacity and source/input-feed or "intel") is expanded, encompassing a field comprising not just literature but also visual art (most notably the work of the surrealists), cinema, psychoanalysis, sociology, and technological invention. Given his much-repeated claim that facts, real-world events, and ever more pervasive media are taking over from fiction, it seems high time that his own copious nonfiction output should be gathered together and laid bare to the same scrutiny—even if he would have rejected the distinction. Here, no less than in the novels, we're treated, on repeat, to the forging of connections that, utterly counterintuitive though they may be, leap out like lightning flashes in their ineluctable lucidity: from the Wright Brothers to the contraceptive pill via "the social and sexual philosophy of the ejector seat"; or from Hitler to the aforementioned Bloom via their common diet of the half-digested reference library, "vague artistic yearnings and clap-trap picked up from popular magazines." And here, no less than in the novels too, Ballard cements his place as one of English prose's finest lyricists, conjuring from "the plane of intersection of the body of this woman in my room with the cleavage of Elizabeth Taylor" an image of "the glazed eyes of Chiang Kai Shek, an invasion plan of the offshore islands"; sounding the desolate immensity of Spain's Rio Seco, "the great deck of the drained river running inland, crossed by the white span of a modern motor bridge" beyond which extend "secret basins of cracked mud the size of ballrooms, models of a state of mind, a curvilinear labyrinth" while "juke-boxes play in the bars of Benidorm" and "the molten sea swallows the shadow of the Guardia Civil helicopter"; or (most haunting of all) affirming in a *credo* which, should I ever become supreme spiritual leader of a postrevolutionary Britain, I will institute as the prime text of national liturgy, replacing the defunct Lord's Prayer:

I believe in the mysterious beauty of Margaret Thatcher, in the arch of her nostrils and the sheen on her lower lip; in the melancholy of wounded Argentine conscripts; in the haunted smiles of filling station personnel; in my dream of Margaret Thatcher caressed by that young Argentine soldier in a forgotten motel watched by a tubercular filling station attendant.

Tom McCarthy, 2023

INTRODUCTION

J. G. Ballard was a journalist for as long as he was a professional writer of fiction. In November 1956, his short story "Prima Belladona" was published in *Science Fantasy*. Around the spring of the following year, John "Ted" Carnell, the editor who'd bought that piece for £8, found him a job as an assistant editor on a trade journal, *British Baker*. In the autumn, he moved on to work for the Society of the Chemical Industry: "I had heard that there was a vacancy as assistant editor at *Chemistry & Industry*, at a much better salary, so I went there . . . I was there for three or four years as assistant editor. I did practically everything."[1] He remembered the job fondly, recalling that he "devoured" the scientific magazines that came into the office, and worked across the process of magazine production, subbing, editing, and pasting layout. "I enjoyed being at the centre of a huge information flow." The salary enabled him to support his young family and to continue to contribute stories to Ted Carnell at *Science Fantasy* and *New Worlds*.

In April 1962, his essay "Which Way to Inner Space?" was published in the May issue of *New Worlds* as a guest editorial, a statement of what Ballard saw as a fresh direction for SF. Declaring that "earth is the only truly alien planet," "Which Way" began the staking out of territory for what would come to be called the New Wave of science fiction, a loose collection of writers, as much as a movement, who were reinventing the form and content of a genre that had been dominated by its debt to H. G. Wells, to alien planets, rocket ships, and tales of interstellar adventure.

---

1. J. G. Ballard, "The Profession of Science Fiction, 26: From Shanghai to Shepperton," *Foundation* 24 (1982): 5–23 (17).

In February 1964, *New Worlds* was sold, and the twenty-three-year-old Michael Moorcock took over as editor on Ted Carnell's recommendation. Moorcock, who described Ballard as "Trotski" to his Lenin, set about transforming the magazine. While Ballard's own stories mutated into the condensed fictions that would be collected as *The Atrocity Exhibition*, a series of review-essays appeared, directing readers' attention to an alternative canon: the art of Salvador Dalí and the surrealists, the experimental fiction of William Burroughs, and the satires of Wyndham Lewis. Alongside these were provocative reviews; of *Mein Kampf*, and a dissection of an example of what Ballard termed "invisible literature," in the form of a popular sexual self-help manual ("Use Your Vagina," this volume, 46).

The jobbing journalist, meanwhile, continued to operate alongside the polemicist. In 1962, Ballard had begun reviewing books for *Chemistry & Industry*, eventually contributing twenty-three pieces to the journal by 1965. From 1965 to 1967, he contributed sixteen reviews to the book pages of the *Guardian*, predominantly round-ups of science fiction, but with a revealing foray into nonfiction territory: Michael Siffre's account of living in a cave for several months was an exemplary exploration of the "inner space" Ballard had declared the concern of his fiction. From then on, allowing for a couple of hiatuses, he was barely out of print in the British broadsheet newspapers until his last piece was published in the *Guardian* in late 2007, a year after the publication of his final novel, *Kingdom Come* (2006).

*

The first part of Ballard's biography is well known, mythologized in the quasi-autobiographical novel *Empire of the Sun* (1984) and Steven Spielberg's 1987 film adaptation. James Graham Ballard was born in 1930 in Shanghai, where his father ran the China Printing and Finishing Company, a subsidiary of the Calico Printers Association. He grew up just beyond the official boundary of the International Settlement.

In 1937, Japan invaded China and the occupying forces captured Shanghai. The Ballards moved to the safer French Concession, and while the international city was left to its own devices, the brutality and violence of the occupying Japanese was visible at the perimeter of their lives.

In December 1941, immediately following the bombing of Pearl Harbor, Japanese troops seized the International Settlement, and in March 1943 the Ballard family were interned in the Lunghua civilian camp, where they remained until August 1945.

Following the end of the war, Ballard shipped back to England, where he encountered a "derelict, dark and half-ruined" country.[2] He was sent to board at the Leys School in Cambridge. In 1949, he began studying medicine at King's College, Cambridge University, dropping out after completing the anatomy course at the end of his second year. He spent two terms studying English literature at Queen Mary's College, then worked as an advertising copywriter, as a porter at Covent Garden Market, and for a period selling the Waverley Encyclopedia door-to-door in the West Midlands. In 1954, he signed on for the RAF, undertaking basic training in Lincolnshire before shipping to Canada for six months flight training in Moosejaw, Saskatchewan.

Looking back on this early life, the writer would identify the formation in these experiences of ideas and images that informed his life's work: the idea that civilization was a stage set, and that at any time the apparent reality of normal life could be stripped away; that powerful unconscious forces could drive entire populations to acts of irrationality and violence; the symbolic resonance of drained swimming pools, atomic bombs, grounded pilots, and enclosed communities. Inspired by the science fiction magazines he read during his downtime in Canada, he landed on a field of literature in which his imagination could work with these impulses.

Shortly after returning to England in 1955, he married Mary Matthews, and early the next year, their son James was born. Their daughters Fay and Bea followed in 1957 and 1959.

Despite early rejections from the American magazines he'd read in Canada, Ballard's short fiction soon found a home in *New Worlds* and *Science Fantasy*, where Ted Carnell championed its innovation: as early as 1957, Carnell was styling him "one of Britain's most promising new writers."[3] Obsessed with the "inner space" of his characters' psychology, conscious

---

2. J. G. Ballard, *Miracles of Life* (London: Harper Perennial, 2008), 122.
3. "Manhole 69," *New Worlds* 22, no. 65 (November 1957): 45.

and unconscious, and how they responded to the physics of the universe and the mysteries of "deep time," Ballard's short fiction explored the intersection of extreme psychic states and alienated landscapes—deserts, bases, atolls, and resorts.

His first novel was written in a two-week holiday from work in order to slingshot his professional career. In 1961, *To Reap the Whirlwind* was sold to Berkley Books in New York, published as *The Wind from Nowhere* in 1962. *The Drowned World*, published in the United States later the same year, and at the beginning of 1963 by Victor Gollancz in the United Kingdom, was the true career breakthrough, attracting the admiration of the British novelist Kingsley Amis, who became a friend and champion in the early years of Ballard's career. In May 1965, *The Drought* was published in the United Kingdom, and *The Crystal World* in 1966. Between his first four novels, Ballard had imagined a world consumed by wind, flood, drought, and, finally, transformed into crystal, as well as a suite of characters who wished to merge with these metamorphic environments.

Just as his career was taking off, his young family suffered the shock of the sudden death of Mary following a rapid illness during a holiday in Alicante, Spain, in 1965. Ballard drove his three children home to bring them up as a single father.

If his work of the preceding decade had taken on the SF establishment, the series of nonlinear, "condensed novels" written between 1966 and 1969 and collected as *The Atrocity Exhibition* (1970) were yet more confrontational. Loosely bound by a series of repeating characters, these borrowed vocabularies from the invisible literatures of scholarly psychology papers and scientific manuals and, using avant-garde cues and techniques, treated celebrities from the media environment and obscene imagery as elements in a clinical collage.

In January 1968, the Unicorn bookshop in Brighton was raided by police, and among the publications seized was a pamphlet copy of one such piece, "Why I Want to Fuck Ronald Reagan." Ballard agreed to appear as a witness for the defense in the subsequent obscenity trial but was stood down on the grounds that he did indeed intend his work to be obscene. The belated discovery of the same piece in the proposed first US edition of *The Atrocity Exhibition* by publisher Nelson Doubleday precipitated the pulping of the entire run.

Through the late 1960s, Moorcock, Ballard, and *New Worlds* were contributors to a thriving counterculture. As fiction editor at *Ambit*, where a number of *The Atrocity Exhibition* pieces had first been published, Ballard ran a competition for the best short story written under the influence of drugs. The winning piece, by Ann Quinn, was written while the author was using the birth control pill. By the end of the decade, Ballard was following a new obsession. In April 1970, he exhibited three wrecked cars at the New Arts Laboratory in Camden, as a way of testing the waters for the book that was coming. The drunken opening night confirmed his suspicion that the car crash was a fertilizing libidinal force.

Crash (1973), in which a group of middle-class professionals pursue anatomical sexual fantasies by instigating collisions and accidents to fuse their bodies with those of cars, described by Simon Sellars as "the blackest intellectual meat," was the first in the "urban disaster trilogy" of the 1970s.[4] Notoriously, a reader for publisher Jonathan Cape reported that "the author is beyond psychiatric help."[5] Next came *Concrete Island* (1974), a Robinsonade in which an architect becomes marooned in the wasteland below the Westway motorway with a tramp and a prostitute. *High-Rise* (1975) imagined the social breakdown of a hierarchically organized tower-block and the changes among its inhabitants as they create new lives within the malfunctioning society. All three novels were characterized by a nerveless refusal to blink from an extreme logic.

At the end of the decade, *The Unlimited Dream Company* (1979) seemed to mark a new phase in his work, turning his hometown of Shepperton into a tropical phantasmagoria, a shifting superfluity of desire, dream, and nature, fertilized by its narrator's unconscious. *Hello America* (1981) transformed the United States into an entropic wasteland ruled by a despot called Charles Manson. *The Day of Creation* (1987) and *Rushing to Paradise* (1994) described ecological fever-dreams of African rivers and Pacific islands. Among these, the novel that made him a household

---

4. Simon Sellars, "Introduction: A Launchpad for Other Explorations," in *Extreme Metaphors: Selected Interviews with J. G. Ballard, 1967–2008*, ed. Simon Sellars and Dan O'Hara (London: Fourth Estate, 2012), xi–xx (xiii).
5. "The reader in question was Catherine Storr (née Peters), second wife of the psychiatrist Anthony Storr." David Pringle, "J. G. Ballard Chronology: 1971–1975," in *Deep Ends 2019* (Powell River: The Terminal Press, 2019), 8–35 (17).

name, *Empire of the Sun*, and its first-person sequel, *The Kindness of Women* (1991), reimagined his own autobiography as mythologized fiction.

A new experiment, *Running Wild* (1988), an illustrated crime novella in documentary form describing the investigation into murders committed by children in a gated community, anticipated his final quartet of novels. Glossy covers disguised *Cocaine Nights* (1996) and *Super-Cannes* (2000) as airport reads for unwary holidaymakers. *Millennium People* (2003) and *Kingdom Come* (2006) brought closer to home his final, enduring theme, of the cosseted middle classes seeking relief from the boredom of insulated contemporary life in acts of violence.

*

The reputation and influence of Ballard's body of work has increased since his death. The contemporary art world paid handsome tribute with the exhibition *Crash* at the Gagosian Gallery in London in early 2010, conceived as a response to his "enormous cultural significance."[6] With Ballard's own *Project for a New Novel* billboard pieces (1958) at its heart, *Crash* collected work by artists most admired by Ballard—Salvador Dalí, Giorgio de Chirico, Paul Delvaux, Francis Bacon—alongside that by contemporary artists directly responsive to his writing—pieces such as Tacita Dean's *Teignmouth Electron, Cayman Brac (Ballard)* (1999), Ed Ruscha's *Fountain of Crystal* (2009), and Jake and Dinos Chapman's multiple edition, the paperback *Bang, Wallop, By J&D Ballard* (2010).

Fan communities, centered around a core of enthusiasts and collectors, active mailing lists, and numerous websites, have flourished. Simon Sellars's Ballardian.com was a hub from 2005 to 2020 and spawned two books: *Extreme Metaphors* (2012), coedited with Dan O'Hara, which collected Ballard's interviews, "a second sun" in the context of his written corpus, that displayed a "disarming mix of full-frontal future-shock and old-world, erudite charm."[7] Sellars's "theory-fiction" *Applied Ballardianism*, a fantastical, hybrid account of his obsession with and academic

---

6. Kay Pallister and Mark Francis, eds., *Crash: Homage to JG Ballard* (London: Gagosian, 2010), 6.

7. "Introduction," in *Extreme Metaphors*, xx.

thought about Ballard's work, was published in 2018.[8] At "The Digital Ballard," Mike Bonsall maintains an online concordance and links to his several twitter bots. The para-academic *Deep Ends* annual issue, published by the collector Rick McGrath since 2014, continues to present work by artists, scholars, and enthusiasts responding to Ballard, providing an ongoing catalog of research and miscellany. Serialized in its pages since the 2015 issue, David Pringle's detailed chronology of Ballard's life and work provides the most comprehensive biographical resource yet published.

Ben Wheatley's critically acclaimed *High-Rise* (2015) was the first new film adaptation of a Ballard novel since Jonathan Weiss's 1998 version of *The Atrocity Exhibition*, a low-budget piece warmly welcomed by the author, who contributed a commentary to the DVD. Wheatley's movie, with its A-list cast, reignited discussions of the political valences of Ballard's 1970s novel at a time when austerity policies in the United Kingdom had resurfaced questions of social inequality. At the time of writing, two new screen adaptations are hotly anticipated: Brandon Cronenberg, the son of director David Cronenberg, whose own adaptation of Ballard's *Crash* was the source of bitter controversy, will helm a serialized *Super-Cannes*. *The Road* director John Hillcoat is making a feature film of *Running Wild*.

The ripples of cultural impact do not end there. In the tradition of the alternative musicians of the 1970s who found inspiration in *The Atrocity Exhibition* and *Crash*—Joy Division, Gary Numan, and The Normal—contemporary releases by bands such as Squid, Danny Brown, and TVAM have continued to pay tribute. Even the fashion industry has signed up to Ballard fandom, with a number of high-profile designers referencing his work.

As indicative of influence as these are, the listing of cultural productions can only take us so far. Writing in the catalog to the *Crash* exhibition, Will Self observes: "When Ballard died, the location of his 'influence' in this genre or that medium was a relatively easy task to undertake; what was more difficult for commentators to grasp was how insidiously in the preceding five decades the Ballardian had become the commonplace."[9] As a writer, Ballard had staked out a distinct territory: the suburbs, the rise

---

8. Simon Sellars, *Applied Ballardianism* (Falmouth: Urbanomic, 2018).
9. "The Bounds of Inner Space," in *Crash: Homage to JG Ballard*, 25–29 (29).

of "politics conducted as a branch of advertising," the alienating effects of technologies, and the idea that boredom would drive the middle classes to acts of violence ("Introduction to the French Edition of *Crash!*," this volume, 13). For many observers, reality has mapped onto the ground he had already occupied.

Examples have not been hard to find as reality television stars have become presidents and the health of prime ministers has been tracked in real time in TV chyrons. Self was among the commentators quick to identify the parallels between Ballard's work and the experiences of enforced isolation during the COVID-19 pandemic, addressing BBC R4's flagship news program *Today*.[10] The next riot in a shopping mall seems perpetually five minutes into the future.

*

Rare are the writers whose careers span so many phases or endure for half a century: from leading genre writer and reformist, through confrontational avant-gardist and countercultural provocateur to garlanded mainstream novelist. Rarer still are those whose aesthetic is so distinct it spawns a commonly used adjectival form. The indexing of a career's worth of obsessions presents an acute difficulty, and if we are to ask what it is about Ballard's work that has achieved this level of imaginative reach and prescience, his short nonfiction is an essential resource.

This collection comes about to answer a need. Exploring the archive of papers donated to the British Library in 2010, I happened across a printout of a catalog essay for a Robert Smithson exhibition, shared with the artist Tacita Dean, with whom Ballard had been corresponding. The piece "Robert Smithson as Cargo Cultist" is a rich appreciation of the canonical works of the land artist, displaying some typical Ballardian nonfictional strategies: a pair of provocative, suggestive, and eloquent questions open an engagement with Smithson's work from within the imaginative world of that work: "What cargo might have berthed at the Spiral Jetty? And

---

10. Will Self, "Today," *BBC R4*, April 14, 2020. See also Mark O'Connell, "Why We Are Living in JG Ballard's World," *New Statesman*, April 1, 2020, https://www.news tatesman.com/long-reads/2020/04/why-we-are-living-jg-ballard-s-world.

what strange caravel could have emerged from the saline mists of this remote lake and chosen to dock at this mysterious harbour?" ("Robert Smithson as Cargo Cultist," this volume, 99).

The Smithson piece had never been collected and was only available in its original publication in an obscure catalog, which is why he had sent a copy to Dean. I began to consider what else might be hard to locate or uncollected. David Pringle's bibliography, including 236 items of short nonfiction, revealed how much new journalism was published in the late 1990s and early 2000s and had therefore escaped capture in the only previous collection, *A User's Guide to the Millennium* (1996).[11]

A new collection, bringing together more of this dispersed writing in a new arrangement, provides a selection of materials to illuminate the full range of Ballard's activities as a reviewer, essayist, journalist, commentator, memoirist, provocateur, compiler of lists, and talking head. The categories under which it is organized have been devised to assist easy navigation; on occasion the hybridity of certain pieces has suggested multiple possible categorizations and, in such instances, the reader's patience is begged: chapter headings are aids and are not intended to be secure or definitive.

The first such categorization is perhaps the most contentious. None of four pieces in the opening section, "Statements," were explicitly issued as manifestoes (though one of them is undeniably a credo). Ballard refused the idea that he had such a formalized approach to his work, responding to Mark Dery in interview: "Some of your questions seem to challenge me on the grounds that I don't have a complete manifesto, a party platform that will address all questions—you know, 'What are your views on the common-market agricultural policy? What are your views on abortion?' I don't have set-piece answers; I have question marks."[12] Yet the work he and Moorcock were undertaking in *New Worlds* was admittedly polemical in nature.

What is indisputable is that a number of pieces have become key points of reference for framing Ballard's work at different stages in his career. These have been pulled out to the front of the book to give a

---

11. "Bibliography," in *Crash: Homage to JG Ballard*, 179–191.
12. Mark Dery, "Sex Drive," in *21C: The Magazine of Culture, Technology and Science* 24 (1997): 40–51 (47).

snapshot not just of the concerns of Ballard's work at the points in time at which they were written, but also a taste of the formal variety that the collection will encompass. These statements provide helpful conceptual orientation: Ballard will refer frequently in his early reviews and essays to "inner space," while the "death of affect," a muting of emotional response to an oversaturated mediascape, becomes a guiding principle for understanding his protagonists. The surrealists, whose images and ideas nourish his oeuvre, will jostle throughout.

Of the manifesto form, Mary Ann Caws writes: "The manifesto was from the beginning, and has remained, a deliberate manipulation of the public view. Setting out the terms of the faith toward which the listening public is to be swayed, it is a document of an ideology."[13] Presented in the first section of this collection is a selection of pieces in which Ballard set out the terms of his faith.

Context and chronology are the guiding principles of organization throughout, and for that reason the remaining *New Worlds* pieces clamor to be collected together. This collation allows us to consider the specifics of *New Worlds*, including its transformative approach to publishing SF during Moorcock's tenure as editor, reflected in the design and layout of the magazine, which under Charles Platt's art direction experimented with typography and the space of the page. That visual character cannot be translated into this collection, but it is hoped that the textual flavor of these pieces is concentrated by grouping them together.

Given the canon-making impulse in the "*New Worlds*" section, the natural successors are the "Commentaries" Ballard wrote for the writers and artists whose work he admired, most often in the form of forewords or catalog essays, but also, on occasion, as newspaper or magazine articles. These allow the visual artists to be promoted to the prominent position they held in the Ballardian imaginary and for patterns of reciprocity to begin to emerge. Introductions and glosses to his own novels and stories give insight into his views on his own practice.

Longer-form "Features and Essays" include a report, commissioned by the AA's *Drive* magazine, of piloting a vintage Mercedes across Europe;

---

13. Mary Ann Caws, "The Poetics of the Manifesto," in *Manifesto: A Century of Isms* (Lincoln: University of Nebraska Press, 2001), xix–xxxi (xix).

speculative pieces for *Vogue*; a travel feature for *The Mail on Sunday*; an account of a visit to an exhibition of the work of Edward Hopper at the Musée Cantini; and essays on airports, cities, directors, and modernist architecture. The sophisticated cultural analyst and theorist apparent from his interviews has considerable free rein in the longer form.

"Lists, Captions, and Glossaries" occupy a significant place in Ballard's work, as the proliferation of lists in *The Atrocity Exhibition* attests. An experimenter in the forms of print media—interview answers divorced from their questions and the paratextual play of an index to an imagined biography are exemplary of the many uses and subversions of textual formats to be found in both his nonfiction and hybrid experiments—Ballard took perfectly seriously the opportunity to indulge this favored form of magazine editors, and later commissioners sought him out for his expertise in the mode to provide glosses or captions.

The "Reviews" come next. To allow space for other sections, these are greatly reduced in number from *A User's Guide to the Millennium* (1996) and aim to give an exemplary selection from Ballard's forty-five years as a professional reviewer. The criteria for selection have been chronological range, the durability of the films, titles, or authors under review, the inclusion of autobiographical detail, and a spread across publications. There are fewer group reviews, because these tend not to allow the space for a reviewer to hit a stride. Here, we read early approaches to SF, engaged but skeptical reviews of books by futurologists, and anecdotes about Steven Spielberg and Quentin Tarantino. Close attention reveals a broad erudition and range of reading. Quotations come from far and wide: the psychoanalyst Edward Glover, William Blake, and Woody Allen.

The peri-millennial run of pieces for the *New Statesman*, published both in print and online, is permitted its own gated environment in which Ballard's legendarily gimlet eye is turned to the state of the United Kingdom around the year 2000. These provide a cultural historical parallel to the final pair of novels, *Millennium People* (2003) and *Kingdom Come* (2006), a user's guide to the birth of the current millennium.

As with "Lists," "Capsule Commentaries" should not be mistaken as superficial in the context of the work of an author who had mastered condensed lexia. Being J. G. Ballard was an essential part of the work and a continuation by different means of the questioning of the boundary between fiction and nonfiction. Ballard seemingly enjoyed appearing straight as a talking head as much as he enjoyed playing provocateur. If you want a snapshot of how he imagined the world might end, his favorite beach, or the state of the room in which he wrote, head straight here, but don't expect the standard fare. Ballard never just dialed it in, even when dialing it (or faxing it) in.

Finally, "Memoirs and Tributes" closes out the collection with a series of generous and modest retrospections. Here he remembers episodes from his life, his friends, and his influences. Among these supplements to the succinct autobiography *Miracles of Life* (2008), readers will also find referents for fictionalized events narrated in *Empire of the Sun* (1984) and *The Kindness of Women* (1991).

*

The question of scope in this collection is an existential one. In the context of the work of J. G. Ballard, peppered with characters called Jim, Ballard, or simply B, what is fiction and what is nonfiction? It is a question that this edition has to consider carefully, and one that Ballard's work continually posed of its readers. In his "Introduction to the French Edition of *Crash!*," Ballard set out a theory: "We live inside an enormous novel. For the writer in particular it is less and less necessary for him to invent the fictional content of his novel. The fiction is already there. The writer's task is to invent the reality" ("Introduction to the French Edition of *Crash!*," this volume, 13–14).

This wasn't simply an observation, but a driving impetus behind his work, resulting in a number of pieces that trouble the fiction/nonfiction border in distinct ways and have caused critics to respond with a mixture of admiration and wariness. Roger Luckhurst summarizes this succinctly: "It seems to me that Ballard . . . exposes the hidden assumptions behind the secure categorizations of literature and literary judgement. . . . The Ballard oeuvre is nothing other than a prolonged meditation on the questions of protocols, boundaries, frames, and the evaluations they set in train."[14]

---

14. Roger Luckhurst, *The Angle between Two Walls* (Liverpool: Liverpool University Press, 1997), xii.

Two examples of pieces that lie outside the scope of this collection illustrate the manner in which such work operates to test standard protocols. "The Secret Autobiography of J. G. Ballard" is a vignette imagining a character called B. settling into life as the sole inhabitant of a deserted world. Despite declaring itself an autobiographical piece, it does not describe the lived events of a life, but rather a fantastic or imagined scene: a dream autobiography, perhaps. "The Side-Effects of Orthonovin G," meanwhile, is composed from a pair of found, first-person texts written by American women who had taken a specific birth control pill. These do describe the empirical events of real lives, but they are not those of the purported author, who contributes only the title and his byline.[15]

Should we characterize the former as nonfiction because it is so identified by the author? Or the latter as fiction because it is signed by J. G. Ballard and set out as a prose poem? Which—if either—should be included in an edition of nonfiction? "The Side-Effects" at first glance has the strongest claim, in that its main texts certainly are nonfictional. Would it be right, however, to include it in a collection of selected nonfiction of J. G. Ballard? What would the true authors of these texts make of that? We are thrown, instead, into questions of authorship and propriety.

The response taken here is to keep in mind such pieces and the questions they pose, while holding them in the wings, allowing only "What I Believe" a starring soliloquy as the sole representative of these hybrids.

Another thorny obstacle for an edition such as this is where to locate itself in relation to scholarly study of Ballard's work. Read his disdainful response to the editors of *Science Fiction Studies* and you are left in no doubt of what he thinks of SF scholarship: "bourgeoisification in the form of an over-professionalized academia with nowhere to take its girlfriend for a bottle of wine and a dance is now rolling its jaws over innocent and naive fiction that desperately needs to be left alone. You [sic] killing us! Stay your hand! Leave us be!" ("A Response to the Invitation to Respond," this volume, 304).

---

15. *Ambit*, 96 (Spring 1984): 2–5; *Ambit*, 50 (Spring 1972): 26–27. "The book from which Ballard took his 'found text' was *Women at Yale: Liberating a College Campus* by Janet Lever and Pepper Schwartz, Indianapolis: Bobbs-Merrill, and London: Allen Lane, The Penguin Press, 1971." David Pringle, "JG Ballard Chronology, 1971–1975," in *Deep Ends: A Ballardian Anthology 2019*, 16.

Those who would follow the word of Ballard should look away now. The scholars vociferously warned off have declined to heed him, with increasing resources available through which to consider his legacy. The archive of his papers at the British Library, while carefully curated, allows researchers to read original manuscripts of his novels and to study his process. Archivist Chris Beckett has used this material to publish a richly illustrated Collector's Edition of *Crash* and a number of genetic studies.[16] The cataloging of Ballard's personal library, not deposited with the archival papers, has led to fresh consideration of his idea of invisible literatures by Catherine McKenna.

Building on the influential studies of scholars such as Roger Luckhurst and Jeannette Baxter, Ballard's work is increasingly read in English Literature Departments in the context of courses on modern and contemporary literature, science fiction, and eco-criticism, a field whose foundational documents consider his first quartet of novels against the backdrop of climate crisis. Architectural scholars have studied his fictional buildings as a critical reflection on, and speculative intervention into, the built environment. A brutalist reading group at the Barbican Centre in London focused on Ballard's interest in modernist architecture, ran in 2018. The political historian Duncan Bell has used Ballard's nonfiction writing to essay an analysis of his politics. Research that reconsiders *New Worlds* as a fertile seedbed for the 1960s avant-garde has expanded the view of that magazine as contributing to both visual and literary culture.[17]

For these interdisciplinary approaches, the nonfiction provides a crucial context against which to read both the fiction and the formation of the Ballardian imaginary. Where books reviewed provide a partial record of Ballard's reading during any given period, his commentary pieces extend, in a more formal register, the opinions expressed in interview. For literary historians and close students of Ballard, a fresh look at the nonfiction provides another opportunity: to reconsider his active image-management and mythmaking.

---

16. Chris Beckett, ed., *Crash: The Collector's Edition* (London: HarperCollins, 2017).
17. Please see the bibliography of suggested further reading for full references to these sources and more.

Perhaps now is the time to regard the warning to keep our tanks off his lawn as an invitation, instead, to perform a finger-tip search.

*

Whether analysts or fans, readers will recognize in these pieces the work of a stylist who honed phrases until they were operating like surgical instruments, and could be redeployed several times over: take, as just one example, from the "Introduction to the French Edition of *Crash!*," the construction "in sex as the perfect arena, like a culture-bed of sterile pus, for all the veronicas of our own perversions." Appearing twice in this collection and used also in the piece "Tolerances of the Human Face," it is a typically arresting combination of subject, metaphor, and diagnosis, deploying biological and emotional vocabularies with care and precision to produce something equally disturbing and delicious ("Introduction to the French Edition of *Crash!*," this volume, 11; "Salvador Dali: the Innocent as Paranoid," this volume, 38).

Repetition is a strategy in Ballard, both practical and determined, at the levels of language, structure, and narrative: it did not impress reviewers of *A User's Guide to the Millennium*, who felt shortchanged, and can either cast a glamour over or frustrate readers of the fiction, who experience the unnerving sense that they've read this one before. The current book allows conscious repetition its head so that it may perform its incantatory function, and enable comparison of key variants, but reduces multiple approaches to topics from the same perspective. For this reason, for example, while Ballard wrote several reviews of books by or about William Burroughs, only the *New Worlds* essay-review "Myth-Maker of the 20th Century," a review of the biography *Literary Outlaw: The Life and Times of William S. Burroughs* by Ted Morgan, and an obituary piece are included, allowing us to read the evolution of his relationship with Burroughs's work across his career.

To enthusiasts it might seem redundant to observe that Ballard was unusually quotable, but newcomers may not be aware of how luminous his phrase-turning could be. The book *J. G. Ballard: Quotes* (2004), published by Re/Search, ultimately functions as a nonfiction collection, so many passages of vivid phrasing and acute observation does it identify and isolate. Keep an alert eye open when reading opinion columns and you may be surprised how frequently journalists reach for a Ballard line. A joy for any reader of the current edition will be to set to the text with a pen and underline the slogans and crisp, killer lines that just keep coming: "We live in a world ruled by fictions of every kind"; "Architecture is a stage set where we need to be at ease in order to perform"; "Psychopathology is fun" ("Introduction to the French Edition of *Crash!*," this volume, 13; "A Handful of Dust," this volume, 148; "Weirdly Wise," this volume, 224).

The adman and caption writer folded this technique into the descriptive language of his fiction, at turns painterly and scientifically accurate. Readers will not want for examples of accomplished figurative prose style. Consider his lilting description of the experience of the female inhabitant of an immersive living/media environment of the future for *Vogue* readers: "The delicate quicksilver loom of her nervous system as she sits at her dressing table, the sudden flush of adrenaline as the telephone rings, the warm arterial tides of emotion as she arranges lunch with her lover . . . The spherical mirror forms the wall of our universe, enclosing us for ever at its heart . . ." ("The Future of the Future," this volume, 121, 123).

Polemics, lyrical visions, droll anecdotes, incisive analysis, and tender tributes. The unconscious, the history of the twentieth century, the phenomenon of celebrity, the impact of technology and the media landscape on the human subject. Access pieces at random or proceed with a linear reading. It matters not. You are inside a spherical mirror.

NOTES ON THE EDITION

Ballard did not archive his journalism, so the pieces collected here are taken from the earliest published edition unless otherwise indicated. Every effort has been made to trace the earliest version and to restore the text where possible. In those instances where it has not been possible to source the earliest publication, the source used has been recorded in a footnote (all notes in the edition are the editor's). The prices and publishing details of books under review have been removed from the body of the text and formatting has been made consistent where original publications used a variety of formats for titles of works, for example. Accents have been maintained. For this reason, the name "Dalí" will sometimes appear unaccented: it is worth noting that Ballard did not use the accent when writing Dalí's name by hand.

As Ballard wrote to David Pringle in 1992: "None of the titles in the *Guardian, Independent, Daily Telegraph*, etc., were mine—all were the editors. Years ago, when I was reviewing for the *Guardian, New Statesman*, etc., I thought up almost all the titles ('The Elephant and the Quasar' etc.), but for some reason I stopped doing this a few years ago—mental laziness, probably."[1] The titles used when pieces were first published have nevertheless been maintained as intertitles and in the bibliography, and these too have been brought into a consistent formatting. In the table of contents if single works or individuals are under discussion, these have been favored for ease of navigation. Dates given in the table of contents refer to the date of publication of the piece itself, rather than the work on which it comments.

---

1. David Pringle, *JGB NEWS* 18 (August 1992).

The term *SF* has been favored in the prefatory materials as the most useful for encompassing the various terms *science fiction, s-f,* and *speculative fiction.*

It has proven impractical for this volume to be comprehensive. Rationales for inclusion and exclusion have been required, as outlined above. The bibliography, which also includes pieces that have not been reproduced here, will direct readers to the many fascinating pieces that it has not been possible to include.

1

STATEMENTS

This opening section provides a snapshot of Ballard's statements of his critical and imaginative concerns at different key stages in his career.

"Which Way to Inner Space?" (1962) became a manifesto for the New Wave of science fiction that was "ignited" in the pages of *New Worlds* magazine in the 1960s. It combines Ballard's trenchant and iconoclastic critique of traditional SF with his diagnosis for reform: "I'd like to see more psycho-literary ideas, more meta-biological and meta-chemical concepts, private time-systems, synthetic psychologies and space-times, more of the remote, sombre half-worlds one glimpses in the paintings of schizophrenics, all in all a complete speculative poetry and fantasy of science." It also coins the memorable slogan, subsequently much-repeated: "The only truly alien planet is Earth."

"Notes from Nowhere" mirrors the formally experimental style toward which Ballard was working in his fiction in the late 1960s, particularly in *New Worlds* and *Ambit*. The elimination of "the elements of sequential narrative" that characterized the condensed novels collected as *The Atrocity Exhibition* is employed structurally: self-reflexive critical analysis of his own methods and work is organized in a numbered list including commands to the reader—"Defend Dali"—queries, statements, apothegms, and quotations. It bears close resemblance, formally, at least, to "Images of the Future: Comments on Some Recent Experiments," written in the same year but unpublished until 1993 in David Pringle's newsletter *JGB News*.

Ballard's original English text for the "Introduction to the French Edition of *Crash!*" (1974), translated by Robert Louit, was published the following year in the SF journal *Foundation*, accompanied by Louit's

interview under the title "some words on *Crash!*" Drawing on Freud, this
gives the fullest account of the concept of the "death of affect" experienced by the subject immersed in the contemporary media landscape.
Ballard would distance himself from the position he took here with
regard to his most controversial novel, preferring later to describe it as
"a warning against the deviant possibilities that 20th century technology
offers to the human imagination," and the piece was not included in *A
User's Guide to the Millennium* (1996) ("Remembering *Crash*," this volume,
317). It shares some paragraphs with the *New Worlds* essay "Salvador Dali:
The Innocent as Paranoid" (1969).

"What I Believe" was written in response to a form question from Daniel Riche, the editor of the French magazine *Science Fiction*, who was inau-
gurating a column entitled "Ce que je crois." David Pringle republished
the English text later the same year in the glossy SF magazine *Interzone*,
reproducing Ballard's handwritten typescript. "What I Believe" is a credo,
an index, a prose poem, and a further engagement in the detournement
of mass media modes that was a continuous strain from the 1958 billboard piece *Project for a New Novel (Mr F is Mr F)* onto 1985's "Answers to
a Questionnaire," which framed the autobiographical answers without
providing the questions, inviting the reader to complete the other half of
the questionnaire in their imagination.

In 2002, a cardboard cut-out of the incapacitated Ballard accompanied
Iain Sinclair's reading of "What I Believe" at the launch for his book *Lon-
don Orbital* at the Barbican in London, and Ballard himself read it for the
ITV arts program *The South Bank Show* in 2006.

WHICH WAY TO INNER SPACE?

New Worlds (1962)

One unfortunate by-product of the Russian-American space race, and the immense publicity given to the rival astronauts, is likely to be an even closer identification, in the mind of the general public, of science fiction with the rocket ships and ray guns of Buck Rogers. If science fiction ever had a chance of escaping this identification—from which most of its present ills derive—that chance will soon be gone, and the successful landing of a manned vehicle on the Moon will fix this image conclusively. Instead of greeting the appearance of the space-suited hero with a deep groan, most general readers will be disappointed if the standard paraphernalia of robot brains and hyper-drives is not present, just as most cinema-goers are bored stiff if a western doesn't contain at least one major gun-battle. A few westerns without guns have been attempted, but they seem to turn into dog and timberland stories, and as a reader of science fiction one of my fears is that unless the medium drastically reinvigorates itself in the near future the serious fringe material, at present its only justification, will be relegated to the same limbo occupied by other withering literary forms such as the ghost and detective stories.

There are several reasons why I believe space fiction can no longer provide the main wellspring of ideas for s-f. Firstly, the bulk of it is invariably juvenile, though this is not entirely the fault of the writers. Mort Sahl has referred to the missile-testing site at Cape Canaveral as "Disneyland East," and like it or not this sums up the attitude of most people towards science fiction, and underlines the narrow imaginative limits imposed by the background of rocket ships and planet-hopping.

A poet such as Ray Bradbury can accept the current magazine conventions and transform even so hackneyed a subject as Mars into an enthralling private world, but science fiction can't rely for its survival on the continued emergence of writers of Bradbury's calibre. The degree of interest inherent in the rocket and planet story—with its confined and psychological dimensions and its limited human relationships—is so slight as to make a self-sufficient fictional form based on it almost impossible. If anything, however, the success of the manned satellites will only tend to establish the limited psychological experiences of their crews—on the whole accurately anticipated, though unintentionally, by s-f writers—as the model of those to be found in science fiction.

Visually, of course, nothing can equal space fiction for its vast perspectives and cold beauty, as any s-f film or comic-strip demonstrates, but a literary form requires more complex and more verbalised ideas to sustain it. The spaceship simply doesn't provide these. (Curiously enough, in the light of the present roster of astronauts, the one authentic element in old-style space opera is its wooden, one-dimensional dialogue. But if one can't altogether blame Commander Shepard for his "Boy, what a ride," Major Titov's dreamless sleep after the first night in space was the biggest let-down since the fall of Icarus—how many s-f writers must wish they had been writing his script!)

But my real objection to the central role now occupied by the space story is that its appeal is too narrow. Unlike the Western, science fiction can't rely for its existence upon the casual intermittent pleasure it may give to a wide non-specialist audience, if it is to hold its ground and continue to develop. As with most specialized media, it needs a faithful and discriminating audience who will go to it for specific pleasures, similar to the audience for abstract painting or serial music. The old-guard space opera fans, although they probably form the solid backbone of present s-f readership, won't be able to keep the medium alive on their own. Like most purists, they prefer their diet unchanged, and unless s-f evolves, sooner or later other media are going to step in and take away its main distinction, the right to be the shop window of tomorrow.

Too often recently, when I've wanted intellectual excitement, I've found myself turning to music or painting rather than to science fiction, and surely this is the chief thing wrong with it at present. To attract a critical readership science fiction needs to alter completely its present content and approach. Magazine s-f was born in the 1930s and like the pseudo-streamlined architecture of the '30s, it is beginning to look old-fashioned to the general reader. It's not simply that time travel, psionics and teleporting (which have nothing to do with science anyway and are so breath-taking in their implications that they require genius to do them justice) date science fiction, but that the general reader is intelligent enough to realise that the majority of the stories are based on the most minor variations on these themes, rather than on any fresh imaginative leaps.

In other words, s-f is becoming academic. Historically, this type of academic virtuosity is a sure sign of decline, and it may well be that the real role science fiction has to play is that of a minor eclectic pastime similar to other baroque amusements such as Grand Guignol melodrama and astrological romances, its few magazines sustained by opportunist editorial swerves after the latest popular-science fad.

Rejecting this view, however, and believing that s-f has a continuing and expanding role as an imaginative interpreter of the future, how can one find a new wellspring of ideas? Firstly, I think science fiction should turn its back on space, on interstellar travel, extra-terrestrial life forms, galactic wars and the overlap of these ideas that spreads across the margins of nine-tenths of magazine s-f. Great writer though he was, I'm convinced that H. G. Wells has had a disastrous influence on the subsequent course of science fiction. Not only did he provide it with a repertory of ideas that have virtually monopolized the medium for the last fifty years, but he established the conventions of its style and form, with its simple plots, journalistic narrative, and standard range of situation and character. It is these, whether they realize it or not, that s-f readers are so bored with now, and which are beginning to look increasingly outdated by comparison with the developments in other literary fields.

I've often wondered why s-f shows so little of the experimental enthusiasm which has characterized painting, music and the cinema during the last four or five decades, particularly as these have become wholeheartedly speculative, more and more concerned with the creation of new states of mind, constructing fresh symbols and languages where the old cease to be valid. Similarly, I think science fiction must jettison its present narrative forms and plots. Most of these are far too explicit to express any subtle interplay of character and theme. Devices such as time travel and telepathy, for example, save the writer the trouble of describing the interrelationships of time and space indirectly. And by a curious paradox they prevent him from using his imagination at all, giving him very little true freedom of movement within the narrow limits set by the device.

The biggest developments of the immediate future will take place, not on the Moon or Mars, but on Earth, and it is inner space, not outer, that needs to be explored. The only truly alien planet is Earth. In the past the scientific bias of s-f has been towards the physical sciences—rocketry, electronics, cybernetics—and the emphasis should switch to the biological sciences, particularly to imaginative and fictional treatments of them, which is what is implied by the term science *fiction*. Accuracy, that last refuge of the unimaginative, doesn't matter a hoot. What we need is not science fact but more science fiction, and the introduction of so-called science fact articles is merely an attempt to dress up the old Buck Rogers material in more respectable garb.

More precisely, I'd like to see s-f becoming abstract and "cool," inventing fresh situations and contexts that illustrate its theme obliquely. For example, instead of treating time like a sort of glorified scenic railway, I'd like to see it used for what it is, one of the perspectives of the personality, and the elaboration of concepts such as the time zone, deep time and archaeopsychic time. I'd like to see more psycho-literary ideas, more meta-biological and meta-chemical concepts, private time-systems, synthetic psychologies and space-times, more of the remote, sombre half-worlds one glimpses in the paintings of schizophrenics, all in all a complete speculative poetry and fantasy of science.

I firmly believe that only science fiction is fully equipped to become the literature of tomorrow, and that it is the only medium with an adequate vocabulary of ideas and situations. By and large, the standards it sets for itself are higher than those of any other specialist literary genre, and from now on, I think, most of the hard work will fall, not on the writer and editor, but on the readers. The onus is on them to accept a more oblique narrative style, understated themes, private symbols and vocabularies. The first true s-f story, and one I intend to write myself if no one else will, is about a man with amnesia lying on a beach and looking at a rusty bicycle wheel, trying to work out the absolute essence of the relationship between them. If this sounds off-beat and abstract, so much the better, for science fiction could use a big dose of the experimental; and if it sounds boring, well at least it will be a new kind of boredom.

As a final text, I'm reminded of the diving suit in which Salvador Dali delivered a lecture some years ago in London. The workman sent along to supervise the suit asked how deep Dali proposed to descend, and with a flourish the maestro exclaimed: "To the Unconscious!" to which the workman replied sagely: "I'm afraid we don't go down that deep." Five minutes later, sure enough, Dali nearly suffocated inside the helmet.

It is that inner space-suit which is still needed, and it is up to science fiction to build it!

NOTES FROM NOWHERE

New Worlds (1966)

Comments on Work in Progress

1. Science fiction, above all a prospective form of fiction, concerned with the immediate present in terms of the future rather than the past, requires narrative techniques that reflect its subject matter. To date almost all its writers, including myself, fall to the ground because they fail to realise that the principal narrative technique of retrospective fiction, the sequential and consequential narrative, based as it is on an already established set of events and relationships, is wholly unsuited to create the images of a future that has as yet made no concessions to us. In *The Drowned World, The Drought* and *The Crystal World* I tried to construct linear systems that made no use of the sequential elements of time—basically, a handful of ontological "myths." However, in spite of my efforts, the landscapes of these novels more and more began to quantify themselves. Images and events became isolated, defining their own boundaries. Crocodiles enthroned themselves in the armour of their own tissues.

2. In *The Terminal Beach* the elements of sequential narrative had been almost completely eliminated. It occurred to me that one could carry this to its logical conclusion, and a recent group of stories—"You and Me and the Continuum," "The Assassination Weapon," "You: Coma: Marilyn Monroe" and "The Atrocity Exhibition"—show some of the results. Apart from anything else, this new narrative technique seems to show a tremendous gain in the density of ideas and images. In fact, I regard each of them as a complete novel.

3. Who else is trying? Here and there, one or two. More power to their elbows. But for all the talk, most of the established writers seem stuck in a rut.

4. Few of them had much of a chance, anyway: not enough wild genes.

5. Of those I have read, Platt's *Lone Zone* (in particular, the first three or four paragraphs, brilliant writing) and Colvin's *The Pleasure Garden* . . . and *The Ruins* are wholly original attempts, successful I feel, to enlarge the scope and subject matter of science fiction.

6. Defend Dali.

7. In fact, the revival of interest in surrealism—after the recent flurry over Dada, there is now a full-scale retrospective of Duchamp at the Tate Gallery—bodes well for science fiction, turning its writers away from so-called realism to a more open and imaginative manner. One hopes that its real aims will be followed. One trouble with Dali is that no one has ever really looked at his paintings. *Goddess Leaning on Her Elbow*, for example, or *Young Virgin Auto-sodomised by Her Own Chastity*, seem to me to be among the most important paintings of the 20th century.

8. The social novel is dead. Like all retrospective fiction, it is obsessed with the past, with the roots of behaviour and background, with sins of omission and commission long-past, with all the distant antecedents of the present. Most people, thank God, have declared a moratorium on the past, and are more concerned with the present and future, with all the possibilities of their lives. To begin with: the possibilities of musculature and posture, the time and space of our immediate physical environments.

9. Fiction is a branch of neurology.

10. Planes intersect: on one level, the world of public events, Cape Kennedy and Viet Nam mimetised on billboards. On another level, the immediate personal environment, the volumes of space enclosed by my opposed hands, the geometry of my own postures, the time-values contained in this room, the motion-space of highways, staircases, the angles between these walls. On a third level, the inner world of the psyche. Where these planes intersect, images are born. With these co-ordinates, some kind of valid reality begins to clarify itself.

11. Quantify.

12. Some of these ideas can be seen in my four recent "novels." The linear elements have been eliminated, the reality of the narrative is relativistic. Therefore place on the events only the perspective of a given instant, a given set of images and relationships.

13. Dali: "After Freud's explorations within the psyche it is now the outer world of reality which will have to be quantified and eroticised." Query: at what point does the plane of intersection of two cones become sexually more stimulating than Elizabeth Taylor's cleavage?

14. Neurology is a branch of fiction: the scenarios of nerve and blood-vessel are the written mythologies of brain and body. Does the angle between two walls have a happy ending?

15. Query: does the plane of intersection of the body of this woman in my room with the cleavage of Elizabeth Taylor generate a valid image of the glazed eyes of Chiang Kai Shek, an invasion plan of the off-shore islands?

16. Of course these four published "novels," and those that I am working on now, contain a number of other ideas. However, one can distin-guish between the manifest content, i.e., the attempt to produce a new "mythology" out of the intersecting identities of J. F. Kennedy, Marilyn Monroe, smashed automobiles and dead apartments, and the latent content, the shift in geometric formula from one chapter to the next. Each section is a symbol in some kind of spinal math-ematics. In fact I believe that one may be able one day to represent a novel or short story, with all its images and relationships, simply as a three-dimensional geometric model. In *The Atrocity Exhibition* one of the characters remarks of a set of Enneper's models ". . . operat-ing formulae, for a doomsday weapon." Cubism, for example, had a greater destructive power than all the explosives discharged during World War I—and killed no one.

17. The analytic function of this new fiction should not be overlooked. Most fiction is synthetic in method—as Freud remarked, rightly I feel, a sure sign of immaturity.

18. Au revoir, jewelled alligators and white hotels, hallucinatory forests, farewell.

19. For the moment it's difficult to tell where this thing will go. One problem that worries me is that a short story, or even, ultimately, a novel, may become nothing more than a three-dimensional geo-metric model. Nevertheless, it seems to me that so much of what is going on, on both sides of the retina, makes nonsense unless viewed in these terms. A huge portion of our lives is ignored, merely because it plays no direct part in conscious experience.

20. No one in science fiction has ever written about outer space. "You and Me and the Continuum": "What is space?" the lecturer concluded, "what does it mean to our sense of time and the images we carry of our finite lives . . . ?" At present I am working on a story about a disaster in space which, however badly, makes a first attempt to describe what space means. So far, science fiction's idea of outer space has resembled a fish's image of life on land as a goldfish bowl.

21. The surrealist painter, Matta: "Why must we await, and fear, a disaster in space in order to understand our own times?"

22. In my own story a disaster in space is translated into the terms of our own inner and outer environments. It may be that certain interesting ideas will emerge.

23. So far, science fiction has demonstrated conclusively that it has no idea of what space means, and is completely unequipped to describe what will no doubt be the greatest transformation of the life of this planet—the exploration of outer space.

24. Meanwhile: the prospect of a journey to Spain, a return to the drained basin of the Rio Seco. At the mouth a delta of shingle forms an ocean bar, pools of warm water filled with sea-urchins. Then the great deck of the drained river running inland, crossed by the white span of a modern motor bridge. Beyond this, secret basins of cracked mud the size of ballrooms, models of a state of mind, a curvilinear labyrinth. The limitless neural geometry of the landscape. The apartment houses on the beach are the operating formulae for our passage through consciousness. To the north a shoulder of Pre-Cambrian rock rises from the sea after its crossing from Africa. The jukeboxes play in the bars of Benidorm. The molten sea swallows the shadow of the Guardia Civil helicopter.

INTRODUCTION TO THE FRENCH EDITION OF *CRASH!*

"Some Words about *Crash!*" in *Foundation* (1973)

The marriage of reason and nightmare which has dominated the 20th century has given birth to an ever more ambiguous world. Across the communications landscape move the spectres of sinister technologies and the dreams that money can buy. Thermonuclear weapons systems and soft drink commercials coexist in an overlit realm ruled by advertising and pseudo-events, science and pornography. Over our lives preside the great twin motifs of the 20th century—sex and paranoia. Despite McLuhan's delight in high-speed information mosaics we are still reminded of Freud's profound pessimism in *Civilization and its Discontents*. Voyeurism, self-disgust, the infantile basis of our dreams and longings—these diseases of the psyche have now culminated in the most terrifying casualty of the [20th] century: the death of affect.

This demise of feeling and emotion has paved the way for all our most real and tender pleasures—in the excitements of pain and mutilation; in sex as the perfect arena, like a culture bed of sterile pus, for all the veronicas of our own perversions; in our moral freedom to pursue our own psychopathology as a game; and in our apparently limitless powers for conceptualization—what our children have to fear is not the cars on the highways of tomorrow but our own pleasure in calculating the most elegant parameters of their deaths. To document the uneasy pleasures of living within this glaucous paradise have more and more become the role of science fiction. I firmly believe that science fiction, far from being an unimportant minor offshoot, in fact represents the main literary tradition of the 20th century, and certainly its oldest—a tradition of imaginative response to science and technology that runs in an intact line through H. G. Wells, Aldous Huxley, the writers of modern American science fiction, to such present-day innovators as William Burroughs.

The main fact of the 20th century is the concept of the unlimited possibility. This predicate of science and technology enshrines the notion of a moratorium on the past—the irrelevancy and even death of the past—and the limitless alternatives available to the present. What links the first flight of the Wright brothers to the invention of the Pill is the social and sexual philosophy of the ejector seat. Given this immense continent of possibility, few literatures seem to be better equipped to deal with their subject matter than science fiction. No other form of fiction has the vocabulary and images to deal with the present, let alone the future. The dominant characteristic of the modern mainstream novelist its sense of individual isolation; its mood of introspection and alienation, a state of mind assumed to be the hallmark of the 20th century consciousness. Far from it. On the contrary, it seems to me that this is a psychology that belongs entirely to the 19th century, part of a reaction against the massive restraints of bourgeois society, the monolithic character of Victorianism and the tyranny of the paterfamilias, secure in his financial and sexual authority. Apart from its marked retrospective bias and its obsession with the subjective nature of experience, its real subject matter is the rationalization of guilt and estrangement. Its elements are introspection, pessimism and sophistication. Yet if anything befits the 20th century it is optimism, the iconography of mass merchandising, naivety and a guilt free enjoyment of all the mind's possibilities.

The kind of imagination that now manifests itself in science fiction is not something new. Homer, Shakespeare and Milton all invented new worlds to comment on this one. The split of science fiction into a separate and somewhat disreputable genre is a recent development. It is connected to the near disappearance of dramatic and philosophical poetry and the slow shrinking of the traditional novel as it concerns more and more exclusively with the nuances of human relationships. Among those areas neglected by the traditional novel are, above all, the dynamics of human societies [the traditional novel tends to depict society as static], and man's place in the universe. However crudely or naively, science fiction at least attempts to place a philosophical and metaphysical frame around the most important events within our lives and consciousness.

If I make this general defense of science fiction it is, obviously, because my own career as a writer has been involved with it for almost 20 years. From the very start, when I first turned to science fiction, I was convinced that the future was a better key to the present than the past. At the time, however, I was dissatisfied with science fiction's obsession with its two principal themes—outer space and the far future. As much for emblematic purposes as any theoretical or programmatic ones, I christened the new terrain I wished to explore inner space, that psychological domain [manifest, for example, in surrealist painting] where the inner world of the mind and the outer world of reality meet and fuse.

Primarily I wanted to write a fiction about the present day. To do this in the context of the late 1950s, in a world where the call sign of Sputnik 1 could be heard on one's radio like the advance beacon of a new universe, required completely different techniques from those available to the 19th century novelist. In fact, I believe that if it were possible to scrap the whole of existing literature, and be forced to begin again without any knowledge of the past, all writers would find themselves inevitably producing something very close to science fiction.

Science and technology multiply around us. To an increasing extent they dictate the languages in which we speak and think. Either we use those languages, or we remain mute.

Yet, by an ironic paradox, modern science fiction became the first casualty of the changing world it anticipated and helped to create. The future envisaged by the science fiction of the 1940s and 1950s is already our past. Its dominant images, not merely of the first Moon flights and interplanetary voyages, but of our changing social and political relationships in a world governed by technology, now resemble huge pieces of discarded stage scenery. For me, this could be seen most touchingly in the film *2001: A Space Odyssey*, which signified the end of the heroic period of modern science fiction—its lovingly imagined panoramas and costumes, its huge set pieces, reminded me of *Gone with the Wind*, a scientific pageant that became a kind of historical romance in reverse, a sealed world into which the hard light of contemporary reality was never allowed to penetrate.

Increasingly, our concepts of past, present and future are being forced to revise themselves. Just as the past itself, in social and psychological terms, became a casualty of Hiroshima and the nuclear age [almost by definition a period where we were all forced to think prospectively], so in its turn the future is ceasing to exist, devoured by the all-voracious present. We have annexed the future into our own present, as merely one of those manifold alternatives open to us. Options multiply around us, we live in an almost infantile world where any demand, any possibility, whether for life-styles, travel, sexual roles and identities, can be satisfied instantly.

In addition, I think that the balance between fiction and reality has changed significantly in the past decade [1960s]. Increasingly their roles are reversed. We live in a world ruled by fictions of every kind—mass merchandising, advertising, politics conducted as a branch of advertising, the instant translation of science and technology into popular imagery, the increasing blurring and intermingling of identities within the realm of consumer goods, the preempting of any free or imaginative response to experience by the television screen. We live inside an enormous novel.

For the writer in particular it is less and less necessary for him to invent the fictional content of his novel. The fiction is already there. The writer's task is to invent the reality.

In the past we have always assumed that the external world around us represented reality, however confusing or uncertain, and that the inner world of our minds, its dreams, hopes, ambitions, represented the realm of fantasy and the imagination. These roles, too, it seems to me, have been reversed. The most prudent and effective method of dealing with the world around us is to assume that it is a complete fiction—conversely, the one node of reality left to us is inside our own heads. Freud's classic distinction between the latent and manifest content of the dream, between the apparent and the real, now needs to be applied to the external world of so-called reality.

Given these transformations, what is the main task facing the writer? Can he, any longer, make use of the techniques and perspectives of the traditional 19th century novel, with its linear narrative, its measured chronology, its consular characters grandly inhabiting domains within an ample time and space? Is his subject matter the sources of character and personality sunk deep in the past, the unhurried inspection of roots, the examination of the most subtle nuances of social behaviour and personal relationships? Has the writer still the moral authority to invent a self-sufficient and self-enclosed world, to preside over his characters like an examiner, knowing all the questions in advance? Can he leave out anything he prefers not to understand, including his own motives, prejudices and psychopathologies?

I feel myself that the writer's role, his authority and license to act, has changed radically. I feel that, in a sense, the writer knows nothing any longer. He has no moral stance. He offers the reader the contents of his own head, he offers a set of options and imaginative alternatives. His role is that of the scientist, whether on safari or in his laboratory, faced with a completely unknown terrain or subject. All he can do is to devise hypothesis and test them against the facts.

Crash! is such a book, an extreme metaphor for an extreme situation, a kit of desperate measures only for use in an extreme crisis. If I am right, and what I have done over the past years is to rediscover the present for myself, *Crash!* takes up its position as a cataclysmic novel of the present day in line with my previous novels of world cataclysm set in the near or immediate future—*The Drowned World, The Drought* and *The Crystal World.*

Crash!, of course, is not concerned with an imaginary disaster, however imminent, but with a pandemic cataclysm institutionalized in all industrial societies that kills hundreds of thousands of people each year and injures millions. Do we see, in the car crash, a sinister portent of a nightmare marriage between sex and technology? Will modern technology provide us with a hitherto undreamed-of means for tapping our own psychopathologies? Is this harnessing of our innate perversity conceivably of benefit to us? Is there some deviant logic unfolding more powerful than that of reason?

Throughout *Crash!* I have used the car not only as a sexual image, but as a total metaphor for man's life in today's society. As such the novel has a political role quite apart from its sexual content, but I would like still to think that *Crash!* is the first pornographic novel based on technology. In a sense, pornography is the most political form of fiction, dealing with how we use and exploit each other in the most urgent and ruthless way. Needless to say, the ultimate role of *Crash!* is cautionary, a warning against that brutal, erotic realm that beckons more and more persuasively to us from the margins of technological landscapes.

WHAT I BELIEVE

Interzone (Summer 1984)

I believe in the power of the imagination to remake the world, to release the truth within us, to hold back the night, to transcend death, to charm motorways, to ingratiate ourselves with birds, to enlist the confidences of madmen.

I believe in my own obsessions, in the beauty of the car crash, in the peace of the submerged forest, in the excitements of the deserted holiday beach, in the elegance of automobile graveyards, in the mystery of multi-storey car parks, in the poetry of abandoned hotels.

I believe in the forgotten runways of Wake Island, pointing towards the Pacifics of our imaginations.

I believe in the mysterious beauty of Margaret Thatcher, in the arch of her nostrils and the sheen on her lower lip; in the melancholy of wounded Argentine conscripts; in the haunted smiles of filling station personnel; in my dream of Margaret Thatcher caressed by that young Argentine soldier in a forgotten motel watched by a tubercular filling station attendant.

I believe in the beauty of all women, in the treachery of their imaginations, so close to my heart; in the junction of their disenchanted bodies with the enchanted chromium rails of supermarket counters; in their warm tolerance of my perversions.

I believe in the death of tomorrow, in the exhaustion of time, in our search for a new time within the smiles of auto-route waitresses and the tired eyes of air-traffic controllers at out-of-season airports.

I believe in the genital organs of great men and women, in the body postures of Ronald Reagan, Margaret Thatcher and Princess Di, in the sweet odors emanating from their lips as they regard the cameras of the entire world.

I believe in madness, in the truth of the inexplicable, in the common sense of stones, in the lunacy of flowers, in the disease stored up for the human race by the Apollo astronauts.

I believe in nothing.

I believe in Max Ernst, Delvaux, Dali, Titian, Goya, Leonardo, Vermeer, Chirico, Magritte, Redon, Duerer, Tanguy, the Facteur Cheval, the Watts Towers, Boecklin, Francis Bacon, and all the invisible artists within the psychiatric institutions of the planet.

I believe in the impossibility of existence, in the humour of mountains, in the absurdity of electromagnetism, in the farce of geometry, in the cruelty of arithmetic, in the murderous intent of logic.

I believe in adolescent women, in their corruption by their own leg stances, in the purity of their disheveled bodies, in the traces of their pudenda left in the bathrooms of shabby motels.

I believe in flight, in the beauty of the wing, and in the beauty of everything that has ever flown, in the stone thrown by a small child that carries with it the wisdom of statesmen and midwives.

I believe in the gentleness of the surgeon's knife, in the limitless geometry of the cinema screen, in the hidden universe within supermarkets, in the loneliness of the sun, in the garrulousness of planets, in the repetitiveness or ourselves, in the inexistence of the universe and the boredom of the atom.

I believe in the light cast by video-recorders in department store windows, in the messianic insights of the radiator grilles of showroom automobiles, in the elegance of the oil stains on the engine nacelles of 747s parked on airport tarmacs.

I believe in the non-existence of the past, in the death of the future, and the infinite possibilities of the present.

I believe in the derangement of the senses: in Rimbaud, William Burroughs, Huysmans, Genet, Celine, Swift, Defoe, Carroll, Coleridge, Kafka.

I believe in the designers of the Pyramids, the Empire State Building, the Berlin Fuehrerbunker, the Wake Island runways.

I believe in the body odors of Princess Di.

I believe in the next five minutes.

I believe in the history of my feet.

I believe in migraines, the boredom of afternoons, the fear of calendars, the treachery of clocks.

I believe in anxiety, psychosis and despair.

I believe in the perversions, in the infatuations with trees, princesses, prime ministers, derelict filling stations (more beautiful than the Taj Mahal), clouds and birds.

I believe in the death of the emotions and the triumph of the imagination.

I believe in Tokyo, Benidorm, La Grande Motte, Wake Island, Eniwetok, Dealey Plaza.

I believe in alcoholism, venereal disease, fever and exhaustion.

I believe in pain.

I believe in despair.

I believe in all children.

I believe in maps, diagrams, codes, chess-games, puzzles, airline time-tables, airport indicator signs.

I believe all excuses.

I believe all reasons.

I believe all hallucinations.

I believe all anger.

I believe all mythologies, memories, lies, fantasies, evasions.

I believe in the mystery and melancholy of a hand, in the kindness of trees, in the wisdom of light.

2

NEW WORLDS

New Worlds began life as a prewar fanzine at the height of the golden age of SF, when the genre was dominated by visions of space travel and rocket ships. It was professionally produced as a small pulp magazine published by Pendulum Publications and edited by John "Ted" Carnell from 1946. When Pendulum collapsed, a consortium of SF writers, editors, and fans, including Carnell and Arthur C. Clarke, formed Nova Publications, which published the magazine under Carnell's editorship from January 1949 to April 1964.

Ballard's first professional story, "Escapement," appeared in *New Worlds* 54 in December 1956. Carnell bought a further eighteen stories for the magazine and, in *New Worlds* 118, published "Which Way to Inner Space?," Ballard's first significant piece of nonfiction. Ballard remembered particularly Carnell's willingness to publish his story "The Terminal Beach," an important development in his work but broadly rejected by American magazines ("A Personal View," this volume, 189–191).

With sales of paperback SF magazines declining in the early 1960s, Nova Publications sold *New Worlds* and its sister title, *Science Fantasy*, to Roberts and Vintner Ltd. Carnell stood down and recommended a twenty-three-year-old writer and editor, Michael Moorcock, as his replacement.

Under Moorcock's editorial control, *New Worlds* shifted toward publishing

a cross-fertilisation of popular sf, science and the work of the literary and artistic avant garde . . . I felt that if the magazine was worth taking over (I had been reluctant to edit a purely sf magazine; I had little relish for most sf) then it should become the vehicle for various ideas I had had for some time. These ideas had been given encouragement and clearer shape by my friendship with

J. G. Ballard, whose enthusiasm vindicated many of my half-hearted attempts to find out what was 'wrong' with the sf genre and most modern literature in general.[1]

Moorcock's first issue demonstrated this intent by leading with Ballard's guest editorial, "Myth Maker of the 20th Century," a summary review of recent work by the novelist William Burroughs, then living in Tangiers and with whom Ballard had corresponded in March of that year.[2] Moorcock had first introduced Ballard to Burroughs's work in 1963, through a copy of the Olympia Press edition of *Naked Lunch* obtained in Paris by Maxim Jakubowski.

In the paperback format, Moorcock's *New Worlds* remained similar in appearance to its Carnell incarnation, but the editorial stance became more polemical and the avant-garde works that interested Moorcock and Ballard were given increasing attention. Ballard's review of the founding Vorticist and novelist Wyndham Lewis's *The Human Age* trilogy, *Chidermass*, *Monstre Gai*, and *The Malign Fiesta*, was occasioned by their publication in paperback by John Calder offshoot Jupiter Books in 1965.

The French director Chris Marker's 1962 black-and-white SF film, the "photo roman" *La Jetée*, was released in the United Kingdom in March 1966: Ballard's review was published as another guest editorial in *New Worlds* 164. The same issue contained his expansive analysis of surrealist painting, under the guise of a review of two books: *Surrealism* (1966) by Patrick Waldberg and *The History of Surrealist Painting* (1960) by Marcel Jean. The subsequent issue featured SF writer John Brunner reviewing Jean-Luc Godard's *Alphaville* (1965).

In summer 1967 the Arts Council of Great Britain awarded *New Worlds* a grant of £150 an issue, which enabled Moorcock to shift format from paperback to a larger magazine with halftone reproduction, allowing the use of photography. Charles Platt became art director. Issue 173, the first in the new format, used M. C. Escher's *Relativity* (1953) on the cover and contained Pamela Zoline's influential story "The Heat Death of the

---

1. Michael Moorcock, "New Worlds: A Personal History," *Foundation* 15 (January 1979): 5–18 (6).
2. This piece would be heavily revised for publication in *Ambit* (Spring 1966) as "Terminal Documents: Burroughs Reviewed."

Universe." Issue 174 included a profile of Eduardo Paolozzi, "Language Mechanisms," written by Christopher Finch, an art critic who had contributed an introductory text to Paolozzi's boxed print edition *Moonstrips Empire News* (1967), and who, from the next issue, became *New Worlds's* art editor.

The experimental form envisaged by Moorcock and Ballard as responsive to changes in the cultural and technological environment of the period was carried through to the visual character of the magazine from mid-1967 to its final iteration in the magazine format in 1970. With Paolozzi's name on the masthead as "Aeronautics Advisor" until 1969, the influence of pop art was clear: Paolozzi's Independent Group colleague Richard Hamilton was profiled in issue 176 and Andy Warhol's films reviewed in 185. Image collage, blurred polaroid photographs, comic strips, and illustrations accompanied formally experimental text pieces encompassing found texts, detournements of documentary forms, and cut-up text collages. Traces of theoretical and critical writing became more prominent in the reviews.

Against the context of increasing interest in obscenity from the United Kingdom's Director of Public Prosecutions, *New Worlds* was embroiled in a brief scandal in early 1968 after the newsagents W. H. Smiths pulled copies of the March issue, reacting belatedly to the serialization of Norman Spinrad's *Bug Jack Baron* (1969) in the magazine, which it deemed obscene. No issues appeared in April or May. The retailer relented in the face of public reaction, but the financial damage to the already uncertain *New Worlds* project was significant.

In early 1969, Ballard's review of J. T. Frazer's *The Voices of Time* (1966) appeared in the same issue as his condensed novel "The Summer Cannibals," which was illustrated by Charles Platt with close-up photographs of female models, cars, crash-test dummies, and motorway systems. The following month an extended essay, "Salvador Dali: The Innocent as Paranoid," was accompanied by images of thirteen of the works under discussion, and a table comparing Dalí to several SF luminaries. Published in the same issue was Ballard's computer print-out, found-text "How Dr Christopher Evans Landed on the Moon."

Reviews of provocative books continued. "Use Your Vagina" analyzed a sexual self-help guide, *How to Achieve Sexual Ecstasy* (1969), published by Christopher Kypreos, whose underground magazine *Running Man* had become *Running Man Press*, and who was subsequently prosecuted in late 1969 under the Obscene Publications Act. The December 1969 issue was a new writers' special, but New Wave names remained. The strapline announced: "Ballard on Hitler" as well as "Sladek on God" and "Harrison on pot." The book reviewed by Ballard, a translation of *Mein Kampf* published by Hutchinson in 1969, was already controversial, having prompted questions in the House of Commons.

Moorcock resigned the editor's role in late 1969, and Charles Platt oversaw the final issues in 1970 before monthly publication ceased with issue 201. There were quarterly paperback editions until issue 212 in Spring 1978, and thereafter irregular issues in samizdat magazine style. The influence of *New Worlds* on SF and magazine culture, and Ballard's contribution to that, is considerable.

MYTH MAKER OF THE 20TH CENTURY

(May–June 1964)

True genius and first mythographer of the mid-20th century, William Burroughs is the lineal successor to James Joyce, to whom he bears more than a passing resemblance—exile, publication in Paris, undeserved notoriety as a pornographer, and an absolute dedication to The Word—the last characteristic alone sufficient to guarantee the hostility and incomprehension of the English reviewers. Burroughs' originality, his "difficulty" as a writer, resides largely in the fact that he is a writer, systematically creating the verbal myths of the mid-century at a time when the oral novel, or un-illustrated cartoon, holds almost exclusive sway. In their range, complexity, comic richness and invention his three novels, *The Naked Lunch*, *The Soft Machine* and *The Ticket that Exploded*, re-worked to form the basis of *Dead Fingers Talk*, display a degree of virtuosity and literary power that places Burroughs on a par with the authors of *Finnegans Wake* and *The Metamorphosis*.

In *Finnegans Wake*, a gigantic glutinous pun, Joyce in effect brought the novel up to date, circa 1940, with his vast cyclical dream-rebus of a Dublin publican who is simultaneously Adam, Napoleon and the heroes of a thousand mythologies. Burroughs takes up from here, and his three novels are the first definite portrait of the inner landscape of our mid-century, using its own language and manipulative techniques, its own fantasies and nightmares, those of

Followers of obsolete unthinkable trades doodling in Etruscan, addicts of drugs not yet synthesised, investigators of infractions denounced by bland paranoid chess players, officials of unconstituted police states, brokers of exquisite dreams . . .

The landscapes are those of the exurban man-made wilderness:

swamps and garbage heaps, alligators crawling around in broken bottles and tin cans, neon arabesques of motels, marooned pimps scream obscenities at passing cars from islands of rubbish.

The almost complete inability of the English critics to understand Burroughs is as much a social failure as a literary one, a refusal to recognise the materials of the present decade as acceptable for literary purposes until a lapse of a generation or so has given to a few brand names an appropriately discreet nostalgia. One result is the detachment of the English social novel from everyday life to a point where it is fast becoming a minor genre as unrelated to common experience as the country house detective story (by contrast, the great merit of science fiction has been its ability to assimilate rapidly the materials of the immediate present and future, although it is now failing in precisely those areas where the future has already become the past).

Whatever his reservations about some aspects of the mid-20th century, Burroughs accepts that it can be fully described only in terms of its own language, its own idioms and verbal lore. Dozens of different argots are now in common currency; most people speak at least three or four separate languages, and a verbal relativity exists as important as any of time and space. To use the stylistic conventions of the traditional oral novel—the sequential narrative, characters "in the round," consecutive events, balloons of dialogue attached to "he said" and "she said"—is to perpetuate a set of conventions ideally suited to a period of great tales of adventure in the Conradian mode, or to an over-formalized Jamesian society, but now valuable for little more than the bedtime story and the fable. To use these conventions to describe events in the present decade is to write a kind of historical novel in reverse, and it is interesting to see that most original social novelists have already dropped these conventions. Kingsley Amis's brilliant novel *One Fat Englishman* is not merely a cyclical work of immense subtlety which can be begun at any point—its portrait of the central character is so fully realised and developed, his progress so non-linear, that the pages of the book could be detached and shuffled.

Burroughs begins by accepting the full implication of his subject matter:

Well these are the simple facts of the case—There were at least two parasites one sexual the other cerebral working together the way parasites will—And why has no one ever asked "What is word?"—Why do you talk to yourself all the time?

Operation Rewrite, Burroughs's own function as a writer, a role recognised by the narrative (there is no pretence that the book has some kind of independent existence), defines the subject matter of *The Ticket that Exploded*:

The Venusian invasion was known as "Operation Other Half," that is a parasitic invasion of the sexual area taking advantage, as all invasion plans must, of an already existing mucked up situation—The human organism is literally consisting of two halves from the beginning, word and all human sex is this unsanitary arrangement whereby two entities attempt to occupy the same three-dimensional coordinate points giving rise to the sordid latrine brawls which have characterised a planet based on "The Word."

Far from being an arbitrary stunt, Burroughs's cut-in method is thus seen as the most appropriate technique for this marriage of opposites, as well as underlining the role of recurrent images in all communication, fixed at the points of contact in the webs of language linking everything in our lives, from nostalgic reveries of "invisible passenger took my hands in dawn sleep of water music—Broken towers intersect cigarette smoke memory of each other" to sinister bureaucratic memos and medicalese. Many of the portmanteau images in the book make no sense unless seen in terms of this merging of opposites, e.g. the composite character known as Mr Bradly Mr Martin, and a phrase such as "rectums merging," which shocked the reviewer in *The London Magazine* to ask "how?"—obviously the poor woman hadn't the faintest idea what the book was about.

The characters who appear in the narrative may be externalised in "three-dimensional terms," as Burroughs puts it, but only so long as they suit the purposes of the subject matter. The "reality" of the books is not some pallid reflection of a hypothetical external scene, its details and local colour stitched into the narrative like poker-work, but the self-created verbal reality of the next sentence and paragraph, like a track-laying train free to move about in all directions on a single set of rails.

In turn, Burroughs's three novels are a comprehensive vision of the individual imagination's relationship to society at large (*The Naked Lunch*), to sex (*The Soft Machine*), and to time and space (*The Ticket that Exploded*).

In *The Naked Lunch* (i.e., the addict's fix), Burroughs compares organized society with that of its most extreme opposite, the invisible society of drug addicts. His implicit conclusion is that the two are not very different, certainly at the points where they make the closest contact—in prisons and psychiatric institutions. His police are all criminals and perverts, while his doctors, like the egregious Dr Benway of Islam Inc., are sadistic psychopaths whose main intention is to maim and disfigure their patients. Most of them, of course, are not aware of this, and their stated intentions may be the very opposite. Benway, a manipulator and co-ordinator of symbol systems, whose assignment in Annexia is T.D.—Total Demoralization—makes it his first task to abolish concentration camps, mass arrest, and "except under certain limited and special circumstances" the use of torture. When out of a job he keeps himself going by per-forming cut-rate abortions in subway toilets, "operating with one hand, beating the rats offa my patients with the other." Likeable and insouci-ant, Benway is full of ingenious ideas for uncovering the spies who infest every nook and cranny:

An agent is trained to deny his agent identity by asserting his cover story. So why not use psychic jiu-jitsu and go along with him? Suggest that his cover story is his identity and that he has no other. His agent identity becomes uncon-scious, that is, out of control . . .

However, questions of identity are highly relativistic. As one spy laments: "So I am a public agent and don't know who I work for, get my instructions from street signs, newspapers and pieces of conversation . . ."

By contrast, the addicts form a fragmentary, hunted sect, only asking to be left alone and haunted by their visions of subway dawns, cheap hotels, empty amusement parks and friends who have committed suicide. "The fact of addiction imposes contact," but in their relationships with one another they at least take no moral stand, and their illusions and ambitions are directed only at themselves. But for its continued comic richness—for much of the way it reads like the Lenny Bruce show rewrit-ten by Dr Goebbels—*The Naked Lunch* would be a profoundly pessimis-tic book, for Burroughs's conclusion is that the war between society and individual freedom, a freedom that consists simply of being individual, can never end, and that ultimately the only choice is between living in one's own nightmares or in other people's, for those who gain control of the system, like Benway and the Nazi creators of the death camps, merely impose their own fantasies on everyone else.

In *The Soft Machine* (the title is an explicit description of the sexual apparatus) Burroughs carries out a vast exploration of the nature of the sexual act, whose magic revivifies everything it touches. In this strange, hallucinatory world everything is translated into sexual terms, and the time is one when "everyone was raising some kinda awful life form in his bidet to fight the Sex Enemy."

What appear to be the science fictional elements in *The Soft Machine*, and to a greater extent in *The Ticket that Exploded*—there are Nova Police, and characters such as the Fluoroscopic Kid, the Subliminal Kid, the delightful Johnny Yen, errand boy from the death trauma, heavy metal addicts, Green boy-girls from the terminal sewers of Venus—in fact play a metaphorical role and are not intended to represent "three-dimensional" figures. These self-satirizing figments are part of the casual vocabulary of the space age, shared by all people born after the year 1920, just as Mata Hari, the Mons Angel, and the dirty men's urinal to the north of Waterloo form part of the semi-comical vocabulary of an older generation. In so far as *The Ticket . . .* is a work of science fiction, it is on a far more serious level. The exploding ticket, i.e., the individual identity in extension through time and space, provides Burroughs with an endless source of brilliant images, of which "the photo flakes falling" is the most moving in the book—moments of spent time, each bearing an image of some experience, drifting down like snow on all our memories and lost hopes. The sad poetry of the concluding chapter of *The Ticket . . .* , as the whole apocalyptic landscape of Burroughs's world closes in upon itself, now and then flaring briefly like a dying volcano, is on a par with Anna Livia Plurabelle's requiem for her river-husband in *Finnegans Wake*.

And zero time to the sick tracks—A long time between suns I held the stale overcoat—Sliding between light and shadow—Cross the wounded galaxies we intersect, poison of dead sun in your brain slowly fading—Migrants of ape in gasoline crack of history, explosive bio-advance out of space to neon Pass without doing our ticket—Mountain wind of Saturn in the morning sky—From the death trauma weary goodbye then.

For science fiction the lesson of Burroughs's work is plain. It is now nearly forty years since the first Buck Rogers comic strip, and only two less than a century since the birth of science fiction's greatest modern practitioner, H. G. Wells, yet the genre is still dominated by largely the same set of conventions, the same repertory of ideas, and, worst of all, by the assumption that it is still possible to write accounts of interplanetary voyages in which the appeal is to realism rather than to fantasy. Once it gets "off the ground" into space all science fiction is fantasy, and the more serious it tries to be, the more naturalistic, the greater its failure, as it completely lacks the moral authority and conviction of a literature won from experience.

Burroughs also illustrates that the whole of science fiction's imaginary universe has long since been absorbed into the general consciousness, and that most of its ideas are now valid only in a kind of marginal spoofing. Indeed, I seriously doubt whether science fiction is any longer the most important source of new ideas in the very medium it originally created. The main task facing science fiction writers now is to create a new set of conventions. Burroughs methods of exploring time and space, for example, or creating their literary equivalents, are an object lesson.

However, Burroughs's contribution to science fiction is only a minor aspect of his achievement. In his trilogy, William Burroughs has fashioned from our dreams and nightmares the authentic mythology of the age of Cape Canaveral, Hiroshima and Belsen. His novels are the terminal documents of the mid-20th century, scabrous and scarifying, a progress report from an inmate in the cosmic madhouse.

William Burroughs,
    I'm with you in Rockland
        where we wake up electrified out of the coma by
        our own soul's airplanes
    I'm with you in Rockland
        in my dreams you walk dripping from a sea-
        journey on the highway across America in tears
        to the door of my cottage in the Western night

LA JETÉE, ACADEMY ONE

(July 1966)

This strange and poetic film, a fusion of science fiction, psychological fable and photo-montage, creates in its unique way a series of bizarre images of the inner landscapes of time. Apart from a brief three-second sequence—a young woman's hesitant smile, a moment of extraordinary poignancy, like a fragment of a child's dream—the thirty-minute film is composed entirely of still photographs. Yet this succession of disconnected images is a perfect means of projecting the quantified memories and movements through time that are the film's subject matter.

The jetty of the title is the main observation platform at Orly Airport. The long pier reaches out across the concrete no man's land, the departure-point for other worlds. Giant jets rest on the apron beside the pier, metallic ciphers whose streamlining is a code for their passage through time. The light is powdery. The spectators on the observation platform have the appearance of mannequins. The hero is a small boy, visiting the airport with his parents. Suddenly there is a fragmented glimpse of a man falling. An accident has occurred, but while everyone is running to the dead man the small boy is looking instead at the face of a young woman by the rail. Something about this face, its expression of anxiety, regret and relief, and above all the obvious but unstated involvement of the young woman with the dead man, creates an image of extraordinary power in the boy's mind.

Years later, World War III breaks out. Paris is almost obliterated by an immense holocaust. A few survivors live in the circular galleries below the Palais de Chaillot, like rats in some sort of abandoned test-maze warped out of its normal time. The victors, distinguished by the strange eye-pieces they wear, begin to conduct a series of experiments on the survivors, among them the hero, now a man of about thirty. Faced with a destroyed world, the experimenters are hoping to send a man through time. They select the young man because of the powerful memory he carries of the pier at Orly. With luck he will home on to this. Other volunteers have gone insane, but the extraordinary strength of his memory carries him back to pre-war Paris. The sequence of images here is the most remarkable in the film, the subject lying in a hammock in the underground corridor as if waiting for some inward sun to rise, a bizarre surgical mask over his eyes—in my experience, the only convincing time travel in the whole of science fiction.

Arriving in Paris, he wanders among the strange crowds, unable to make contact with anyone until he meets the young woman he had seen as a child at Orly Airport. They fall in love, but their relationship is marred by his sense of isolation in time, his awareness that he has committed some kind of psychological crime in pursuing this memory. As if trying to place himself in time, he takes the young woman to museums of palaeontology, and they spend days among the fossil plants and animals. They visit Orly Airport, where he decides that he will not go back to the experimenters at Chaillot. At this moment three strange figures appear. Agents from an even more distant future, they are policing the time-ways, and have come to force him back. Rather than leave the young woman, he throws himself from the pier. The falling body is the one he glimpsed as a child.

This familiar theme is treated with remarkable finesse and imagination, its symbols and perspectives continually reinforcing the subject matter. Not once does it make use of the time-honoured conventions of traditional science fiction. Creating its own conventions from scratch, it triumphantly succeeds where science fiction invariably fails.

THE COMING OF THE UNCONSCIOUS

(July 1966)

The images of surrealism are the iconography of inner space. Popularly regarded as a lurid manifestation of fantastic art concerned with states of dream and hallucination, surrealism is in fact the first movement, in the words of Odilon Redon, to place "the logic of the visible at the service of the invisible." This calculated submission of the impulses and fantasies of our inner lives to the rigours of time and space, to the formal inquisition of the sciences, psychoanalysis pre-eminent among them, produces a heightened or alternate reality beyond and above those familiar to either our sight or our senses. What uniquely characterises this fusion of the outer world of reality and the inner world of the psyche (which I have termed "inner space") is its redemptive and therapeutic power. To move through these landscapes is a journey of return to one's innermost being.

The pervasiveness of surrealism is proof enough of its success. The landscapes of the soul, the juxtaposition of the bizarre and familiar, and all the techniques of violent impact have become part of the stock-in-trade of publicity and the cinema, not to mention science fiction. If anything, surrealism has been hoisted with the petard of its own undisputed mastery of self-advertisement. The real achievements of Ernst, Tanguy and Magritte have only just begun to emerge through the mêlée of megaphones and manifestos. Even in the case of a single painter, such as Salvador Dali, the exhibitionistic antics which the Press have always regarded as "news" have consistently obscured the far more important implications of his work.

These contradictory elements reflect the dual origins of surrealism—on the one hand in Dada, a post–World War I movement not merely against war and society, but against art and literature as well, out to perpetrate any enormity that would attract attention to its mission—the total destruction of so-called "civilised" values. The rise of Hitler, a madman beyond the wildest dreams even of the Dadaists, shut them up for good, although the influence of Dada can still be seen in "happenings," in the obscene tableau-sculptures of Keinholz and in the critical dictats of Andre Breton, the pope of surrealism, that "surrealism is pure psychic automatism." Far from it.

The other, and far older, source of surrealism is in the symbolists and expressionists of the 19th century, and in those whom Marcel Jean calls "sages of dual civilisation"—Sade, Lautréamont, Jarry and Apollinaire, synthesist poets well aware of the role of the sciences and the industrial societies in which they lived. Sade's erotic fantasies were matched by an acute scientific interest in the psychology and physiology of the human being. Lautréamont's *Song of Maldoror*, almost the basic dream-text of surrealism, uses scientific images: "beautiful as the fleshy wattle, conical in shape, furrowed by deep transverse lines, which rises up at the base of the turkey's upper beak—beautiful as the chance meeting on an operating table of a sewing machine and an umbrella." Apollinaire's erotic-scientific poetry is full of aircraft and the symbols of industrial society, while Jarry, in "The Passion considered as an Uphill Bicycle Race," unites science, sport and Christianity in the happiest vein of anti-clerical humour.

This preoccupation with the analytic function of the sciences as a means of codifying and fractionating the inner experience of the senses is seen in the use surrealism made of discoveries in optics and photography—for example, in the physiologist E. J. Marey's Chronograms, multiple-exposure photographs in which the dimension of time is perceptible, *the moving figure of a man represented as a series of dune-like lumps*. Its interest in the peculiar time-values of oceanic art, in the concealed dimensions hinted at by Rorschach tests, culminated in psychoanalysis. This, with its emphasis on the irrational and perverse, on the significance of apparently free or random associations, its symbolism and whole concept of the unconscious, was a complete mythology of the psyche—moreover, a functional mythology which could be used for the systematic exploration of the inner reality of our lives.

Something of the ferment of ideas that existed by 1924, when Andre Breton issued the First Surrealist Manifesto, can be seen from both these histories. What seems particularly extraordinary is the sheer volume of activity, the endless stream of experimental magazines, pamphlets, exhibitions and congresses, films and bizarre frolics, as well as a substantial body of paintings and sculpture, all produced by a comparatively small group (far smaller, for example, than the number of writers in science fiction here and in the U.S.A.).

Equally, the movement is noted for the remarkable beauty of its women—Georgette Magritte, demure sphinx with the eyes of a tamed Mona Lisa; the peerless Meret Oppenheim, designer of the fur-lined cup and saucer; Dorothea Tanning, with her hieratic eyes; the mystic Leonora Carrington, painter of infinitely frail fantasies; and presiding above them all the madonna of Port Lligat, Gala Dali, ex-wife of the poet Paul Eluard, who described her before his death as the one "with the look that pierces walls." One could write a book, let alone a review, about these extraordinary creatures—nymphs of another planet, in your orisons be all my dreams remembered.

In so far as they have a direct bearing on the speculative fiction of the immediate future, the key documents of surrealism seem to me to be the following. Together they share an explicit preoccupation with the nature of that reality perceived by the inner eye, with our notions of identity and the metaphysics of our lives.

Chirico: *The Disquieting Muses.* An undefined anxiety has begun to spread across the deserted square. The symmetry and regularity of the arcades conceals an intense inner violence; this is the face of catatonic withdrawal. The space within this painting, like the intervals within the arcades, contains an oppressive negative time. The smooth, egg-shaped heads of the mannequins lack all features and organs of sense, but instead are marked with cryptic signs. These mannequins are human beings from whom all transitional time has been eroded, they have been reduced to the essence of their own geometries.

Max Ernst: *The Elephant of Celebes*. A large cauldron with legs, sprouting a pipe that ends in a bull's head. A decapitated woman gestures towards it, but the elephant is gazing at the sky. High in the clouds, fishes are floating. Ernst's wise machine, hot cauldron of time and myth, is the tutelary deity of inner space, the benign minotaur of the labyrinth.

Magritte: *The Annunciation*. A rocky path leads among dusty olive trees. Suddenly a strange structure blocks our way. At first glance it seems to be some kind of pavilion. A white lattice hangs like a curtain over the dark façade. Two elongated chess-men stand to one side. Then we see that this is in no sense a pavilion where we may rest. This terrifying structure is a neuronic totem, its rounded and connected forms are a fragment of our own nervous systems, perhaps an insoluble code that contains the operating formulae for our own passage through time and space. The annunciation is that of a unique event, the first exter-nalisation of a neural interval.

Dali: *The Persistence of Memory*. The empty beach with its fused sand is a symbol of utter psychic alienation, of a final stasis of the soul. Clock time here is no longer valid, the watches have begun to melt and drip. Even the embryo, symbol of secret growth and possibility, is drained and limp. These are the residues of a remembered moment of time. The most remarkable elements are the two rectilinear objects, formalisations of sections of the beach and sea. The displacement of these two images through time, and their marriage with our own four-dimensional continuum, has warped them into the rigid and unyield-ing structures of our own consciousness. Likewise, the rectilinear structures of our own conscious reality are warped elements from some placid and harmonious future.

Oscar Dominguez: *Decalcomania*. By crushing gouache Dominguez pro-duced evocative landscapes of porous rocks, drowned seas and corals. These coded terrains are models of the organic landscapes enshrined in our central nervous systems. Their closest equivalents in the outer world of reality are those to which we most respond: igneous rocks, dunes, drained deltas. Only these landscapes contain the psychologi-cal dimensions of nostalgia, memory and the emotions.

Ernst: *The Eye of Silence*. This spinal landscape, with its frenzied rocks tow-
ering into the air above the silent swamp, has attained an organic life
more real than that of the solitary nymph sitting in the foreground.
These rocks have the luminosity of organs freshly exposed to the light.
The real landscapes of our world are seen for what they are—the palaces of flesh and bone that are the living facades enclosing our own
subliminal consciousness.

The sensational elements in these paintings are merely a result of
their use of the unfamiliar, their revelation of unexpected associations.
If anything, surrealist painting has one dominant characteristic: a glassy
isolation, as if all the objects in its landscapes had been drained of their
emotional associations, the accretions of sentiment and common usage.

What they demonstrate conclusively is that our commonplace notions
of reality—for example, the rooms we occupy, the rural and urban landscapes around us, the musculatures of our own bodies, the postures we
assume—may have very different meanings by the time they reach the
central nervous system. Conversely, the significance of the images projected from within the psyche may have no direct correlation at all to
their apparent counterparts in the world outside us. This is commonplace
enough as far as the more explicit symbols of the dream are concerned—
the snakes, towers and mandalas whose identity Freud and Jung revealed.
Surrealism, however, is the first systematic investigation of the significance of the most unsuspected aspects of both our inner and outer lives—
the meaning, for example, of certain kinds of horizontal perspective, of
curvilinear or soft forms as opposed to rectilinear ones, of the conjunction of two apparently unrelated postures.

The techniques of surrealism have a particular relevance at this
moment, when the fictional elements in the world around us are multiplying to the point where it is almost impossible to distinguish between
the "real" and the "false"—the terms no longer have any meaning. The
faces of public figures are projected at us as if out of some endless global
pantomime, they and the events in the world at large have the conviction and reality of those depicted on giant advertisement hoardings. The
task of the arts seems more and more to be that of isolating the few elements of reality from this mélange of fictions, not some metaphorical

"reality," but simply the basic elements of cognition and posture that are the jigs and props of our consciousness.

Surrealism offers an ideal tool for exploring these ontological objectives: the meaning of time and space (for example, the particular significance of rectilinear forms in memory), of landscape and identity, the role of the senses and emotions within these frameworks. As Dali has remarked, after Freud's explorations within the psyche it is now the *outer* world which will have to be eroticised and quantified. The mimetising of past traumas and experiences, the discharging of fears and obsessions through states of landscape, architectural portraits of individuals—these more serious aspects of Dali's work illustrate some of the uses of surrealism. It offers a neutral zone or clearing house where the confused currencies of both the inner and outer worlds can be standardised against each other.

At the same time we should not forget the elements of magic and surprise that wait for us in this realm. In the words of Andre Breton: "The confidences of madmen: I would spend my life in provoking them. They are people of scrupulous honesty, whose innocence is only equalled by mine. Columbus had to sail with madmen to discover America."

THE THOUSAND WOUNDS AND FLOWERS

(January 1969)

If an Einstein Memorial Time Centre is ever founded, it should take its first premises in the Museum of Modern Art. The hidden perspectives hinted at in even the most anecdotal paintings of Picasso and Braque, not to mention the time-saturated images of the surrealists, say more about the subject than anything the natural sciences can provide, for the clear reason that the sciences are not equipped to deal with the metaphor. The thousand wounds and flowers opened in our sides every day irrigate themselves from a very different watershed.

Given this virtually total handicap, the collection of essays edited (or more exactly, "edited up") by J. T. Frazer is interesting chiefly for its marginal information. The bulk of this book is concerned, not with time, but with duration, succession, the "representation" of events, coexistence and the like, topics that soon float adrift on the verbal level, if they ever had any existence at all on any other. Enough glosses on Heraclitus, Parmenides, Newton, Shakespeare's Sonnets, Kant, Bergson and William James are provided to pump the British Museum Library into the world's largest hot air balloon, although in other senses the book has a certain charm, like an imaginary Borges story about a history of histories of time. Charm, though, is probably too light a word to use—this book may not have depth but it undoubtedly has width. Laid side by side, the tongues of its garrulous authors would pave all the roads to Babel.

The succession of banal misstatements of the obvious soon becomes wearying. "Man is confronted by a world which he commonly describes through two characteristics: on the one hand, objects are spread out in space; on the other hand, events succeed each other and endure for shorter or longer periods of *time*." J. T. Frazer. And, "At some time during childhood each normal human being makes two discoveries of profound personal significance: they are those of the facts of birth and death." S. G. F. Brandon. Both these statements make one wonder how the publishers ever passed the book to the typesetters—perhaps they were hoping for a printer's strike.

Various questions seem to me to be of interest.

1) To take a literary example, why do so many of Shakespeare's heroes exhibit signs of "narrative delay"; Hamlet notably, Macbeth and Lear (both archetypical ward bosses presumably well educated in the realpolitik of when to put the knife in or back out gracefully), even Caesar and Prospero, world-weary intellectuals not notably tolerant of fools? The great majority of Shakespeare's heroes show all the signs of immaturity rather than psychopathology, but it seems to me that the "time delay" device may well reflect some subtle dislocation of one's normal processes of recognition and action during situations of extreme danger or hazard, like the suspended time of Warhol's "Death and Disaster" series—a deliberate holding of the camera frame for the purposes of one's own conceptual understanding. At times of crisis or bereavement one may well "hold" events in the camera of one's mind in order to accept all the parameters of the situation, a calculated dramatising of experience, however painful.

2) At London's Charing Cross Hospital, and a number of other enlightened maternity homes, the father is present at his wife's delivery, an extraordinary experience, by any standards, of the new-born child's

remarkable age; lying between his mother's legs, older than pharaoh, older in fact than the great majority of his so-called biological contemporaries. From where does this sense of time come, like the sense of space one feels while looking at the Milky Way?

3) The time-values contained in the paintings of Tanguy, Delvaux, Chirico, quite apart from those of the more "psychological" of the Renaissance masters—Gentile Bellini, Leonardo, Piero della Francesca. The geometry of landscape and situation seems to create its own systems of time, the sense of a dynamic element which is cinematising the events of the canvas, translating a posture or ceremony into dynamic terms. The greatest movie of the twentieth century is the Mona Lisa, just as the greatest novel is Gray's Anatomy.

4) Are there reasons to believe that our apprehension of the future is intimately associated with the origins of human speech, and that the imaginary reconstruction of events necessary for our recognition of the past is also linked with the invention of language?

In the Korsakov Syndrome, as a result of organic brain disturbance, memories fall out of place and there is no comprehension of succession and duration. Disturbance in chronology is often a first symptom of an oncoming psychotic phase. Schizophrenics may either deny the existence of time (on the basis of their infantile delusions of omnipotence), or deny that they lived at all before the onset of their psychosis. Compulsion neurotics stick to a tyrannical inner schedule out of a fear of real time. *Déjà vu* may be prompted by forbidden infantile wishes of which the possessor has become subliminally aware. In serious brain disturbances there can be extreme feelings of confusion which stem from the inability to "file" daily events (From *The Time Sense in Psychiatry* by J. A. M. Meerloo, one of the few interesting papers in the book).

"Time does not exist for those who are absolutely without anxiety." Kierkegaard. A melancholy prescription for immortality.

Counting rhythms are increased by rises in temperature. Psilocybin or LSD not only raise the body temperature and thus produce an overestimation of clock time, "clock contraction," but a simultaneous expansion of space. The speed of nervous conduction is raised by three milliseconds for every degree Centigrade.

Certain patients with severe brain damage are unable to distinguish whether they are awake or dreaming.

SALVADOR DALI: THE INNOCENT AS PARANOID

(February 1969)

The art of Salvador Dali is a metaphor that embraces the 20th century. Within his genius the marriage of reason and nightmare is celebrated across an altar smeared with excrement, in an order of service read from a textbook of psychopathology. Dali's paintings constitute a body of prophecy about ourselves unequalled in accuracy since Freud's *Civilization and its Discontents*. Voyeurism, self-disgust, biomorphic horror, the infantile basis of our dreams and longings—these diseases of the psyche which Dali rightly diagnosed have now culminated in the most sinister casualty of the century: the death of affect.

This demise of feeling and emotion has paved the way for all our most real and tender pleasures—in the excitements of pain and mutilation; in sex as the perfect arena, like a culture-bed of sterile pus, for all the veronicas of our own perversions; in our moral freedom to pursue our own psychopathology as a game; and in our ever-greater powers of abstraction—what our children have to fear are not the cars on the freeways of tomorrow but our own pleasure in calculating the most elegant parameters of their deaths.

Dali's paintings not only anticipate the psychic crisis that produced this glaucous paradise, but document the uneasy pleasures of living within it. The great twin leitmotifs of the 20th century—sex and paranoia—preside over his life, as over ours. With Max Ernst and William Burroughs he forms a trinity of the only living men of genius. However, where Ernst and Burroughs transmit their reports at midnight from the dark causeways of our spinal columns, Dali has chosen to face all the chimeras of his mind in the full glare of noon. Again, unlike Ernst and Burroughs, whose reclusive personalities merge into the penumbra around them, Dali's identity remains entirely his own. Don Quixote in a silk lounge suit, he rides eccentrically across a viscous and overlit desert, protected by nothing more than his furious moustaches.

For most people, it goes without saying, Dali is far too much his own man. Although the pampered darling of jet-set aristocracy, many of whom, like Edward James and the Vicomte de Noailles, have done their intelligent best by him, forking out large amounts of cash when he most needed it, the general response to Dali is negative—thanks, first, to the international press, which has always encouraged his exhibitionist antics, and second, to the puritanical intelligentsia of Northern Europe and America, for whom Dali's subject matter, like the excrement he painted in *The Lugubrious Game*, reminds them far too much of all the psychic capitulations of their childhoods.

Admittedly Dali's chosen persona—part comic-opera barber, part mad muezzin on his phallic tower crying out a hymn of undigested gobbets of psychoanalysis and self-confession (just the kind of thing to upset those bowler-hatted library customs clerks), part genius with all its even greater embarrassments—is not one that can be fitted into any handy category. Most people, even intelligent ones, are not notably inventive, and the effort of devising a wholly new category, and one at that to be occupied by only one tenant, demoralizes them even before they have started.

At the same time it seems to me that the consistent failure, during the past thirty years, to grasp the immense importance of Dali's work has a significance that extends far beyond any feelings of distaste for his personal style. Painter, writer, engraver, illustrator, jeweller, personality—his polymath genius is on a par with Leonardo's. What mars it is not himself, but the cracks running across a million eyeballs.

SURREALISM THE MAIN VISUAL TRADITION OF THE 20TH CENTURY; SCIENCE FICTION THE MAIN LITERARY TRADITION

Already one can see that science fiction, far from being an unimportant minor offshoot, in fact represents the main literary tradition of the 20th century, and certainly its oldest—a tradition of imaginative response to science and technology that runs in an intact line through Wells, Aldous Huxley, the writers of modern American science fiction, and such present-day innovators as William Burroughs and Paolozzi.

The main "fact" of the 20th century is the concept of the unlimited future. This predicate of science and technology enshrines the notion of a moratorium on the past, on the one hand, and on the other the limitless possibilities of even the most trivial situation. Above all, the 20th century is the first to realise the notion of the concept as a programmatic device, whether applied to the largest topics—space exploration, the neutralisation of emotion contained in what I have called "the death of affect"—or in the most unimportant, such as the gesture of uncrossing one's legs, the geometry of a motor car fender, or what you will.

In the face of this immense continent of possibility, all literatures other than science fiction are doomed to irrelevance. None have the vocabulary of ideas and images to deal with the present, let alone the future. One of the conventions of the past thirty years has been that the so-called Modern Movement—i.e., the literary tradition running from Baudelaire and Rimbaud through Joyce and Eliot to Hemingway and Camus, to name a few landmarks—is the principal literary tradition of the 20th century. The dominant characteristic of this movement is its sense of individual isolation, its mood of introspection and alienation, a state of mind always assumed to be the hallmark of the 20th century consciousness.

Far from it. On the contrary, it seems to me that the Modern Movement belongs to the nineteenth century, a reaction against the monolithic philistine character of Victorianism, against the tyranny of the paterfamilias, secure in his financial and sexual authority, and against the massive constraints of bourgeois society. In no way does the Modern Movement have any bearing on the facts of the 20th century, the first flight of the Wright brothers, the invention of the Pill, the social and sexual philosophy of the ejector seat. Apart from its marked retrospective bias, its obsession with the subjective nature of experience, its real subject matter is the rationalization of guilt and estrangement. Its elements are introspection, pessimism and sophistication. Yet if anything befits the 20th century it is optimism, the iconography of mass-merchandizing, and naivety.

This long-standing hostility to science fiction, and the inability to realize that the future provides a better key to the present than does the past, is reflected in a similar attitude to surrealism as a whole. Recently, as part of a general rejection and loss of interest in the past, both science fiction and surrealism have enjoyed a sudden vogue, but Dali still remains excluded. He is popular as ever only with the rich—who presumably feel no puritan restraints about exploring the possibilities of their lives—and a few wayward spirits like myself.

THE BIRTH OF LIQUID DESIRES
Dali's background was conventional. Born in 1904, the second son of a well-to-do lawyer, he had a permissive childhood, which allowed him a

number of quasi-incestuous involvements with governesses, art masters, old beggar women and the like. At art school he developed his precociously brilliant personality, and discovered psychoanalysis.

By this time, the late 1920s, surrealism was already a mature art. Chirico, Duchamp and Max Ernst were its elder statesmen. Dali, however, was the first to accept completely the logic of the Freudian age, to describe the extraordinary world of the 20th century psyche in terms of the commonplace vocabulary of everyday life—telephones, wristwatches, fried eggs, cupboards, beaches. What distinguishes Dali's work, above everything else, is the hallucinatory naturalism of his renaissance style. For the most part the landscapes of Ernst, Tanguy or Magritte describe impossible or symbolic worlds—the events within them have "occurred," but in a metaphoric or spinal sense. The events in Dali's paintings are not far from our ordinary reality.

This reflects Dali's total involvement in Freud's view of the unconscious as a narrative stage. Elements from the margins of one's mind—the gestures of minor domestic traffic, movements through doors, a glance across a balcony—become transformed into the materials of a bizarre and overlit drama. The Oedipal conflicts we have carried with us from childhood fuse with the polymorphic landscapes of the present to create a strange and ambiguous future. The contours of a woman's back, the significance of certain rectilinear forms, marry with our memories and desires. The roles of everything are switched. Christopher Columbus comes ashore, just having discovered a young woman's buttocks. A childhood governess still dominates the foreshore of one's life, windows let into her body as in the walls of one's nursery. Later, in the mature Dali, nuclear and fragmentary forms transcribe the postures of the Virgin, tachist explosions illuminate the cosmogony of the H-bomb, the images of atomic physics are recruited to represent a pietist icon of a Renaissance madonna.

Given the extraordinary familiarity of Dali's paintings, it is surprising that so few people seem ever to have looked at them. If they remember them at all, it is in some kind of vague and uncomfortable way, which indicates that it is not only Oedipal and other symbols that frighten us, but any dislocation of our commonplace notions about reality. The latent significance of curvilinear as opposed to rectilinear forms, of soft as opposed to hard geometries, are topics that disturb us as much as any memory of a paternal ogre. Applying Freud's principle, we can see that reason safely rationalizes reality for us. Dali pulls the fuses out of this comfortable system.

In addition, Dali's technique of photographic realism and the particular cinematic style he adopted involve the spectator too closely for his own comfort. Where Ernst, Magritte and Tanguy relied very much on a traditional narrative space, presenting the subject matter frontally and with a generalized time structure, Dali represents the events of his paintings as if each was a single frame from a movie.

Although he is now famous for his paintings of the late 1920s and early 1930s, such as *The Persistence of Memory*, at the time Dali was close to penury. Picasso, Braque and Matisse held a monopoly of the critics' attention; the great battle being fought then, older than any Uccello painted, was between a philistine public and the cubist painters. Faced with this position, Dali, assisted by his ruthless and ambitious wife Gala, set out to use that other developing popular art of the 20th century—publicity, then shunned by intellectuals and the preserve of newspapers, film companies and the like. Dali's originality lay in the way he used the techniques of publicity for private purposes, to propound his own extremely private and conceptual ideas. Here he anticipated Warhol and a hundred other contemporary imitators.

Applying himself to a thousand and one stunts, he soon achieved the success he needed. At the start of World War II he moved to America, and his autobiography (*The Secret Life of Salvador Dali*) was written in the New England home of one of his first American patrons. Without doubt one of the great books of the century, *The Secret Life* was first published in England in 1948. Here Dali reveals his mastery as a writer. More than this, he invents a completely new alphabet, vocabulary and grammar of ideas, rich in psychoanalytic allusions but freighted also with an immense weight of reference to geology, aesthetic theory, metaphysics, metabiology, Christian iconography, haute couture, mathematics, film criticism, heraldry, politics—melded together into a unique alloy. This new language, which few people seem willing to read, just as they refuse to look at his paintings, allowed him to enlarge verbally on his visual subject matter, and was formalized above all in his so-called paranoic-critical method, i.e., the systematic and rational interpretation of hallucinatory phenomena.

Some idea of the richness and seriousness of this language can be seen in the titles of Dali's paintings:

Gala and the Angelus of Millet immediately preceding the arrival of the conic anamorphosis.

Suburbs of the Paranoic-Critical town: Afternoon on the outskirts of European history.

The flesh of the decollete of my wife, clothed, outstripping light at full speed.

Velazquez painting the Infanta Margarita with the lights and shadows of his own glory.

The Chromosome of a highly coloured fish's eye starting the harmonious disintegration of the Persistence of Memory.

Although apparently comic masterpieces at first sight, each of these titles, like dozens of others, exactly describes the subject matter of the painting. More than that, each illuminates its painting. To describe the landscapes of the 20th century, Dali uses its own techniques—its deliberate neuroticism, self-indulgence, its love of the glossy, lurid and bizarre. Behind these, however, is an eye as sharp as a surgeon's. Dali's work demonstrates that surrealism, far from being a gratuitous dislocation of one's perceptual processes, in fact represents the only reasonable technique for dealing with the subject matter of the century.

THE PAINTINGS

1) The classic Freudian phase. The trauma of birth, as in *The Persistence of Memory*, the irreconcilable melancholy of the exposed embryo. This world of fused beaches and overheated light is that perceived by the isolated child. The nervous surfaces are wounds on the cerebral cortex. The people who populate it, the Oedipal figures and marooned lovers, are those perceived through the glass of early childhood and adolescence. The obsessions are: excrement, the flaccid penis, anxiety, the timeless place, the threatening posture, the hallucinatory over-reality of tables and furniture, the geometry of rooms and stairways.

2) The metamorphic phase. A polyperverse period, a free-for-all of image and identity. From this period, during the late 1930s, come Dali's

obsessions with Hitler (the milky breasts of the Fuhrer compressed by his leather belt) and Lenin's buttocks, elongated like an immense sexual salami. Here, too, are most of the nightmare paintings, such as *The Horrors of War*, which anticipates not only Hiroshima and the death camps, but the metamorphic horrors of heart surgery and organ transplants, the interchangeability and dissolving identities of our own organs.

3) The Renaissance phase. Dali's penchant for a wiped academic style, Leonardoesque skies and grottoes, comes through strongly during the 1940s and 1950s in paintings such as his *Hypercubic Christ*. These images of madonnas and martyred Christs, quantified by a formal geometry, represent a pagan phase in Dali's art.

4) The Cosmogonic-religious phase. In the fifties Dali embarked on a series of explicitly religious paintings (most of them apparently on secular topics), such as those using the central figure of Christopher Columbus. Here the iconography of nuclear physics is used to invest his religious heroes with the unseen powers of the universe.

5) The phase of Analytic Geometry. The masterworks of this period, among the greatest in Dali's art, are the famous *Young Virgin Autosodomized by Her Own Chastity*, and *Goddess Leaning on Her Elbow*. Here the quantification of time and space is applied to the mysterious geometry of our own morphology and musculature.

6) Nuclear phase. Dali's marriage with the age of physics. Many of his most serene paintings, such as *Raphaelesque Head Exploding*, date from this recent period.

Notwithstanding the immense richness and vitality of this work, Dali still invites little more than hostility and derision. All too clearly one can see that polyperverse and polymorphic elements, acceptable within, say, automobile styling, are not acceptable when they explicitly refer to the basic props and perspectives of our consciousness.

DALI THE NAIVE
At the same time, other factors explain this hostility, above all the notion of the naive. Too often, when we think of the naive, we shed a sentimental tear for the Douanier Rousseau or the Facteur Cheval (the eccentric country postman who built with his own hands a dream palace in

pebbles and cement that rivals Ankor). Both these men, naives of genius, for the most part lonely, ignored and derided during their lifetimes, lit conveniently into our idea of the naive—amiable simpletons with egg on their ties. We can reassure ourselves that Jarry, Apollinaire and Picasso laughed at Rousseau, and admit that we too might laugh faced with so odd a departure from the accepted norm.

What we fail to realize is that science fiction, like surrealism, provides just this departure, and is an example of an art of the naive in mid-20th century terms. None of us have egg on our ties (more likely crepe suzette, given Playboy prices), nor are we particularly amiable, but like Dali we may well be simpletons. I regard Dali, like Wells and the writers of modern science fiction, as true naives, i.e. those taking imagination and reality at their face value, never at all sure, or for that matter concerned, which is which. In the same category I place many other notable originators, such as William Burroughs—certainly a naive, with his weird delusions, possibly correct, that Time magazine is out to subvert our minds and language—and Andy Warhol, a faun-like naive of the media landscape, using the basic techniques of 20th century mass communications, cinema and colour reproduction processes, for his own innocent and childlike amusement, the invention of conceptual games that delight the child in all of us.

Dali is a good example of the sophisticated naive, with an immense vocabulary of ideas and imagery, taking the "facts" of psychoanalysis at their face value and applying them like a Sunday painter to the materials of 20th century life—our psychopathology, our electric gardens, our switchboards of emotion and orgasm. Rousseau's enchanted botanical forests have been replaced by flyovers and production lines, but Dali's paintings still remain a valid image of the interior landscape of our minds.

That other naive, Henri Rousseau, a minor customs official, died alone and in poverty in 1910. His friends who had laughed at him then realized his true worth. Two years later he was reburied in a decent grave. The great sculptor, Brancusi, became a simple engraver and inscribed on the tomb an epitaph written by Apollinaire:

Dear Rousseau, can you hear us?
. . . let our luggage pass through the doors of heaven
Without paying duty . . .

Let us hope that on Dali's death a suitable epitaph is written to celebrate this unique and undervalued genius, who has counted for the first time the multiplication tables of obsession, psychopathology and possibility.

USE YOUR VAGINA

(June 1969)

Books like this one are never reviewed, although their sales—through mail order and under-the-counter outlets—are among the largest of all time, part of a huge invisible literature ignored by the critics. A factual reappraisal of these sexual handbooks, not merely as a subject for arch or clever comment, is long overdue. Most of them are profoundly earnest in tone, and deserve to be taken on their own terms in exactly the same way as the latest Ford Zephyr maintenance manual. How far any of them reflect the real world of sex is for each of us to judge. As basic primers they have the same unreality as the sort of colloquial French found in tourist guides, but this is less the fault of the publishers and authors than the impossibility of compressing the subject matter within the pages of a book.

How to Achieve Sexual Ecstasy was launched recently in a series of mail-order advertisements in magazines and underground newspapers. Elegant typography and a naked photographic model kicking up her heels suggested that this would be a fresh attempt to deal with an old subject matter. Some of the chapter titles, such as "Beyond Sexual Infinity" and "Threshold of the Sexual Psyche," seemed to describe a sexual version of *2001*, conjuring up a vision of a Panavision penis driving towards all the bedposts of eternity, while the Blue Danube played from the mattress vents. The book itself is far more conservative. Although its first publication is given as 1969, it is difficult to tell when it was written. So successful have these handbooks been over the last fifty years that many of them have been revised and reprinted dozens of times. This one is American in origin, the bulk of it probably written in the late fifties, although in one section comments are made on the Masters-Johnson studies. The author's attitude is one of permissiveness governed by a strict moral code. Throughout, his text enshrines the notion that complete sexual happiness is the right of everyone in terms of that self-defeating paradox, normal sexual behaviour.

The hypothetical reader is difficult to visualize, although the sales of this book have already been enormous. Who in fact would want to read it? Who would gain information from it? The preface describes it as a handbook of sex technique, though most of the amatory techniques and sexual positions described are known to any adolescent. At times one wonders whether these books are intended as fact or fiction. The lengthy description of acts of intercourse couched in detailed narrative terms are much more reminiscent of erotic fiction than they are of any handbook. However, in one sense it seems to me that these books of so-called sexual expertise provide what J. B. S. Haldane called a kinesthetic language, in this case a kinesthetic language of sex, a set of terms and descriptions by which ordinary people can describe a series of important experiences and activities for which no vocabulary previously existed.

A key to the book may come in the first chapter, in a section entitled "Arousing the Unresponsive Wife," a suggestion that perhaps the book is designed for married couples who have begun to find a monogamous sexual relationship something of a bore. The description of an idealized sexual encounter, the set piece of the book, is presented with enormous detail, with a great deal of attention paid to the mise-en-scene: "The place should be agreeable to both participants. If it is to be a public place such as an hotel or motel, care should be taken to ensure availability of accommodation, by reservation if possible." Warnings are given about the hazards offered by paper-thin walls, corridor noises and highway traffic, as well as public places which cater for "illicit sex traffic, which should be avoided for aesthetic as well as practical reasons."

Given the appropriate situation, all is well, and the extended description of the sex act becomes a kind of seduction of the reader, presented with a notable simplicity and warmth. Careful attention is paid to the needs of elaborate foreplay and a concern for the partner's responses. Repeatedly the book stresses the traditional view of the supposed slowness of women's responses (how times have changed). However, those of us who tend to rush our fences could surely learn something from the descriptions of how to kiss our partner's elbows and savour the delights of the navel. "Under the impetus of these attentions," the author assures us, "the woman will quickly reach a high level of passionate abandon. Her breath will begin to come in gasps (or sobs) and her hips will be in continuous motion. She may ask you to 'put it in me' or she may say something like 'Hurry, hurry.' At this point you should roll her onto her back."

An interesting comment on the psychology of the book is seen in what the author terms "the clean-up operation immediately following the afterplay period." He warns his readers that certain substances secreted under the duress of passion are often found offensive by both partners as passion wanes. It is wise, the author states, that clean-up begin before any feelings of revulsion may set in.

After this first extended narrative seen from the man's point of view a similar chapter follows from the standpoint of the woman. What characterizes the text is the immense concern that the author attributes to his two idealized partners. Both are so busy caring for the feelings of the other that they can have little time for any real passion, let alone the aggression and cruelty that drive in the same harness as love and tenderness.

In the second chapter, "Specialized Coital Positions," hints are given on how to derive the maximum of pleasure from the classic sexual positions. The language throughout is simple and matter-of-fact, under headings such as "Penetration is too shallow," "Fit is too loose" or "Fit is too tight." Again, enormous attention is given to the need to satisfy the woman partner, a problem primarily solved in terms of a series of elaborate devices for bringing the clitoris into direct and continuous contact with the shaft of the penis. This continuous deference towards women reveals the archaeology of the book, that first realization of the immense sexuality of women that stunned the generation of Freud and D. H. Lawrence.

Other problems discussed are those of intercourse where the man is much taller than the woman, where the woman's buttocks are particularly large, or where, given an unusually big penis, a fuller range of sexual pastimes is possible. The author recommends what he terms "riding high," and places great stress on the so-called "wheelbarrow position," strongly recommending it for those women who have difficulty in achieving complete orgasm. However, he points out the hazards of using the inverted-vulva positions during pregnancy. Again and again he emphasizes the need for women to make the most of their sexual

pleasure, at times even at the expense of their male partners. "Use your
vagina," he writes, "use it for sexual pleasure. Do not hasten towards his
climax, but towards *yours*."

Good advice, but at one point the author contrasts his idealized sexual
experience with what he terms the usual and tragic pattern of sex in our
society—masturbation, illicit adventures, frigidity, perversions, disenchantment, divorce, neuroses, psychoses, alcoholism and drug addiction,
prostitution and sex crimes. What the book completely ignores is the
fact that these activities are those which most people now seem to prefer,
that sexuality is expressed more and more in terms only of its perversions
and disenchantments rather than of those platonic embraces the book so
humanely and affectionately describes. Too many of us would rather be
involved in a sex crime than in sex. Sadly, the conceptualization of sex
which has taken place along with everything else leads us away from precisely those idealized sexual encounters which these handbooks describe.
To a large extent this book, like many others, is a nostalgic hymn to a
kind of sexual Garden of Eden, whose doors Havelock Ellis, Marie Stopes
and numerous other pioneers tried for so many years to re-open. Alas, the
original tenants are no longer interested. In all probability what will put
an end to the population explosion will be not birth control but buggery.
Sex does not exist, only eroticism.

For all its good intentions, and its broadminded concern for our sexual
happiness, *How to Achieve Sexual Ecstasy* has a strangely period quality.
Above all it is a monument to marriage and the monogamous sexual relationship, and to the somewhat old-fashioned notion that someone else's
pleasure is more important than our own. Far from being sent out under
plain wrappers, books of this kind should be read in schools, though how
far this would prepare our children for the real world seems doubtful, particularly to a generation of sub-teens brought up on Zap comics. When
one thinks of successful marriages today one thinks in terms of couples
who have worked out successful extra-marital relationships. A modern
and much more relevant version of this manual would be concerned with
the sexual perversions (some so bizarre that they have ceased to have
any connection with sex), with the effects of drugs and pot on sexual
behaviour, and the whole gamut of real and vicarious couplings possible
when more than two people are present. It would also provide accounts

of sexual intercourse with prostitutes, a specialized sub-category of sexual experience that requires its own expertise and mental attitudes. Needless to say, these ecstasies are of a very different kind, of the white tile smeared with pus. And if only by way of a pause, I recommend Stephan Gregory's book.

ALPHABETS OF UNREASON

(December 1969)

The psychopath never dates. Hitler's contemporaries—Baldwin, Chamberlain, Herbert Hoover—seem pathetically fusty figures, with their frock coats and wing collars, closer to the world of Edison, Carnegie and the hansom cab than to the first fully evolved modern societies over which they presided, areas of national consciousness formed by mass-produced newspapers and consumer goods, advertising and tele-communications. By comparison Hitler is completely up to date, and would be equally at home in the sixties (and probably even more so in the seventies) as in the twenties. The whole apparatus of the Nazi superstate, its nightmare uniforms and propaganda, seems weirdly turned-on, providing just that element of manifest insanity to which we all respond in the H-bomb or Vietnam—perhaps one reason why the American and Russian space programmes have failed to catch our imaginations is that this quality of explicit psychopathology is missing.

Certainly, Nazi society seems strangely prophetic of our own—the same maximizing of violence and sensation, the same alphabets of unreason and the fictionalizing of experience. Goebbels in his diaries remarks that he and the Nazi leaders had merely done in the realm of reality what Dostoevski had done in fiction. Interestingly, both Goebbels and Mussolini had written novels, in the days before they were able to get to grips with their real subject matter—one wonders if they would have bothered now, with the fiction waiting to be manipulated all around them.

Hitler's "novel," *Mein Kampf* was written in 1924, nearly a decade before he came to power, but is a remarkably accurate prospectus of his intentions, not so much in terms of finite political and social aims as of the precise psychology he intended to impose on the German people and its European vassals. For this reason alone it is one of the most important books of the 20th century, and well worth re-printing, despite the grisly pleasures its anti-Semitic ravings will give to the present generation of racists.

How far does Hitler the man come through the pages of this book? In the newsreels Hitler tends to appear in two roles—one, the demagogic orator, ranting away in a state apparently close to neurotic hysteria, and two, a benevolent and slightly eccentric *kapellmeister* sentimentally reviewing his SS bodyguard, or beaming down at a picked chorus of blond-haired German infants. Both these strands are present in *Mein Kampf*—the hectoring, rhetorical style, shaking with hate and violence, interspersed with passages of deep sentimentality as the author rhapsodizes to himself about the mystical beauty of the German landscape and its noble, simple-hearted peoples.

Apart from its autobiographical sections, the discovery by a small Austrian boy of his "Germanism," *Mein Kampf* contains three principal elements, the foundation stones, walls and pediment of a remarkably strong paranoid structure. First, there are Hitler's views on history and race, a quasi-biological system which underpins the whole basis of his political thought and explains almost every action he ever committed. Second, there are his views on the strict practicalities of politics and the seizure of power, methods of political organization and propaganda. Third, there are his views on the political future of the united Germanies, its expansionist foreign policy and general attitude to the world around it.

The overall tone of *Mein Kampf* can be seen from Hitler's original title for the testament: *A Four and a Half Years' Struggle Against Lies, Stupidity and Cowardice: A Reckoning with the Destroyers of the Nazi Party Movement*. It was the publisher, Max Amann, who suggested the shorter and far less revealing *Mein Kampf,* and what a sigh he must have breathed when Hitler agreed. Hitler's own title would have been far too much of a giveaway, reminding the readers of the real sources of Hitler's anti-Semitic and racialist notions.

Reading Hitler's paranoid rantings against the Jews, one is constantly struck by the biological rather than political basis of his entire thought and personality. His revulsion against the Jews was physical, like his reaction against any peoples, such as the Slavs and Negroes, whose physique, posture, morphology and pigmentation alerted some screaming switchboard of insecurity within his own mind.

What is interesting is the language in which he chose to describe those obsessions—primarily faecal, one assumes, from his endless preoccupation with "cleanliness." Rather than use economic, social or political arguments against the Jews, Hitler concentrated almost solely on this inflated biological rhetoric. By dispensing with any need to rationalize his prejudices, he was able to tap an area of far deeper unease and uncertainty, and one moreover which his followers would never care to expose too fully to the light of day. In the unanswerable logic of psychopathology, the Jews became the scapegoats for all the terrors of toilet-training and weaning. The constant repetition of the words "filth," "vileness," "abscess," "hostile," "shudder," endlessly reinforce these long-repressed feelings of guilt and desire.

In passing, it is curious to notice that Hitler's biological interpretations of history have a number of striking resemblances to those of Desmond Morris. In both writers one finds the same reliance on the analogy of the lower mammals, on a few basic formulas of behaviour such as "struggle," "competition," "defence of territory." There is the same simple schematic view of social relations, the same highly generalised assertions about human behaviour that are presented as proven facts. Hitler talks without definition of "lower races" in the same way that Morris refers to "primitive societies" and "simple communities." Both are writing for half-educated people whose ideas about biology and history come from popular newspaper and encyclopaedia articles, and whose interest in these subjects is a barely transparent cover for uneasy fantasies about their own bodies and emotions.[3]

In his preface, the translator of *Mein Kampf* describes it as written in the style of a self-educated modern South German with a talent for oratory. In this respect Hitler was one of the rightful inheritors of the twentieth century—the epitome of the half-educated man. Wandering about the streets of Vienna shortly before the First World War, his head full of vague artistic yearnings and clap-trap picked up from popular magazines, whom does he most closely resemble? Above all, Leopold Bloom, his ostensible arch-enemy, wandering around Joyce's Dublin at about the

---

3. This paragraph was omitted from *A User's Guide to the Millennium* (1997).

same time, his head filled with the same clap-trap and the same yearnings. Both are the children of the reference library and the self-improvement manual, of mass newspapers creating a new vocabulary of violence and sensation. Hitler was the half-educated psychopath inheriting the lavish communications systems of the 20th century. Forty years after his first abortive seizure of power he was followed by another unhappy misfit, Lee Harvey Oswald, in whose *Historic Diary* we see the same attempt by the half-educated to grapple with the information overflow that threatened to drown him.

3

COMMENTARIES

ON OWN WORK: NOVELS

Ballard wrote few introductions to his own novels, so the four here are all the more valuable for the insight they give into his reflections on his own practice.

A feature article originally published in *The Woman Journalist*, the small, card-bound "organ of the Society of Women Journalists and Writers," as "Time, Memory, Inner Space" acts as a commentary on *The Drowned World*. The Danish "Forord [foreword]" to *Grusomhedsudstillingen* [*The Atrocity Exhibition*] is the only piece from a foreign edition: we are fortunate that Ballard's original text, which bears intriguing comparison with the later "Introduction to the French Edition of *Crash!*," remains.[1] Ballard sent the English text to his Danish translator Jannick Storm on June 11, 1969. When assisting with the sale of Storm's archive, his friend Arne Herløv Petersen kept a copy, which was recovered for publication by Bernard Sigaud in 2014.[2]

The introductions to *Concrete Island* and *Hello America* were written for the 1994 Vintage reprints of these novels.

---

1. *The Atrocity Exhibition* (San Francisco: RE/Search, 1990) includes Ballard's marginal annotations, a sustained paratextual commentary that constitutes a comprehensive work in its own right. It makes little sense to include that here, so integrated is it with the text to which it responds: readers interested in that are urged to seek it out in any of the editions that have subsequently reproduced it; the RE/Search edition is highly recommended as being closest to Ballard's original wish for the collection to be published in a hybrid form with illustrations.

2. Bernard Sigaud, "The 'Forord' to the Danish Edition of *The Atrocity Exhibition*," in *Deep Ends: The J. G. Ballard Anthology 2015* (Toronto: The Terminal Press, 2015), 118–125.

THE DROWNED WORLD

"Time, Memory, Inner Space," *The Woman Journalist* (1963)

How far do the landscapes of one's childhood, as much as its emotional experiences, provide an inescapable background to all one's imaginative writing? Certainly my own earliest memories are of Shanghai during the annual long summer of floods, when the streets of the city were two or three feet deep in a brown silt-laden water, and where the surrounding countryside, in the center of the flood-table of the Yangtze, was an almost continuous mirror of drowned paddy fields and irrigation canals stirring sluggishly in the hot sunlight. On reflection it seems to me that the image of an immense half-submerged city overgrown by tropical vegetation, which forms the centerpiece of *The Drowned World*, is in some way a fusion of my childhood memories of Shanghai and those of my last 10 years in London.

One of the subjects of the novel is the journey of return made by the principal characters from the 20th century back into the paradisal sun-filled world of a second Triassic age, and their gradually mounting awareness of the ambivalent motives propelling them into the emerging past. They realize that the uterine sea around them, the dark womb of the ocean mother, is as much the graveyard of their own individuality as it is the source of their lives, and perhaps their fears reflect my own uneasiness in re-enacting the experiences of childhood and attempting to explore such dangerous ground.

Among the characteristic fauna of the Triassic age were the crocodiles and alligators, amphibian creatures at home in both the aquatic and terrestrial worlds, who symbolize for the hero of the novel the submerged dangers of his quest. Even now I can vividly remember the enormous ancient alligator housed in a narrow concrete pit, half-filled with cigarette packets and ice-cream cartons in the reptile house at the Shanghai Zoo, who seemed to have been jerked forward reluctantly, so many tens of millions of years into the 20th century.

In many respects this fusion of past and present experiences, and of such disparate elements as the modern office buildings of central London and an alligator in a Chinese zoo, resembles the mechanisms by which dreams are constructed, and perhaps the great value of fantasy as a literary form is its ability to bring together apparently unconnected and dissimilar ideas. To a large extent all fantasy serves this purpose, but I believe that speculative fantasy, as I prefer to call the more serious fringe of science fiction, is an especially potent method of using one's imagination to construct a paradoxical universe where dream and reality become fused together, each retaining its own distinctive quality and yet in some way assuming the role of its opposite, and where by an undeniable logic black simultaneously becomes white.

Without in any way suggesting that the act of writing is a form of creative self-analysis, I feel that the writer of fantasy has a marked tendency to select images and ideas which directly reflect the internal landscapes of his mind, and the reader of fantasy must interpret them on this level, distinguishing between the manifest content, which may seem obscure, meaningless or nightmarish, and the latent content, the private vocabulary of symbols drawn by the narrative from the writer's mind. The dream worlds, synthetic landscapes and plasticity of visual forms invented by the writer of fantasy are external equivalents of the inner world of the psyche, and because these symbols take their impetus from the most formative and confused periods of our lives they are often time-sculptures of terrifying ambiguity.

This zone I think of as "inner space," the internal landscape of tomorrow that is a transmuted image of the past, and one of the most fruitful areas for the imaginative writer. It is particularly rich in visual symbols, and I feel that this type of speculative fantasy plays a role very similar to that of surrealism in the graphic arts. The painters de Chirico, Dali and Max Ernst, among others, are in a sense the iconographers of inner space, all during their most creative periods concerned with the discovery of images in which internal and external reality meet and fuse. Dali, regrettably, is now in total critical eclipse, but his paintings, with their soft watches and minatory luminous beaches, are of almost magical potency, suffused by that curious ambivalence that one can see elsewhere only on the serpentine faces in the paintings of Leonardo.

It is a curious thing that the landscapes of these painters, and of Dali in particular, are often referred to as dream-like, when in fact they must bear no resemblance to the vast majority of dreams, which in general take place within confined indoor settings, a cross between Kafka and Mrs Dale's Diary, and where fantastic images, such as singing flowers or sonic sculpture, appear as infrequently as they do in reality. This false identification, and the awareness that the landscapes and themes are reflections of some interior reality within our minds, is a pointer to the importance of speculative fantasy in the century of Hiroshima and Cape Canaveral.

THE ATROCITY EXHIBITION (1970)

"Forord" in *Grusomhedsudstillingen* (1969)

The marriage of reason and nightmare which has dominated the 20th century has given birth to an ever more surreal world. Within my own lifetime the Nagasaki mushroom cloud has given place on the psychic menu to Oldenburg's giant hamburgers. The assassins of presidents and cities become media personalities, flattered by interviewers, their tics and stutters fascinating millions. The Viet Nam war has become TV wallpaper. Sigmund Freud's profound pessimism in *Civilization and Its Discontents* has been replaced by McLuhan's delight in high-speed information mosaics. The H-bomb is a potency symbol. Our moral right to pursue our own psychopathology as a game is enshrined in almost every mass-magazine, motion picture and experimental play. Stylized violence in *Bonnie and Clyde* provides a viable iconography for department-store fashion displays. *Mondo Cane* finds a huge new market for the merchandising of pain. The furthest fantasies of science fiction and comic-strips have become the reality of the commonplace.

More and more the external landscape of our lives is now fictional, invented to serve some imaginative or conceptual end. Half a century ago, to go back no further, a fairly clear distinction existed between so-called reality—the world of work, of commerce and industry, of our personal relations with one another—and that of fantasy, our dreams, hopes, ideals and so on. This relationship has now been almost completely reversed. The locus solus of reality exists only within our skulls. Meanwhile the external world is completely the creation of advertising, politics conducted as advertising, peopled by characters more bizarre and incredible than any a mere writer could produce. As far as the limited world of literature is concerned, the greatest producer of fiction is now science—the social and psychological sciences between them produce a vast volume of material that belongs more in the realm of imagination than of impersonal investigation. Where science once took its raw materials from nature, calculating the boiling point of a gas or the magnitude of a star, it now takes its raw materials from its own defined subject matter, proposing studies, for example, of how and where college students touch each other, how the sexual behaviour of middle-income housewives is influenced by TV war newsreels or the purchase of a new car.

The Atrocity Exhibition is a fiction for the 1970s. In general it seems clear to me that the direction of next decade is towards the *total* fictionalizing of all, whether that of the external environment or the world inside our own heads. However, it seems to me that one can distinguish various elements in this goulash of fictions. First, there is the world of public events, as transmitted by television, mass-magazines, advertising and so on. Second, there is the realm of our own personal relationships. Third, the interior universe of our minds. Continuously, all these interact. Where these various levels intersect are the only points of reality we can know. *The Atrocity Exhibition* offers a new geometry by which to perceive the elements in this three-dimensional atlas. By means of it I hope the reader may navigate into the deep waters of his own experience, a journey undertaken without the consolations of grace.

CONCRETE ISLAND (1974)

"Introduction" (1994)

The day-dream of being marooned on a desert island still has enormous appeal, however small our chances of actually finding ourselves stranded on a coral atoll in the pacific. But *Robinson Crusoe* was one of the first books we read as children, and the fantasy endures. There are all the fascinating problems of survival, and the task of setting up, as Crusoe did, a working replica of bourgeois society and its ample comforts. This is the desert island as adventure holiday. With a supplies-filled wreck lying conveniently on the nearest reef like a neighbourhood cash and carry.

More seriously, there is the challenge of returning to our more primitive natures, stripped of the self-respect and the mental support systems with which civilisation has equipped us. Can we overcome fear, hunger and isolation, and find the courage and cunning to defeat anything that the elements can throw at us?

At an even deeper level there is the need to dominate the island, and transform its anonymous terrain into an extension of our minds. The mysterious peak veiled by cloud, the deceptively calm lagoon, the rotting mangroves and the secret spring of pure water together become outstations of the psyche, as they must have done for our primeval forbears, filled with lures and pitfalls of every kind.

The Pacific atoll may not be available, but there are other islands far nearer to home, some of them only a few steps from the pavements we tread every day. They are surrounded, not by sea, but by concrete, ringed by chain-mail fences and walled off by bomb-proof glass. All city-dwellers know the constant subliminal fear of being marooned by a power failure in the tunnels of a subway system, or trapped over a holiday weekend inside a stalled elevator on the upper floors of a deserted office building.

As we drive across a motorway intersection, through the elaborately signalled landscape that seems to anticipate every possible hazard, we glimpse triangles of waste ground screened off by steep embankments. What would happen if, by some freak mischance, we suffered a blow-out and plunged over the guard-rail onto a forgotten island of rubble and weeds, out of sight of the surveillance cameras?

Lying with a broken leg beside our overturned car, how will we survive until rescue comes? But what if rescue never comes? How do we attract attention, signal to the distant passengers speeding in their coaches towards London Airport? How, when faced with the task, do we set fire to our car?

But as well as the many physical difficulties facing us, there are the psychological ones. How resolute are we, and how far can we trust ourselves and our own motives? Perhaps, secretly, we hoped to be marooned, to escape our families, lovers and responsibilities. Modern technology, as I tried to show in *Crash* and *High-Rise*, offers an endless field-day to any deviant strains in our personalities. Marooned in an office block or on a traffic island, we can tyrannise ourselves, test our strengths and weaknesses, perhaps come to terms with aspects of our characters to which we have always closed our eyes.

And if we find that we are not alone on the island, the scene is then set for an encounter of an interesting but especially dangerous kind . . .

HELLO AMERICA (1981)

"Introduction" (1994)

The United States has given birth to most of our century's dreams, and to a good many of its nightmares. No other country has created such a potent vision of itself, and exported that vision so successfully to the rest of the world. Skyscrapers and freeways, Buicks and blue jeans, film stars and gangsters, Disneyland and Las Vegas have together stamped the image of America onto the maps of our imaginations.

Recently the American dream may have faded a little, exposed to the harsh reality of violent crime and decaying inner cities, but throughout the rest of the world the core appeal of the American way of life is as strong as ever. Above all, Hollywood still rules our entertainment culture, projecting a fictional image of America far more powerful than the reality.

Whenever I visit the United States I often feel that the real "America" lies not in the streets of Manhattan and Chicago, or the farm towns of the mid-west, but in the imaginary America created by Hollywood and the media landscape. Far from being real, the sidewalks and filling stations and office blocks seem to imitate the images of themselves in countless movies and TV commercials. Even the American people one meets in hotel lobbies and department stores seem like actors in a huge televised sit-com. "U.S.A." might well be the title of a 24 hours a day virtual reality channel, broadcast into the streets and shopping malls and, perhaps, the White House itself—certainly during the Presidency of Ronald Reagan, whose first year in office coincided with the original publication of *Hello America*.

Cadillacs, Coca Cola and cocaine, presidents and psychopaths, Norman Rockwell and the mafia . . . the dream of America endlessly unravels its codes, like the helix of some ideological DNA. But what would happen if we took the United States at its face value and constructed an alternative America from all these images? The simulacrum might well reveal something of the secret agenda that lies beneath the enticing surface of the American dream.

A curious feature of the United States is that this nation with the most advanced science and technology the world has ever seen, which has landed men on the moon and created the super-computers that may one day replace us, amuses itself with a comic-book culture aimed for the most part at bored and violent teenagers. In *Hello America* I suggest that the hidden logic of the American dream might one day lead to a President Manson playing nuclear roulette in Las Vegas, a less far-fetched notion than it seems, bearing in mind the Hollywood actor who occupied the White House through most of the 1980s, his head filled with the debris of old movies as he dreamed his Star Wars fantasies of laser-armed missiles.

Nonetheless, as the reader will find, *Hello America* is strongly on the side of the U.S.A., and a celebration of its optimism and self-confidence, qualities that we Europeans so conspicuously lack. For all my fears of a President Manson, the story ends in the triumph of those 19th century Yankee virtues embodied in my old glass airplane-building inventor. However hard we resist, our dreams still carry the legend "Made in U.S.A."

ON OWN WORK: STORIES AND COLLECTIONS

Glosses on Ballard's short fiction cover many of the key stories produced in the first half of his career thanks to a convention adopted by certain publications and anthology series in the period to invite writers to introduce their own work.

The paragraph on "Storm-Wind" (1961) was presented as an interview profile of the author on the inside front cover of *New Worlds* 111, in which the second part of the story was serialized. "Storm-Wind" was an alternative version of the story that was published in novel form as *The Wind from Nowhere*, regarded by Ballard as a hack piece.

An introductory gloss to "You and Me and the Continuum" is from the March 1966 issue of *Impulse: The New Science Fantasy*, a monthly paperback anthology edited by Kyril Bonfiglioni. Two further commentaries are from anthologies: a personal note on "End-Game," originally published in *Backdrop of Stars* (1968), edited by Harry Harrison, and a gloss to "Report on an Unidentified Space Station" published in *Top Fantasy: The Author's Choice* (1985), edited by Josh Pachter.

A piece originally published in the "Second Thoughts" slot in the *Times* is appended to the "Preface" to the 1973 Cape edition of *Vermillion Sands*. A Norwegian "Forord" to the 1972 edition is not included.

For the reissue of *Myths of the Near Future* (1982) by Vintage in 1994, Ballard wrote a new introduction to the collection containing the title story and seven others from the late 1970s and early 1980s: "Having a Wonderful Time" (1978); "A Host of Furious Fancies" (1980); "Zodiac 2000" (1978); "News from the Sun" (1981); "Theatre of War" (1977); "The Dead Time" (1977); "The Smile" (1976); "Motel Architecture" (1978); "The Intensive Care Unit" (1977).

In a 1996 special issue of *Interzone* devoted to Ballard's work, David Pringle compiled "J. G. Ballard's Comments on His Own Fiction" from collections of short stories, including those from *The Best of J. G. Ballard* (1977) and a French anthology in the *Livre d'or* (1980) series, edited by Robert Louit. These pieces have been grouped together under the titles in which they originally appeared, and the French introductions that do not appear in the English collection have been afforded fresh back-translations. A small number of glosses extracted by Pringle from films and interviews have not been included.

The introduction for the first edition of *The Complete Short Stories* (2001) gives a summary, retrospective view of the short form.

"STORM-WIND"

"J. G. Ballard: Shepperton, Middx," *New Worlds* (1961)

The cataclysmic story is particularly interesting because it shows how even a minor variation in one of the physical constants of the environment can make life totally untenable—a corollary of the biological rule that the more specialized the organism the narrower the margin of safety.

Perhaps because of their climate, English writers seem to have a virtual monopoly of the genre, one or two of the contemporary ones producing almost nothing else. Analysing the author's hidden motives is one of the quieter pleasures of reading—and writing—science fiction, and from the deluge in the Babylonian zodiac myth of Gilgamesh, from which come Noah and the sign of Aquarius, all the way down to *The War of the Worlds*, the real significance of the cataclysmic story is obviously to be found elsewhere. "Storm-Wind" is no exception, and anyone wondering why I've chosen to destroy London quite so thoroughly should try living there for ten years. I'm only sorry that I couldn't call it "Gone with the Wind."

"YOU AND ME AND THE CONTINUUM"

Impulse (1966)

The theme of sacrifice led me to think of the Messiah, or more exactly, the idea of the second coming and how this might take place in the twentieth century. In my version, which I would describe as a botched second coming, the Messiah never quite managing to come to terms with the twentieth century, I have used a fragmentary and non-sequential technique . . . and have tried to invoke some of the images that a twentieth century Messiah might see. You'll notice that the entries are alphabetised.

"END-GAME"

"Comment on End-Game" in *Backdrop of Stars* (1968)

The psychology of guilt and rebellion is barely looked at by science fiction. By and large a literature of optimism, and much the worse for it, science fiction assumes that the chief obstacles in the way of human liberty and progress are faults in social and political institutions, and that once these have been corrected a millennial age will dawn. Of course, nothing could be further from the truth. At the best (and worst) of times it is difficult to know which side of the bars we are, for the simple reason that we can never be sure which side we want to be.

These inversions, one of which "End-Game" illustrates, can take place within a society, an institution, or even a marriage. During the second World War, I was interned with some 2,000 British and American civilians in a Japanese prison camp ten miles from Shanghai. For most of the three-year period the camp was guarded by no more than a dozen Japanese. Apart from a few atrocities committed during the last months of the war, the main energies of the guards were devoted to helping the inmates strengthen the barbed-wire fence which kept out the starving Chinese trying to get into the camp and share the vegetables grown there on every square inch of available soil. Roll-calls, curfews and the like were organized by the inmates—the guards barely put in an appearance, realizing that left to themselves the inmates would devise a more regimented and impregnable prison within a prison than any they could hope for.

Three weeks after the war ended I walked back to the camp along the Shanghai-Nanking railway line. At the small wayside station an abandoned platoon of Japanese soldiers were squatting on the platform, watching one of their number string up a Chinese youth with telephone wire. Four hundred yards away, on a tank-trap embankment, a group of Kuomintatg (Allied) Chinese troops were feeding themselves on the Spam and Nescafé mis-dropped by the B-29's three miles from the camp. Neither of these groups did more than look at me as I walked past. When I reached the camp I found the gates guarded by an American merchant sailor with a Mauser on his hip. Although he had lived in the camp with me for three years, he apparently failed to recognize me, and for half an hour I was unable even to convince him that I was English, let alone get in. The remaining inmates, some 600 in number, had formed an authoritarian regime, with a camp commander, block leaders and so on, and supported themselves by armed forays to retrieve the B-29 food canisters in the surrounding paddy-fields. Six months later I was told that they were still there.

The situation in "End-Game" reflects ambiguities and motives of a similar kind, although in a more domestic and confined context. Here questions of guilt and responsibility complicate matters. (In passing, it occurs to me that the psychology of civilian internees during wartime would make an interesting study. Unlike military personnel, the only reason for their long terms of imprisonment, during which they have to undergo sustained periods of hunger, abuse and their own company, is the notional crime of being enemy nationals—they suffer a wholly abstract form of imprisonment.)

Constantin, the convicted hero of "End-Game," begins by accepting the fact of his guilt. A true child of the 20th century, he has no doubts whatever about the justice, both moral and legal, of his trial and impending execution. Unlike the heroes of Kafka's *Trial* and *Metamorphosis*, who at least begin by assuming their innocence and rebel against the nightmares in which they find themselves, Constantin accepts his situation completely. At first his plans to escape are concerned with his own physical survival, but later he conceives of the moral notion of his own "innocence." Imperceptibly the failed political opportunist transforms himself into a martyr to his own innocence, a credo which he erects into a cathedral. Constantin is now an internal escapee.

It is Constantin's absolute conviction of his innocence for which Malek, his executioner, is waiting. "Only a truly innocent man can know the meaning of guilt," Constantin remarks, but Malek knows full well that the reverse is true. Only a truly guilty man can conceive of the concept of innocence at all, or hold it with such ferocity.

Perhaps I have misread my own story, and its real significance, if any, may lie in another direction altogether. Nonetheless it seems to me that a significant moral and psychological distance now separates us from Kafka's heroes, who succumbed in the end to their own unconscious feelings of guilt and inferiority. We, by contrast, in an age of optimism and promise, may fall equal victims to our notions of freedom, sanity and self-sufficiency.

VERMILION SANDS (1971)

"Preface" (1973)

Vermilion Sands is my guess at what the future will actually be like. It is a curious paradox that almost all science fiction, however far removed in time and space, is really about the present day. Very few attempts have been made to visualize a unique and self-contained future that offers no warnings to us. Perhaps because of this cautionary tone, so many of science fiction's notional futures are zones of unrelieved grimness.

By contrast, Vermilion Sands is a place where I would be happy to live. I once described this over-lit desert resort as an exotic suburb of my mind, and something about the word "suburb"—which I then used pejoratively—now convinces me that I was on the right track in my pursuit of the day after tomorrow. As the countryside vanishes under a top-dressing of chemicals, and as cities provide little more than an urban context for traffic intersections, the suburbs are at last coming into their own. The skies are larger, the air more generous, the clock less urgent, Vermilion Sands has more than its full share of dreams and illusions, fears and fantasies, but the frame for them is less confining. I like to think, too, that it celebrates the neglected virtues of the glossy, lurid and bizarre.

Where is Vermilion Sands? I suppose its spiritual home lies somewhere between Arizona and Ipanema Beach, but in recent years I have been delighted to see it popping up elsewhere—above all, in sections of the 3,000-mile-long linear city that stretches from Gibraltar to Glyfada Beach along the northern shores of the Mediterranean, and where each summer Europe lies on its back in the sun. That posture, of course, is the hallmark of Vermilion Sands and, I hope, of the future—not merely that no-one has to work, but that work is the ultimate play, and play the ultimate work.

The earliest of these tales, "Prima Beladonna," was the first short story I published, seventeen years ago, and the image of this desert resort has remained remarkably constant ever since. I wait optimistically for it to take concrete shape around me.

"Second Thoughts: Sculptors Who Carve the Clouds," *Independent* (1992)

The short stories that make up this collection were written between 1956 and 1970, and once they were published in a single volume I never returned, regrettably, to this genial playground. By sealing one's imagination between hard covers one can close the door forever on a still vivid private world. I'm glad that I began my career by writing short stories, when I was free to chase any passing hare in a way that is no longer possible, and without over-committing myself to a single idea. Fiction today is dominated by career novelists locked into their publishers' contracts like the prematurely middle-aged encumbered by mortgages and pension plans. Irresponsibility, especially the agreeable variety displayed in Vermilion Sands, has a great many neglected virtues.

One of the stories in the collection, "Prima Belladonna," was the first piece of fiction that I ever published, and I can still remember the thrill of receiving the cheque for £8. At last I was a professional writer, and my wife and I celebrated by using the money to buy our baby son a new pram. Pushing it past the department stores in Chiswick High Street, a hundred ideas in my head, I felt that I had found the philosopher's stone.

Looking back, it seems curious that my first short story was set in an imaginary beach resort as far removed from the grey, shabby Britain of the 1950s as one could go without actually leaving the planet. By 1956 I had spent 10 years in England, but clearly had yet to put down any real roots.

Where is Vermilion Sands? Somewhere, I suppose, between Palm Springs and Ipanema Beach. The notion of a future entirely devoted to leisure is now commonplace, but it seemed less obvious in the Fifties, as Europe dragged itself wearily into the post-war world. I had just spent nearly a year in North America, and had seen American prosperity unrolling across the continent like the new interstate highways. Work, I guessed, would one day become the ultimate play, and play the ultimate work.

All this leisure, of course, raises its own set of moral dilemmas, which I look at in Vermilion Sands. To fill their timeless days, the inhabitants of my desert resort divert themselves with a number of playthings. There are computers that compose poetry, sand-yachts and sound-emitting sculptures, which seemed to be fantasies in the 1950s but have long since come to pass. I trust that my other inventions, like the houses sensitive to their owners' moods, and the sculptors who carve the clouds, will soon follow. One day in the near future, perhaps, in Arizona or the south of France, I will wake up and realise that the world I longed for all those decades ago has taken concrete shape around me.

THE BEST SCIENCE FICTION OF J. G. BALLARD (1977)

Science fiction now enjoys enormous freedom, and is one of the most vital forms of modern fiction. So generous is its appeal to the imagination that many leading contemporary writers have temporarily deserted the mainstream novel and have produced books that are either straight science fiction or heavily influenced by it—Anthony Burgess (*Clockwork Orange*) [*sic*], William Burroughs (*The Naked Lunch*), and Kingsley Amis (*The Alteration*), to name only three. Aggressive and exuberant, ranging over the whole of time and space, science fiction talks back to the late twentieth century in its own language.

So open is science fiction now, and so widely read by an ever-increasing audience, that it is difficult to remember how much it has changed in recent years. Twenty years ago, when I first began writing, science fiction was a closed and restricted world. Although there were literally dozens of magazines both in Britain and the United States, and a small but dedicated readership that kept them alive, science fiction was totally dominated by a set of rigid and unvarying formulas. Outer space, interplanetary travel, galactic empires, alternate universes—these were the basic themes on which the writer was expected to work an endless series of variations. He might add some minor personal detail, a fresh twist to telepathy or time travel, a new kind of space drive, but the basic conventions of the s-f formula had to be respected. Even setting a story in the present day made editors and readers nervous. And to try a radically new approach outside those conventions simply meant one thing—you were not published.

Even before I started writing science fiction I was certain that this had to change. So much that was going on in the world desperately needed science fiction to describe it. Computers and communications satellites, pollution and a host of environmental problems, over-population, transplant surgery and psychedelic drugs—these and a dozen other subjects that should have been at the centre of science fiction were in fact excluded altogether or treated at a hundred removes in some imaginary galactic setting. It was like watching everything on the television news bulletins during an international crisis re-enacted as a Star Trek episode.

I was determined that science fiction should turn its back on outer space and the far future and return to where it was most needed—the present. Although the American magazines were effectively closed to me, there fortunately existed in this country one magazine whose editor felt the same way that I did. Ted Carnell, the editor of *New Worlds*, knew that the time had come for a change. By the late 1950s American science fiction, for all the great achievements of writers such as Ray Bradbury, Frederik Pohl, James Blish and Robert Sheckley, had sealed itself into its own world. When I sent him the first of my short stories Ted Carnell encouraged me to follow my own path. From this open-mindedness came the New Wave and a fresh direction for science fiction.

The seventeen stories in this collection are my selection of what I feel to be my best science fiction stories. They are printed in the order in which I wrote them, and I have prefaced them with a few comments that place the stories in the context of their time.

"The Concentration City"

"The Concentration City" was published in 1957, the year of Sputnik I, and the dawn of the Space Age. Remembering the shiver of excitement that went through everyone then—far greater than anything we later felt even during Armstrong's landing on the moon—it must have seemed the worst time for a novice writer to turn his back on interplanetary travel and set off in a radically new direction, inwards into the mind and deep time rather than outwards into deep space. But right from the start—and this was only my third story—I was convinced that to survive science fiction needed to keep one step ahead of reality. If the Space Age had arrived for the rest of the world, for the science-fiction writer it was over. "The Concentration City" is the first story of what I termed Inner Space, the picture of a super-city that is almost literally an infinitely expanded brain.

"Manhole 69"

"Manhole 69" is another inner space story. Here the subject is psycho-surgery, of a particularly sinister kind. In the ten years after World War II everyone was becoming more and more aware of the widespread increase of advanced techniques for the direct manipulation of the mind—brainwashing, pre-frontal lobotomy, the use of new drug-families such as the tranquillizers and synthetic hallucinogens. "Manhole 69" takes a look at what seems to be a responsible scientific attempt to eliminate the function of sleep. The title, by the way, is the name of a complex type of self-regulating manhole used in deep-level drainage systems which shuts off the flow when the pressure becomes too great.

"The Waiting Grounds"

"The Waiting Grounds" is among the few of my stories set on an alien planet. The idea that we in this solar system may be late-comers to a universe whose life is virtually over has always intrigued me, though given a cynical view of things it may be hard to decide whether we are the last guests at the party or the first to arrive at the next. One problem which I had to face, like all s-f writers, was how to describe aliens. The answer, of course, is . . .

"The Sound-Sweep"

"The Sound-Sweep" is the longest of the stories I have written, and in some ways—especially in the relationship between the ageing opera star and the young mute sound-sweep—is more like a novel. Many of my short stories have been extremely long by the standards of the genre, and I sometimes think that I began by writing novels in the form of short stories ("The Sound-Sweep," "Chronopolis" and "The Voices of Time"), and then went on to write short stories in the form of novels—*Concrete Island* and *High-Rise*. Perhaps if I have the time one day I will rewrite them all and get everything the right way round.

"Chronopolis"

By 1960, when "Chronopolis" was published, post-war austerity was over and England was showing all the strains of the consumer-goods society—overloaded transit systems, ruthless competition for housing, soaring urban populations, and the sense that the whole of a city like London might seize up in a gigantic physical and mental traffic jam. One way of controlling a huge metropolitan population might be by rationing time as well as space, particularly as psychological control systems are so effective because they play on barely understood and paradoxical needs. In

"Chronopolis" those who have over-thrown one external tyranny soon substitute an internal one.

"The Voices of Time"

If I were asked to pick one piece of fiction to represent my entire output of seven novels and 92 short stories it would be "The Voices of Time," not because it is the best (I leave that for the reader to judge), but because it contains almost all the themes of my writing—the sense of isolation within the infinite time and space of the universe, the biological fantasies and the attempt to read the complex codes represented by drained swimming pools and abandoned airfields, and above all the determination to break out of a deepening psychological entropy and make some kind of private peace with the unseen powers of the universe.

"The Overloaded Man"

How far is everything one writes autobiographical? "The Overloaded Man" was the first story in which I described a modern marriage in more or less realistic terms, and it prefigures many of the relationships (or confrontations, more exactly) between men and women which appear in my later writing. I remember my wife being outraged when she read this story, and rightly so—the marriage described here, like all those that follow it, has no basis in my own life. Yet from what forgotten experience stems this obsessive and often repeated image of the predatory woman and the husband retreating into his own mind?

"Billennium"

"Billennium" was the favourite story of the late Ted Carnell, the editor of *New Worlds* who published more than half the stories in this book and made possible a new kind of science fiction—the New Wave. By the time he published "Billennium" in 1961 the vague murmurings of discontent from the old-guard readers that had greeted my short stories over the previous four years suddenly broke into outright hostility. Although this was the year of Gagarin's first orbital flight, sales of traditional science fiction were declining everywhere, and the emergence of a new kind of sf threatened the security of the ghetto.

"The Insane Ones"

"The Insane Ones" was one of the first stories I sold to the American magazines. Although most people assume that science fiction, like its main inspiration—science itself—is dedicated to change and experiment, American science fiction in general and its magazines in particular have always been deeply conservative, nervous of anything outside their rigid conventions. Appropriately, perhaps, "The Insane Ones" takes a look at fanaticism. Is the deranged assassin who murders a tyrant the only sane man in his society? Do we need the insane to perform justifiable and necessary acts we are too rational to commit?

"The Garden of Time"

Time is one of the great themes of all science fiction, and one that has dominated most of my own writing. With the exception of the time machine itself, it is one of the few subjects that requires no gadgetry, and the best time stories, those by Ray Bradbury or Richard Matheson, are as simple and mysterious as sundials.

"Thirteen to Centaurus"

By 1962 the first manned spaceflights had taken place and it was clear that within a few years men would land on the Moon, and begin the first of the journeys that will carry us during the next few centuries to all the planets of the solar system. What interested me at the time, but seemed to be ignored by the NASA planners, was to what extent the experience of total confinement and self-immersion in a spacecraft would play into the hands of unexpected psychological impulses. Interestingly, in the last few years we have seen a glimpse of the hidden effects of space travel in the subsequent lives of many of the Apollo astronauts.

"The Subliminal Man"

Given the voracious needs of the modern consumer-goods society, who can blame the merchandisers for doing their best to keep up with us? The kind of psychological force-feeding that I describe in "The Subliminal Man" isn't that different from the efforts I was making at the time cramming large amounts of what seemed to be up-market pet-foods down the throats of my three infants. Even the most extreme stratagem was, after all, for their own good. I mention this because I don't see the central character of the story as entirely a victim.

"Passport to Eternity"

Of my ninety-two stories, "Passport to Eternity" gave me the greatest pleasure to write. This may seem surprising, as it is the one story that stands apart from all the others—this is out-and-out wide-screen super-science, wringing every variant I could conceive from the repertory of interplanetary s-f. In fact, the original draft was written well before the first science fiction story of mine to be published. Just before I left the R.A.F. in 1955 I tapped this out on a borrowed typewriter at R.A.F. Booker, where cashiered air-crew sat around in under-heated huts at a disused airfield. One of my regrets is that I have never written more stories like it.

"The Cage of Sand"

Science-fiction writers in recent years have usually disclaimed the gift of prophecy, at the same time showing a quiet pride when their predictions come true. "The Cage of Sand" was written a year after Gagarin's first flight and in the heyday of Cape Canaveral, when hundreds of square miles of swamp and sand-dune were turned into the world's newest and greatest complex of communications and space technology. Even before the Space Age had begun I had a hunch it would be short-lived—basically because NASA and the Russians had left the imagination out of space, one mistake the sf writers never made. By the early 70s my prophecy bore fruit. The Space Age is virtually over. Large tracts of Cape Kennedy are now rusting and abandoned, the launch pads are deserted, for-sale signs hang over the empty supermarkets and motels. But there is still magic to be found there.

"A Question of Re-Entry"

Few sights, since I looked up as a startled 14-year-old in a Japanese camp near Shanghai at a sky filled with hundreds of B-29's, have moved me as much as that of the Echo I satellite traversing the night sky in the early 60's. The first of a series of huge aluminium balloons, it sped like a surfer through the start-sea, the first tangible evidence of the Age of Space. (It was sad, some ten years later, to point out to a neighbour the speeding light-point of the last Skylab mission, whose crew had been circling the globe for three months. "Who?" he asked, taking for granted that things move in the sky. I knew then that Space Age was over.) What interested me was the effect the visible satellites might have on the imprinted star-maps of migratory birds, or even ourselves. Albatross might roost in England in winter, some latter-day remittance man might find himself running half the Amazon . . .

"The Terminal Beach"

"The Terminal Beach" was the last story of mine to be printed by Ted Carnell, and is for me the most important story I have written. It marks the link between the science fiction of my first ten years, and the next phase of my writings that led to *The Atrocity Exhibition* and *Crash*. What impresses me most now is that the story was ever printed in the first place—*New Worlds* was, after all, a wholly commercial s-f magazine. These were the days before the modern literature departments had begun to erect their plywood partitions around the chafed elbows of science-fiction writers.

"The Day of Forever"

"The Day of Forever" is another favourite story of mine, for reasons I have never understood. Perhaps the young man running around those abandoned hotels reminds me of my own adolescence, and that strange interregnum in Shanghai in 1942, and again in 1945, when one side in World War II had moved out and the other had yet to move in. As a child among the Japanese military one had an extraordinary immunity, we moved like pilot fish in front of them as they wandered through empty apartment blocks and disused seaplane bases, peered into drained swimming pools with that deep melancholy all Japanese seem to have. This was my first story to be published by the second great editor of *New Worlds*, Michael Moorcock, and the start of a completely new chapter . . .

LE LIVRE D'OR DE LA SCIENCE-FICTION: J. G. BALLARD (1980)

"The End of the Party"

The search for unconscious guilt that plays out in the police station, the confessional, or on the psychiatrist's couch has long been a weapon in the arsenal of the qualified interrogator. Perhaps the subject is a victim of terrorism, a believer, or mentally ill, but one assumes that the game is up from the moment that his unconscious accepts the idea of his own guilt (without taking account of his actual innocence—if these terms even have any sense): the victim, morally and psychologically, is forever at the mercy of his interviewer. In "The End of the Party," I've inverted this scheme. In everyday life, it seems to me that, far from assuming ourselves innocent, we consciously take our guilt as an accepted fact. The competent interrogator will wait for the idea of his innocence to develop in the mind of his victim before pronouncing his certain guilt.

"Tomorrow Is a Million Years"
Transition zones have always fascinated me. This is perhaps due to my own childhood in the Far East, during the Second World War. The war, the invasion and the occupation brought with them cataclysmic changes in landscape and psyche. Like all the extremes of experience, intermediate zones, armistices and interregnums seem endowed with a particular power—a flight of stairs descending into a river, the refraction of the fuselage of a semi-submerged plane, the interval that separates night from day.

"The Gentle Assassin"
Time is the ultimate mystery for me, stranger and yet more pitiless than the fear aroused by the sexual drive or the idea of our own death. Its apparently linear flux, in the form that Renaissance perspective imposes on our lives, reveals itself in the final analysis to be an immense curvilinear system around which we spin, like blind motorists trapped on a freeway, passing again and again points in space that we have already traversed an infinite number of times. On this indistinct web, our most profound desires and feelings take on the intermittent brilliance of fireflies.

"The Lost Leonardo"
While not underestimating the plight of its central character, I wrote The Lost Leonardo as a distraction. In fact, some readers—especially in the United States, where the story first appeared—have supposed that the painting described, da Vinci's "Crucifixion," actually exists. Some have even tried to track it down in the museums of Europe. In turn, I've almost become persuaded of its reality. I half expect to come across it when I next visit the Prado, the Palais Uffizi or the Louvre . . .

"The Escapement"
This was my first science-fiction story, published in *New Worlds* more than twenty years ago. Conflicting time systems collide and destroy each other as if in an asylum where hungry clocks tear each other to pieces. Unintentionally, the story also provides a more or less faithful picture of my first year of marriage.

"The Drowned Giant"
Gulliver's Travels is a classic of the literature of the imagination. I've always wondered what would have happened had Gulliver washed up dead, rather than alive, on the shore of Lilliput. In writing this story, I

was not at all concerned to produce a moral tale about man's inhumanity and lack of pity. Even today, I think that "The Drowned Giant" is more concerned with time, the decay that affects even the most abstract universe. No system can vanquish the entropy inherent within it. The end of the giant strikes me as particularly serene. Laid out on a beach, at the edge of the ocean, I sometimes imagine myself in his place, quite content.

"The Singing Statues"

This story is part of the *Vermillion Sands* cycle. Vermillion Sands: an imaginary resort, a kind of desert Riviera. Without exaggerating, I think that our future will take this form—and not that of *1984* or *Brave New World*, despite the visionary power of those masterpieces. I imagine myself in a country-club paradise, where leisure is the final form of work and work the final form of leisure. Where is Vermillion Sands? Without doubt, it is somewhere between Palm Springs and Ipanema, Miami and La Grande Motte.

"Love and Napalm: Export USA"

At the end of the 60s, when I was writing *The Atrocity Exhibition*, I was driven to measure the increasingly important—and sometimes sinister— role that science was playing in the creation of those vast fictions that more and more govern our existence. We all live inside an enormous horror novel. Scientists no longer extract their material from nature, but from their own dreams, or their fantasy of nature. Over the course of the 70s, the experiences that I describe and the conclusions at which I arrive, have become common currency in the scientific journals.

MYTHS OF THE NEAR FUTURE (1982)

As the year 2000 approaches, releasing a rush of millennial hopes and fears, I take for granted that the future will once again play a dominant role in our lives. Sadly, at some point in the 1960s our sense of the future seemed to atrophy and die. Over-population and the threat of nuclear war, environmentalist concerns for our ravaged planet and unease at an increasingly wayward science together made everyone fearful of the future. Like passengers on a ship blown towards a rocky coast, we retreated to our cabins and drew the curtains over the portholes.

Yet I can remember when people throughout the world were intensely interested in the future, and convinced that it would change their lives for the better. In the years after the Second World War the future was the air that everyone breathed. Looking back, we can see that the blueprint of the world we inhabit today was then being drawn—television and the consumer society, computers, jet travel and the newest wonder drugs transformed our lives and gave us a powerful sense of what the 20th century could do for us once we freed ourselves from war and economic depression.

In many ways, we all became Americans, turning our backs on the past and confident that we could shape our world in any way we wished, dream any dream and see it come to life. For the first time the future was a better key to the present than was the past. All this had ended by the 1970s, though a few romantics like myself still believe that our sense of the future remains intact, a submerged realm of hopes and dreams that lies below the surface of our minds, ready to wake again as one millennium closes and the next begins.

Myths of the Near Future is a set of windows onto this future world, an observation car from which we can look out at the intriguing and uncertain terrain where we will spend the rest of our lives. The title story, and its companion piece "News from the Sun," are attempts to free us from the tyranny of time, or at least from our limited sense of linear time that runs into the future like a narrow-gauge scenic railway. Here a drained swimming-pool in a deserted Florida beach resort can become a time-machine, transporting the central characters into a zone where past, present and future meet and fuse.

As the reader will find, one story in this collection is not set in the near future, but in a remote corner of the Second World War on the eastern edge of Asia. "The Dead Time," written in 1977, takes place in and near Lunghua camp, a few miles from Shanghai, where I was interned as a boy by the Japanese. Until then I had never written about my war-time experiences, and "The Dead Time" is the gene from which *Empire of the Sun* was to grow a few years later.

I hope that the stories in this collection together form a chromosome of the future which will divide and grow in the reader's mind, dreams of the day after tomorrow waiting to enfold us as we move like sleepwalkers towards them.

"REPORT ON AN UNIDENTIFIED SPACE STATION" (1982)

Top Fantasy: The Author's Choice (1985)

"Report on an Unidentified Space Station" is one of the very few stories I have written to be set in that happy hunting ground of traditional science fiction—outer space. Out of some hundred or more of my short stories, which fill some ten volumes, this is only the third to take place in deep space. Perhaps the silence of those infinite spaces, which so terrified Pascal, has at last begun to get through to me. However, readers of the story will see that this is, after all, a special kind of space, far closer to terra firma than it might seem at first, and even perhaps to inner space itself.

The story is also one of the very few of mine to be directly inspired by a dream—in this case, a nightmare of extreme anguish, though I like to think that the mood of the story is one of serenity and peace, part of the difference, it may be, between dream and imagination.

J. G. BALLARD: THE COMPLETE SHORT STORIES (2001)

Short stories are the loose change in the treasury of fiction, easily ignored beside the wealth of novels available, an over-valued currency that often turns out to be counterfeit. At its best, in Borges, Ray Bradbury and Edgar Allan Poe, the short story is coined from precious metal, a glint of gold that will glow for ever in the deep purse of your imagination.

Short stories have always been important to me. I like their snapshot quality, their ability to focus intensely on a single subject. They're also a useful way of trying out the ideas later developed at novel length. Almost all my novels were first hinted at in short stories, and readers of *The Crystal World*, *Crash* and *Empire of the Sun* will find their seeds germinating somewhere in this collection.

When I started writing, fifty years ago, short stories were immensely popular with readers, and some newspapers printed a new short story every day. Sadly, I think that people at present have lost the knack of reading short stories, a response perhaps to the baggy and long-winded narratives of television serials. Young writers, myself included, have always seen their first novels as a kind of virility test, but so many novels published today would have been better if they had been recast as short stories.

Curiously, there are many perfect short stories, but no perfect novels. The short story still survives, especially in science fiction, which makes the most of its closeness to the folk tale and the parable. Many of the stories in this collection were first published in science fiction magazines, though readers at the time loudly complained that they weren't science fiction at all.

But I was interested in the real future that I could see approaching, and less in the invented future that science fiction preferred. The future, needless to say, is a dangerous area to enter, heavily mined and with a tendency to turn and bite your ankles as you stride forward. A correspondent recently pointed out to me that the poetry-writing computers in Vermilion Sands are powered by valves. And why don't all those sleek people living in the future have PCs and pagers? I could only reply that Vermilion Sands isn't set in the future at all, but in a kind of visionary present—a description that fits the stories in this book and almost everything else I have written. But oh, for a steam-powered computer and a wind-driven television set. Now, there's an idea for a short story.

ON WORK OF OTHERS: LITERATURE

Ballard contributed forewords and introductions to a number of published works, and appreciations of key influences appeared in newspapers or magazines. His personal canon remained largely stable, as evidenced in "My Favourite Books" and *The Test of Time*.

The Visual Encyclopedia of Science Fiction, edited by Brian Ash, was a richly illustrated guide to generic SF, approached through four sections: "Program," a timeline of key works and events up to 1976; "Thematics," including "Galactic Empires," "Future and Alternative Histories," "Time and Nth Dimensions"; three longer essays, or "Deep Probes"; and a section documenting "Fandom and Media." Ballard was among a host of the most recognizable names in SF to contribute a "Thematic" introduction: Isaac Asimov, Arthur C. Clarke, and Harry Harrison were others.

The piece on Graham Greene, "Visa pour la réalité," was published in the French *Magazine littéraire*, for which it was translated by Robert Louit. Louit, director of the Dimensions SF anthology series at Calmann-Lévy and Etoiles Doubles at Denoël, had in 1974 translated *Crash!* into French and interviewed Ballard for *Magazine littéraire* at that time. He would later subtitle Cronenberg's adaptation, and also translated Greene into French. The original English text was retained by Ballard's agent John Wolfers and passed on to David Pringle.

Ballard's account of his youthful reading of James Joyce—in his first author profile accompanying a story in *New Worlds* he noted approvingly that "James Joyce still remains the wordmaster"—was published in the short, weekly "First Impressions" column in the *Guardian* Books section, in which authors described formative encounters with literature. "On the Shelf" was a similarly conceived column in *The Sunday Times* Books section, in which authors would highlight a favorite novel.

The brief foreword to Aldous Huxley's *The Doors of Perception* (1954), an account of the experience of taking mescalin—"I was now a Not-self, simultaneously perceiving and being the Not-self of the things around me" (19)—was written for the Flamingo paperback reissue of the text in an edition with its follow-up essay *Heaven and Hell* (1956).

"CATACLYSMS AND DOOMS" IN *THE VISUAL ENCYCLOPEDIA OF SCIENCE FICTION* (1977)

Visions of world cataclysm constitute one of the most powerful and most mysterious of all the categories of science fiction, and in their classic form predate modern science fiction by thousands of years. In many ways, I believe that science fiction is itself no more than a minor offshoot of the cataclysmic tale. From the deluge in the Babylonian zodiac myth of Gilgamesh to contemporary fantasies of twentieth-century super-science, there has clearly been no limit to our need to devise new means of destroying the world we inhabit. I would guess that from man's first inkling of this planet as a single entity existing independently of himself came the determination to bring about its destruction, part of the same impulse we see in a placid infant who wakes alone in his cot and sets about wrecking his entire nursery.

Psychiatric studies of the fantasies and dream life of the insane show that ideas of world destruction are latent in the unconscious mind. The marvels of twentieth-century science and technology provide an anthology of destructive techniques unrivalled by even the most bizarre religions. As Edward Glover comments in *War, Sadism and Pacifism* (1947), "Nagasaki destroyed by the magic of science is the nearest man has yet approached to the realisation of dreams that even during the safe immobility of sleep are accustomed to develop into nightmares of anxiety."

As an author who has produced a substantial number of cataclysmic stories, I take for granted that the planet the writer destroys with such tireless ingenuity is in fact an image of the writer himself. But are these deluges and droughts, whirlwinds and glaciations no more than overextended metaphors of some kind of suicidal self-hate? Though I am even more suspicious of my own motives than of other people's, I nevertheless think not. On the contrary, I believe that the catastrophe story, whoever may tell it, represents a constructive and positive act by the imagination rather than a negative one, an attempt to confront a patently meaningless universe by challenging it at its own game. Within the realm of fiction, the writer of the catastrophe story illustrates, in the most extreme and literal way, Conrad's challenge—"Immerse yourself in the most destructive element—and swim!" Each one of these fantasies represents an arraignment of the finite, an attempt to dismantle the formal structure of time and space which the universe wraps around us at the moment we first achieve consciousness. It is the inflexibility of this huge reductive machine we call reality that provokes infant and madman alike, and in the cataclysm story the science fiction writer joins company with them, using his imagination to describe the infinite alternatives to reality which nature itself has proved incapable of inventing. This celebration of the possibilities of life is at the heart of science fiction.

GRAHAM GREENE

"Visa pour la réalité," *Magazine littéraire* (1978)

Parochialism seems to me to be the besetting sin of contemporary English fiction, a fault of which Graham Greene has always been completely free. Writers, of course, can make any number of angels dance on the head of a pin and create a universe out of a nut-shell or a single room. The greatest and most influential French writers of the past fifty years—Sartre, Celine, Camus and Genet—seem, to me at least, to have taken their subject matter and inspiration from France and her territories alone, in the geographical sense, and from the most intense focus on a sometimes narrow aspect of French life, a small social class, a provincial city, a criminal milieu.

For English writers, however, a similar concentration on the life of their own country seems invariably to lead them into all the worst defects of provincialism—an obsession with obscure social nuances, with the minutiae of everyday language and behaviour, and a moralizing concern for the limited world of their own parish that would do credit to an elderly spinster peering down at her suburban side-street through her lace curtains. The bourgeois novel flourishes in England now as nowhere else, its narrowing walls crushing its writers against their airless and over-stuffed furnishings. With few exceptions—Graham Greene pre-eminent among them—the English novel seems to me to be a branch of provincial fiction, relevant to nothing but itself. The novels of Kingsley Amis, Anthony Powell and C. P. Snow represent the last stale gas leaking from the corpse of the 19th century novel.

I feel that it is no coincidence that the English novelists who triumphantly escape from this limited, entropic realm—Graham Greene,

Lawrence Durrell, Anthony Burgess—are not only emigrants in the literal sense from England itself, but have taken a large part of their inspiration from the world at large. Faced with the suffocating character of English life, the writer has two stark choices—internal emigration, following the route laid down by Kafka, into one's own spinal column; or a one-way ticket from the nearest airport. Now that Britain shows all too many signs of becoming an after-thought of Europe, it may be that the best British writers of the present day, like the best Irish writers of half a century ago, Joyce and Beckett, are forced by internal necessity to seek their imaginative fortunes elsewhere than in their own countries.

I first began to read Graham Greene in the mid-1950s, and will never forget the sense of liberation his novels gave me. This was the heyday of the so-called Angry Young Men—John Osborne, Kingsley Amis, John Braine, and a fraternal American colleague, J. P. Donleavy—morose recipients of a welfare state education from the wrong side of the social tracks who railed against the restrictions of English life (rich men all of them now, they sit in their grand houses, literally in some cases on top of the very hills they once sought to assault). I remember turning from *Look Back in Anger* and *Lucky Jim* to Graham Greene's *The Heart of the Matter*, and then rapidly in the coming years through *The Power and the Glory*, *The Quiet American*, *Our Man in Havana*, and *The Comedians*, to the recent *An Honorary Consul*.

These remarkable novels, whether serious or "entertainments" as Greene likes to call them, had all the tonic effect of stepping from an aircraft on to the airport tarmac of a strange country. In the novels of Graham Greene one was no longer smothered within the red-brick and lace-curtain world of English life, with its endless moral proscriptions upon everything. Instead, one could see the sights and scent the smells of the whole world. As a reluctant emigrant to England from the Far East in 1946, for me Greene's novels were an indefinite visa to reality. In his novels over the years one has been able to see the shape of the post-war world as it emerged in Africa and the Far East, in Central America and the Caribbean, just as one saw the hard reality and moral ambiguities of postwar Europe in his film *The Third Man*.

As a writer myself, I have been enormously influenced by Greene's style, by his method of setting out the psychological ground on which his narratives rest. Within the first paragraph of a Graham Greene novel one has an unmistakable feeling for the imaginative and psychological shape of what is to come. The opening picture of a narrator/hero standing on a jetty watching the sampans drift down river and waiting with rather ambiguous feelings for his sick wife to come ashore, the bored police chief slapping the fly on his neck, together stamp an indelible image on the reader's mind.

And for all his most serious concern for the psychological and spiritual dilemmas of his characters, Greene never moralizes about his subject matter in that way so beloved by the English provincial writer. Their strengths and weaknesses, their dubious motives and social backgrounds are accepted without comment like the grease on the fan, the dirt under one's fingernails.

With Lawrence Durrell and Anthony Burgess, Greene keeps alive the largest and most admirable traditions of the English novel. The robustness and strength of his vision are clearly demonstrated by the fact that after half a century, and now well into his seventies, he is still producing great works of fiction.

JAMES JOYCE

"James the Great," *Guardian* (1990)

James Joyce's *Ulysses* had an immense influence on me—almost entirely for the bad. I read Joyce's masterpiece as an eighteen-year-old medical student dissecting cadavers at Cambridge, then a bastion of academic provincialism and self-congratulation. *Ulysses* opened my eyes to an infinitely richer and more challenging world. Here, I knew, was the authentic voice of heroic modernism that rang through the European and American writers I had devoured at school while trying to recover from the shock of arriving in England—Dostoevsky, Rimbaud, Kafka, Camus and Hemingway. Reading them at too early an age, long before I had the experience to understand them, was probably another mistake.

But *Ulysses* overwhelmed me. It might be set in a single day in a provincial European city, but in Joyce's eye Dublin was the whole world, and that single day lasted longer than a century. Joyce's text seemed to exhaust every conceivable possibility of narrative technique—in fact, technique became the real subject of the novel (a dead end, as the post-modernist writers demonstrate). *Ulysses* convinced me to give up medicine and become a writer, but it was the wrong example for me, an old-fashioned story-teller at heart, and it wasn't until I discovered the surrealists that I found the right model.

I read *Ulysses* again last year and was even more impressed than I was forty years ago, though clearly it's excessively interiorized, is curiously lacking in imagination and fails to engage the reader's emotions, defects that of course recommend it to academia. But if not the greatest novel of the twentieth century it is certainly the greatest work of fiction.

NATHANAEL WEST

"On the Shelf," *Sunday Times* (1993)

Few novelists today dream of emigrating to Hollywood, following the shadows of Scott Fitzgerald and Aldous Huxley to the writers' building on the studio lot and scripting popular adaptations of *The Magic Mountain* or *The Brothers Karamazov*. Jet travel, the fax machine and the demise of the studio system mean that British novelists write their commissioned scripts at home in Maida Vale or Holland Park, which may say something about the sorry state of today's cinema.

Forty years ago, as I mused over my first rejection slips, working as a Hollywood scriptwriter seemed the sweetest way for a novelist to sell his soul, and a vast literature already existed about the moral agonies of being paid $3,000 a week to do so. I couldn't wait to be summoned to that city of man-made sunsets, where the twentieth century created its greatest myths, even if I ended face down in a swimming pool in Beverly Hills, a small price to pay for true celebrity.

Nathanael West's *The Day of the Locust*, first published in 1939 remains the best of the Hollywood novels, a nightmare vision of humanity destroyed by its obsession with film. West, the author of *Miss Lonelyhearts* and *A Cool Million*, had worked as a scriptwriter in Hollywood for five years, but wisely made the hero of his novel a painter rather than a writer, accepting that in film, if not everywhere else, the image mattered more than the word.

His young hero, Tod Hackett, is a promising artist who has been brought to Hollywood to work in the design department of a major studio. The novel opens as he watches a rehearsal of the Battle of Waterloo, taking place on a studio lot crowded with stuffed dinosaurs, Egyptian temples and Mississippi steamboats. The costumes of the hussars and grenadiers, thanks to his scrupulously researched designs, are authentic replicas, but beyond the studio, in the streets of Los Angeles, absolutely nothing else is real.

His apartment building in the Hollywood Hills is surrounded by luxury homes that resemble Rhineland castles, Swiss chalets and Tudor mansions, built not of stone or brick, but of plaster, lath and paper. Yet crowds of sightseers are drawn to Los Angeles from all over America, and for them the spectacle provides the only reality in their stunted lives.

Hackett watches them as they loiter on Hollywood Boulevard, waiting for even the briefest glimpse of their screen idols. He notices that their eyes are filled with envy and a sullen hate, as if they are aware that their dreams are as insubstantial as the painted glue around them. Having nothing else in their lives, they are desperate to seize the sources of their dreams and even, perhaps, destroy them. In his spare time, Hackett is at work on a visionary painting, "The Burning of Los Angeles," which will portray the destruction of the city by this alienated horde. Throughout the novel, West brilliantly counterpoints scenes from Hackett's apocalyptic canvas with events that he observes in the Hollywood demi-monde and its cast of weird and shiftless characters. Among them are a drugstore cowboy who makes a modest living in westerns; a lonely accountant, Homer, who has abandoned his job in Iowa; a failed vaudeville performer reduced to selling polish door to door; and his beautiful daughter Faye, a part-time film extra.

Faye bears a resemblance to the young Marilyn Monroe that is uncannily prophetic. With her platinum hair and affected little-girl wisdom, her nights spent as a call-girl and her determined dreams of becoming a serious actress, Faye is a remarkable portrait of the young Monroe during her first unhappy years in Hollywood.

Powerful set-pieces fill the pages, like the brutal but enthralling cock-fight staged in Homer's garage, which not even Hemingway could have bettered, and the filmed Waterloo that turns into a catastrophic rout of collapsing scenery and injured stuntmen. Most impressive of all is the final chapter when Hackett is trapped and nearly killed by a crowd outside a Hollywood premiere.

This delirious and vengeful mob seems to have stepped straight from his painting of Los Angeles in flames. The fury of the crowd, unable to find an enemy and so turning on itself is chillingly conveyed in West's spare and unemotional prose. Much of the novel's force stems from the reader's sense that, fifty years later, Hollywood's power over our imaginations is undiminished, and that his vacant and restless sightseers are proxies for all of us.

Sadly, West and his wife died in a car crash in 1940. One wonders what he would have made of Hollywood Boulevard today—tacky and faded, the haunt of hookers, drug dealers and edgy tourists, waiting for Tod Hackett's great fire to surge up from the wastelands of central LA and at last destroy the city of dreadful night.

ALDOUS HUXLEY

"Foreword" in *The Doors of Perception* and *Heaven and Hell* (1994)

If *Brave New World* is Aldous Huxley's greatest novel, then *The Doors of Perception* is his most important work of non-fiction, and I suspect that together they will outlast everything else written by him during his long and restless life. *Brave New World*'s unsettling picture of a scientifically engineered utopia, with its recreational drugs and test-tube babies, its "feelie" cinemas that anticipate virtual reality, now seems a shrewder guess at the future than George Orwell's vision of Stalinist terror in *Nineteen Eighty-Four*.

Yet *The Doors of Perception* may prove to be even more prophetic than *Brave New World*. All his life Huxley was driven by a need to understand the mystery of human consciousness, a quest that led him from Christian mysticism to the religions of the Far East and the pseudo-religions of California. Unusually for a literary intellectual, of his day or ours, Huxley was intensely interested in science, and much of his original work lies in the border zone between religion, art and science.

The Doors of Perception sits in the centre of this magnetic ground. Huxley was fascinated by early research in the neurosciences, and in particular by the role of neurotransmitters in our brains and the way in which these chemical messengers control our view of ourselves and the world around us. Despite the wonders of human consciousness, Huxley believed that our brains have been trained during the evolutionary millennia to screen out all those perceptions that do not directly aid us in our day-to-day struggle for existence. We have gained security and survival, but in the process have sacrificed our sense of wonder.

The dismantling of these screens and the revelation of the richer world beyond them has long been the task of art and religious mysticism, but Huxley suspected that modern pharmacology possessed even stronger weapons in its armoury of psycho-active drugs. In *The Doors of Perception* he describes an afternoon in Los Angeles in 1953 when he first ingested mescalin, the active principle of the sacred cactus known to the Mexicans as peyotl, and saw the gates of a new world open before him.

From the start he realised that his insights were not into himself and his modest personal history, but into the universe around him. Over the years there have been endless accounts of mescalin and LSD trips, but none can match Huxley's description of the hallucinatory realm that expanded before his eyes. The shutters around his mind at last fell away, revealing the wonders of existence to his self-centred and earth-bound mind.

In *The Doors of Perception* and its sequel, *Heaven and Hell*, Huxley speculates that human beings will always need some sort of chemical aid to free themselves from the inherited limitations of their own nervous systems. Fifty years after his mescalin trip beside a Hollywood garden, when we have flown to the moon and girdled our planet with an entertainment culture more suffocating than anything visualised in *Brave New World*, we may be right to think that the expedition Huxley undertook into his own brain is the last journey waiting for all of us, whether by chemical means or through some less hazardous door, the inward passage to our truer and richer selves.

ON WORK OF OTHERS: ART

Ballard's relationship with visual art was deep and reciprocal. As documented throughout this collection, his first and most enduring love was surrealism, which lent his work a grammar and aesthetic that persisted from *The Drowned World* (1962) to *Kingdom Come* (2006). From schoolboy experiments and spending hours visiting art galleries on his arrival in London in 1951, visual art of all kinds nourished Ballard's life and work, the rollcall in "What I Believe" giving one version of a canon: "Max Ernst, Delvaux, Dali, Titian, Goya, Leonardo, Vermeer, Chirico, Magritte, Redon, Duerer, Tanguy, the Facteur Cheval, the Watts Towers, Boecklin, Francis Bacon." In the late 1960s, he maintained an association with the Institute of Contemporary Arts, and became a trustee of the New Arts Laboratory, a shortlived counter-cultural events space in North London, where in April 1970 his own exhibition of "Crashed Cars" was shown.

In 1956, Ballard visited the Independent Group exhibition *This Is Tomorrow* at the Whitechapel Gallery, a formative encounter with the emergent pop art and the work of Eduardo Paolozzi, whose "Terminal Hut" made a lasting impression. Following a meeting at an Italian restaurant on the King's Road in 1967, documented in polaroid photographs reproduced in *New Worlds* 178, the two became friends, and went on to collaborate at *New Worlds* and *Ambit*, where Ballard, as prose editor, introduced Paolozzi. The introductory text for *General Dynamic F.U.N.*, was included as one leaf in the edition of prints contained in a tinted Perspex box, produced by Editions Alecto in 1970. Readers will note parallels and echoes in its phrasing to the introduction to *The Atrocity Exhibition* and "Some Words about *Crash!*"

The existence of a foreword for the book *Waves and Light* (1980), showing the work of the Japanese photographer Ikko Narahara and the sculptor Kyoko Asakura, might have gone unremarked in the English language until its rediscovery by Mike Holliday and acquisition by the collector and editor Rick McGrath in 2015. Certainly, the piece was unknown to the Ballard Estate before that time. Narahara writes in his introduction: "I cannot forget the great joy when I got the poetic foreword of the SF writer, Mr. J. G. Ballard, whom I respect so very much. May 17, 1979 in Tokyo." This prose poem, written while Ballard was working on *The*

Unlimited Dream Company (1979), responds suggestively to Narahara's photographs of Asakura's sculptures submerged under sea or half-buried in sand or snow.

When Brigid Marlin's painting *The Rod* (1973) was published in the December 1974 issue of *Science Fiction Monthly*, Ballard opened a correspondence with the artist. In June 1986, Marlin invited Ballard to a new show, sending him postcard reproductions of recent works. In response, he asked if she would consider a commission to reproduce two early Paul Delvaux paintings destroyed in the war, writing: "If this seems offensive, may I say that I wouldn't in the least mind accepting a comparable commission to write a copy of Moby Dick from memory, assuming that all existing versions were destroyed—and I believe Dali accepted commissions to produce exact copies of Vermeers."[3]

The first commission was completed in 1986 and Marlin made a reciprocal request before agreeing to the second: that Ballard sit for a portrait. The reluctant sitter visited her studio in 1987, and the resulting painting was purchased by the National Portrait Gallery in 1989.

An appreciation of Delvaux himself was commissioned by Nicholas Royle for a *Time Out* magazine city guide to Brussels, where it was illustrated with Delvaux's painting *Venus Endormie* (1944).

By the late twentieth century, more artists were in turn responding to Ballard's fiction. His correspondence with Tacita Dean documented Dean's research into the land artist Robert Smithson, and the fact that Smithson's library contained copies of Ballard's books, research which itself produced a show at the Frith Street gallery in 2013. Ballard had earlier been invited by the curators at Pierogi 2000, a gallery then based in Williamsburg, New York, to contribute to a catalog accompanying their *Dead Tree* installation, a recreation of the Robert Smithson work originally shown in Dusseldorf's Kunsthalle in 1969.[4]

---

3. J. G. Ballard to Brigid Marlin, personal letter, dated June 19, 1986.
4. Smithson's 1966 essay "Quasi-infinities and the Waning of Space" opens with an epigram from Ballard's story "The Overloaded Man": "Without a time sense consciousness is difficult to visualize." The later unpublished essay, "The Artist as Site-Seer; or, A Dintrophic Essay," written sometime in 1966–1967, opens with an entire paragraph from "The Terminal Beach." Robert Smithson, *The Collected Writings*, ed. Jack Flam (Berkeley: University of California Press, 1996), 35, 340.

Ed Ruscha's painting *The Music from the Balconies* (1984, oil on canvas) features a line of text from *High-Rise*: "The Music from the Balconies Nearby Was Overlaid by the Noise of Sporadic Acts of Violence"; *Fountain of Crystal* (2009, oil on canvas) features the text "A Fountain of Spraying Crystal Erupted Around them" from *Crash. Fountain of Crystal* sold in auction for $1,335,000 in May 2018.

Ruscha has said of Ballard's influence on his work: "[He] had a way of describing what we all ignore—these roadways, ramps and utility items in our lives, which we tend to overlook. I'm not directly driven by his writing—but this man glorified something that people forget or put out of their minds. Maybe that's what I'm trying to do, and in some ways that makes a direct line from him to me."[5]

The short text on Francis Bacon is reproduced from *J. G. Ballard: Quotes* (2004), where it was attributed simply to *Tate* (2000). Bacon demands inclusion here. As Ballard wrote in a chapter of *Miracles of Life* titled "Screaming Popes": "I still think of Bacon as the greatest painter of the post-War world."[6]

---

5. Charlotte Cripps, "J G Ballard: High Impact on Artists," *Independent*, February 10, 2010, 14–15.
6. Ballard, *Miracles of Life*, 156. In the bibliography to *Crash: Homage to JG Ballard* (2010), David Pringle speculates that the Bacon paragraph may originate from an exhibition catalog, but it has not been possible to locate the source text.

EDUARDO PAOLOZZI

"Introductory text" in *General Dynamic F.U.N. 1965–1970* (1970)

The marriage of reason and fantasy which has dominated the 20th century has given birth to an even more ambiguous world. Across the communications landscape move the spectres of sinister technologies and the dreams that money can buy. Thermo-nuclear weapons systems and soft-drink commercials coexist in an overlit realm ruled by advertising and pseudo-events, science and pornography.

In *Moonstrips Empire News* Eduardo Paolozzi brilliantly explored the darker side of this mysterious continent. By contrast, in *General Dynamic F.U.N.* he brings together the happiest fruits of a benevolent technology. The leitmotif is the California girl sunbathing on her car roof. The mood is idyllic, at times even domestic. Tactile values are emphasised, the surface pleasures to be found in confectionary, beauty parlours and haute couture fabrics. Children play in a garden pool, a circus elephant crushes a baby Fiat. Varieties of coleslaw are offered to our palates, far more exciting than the bared flesh of the muscle men and striptease queens. Mickey Mouse, elder statesman of Paolozzi's imagination, presides over this taming of the machine. The only factories shown here are manufacturing dolls. Customised motorcycles and automobile radiator grills show an amiable technology on its vacation day.

Despite this pleasant carnival air, a tour de force of charm and good humour, Paolozzi's role in providing our most important visual abstracting service should not be overlooked. Here the familiar materials of our everyday lives, the jostling iconographies of mass advertising and consumer goods, are manipulated to reveal their true identities. For those who can read its pages, *General Dynamic F.U.N.* is a unique guidebook to the electric garden of our mind.

IKKO NARAHARA

"Crystal of the Sea" in *Waves and Light* (1980)

Is the sea a living creature that has drowned in its own spirit? Are we merely the dreams in human form of this great sleeping being? By returning ourselves to the sea we can provide perhaps the key that will turn in its liquid lock and thus wake it from its sleep? The sea-floor, that strangest of all domains, seems like the wrinkled forehead of this dormant giant, the absolute base-line of our conscious world. On the sea-floor all becomes possible, reverie and reality meet with no preconceptions. Its deep corrugations and the written history of unrealized futures, re-scripted each hour by the invisible tide. But we move here at our own risk. At any moment light and liquid may fuse together into a crystalline mass as beautiful but as unforgiving as a jewel. The crystal of the sea takes time from us, freezing each of us into a statue as eternal as a single second.

Be careful! A threatening fauna has sprung from this transient domain, from the wrinkled forehead of this sleeping giant. Are these strange creatures extensions of ourselves as we will be in the future, our never-to-be realized identities deformed by the immense passage of unused time? With regret we move towards the surface, waking from another's dream, like the lover of a deranged woman drawing away from their shared slumber. Here in the shallows, at the transit zone between two universes, we pause and rest. The shallow water takes on the intimate character of our own bloodstream, protecting us from the strange realm of the air. After the infinite immersions of the sea, we realize that space is flat, and that its apparent limitless depth is in fact an illusion, a dream of our waking minds. A powdery light clings to our waists, the crystal of the sea dissolves in a silken froth. Without any preparation we find ourselves stranded on the sea-shore. After the certainties of the sea the geometry of the unbroken sand is a model of countless ambiguities, of an imminent psychosis.

Castaway onto the shore of our own consciousness, we try to recover some of that lost time drained from us by the sea. A profound pity and sense of isolation overcomes us, like that of an abandoned child, as well as a determination to impose ourselves on this rigid world. Immediately, as if in response, strange forms begin to appear around us, huge heaps of white crystal that seem like condensed time mined from the unseen possibilities of our lives. More time condenses, forming white hills, a headland of the future, which might evaporate if we could find the process to unlock their energies. Condensed into these white hills are all our hopes, dreams, fears, a thousand encounters, passions, memories. We move among them, searching for some means to release them into this silent air.

But wait! A strange crystal has presented itself to us, some kind of enigma that has emerged out of its own being and now lies on the shore. Already the sea has begun to recede, a deepening sleeper returning to its own dream. Safe at last, we hold in our hand a fragment of our future, a crystal sword which will open the world around us and set us free.

BRIGID MARLIN

"An Appreciation" in *Paintings in the Mische Technique* (1990)

The art of Brigid Marlin describes a visionary world of almost unlimited dimensions and self-sufficiency. Fifteen years ago, when I first saw *The Rod*, one of her most ambitious paintings, reproduced in a magazine, I was so impressed by its imaginative sweep that I sent an enthusiastic letter of appreciation to her, the only fan letter I have ever sent to a painter. The sense of a clearly realised poetic universe, in which every detail, however modest, was accorded equal attention, was what most gripped my imagination.

Surrealism, which had played a large part in forming my own view of the world, had seemed to falter with the death or old age of its greatest practitioners—Max Ernst, Magritte, Dali and Delvaux—and here in Brigid Marlin was a painter who might be the first of the next generation. I remember writing to her with as much excitement as I felt when I came across the paintings of Francis Bacon in the 1950s. The surrealist dream of remaking the world and revealing its true nature seemed to live on in the work of this woman painter, about whom I knew nothing—I assumed that the wistful and even ethereal figure who appeared in many of the paintings was a self-portrait of the artist.

In fact, I was quite wrong, just as I was wrong to think of Brigid Marlin as a surrealist, though I am sure that a great deal of the surrealist world-view is subsumed within her own vision. In the ten years after my fan letter to her I kept a close watch for any further reproductions of her work, and I was delighted when, out of the blue, I one day received from her an invitation to a private view at the London gallery showing her latest work. She told me that she would be there, and I looked forward to meeting my ethereal poetess.

As it happened, Brigid Marlin was a tall and attractive American woman with a strong personality and a lively sense of humour, a superb mimic and robust antagonist in any argument who was always ready to fight her own corner. I liked her immediately. Looking back on our first meeting, I compliment her on the charity and forbearance she showed in ignoring an unintended piece of rudeness on my part. Some time earlier, while going through a collection of Delvaux reproductions, I noticed several black and white photographs of paintings that had been destroyed during the second World War. When I met Brigid Marlin at her gallery I omitted to ask for the prices of her own works and tactlessly suggested that she accept a commission from me to recreate two of the lost Delvaux paintings.

She gracefully accepted, and on my visits to her studio in Hemel Hempstead I got to know this remarkable American woman, saw many more of her paintings and learned a great deal about her unique visionary imagination. Later still, she painted my portrait, which is now part of the National Portrait Gallery collection in London.

Robust conversationalist and restless traveller, moving one week to the Himalayas and the next to Chicago or Los Angeles, Brigid Marlin is also a deeply religious woman, with a strong Christian faith that has been tested and proved by certain unhappy events in the life of her family, sadnesses that now lie in the past. What I had seen as the surrealist elements in her painting were, rather, the transformations brought about by the power of faith and her religious experience of that far richer world that lies beyond the world of appearances. In the best and most ambitious of her paintings we see clearly her dramatic and visionary remaking of the world, but this regeneration of life and space and spirit is present even in her smallest and most domestic images. In her work, as in the greatest of the surrealists, archaic myth and spiritual apocalypse meet and fuse.

PAUL DELVAUX

"Eyes Wide Shut: J. G. Ballard on Paul Delvaux's Landscapes of Nostalgia and Desire" in *Time Out Brussels Guide* (1996)

Each of Delvaux's paintings is a doorway into a unique and enchanting dream, one of the most mysterious realms in twentieth-century art.

Under an evening or late afternoon sky, the temples and palaces of a Renaissance city stand in their own shadows, the stage-sets for a drama of the unconscious that has yet to begin or may have ended decades beforehand. The perspectives are exact, and every cornice and column is strictly in place. Only time is absent, banished from the unearthly light and replaced by memory and a pervading nostalgia.

Almost without exception, this is a city of women. Calm and bare-breasted, they stand or recline in the posture of mannequins, but each has the dormant power of a sleeping goddess. The few men who enter this realm are timid, uneasy figures, like toddlers who have strayed into their mothers' boudoirs and glimpsed a fearful but fascinating beauty. The women guard each other, but now and then a violent panic seems to threaten them. They signal wildly to the dark air, as if the sleeper whose mind encloses them has stirred uncomfortably in his dream.

For the most part, though, a deep and reassuring calm presides over this twilit space. It emanates from the broad hips and heavy breasts of these stately women, and from their placid contemplation of some inner world glimpsed within their large and unflinching eyes. As we observe them we feel an intense yearning for a richer and more real domain that may have existed on the far side of the womb. Our memories of the oedipal conflicts of our childhoods are assuaged by these impassive beings, and our deepest passion for womanhood seems sanctioned by their welcoming gaze.

Delvaux is generally considered to be a surrealist but he had little in common with other members of that restless and international move-ment. Unlike Dalí, Ernst and Tanguy who travelled ceaselessly, he rarely left his native city, took almost no part in the surrealists group activities and spent his life working quietly in his studio, content to embark each day on his solo voyage into his imagination.

He was born in 1897, the son of a Brussels lawyer, and seems to have been dominated by his strong-willed mother. It was only after her death, when he was in his mid-thirties, that the heavy curtains across his mind drew back and he saw clearly for the first time the luminous world that he was to make his own. As a young artist he painted in a loosely expression-ist way, but after a trip to Italy he was deeply impressed by its Classical architecture and by the poetic perspectives in the works he had seen on show by de Chirico.

From then on Delvaux's art scarcely varied for more than half a century. A childhood fascination with trains sometimes revealed itself, and he meticulously painted the stationary carriages pausing at a quiet suburban station before setting off to some destination we will never know, that terminus at the dream's end. During World War II his painting became populated by skeletons, sinister visitors who stand beside his placid nudes, male intruders from the fields of death that the horrors of wartime Europe had driven into the dreamer's mind.

For the most part, Delvaux remained true to his vision of a twilight paradise, in many ways an Edenic image that only a male imagination could evoke. As a result, accusations of voyeurism have made Delvaux less familiar to British gallery-goers than to those on the Continent. But his unselfconscious and consoling women, immersed in their tribal solidarity, in many ways meet all the demands for a nurturing and self-sufficient feminist collective, a world of women content to be without men.

During a century dominated by formalist experiment in the arts, surrealism has been almost alone in its dedication to the poetic imagination, a faculty that may have atrophied among the British audience brought up on concept and installation art. Delvaux's world is as far removed from those of Duchamp and Damien Hirst (where no one ever feels an emotion or has an erection), but his appeal lies in that realm of memory, eroticism and desire that has its roots far beyond the retina and the front lobes in the archaic deeps of the brain.

ROBERT SMITHSON

"Robert Smithson as Cargo Cultist" in *Robert Smithson: A Collection of Writings on Robert Smithson on the Occasion of the Installation of Dead Tree at Pierogi 2000* (1997)

What cargo might have berthed at the Spiral Jetty? And what strange caravel could have emerged from the saline mists of this remote lake and chosen to dock at this mysterious harbour? One can only imagine the craft captained by a rare navigator, a minotaur obsessed by inexplicable geometries, who had commissioned Smithson to serve as his architect and devise this labyrinth in the guise of a cargo terminal.

But what was the cargo? Time appears to have stopped in Utah, during a geological ellipsis that has lasted for hundreds of millions of years. I assume that that cargo was a clock, though one of a very special kind. So many of Smithson's monuments seem to be a patent amalgam of clock, labyrinth and cargo terminal. What time was about to be told, and what even stranger cargo would have landed here?

The Amarillo Ramp I take to be both jetty and runway, a proto-labyrinth that Smithson hoped would launch him from the cramping limits of time and space into a richer and more complex realm.

Fifty thousand years from now our descendants will be mystified by the empty swimming pools of an abandoned southern California and Cote d'Azur, lying in the dust like primitive time machines or the altar of some geometry obsessed religion. I see Smithson's monuments belonging in the same category, artefacts intended to serve as machines that will suddenly switch themselves on and begin to generate a more complex time and space. All his structures seem to be analogues of advanced neurological processes that have yet to articulate themselves.

Reading Smithson's vivid writings, I feel he sensed all this. As he stands on the Spiral Jetty he resembles Daedalus inspecting the ground plan of the labyrinth, working out the freight capacity of his cargo terminal, to be measured in the units of a neurological deep time. He seems unsure whether the cargo has been delivered.

His last flight fits into the myth, though for reasons of his own he chose the wrong runway, meeting the fate intended for his son. But his monuments endure in our minds, the ground plans of heroic psychological edifices that will one day erect themselves and whose shadows we can already see from the corners of our eyes.

TACITA DEAN

"Time and Tacita Dean" in *Tacita Dean* (2001)

Tacita Dean's films are surveillance footage taken in some of the strangest spaces of the mind. At first sight the settings seem to be located in the real world—steam baths in Hungary, an abandoned trimaran on a Caribbean island, a futuristic beach-house still waiting for its real owners to arrive. The spectator's imagination flows into these cryptic and eventless spaces, trying to decode and make sense of them. I assume that Tacita's films are deliberate attempts to explore a mysterious agenda of her own. A hint of what this might be first came to me when she wrote from Utah describing her attempts to find Robert Smithson's *Spiral Jetty* (1970), a pioneering work of Earth art that had disappeared below the surface of an immense saline lake. She included a set of instructions on how to find the jetty, published by the Utah Arts Council. The directions are so complex that they seem designed to mislead anyone searching for the jetty. Tacita believes that the instructions were provided by Smithson himself. One could guess that Smithson, who was soon to die in a plane crash, was posthumously protecting his unique memorial.

In an article about the jetty, I tried to answer the question: what conceivable cargo could be landed at this bizarre, self-enclosed wharf? I concluded that the cargo was probably a time-machine, though not the kind found in science fiction, but a device for manipulating time and space, and that all Smithson's Earthworks were similar "metaphors" working in parallel.

It intrigued me that Tacita was so interested in Smithson. I was struck by the thought that all Tacita's films are obsessed with time. The clearest example of this is her interest in Donald Crowhurst, who disappeared at sea in 1969, while ostensibly taking part in a non-stop race around the world. As was soon known, Crowhurst never left the Atlantic, radioing in false reports of his positions. Eventually he despaired and jumped overboard, and the trimaran later found itself in Cayman Brac, a Caribbean island where Tacita filmed its rotting hulk.

Tacita writes well—perhaps too well for an artist—and has described Crowhurst's tragic story in vivid and gripping prose. She refers to the rumours of collusion between Crowhurst and certain unnamed people in Teignmouth, his home port. Her history of the abandoned trimaran's subsequent career is a tour de force of melancholy reporting, brought out most tellingly in her film. Nearby is the strange beach-house, standing like a piece of the furniture that has arrived too early.

But what most interests Tacita is the fate of Crowhurst's marine chronometer, which he seems to have taken with him when he jumped to his death. Tacita suggests that Crowhurst had run out of time, and that the chronometer was no longer telling any kind of time that made sense to him. After circling the Atlantic for months, he was psychologically and spiritually exhausted. The timeless void of an ocean death was all that was left to him.

There's no doubt that, for Tacita, the trimaran also lies outside time, like so many of the subjects she has filmed. She told me recently that the saline lake in Utah has fallen by several feet, revealing the labyrinth of the spiral jetty. I'm confident that Tacita will be on hand with her camera when the cargo is at last unloaded.

ED RUSCHA

"The Coolest Gaze in Pop Art," *Guardian* (2001)

Ed Ruscha has the coolest gaze in American art. The work of his contemporaries, such as Lichtenstein and Rosenquist, is raw and hot, with the visceral energy of the comic strip and the giant billboard, but as tiring as a hyperactive child screaming a catchphrase picked from a TV ad. Warhol's prints of electric chairs and car crashes are eerily blank and autistic, fictions wholly dependent on the mass-media images that are themselves an even greater fiction.

Ruscha is far calmer, as unflamboyant but as penetrating as a sniper looking at the world through a telescopic sight. If Lichtenstein's *Wham* and Rosenquist's *F 111* are the rowdy Sistine ceiling of American art in the 20th century, then Ruscha is closer in spirit to Vermeer, who quietly compressed a universe of experience and sensibility into his modest domestic interiors.

Ruscha transforms the whole of outdoor America into a private domestic interior. The equivalent of Vermeer's virginal is the filling station in his painting Standard Station, Amarillo, Texas. Nothing moves in Ruscha's art or is overly demonstrative. His paintings that use words, like *Honk* and *Radio*, never clamour for attention, and are the icons of an inverted and ominous commerce. His remarkable set of published books have catalogued the insoluble mystery of the ordinary. *Twenty-Six Gas Stations* and *Some Los Angeles Apartments* convey the planetary emptiness of America as unsparingly as Edward Hopper. The filling stations become strange and arbitrary structures, signposts to a forgotten world. An unknown people paused at these wayside stops before moving on to destinations we will never visit. Ruscha shows that we inhabit the immense emptiness they leave behind them.

Every Building on the Sunset Strip is Ruscha's masterpiece, the image of a single street that defuses the dream of the ultimate dream-city. We unfold the extended pages, moving through the suburbs of north Los Angeles, we scan the original chromosome of urban life, the collective genome of the city from which all others have been reproduced.

Ruscha's images are mementos of the human race taken back with them by visitors from another planet, as unsettling as his typewriter lying in a dusty road, the airless cathedral of his Texas filling station, the lettered symbols of his commercial signs that say everything and tell us nothing.

FRANCIS BACON

"Francis Bacon" in *J. G. Ballard: Quotes* (2004)

Death sits facing us, his legs straddling a garden chair, a machine-gun resting on a nearby table. His head and left shoulder have vanished, sinking into a psychological abyss that leaves a black hole in the centre of the painting. But his gaze is unmistakable, and reminds us of those quiet and patient killers who waited beside the execution pits of the 20th century. Francis Bacon painted this fearful vision in 1945, the year of Hiroshima and Nagasaki, when the full nightmare of the Nazi death-camps became known. But Bacon scarcely needed the second World War to supply him with a feast of horror. Being human was enough, and together his paintings constitute a vast bestiary in which mankind (and it is mostly men; very few women appear in his paintings) is stripped to its core of pain and despair. After the screaming popes and trapped executives, Bacon set out the private space that dominated his later paintings, an airless interior like a television hospitality room where the guests have been left alone too long. One senses that they are frightened to leave, aware that the headless man with a machine-gun is waiting for them in a quiet park not too far away. Francis Bacon is, for me, the greatest British painter of the last century, unflinching in the way he returned the Gorgon's stare.

4

FEATURES AND ESSAYS

In the period between the UK publication of *The Atrocity Exhibition* (1969) by Jonathan Cape and the completion of *Crash* in early 1972, Ballard published three significant feature-essays.

Books and Bookmen was a literary magazine based in London and published by Philip Dosse from 1956 to 1980. The magazine paid contributors little but gave them considerable leeway, attracting over its life a roster of establishment contributors including Auberon Waugh and King Charles. Ballard's piece "Fictions of Every Kind," a review of *The Shattered Ring* (1970), a Christian reading of fantasy literature, paid that book little attention in its assessment of, and predictions for, the role of SF in a rapidly changing society: "science fiction is likely to be the only form of literature which will cross the gap between the dying narrative fiction of the present and the cassette and videotape fictions of the near future." Ballard had been interviewed by the journalist Douglas Reed at home in Shepperton in late 1970, and that interview would run in the same magazine in April 1971.

Ink—"The Other Newspaper"—was an underground weekly founded by Richard Neville, editor of *Oz* magazine, in May 1971. *Ink* switched to fortnightly publication after fourteen issues and closed after twenty-nine. Ballard's essay considered the American author and activist Ralph Nader, who had become a household name in the United States for his 1965 analysis of road safety, *Unsafe at Any Speed*, and his ongoing investigations into the Federal Trade Commission. Ballard had used Nader's name repeatedly in the pieces "The Death Module" (1967) and "The University of Death" (1968), and in April 1971 he had received a lawyer's letter from Dutton, the second publisher to consider *The Atrocity Exhibition* for

American publication, requesting that he remove all mentions to Nader from the text: "The whole essence of the book is contained in these sexual fantasies about public figures. . . . I felt that I couldn't go along with that, so I said 'Sorry,' and there we are now."[1]

In a surprising commission for *Drive*, the magazine produced by the Automobile Association (AA) for its members, Ballard was invited to join a veteran car rally across Europe, from Harwich to Stuttgart, in April 1971. The article was accompanied by a photograph of the author in car-coat and driving gloves at the wheel of a 1904 Renault.

In the late 1970s Ballard's short fiction was appearing regularly in *Bananas*, the literary newspaper edited by Emma Tennant, and his book reviews in the *New Statesman*. The first piece for UK *Vogue* appeared while he was working on *The Unlimited Dream Company* (1979). "The Future of the Future" was a sustained piece of speculative futurology, imagining "the dream house of the year 2000." "The Diary of a Mad Space Wife" revisited the speculative mode for the same magazine two months after the publication of *The Unlimited Dream Company*, while Ballard was working on *Hello America* (1981). On this occasion the imagined environment was an orbiting space-habitat, in which Judith, the space wife of the title, experiences "a creeping malaise, that sinister combination of boredom, listlessness and self-regard which in the previous century affected Norwegian and Swedish settlers living above the Arctic Circle."

Ballard's interest in Edward Hopper was ignited by his visit to the Musée Cantini in Marseille in 1989 to review the Hopper exhibition for the *Guardian*: Hopper garners a brief mention in the story "Memories of the Space Age" (1982) but after this review becomes a reference point, alongside Ed Ruscha, for American visual art. In a 1997 review Ballard wrote: "But the true poet of metropolitan America, the melancholy observer of provincial offices, empty movie theatres and anonymous bars, was Edward Hopper, for me the greatest of all American painters and one of the few prepared to draw the shadows that fell from the shoulders of American power and confidence."[2]

---

1. Jerome Tarshis, "Kraft-Ebing Visits Dealey Plaza," *Evergreen Review* 96 (Spring 1973): 145–146.
2. "American Dreams," *Sunday Times*, August 31, 1997, 2.

The passing reference in the Hopper piece to his apartment in Juan-les-Pins on the Cote d'Azur was expanded in a feature for the travel section of the *Mail on Sunday* published the year before *Cocaine Nights* (1996). It hymns the modern version of the French Riviera, as represented by science park Sophia-Antipolis, close neighbor to the imagined complex of *Super-Cannes* (2000).

The 1997 essay, commissioned for the book *Airport* (1997), edited by Jeremy Millar for the Photographer's Gallery, is a key piece of armchair social geography, a celebration of airports and air travel: "The concourses are the ramblas and agoras of the future city, time-freeze zones where all the clocks of the world are displayed, an atlas of arrivals and destinations forever updating itself, where briefly we become true world citizens." Alongside the airport, the suburb: "The Virtual City," for the *Tate* magazine, considers Shepperton as an exemplary "alienated zone."

"The Prophet" adds Michael Powell to the Ballardian canon of filmmakers, in a career retrospective for the *Guardian* that reflects on the author's cinema-going and considers the ambiguous psychology of Powell's characters in relation to fiction: "My guess is that the serious novel of the future will be serious in the way that Powell's and Hitchcock's films are serious, where the psychological drama has migrated from inside the characters' heads to the world around them."

An appreciation of modernist architecture, grounded in memoir, provides additional context to the story "One Afternoon on Utah Beach" (1978) and a long-standing admiration of Le Corbusier. A retrospective of the career of Salvador Dalí for the *Guardian's* Saturday *Review* section focused on his film in anticipation of the opening of the exhibition *Dalí and Film* at the Tate Modern on June 1, 2007. Finally, a valedictory travelogue describing a visit to the newly opened Guggenheim in Bilbao, written after his diagnosis with cancer, draws together architectural analysis, thoughts on contemporary art, and a cool farewell: "From the far side of the Styx I'll look back on it with awe."

FICTIONS OF EVERY KIND

Books and Bookmen (1971)

Everything is becoming science fiction. From the margins of an almost invisible literature has sprung the intact reality of the 20th century. What the writers of modern science fiction invent today, you and I will do tomorrow—or, more exactly, in about 10 years' time, though the gap is narrowing. Science fiction is the most important fiction that has been written for the last 100 years. The compassion, imagination, lucidity and vision of H. G. Wells and his successors, and above all their grasp of the real identity of the 20th century, dwarf the alienated and introverted fantasies of James Joyce, Eliot and the writers of the so-called Modern Movement, a 19th century offshoot of bourgeois rejection. Given its subject matter, its eager acceptance of naiveté, optimism and possibility, the role and importance of science fiction can only increase. I believe that the reading of science fiction should be compulsory. Fortunately, compulsion will not be necessary, as more and more people are reading it voluntarily. Even the worst science fiction is better—using as the yardstick of merit the mere survival of its readers and their imaginations—than the best conventional fiction. The future is a better key to the present than the past.

Above all, science fiction is likely to be the only form of literature which will cross the gap between the dying narrative fiction of the present and the cassette and videotape fictions of the near future. What can Saul Bellow and John Updike do that J. Walter Thompson, the world's largest advertising agency and its greatest producer of fiction, can't do better? At present science fiction is almost the only form of fiction which is thriving, and certainly the only fiction which has any influence on the world around it. The social novel is reaching fewer and fewer readers, for the clear reason that social relationships are no longer as important as the individual's relationship with the technological landscape of the late 20th century.

In essence, science fiction is a response to science and technology as perceived by the inhabitants of the consumer goods society, and recognizes that the role of the writer today has totally changed—he is now merely one of a huge army of people filling the environment with fictions of every kind. To survive, he must become far more analytic, approaching his subject matter like a scientist or engineer. If he is to produce fiction at all, he must out-imagine everyone else, scream louder, whisper more quietly. For the first time in the history of narrative fiction, it will require more than talent to become a writer. What special skills, proved against those of their fellow members of society, have Muriel Spark or Edna O'Brien, Kingsley Amis or Cyril Connolly? Sliding gradients point the way to their exits.

It is now some 15 years since the sculptor Eduardo Paolozzi, a powerful and original writer in his own right, remarked that the science fiction magazines produced in the suburbs of Los Angeles contained far more imagination and meaning than anything he could find in the literary periodicals of the day. Subsequent events have proved Paolozzi's sharp judgment correct in every respect. Fortunately, his own imagination has been able to work primarily within the visual arts, where the main tradition for the last century has been the tradition of the new. Within fiction, unhappily, the main tradition for all too long has been the tradition of the old. Like the inmates of some declining institution, increasingly forgotten and ignored by the people outside, the leading writers and critics count the worn beads of their memories, intoning the names of the dead, dead who were not even the contemporaries of their own grandparents.

Meanwhile, science fiction, as my agent remarked to me recently in a pleasant tone, is spreading across the world like a cancer. A benign and tolerant cancer, like the culture of beaches. The time-lag of its acceptance narrows—I estimate it at present to be about 10 years. My guess is that the human being is a nervous and fearful creature, and nervous and fearful people detest change. However, as everyone becomes more confident, so they are prepared to accept change, the possibility of a life radically different from their own. Like green stamps given away at the supermarkets of chance and possibility, science fiction becomes the new currency of an ever-expanding future.

The one hazard facing science fiction, the Trojan horse being trundled towards its expanding ghetto—a high-rent area if there ever was one in fiction—is that faceless creature, literary criticism. Almost all the criticism of science fiction has been written by benevolent outsiders, who combine zeal with ignorance, like high-minded missionaries viewing the sex rites of a remarkably fertile aboriginal tribe and finding every laudable influence at work except the outstanding length of penis. The depth of penetration of the earnest couple, Lois and Stephen Rose, is that of a pair of practicing Christians who see in science fiction an attempt to place a new perspective on *"man, nature, history and ultimate meaning."* What they fail to realize is that science fiction is totally atheistic: those critics in the past who have found any mystical strains at work have been blinded by the camouflage. Science fiction is much more concerned with the significance of the gleam on an automobile instrument panel than on the deity's posterior—if Mother Nature has anything in science fiction, it is VD.

Most critics of science fiction trip into one of two pitfalls—either, like Kingsley Amis in *New Maps of Hell*, they try to ignore altogether the technological trappings and relate SF to the "mainstream" of social criticism, anti-utopian fantasies and the like (Amis's main prophecy for science fiction in 1957 and proved wholly wrong), or they attempt to apostrophize SF in terms of individual personalities, hopelessly rivalling the far-better financed efforts of American and British Publishers to sell their fading wares by dressing their minor talents in the great-writer mantle. Science fiction has always been very much a corporate activity, its writers sharing a common pool of ideas, and the yardsticks of individual achievement do not measure the worth of the best writers, Bradbury, Asimov, Bernard Wolfe (*Limbo 90*) and Frederik Pohl. The anonymity of the majority of 20th-century writers of science fiction is the anonymity of modern technology; no more "great names" stand out than in the design of consumer durables, or for that matter Rheims Cathedral.

Who designed the 1971 Cadillac El Dorado, a complex of visual, organic and psychological clues of infinitely more subtlety and relevance, stemming from a vastly older network of crafts and traditions than, say, the writings of Norman Mailer or the latest Weidenfeld or Cape miracle? The subject matter of SF is the subject matter of everyday life: the gleam on refrigerator cabinets, the contours of a wife's or husband's thighs passing the newsreel images on a color TV set, the conjunction of musculature and chromium artefact within an automobile interior, the unique postures of passengers on an airport escalator—all in all, close to the world of the Pop painters and sculptors. Paolozzi, Hamilton, Warhol, Wesselmann, Ruscha, among others. The great advantage of SF is that it can add one unique ingredient to this hot mix—words. Write!

THE CONSUMER CONSUMED

Ink Magazine (1971)

Could Ralph Nader, the consumer crusader and scourge of General Motors, become the first dictator of the United States? The question isn't entirely frivolous. Now in his sixth year as the most articulate and determined champion of the ordinary consumer, Nader already reveals an ominous degree of self-denying fanaticism that links him to the last of the old-style populist demagogues and may be making him the first of the new. Given that party and presidential politics in the USA are no longer flexible enough to admit any true outsider (the next five US presidents will probably come from a tiny pool of a hundred or so professional politicians), one would expect any real maverick with a headful of obsessions to home in on us from an unexpected quarter of the horizon.

The technological landscape of the present day has enfranchised its own electorates—the inhabitants of marketing zones in the consumer society, television audiences and news magazine readerships, who vote with money at the cash counter rather than with the ballot paper in the polling booth. These huge and passive electorates are wide open to any opportunist using the psychological weaponry of fear and anxiety, elements that are carefully blanched out of the world of domestic products and consumer software. For most of us the styling and efficiency of a soup-mix or an automobile are far more real, and far more reassuring, than the issues of traditional politics: East of Suez, balance of payments, trade union reform. Anyone who can take a housewife's trusting relationship with her Mixmaster or my own innocent rapport with my automobile and feed into them all his obsessions and unease is clearly going to be in business.

The son of immigrant Lebanese parents, Ralph Nader decided to become a defender of the common people, according to his own biography, at the age of eight. In the established tradition of populist leaders he took up his law books in their defence, but at Harvard Law School discovered that the young lawyers were being trained to defend the big corporations, not the small consumer. Nader's confrontation with the biggest of the big corporations, General Motors, contains the entire psychology of his method, and represents no mean achievement—for the first time, he made Americans feel guilty about their greatest dream image and totem object: the motor car.

At the time, Americans were so busy worrying about their cars that few of them had a chance to look at Nader's book *Unsafe at Any Speed* and the charged and emotive language he uses. This is the opening sentence: "For over half a century the automobile has brought death, injury and the most inestimable sorrow and deprivation to millions of people."

From this point, Nader never looked back, tapping a huge fund of insecurity about modern technology which has mushroomed into the present concern for pollution and road safety (similar efforts are now being made in Britain to make people feel uneasy over the enormous advances in sexual freedom).

What is interesting about Nader is that this champion of the consumer is himself a non-consumer. His annual income is estimated to be more than $100,000, but he lives on a minute fraction of this in a boarding house room, without a car or a TV set. If one can divide dictators into smokers and non-smokers, Nader's potential for dictatorship is clearly of the puritanical, non-smoking kind. Described as harsh and almost unfeeling in his dedication, Nader insists over and over again that his only concern is with "justice"—love, needless to say, has no place in his scheme of things. "If you want to be loved, you'll be co-opted." None of us can say we haven't been warned.

Many of Nader's targets seem ludicrously puny—did any of us, for example, ever regard breakfast cereals as anything but a good-humoured method of blocking the infant's trumpeting mouth as we recovered from our hangovers? The important point, though, is that Nader is unloading a powerful sense of anxiety and guilt on to a huge range of commonplace activities. Sooner or later, I would guess, these will crystallize around one major subject, a simple formula of antagonism, unease and wish-fulfilment that will play the same role in the technological landscape that cruder formulas played in the political landscape. Inevitably, I suppose, the consumer society must produce its own unique demagogue, but this sort of dictator may well be difficult to recognize and unseat.

As I've found to my own cost, Nader is already being taken more seriously than many politicians, precisely because the real motives at work are so hard to identify. A year ago my novel *The Atrocity Exhibition* was due to be published in the United States by Doubleday, but two weeks before publication the entire edition was withdrawn and destroyed on the orders of the firm's boss, Nelson Doubleday, an old boy of extreme right-wing views who has donated a helicopter to the California police (a nice twist—the rich man no longer bequeaths a Rubens to King's College but a riot-control weapon to keep down the student body).

What had blown Nelson Doubleday's fuses was a section of the book entitled "Why I want to fuck Ronald Reagan." The next firm to take the book, E.P. Dutton, were delighted with this piece, and thought seriously of using it as the book's title. That was last August. They were due to publish this month, but now they too have had cold feet. I was interested to learn that among the things that most bothered them were "sixteen references to Ralph Nader." In vain did I protest that anyone in public life attempting to involve us in his fantasies can hardly complain if we involve him in ours. In *The Atrocity Exhibition* a large number of public figures—Jackie Kennedy, Reagan, Elizabeth Taylor, Princess Margaret, and so on—are involved in the sexual fantasies of the hero. Although there have been threats and complaints about various sections of the book (the first publisher of the Reagan piece, Bill Butler, was tried and fined; the US Embassy put pressure on the Arts Council to stop its grant to *Ambit*, which published the Jackie sex-fantasy), these figures are generally regarded as open targets. Nader, significantly, is still considered to be on our side.

THE CAR, THE FUTURE

Drive (1971)

Think of the twentieth century—what key image most sums it up in your mind? Neil Armstrong standing on the moon? Winston Churchill giving the V-sign? A housewife in a supermarket loading her trolley with brightly coloured food packs? A television commercial? For me, none of these. If I were asked to condense the whole of the present century into one mental picture I would pick a familiar everyday sight: a man in a motor car, driving along a concrete highway to some unknown destination. Almost every aspect of modern life is there, both for good and for ill—our sense of speed, drama and aggression, the worlds of advertising and consumer goods, engineering and mass manufacture, and the shared experience of moving together through an elaborately signalled landscape.

We spend a large part of our lives in the car, and the experience of driving involves many of the experiences of being a human being in the 1970s, a focal point for an immense range of social, economic and psychological pressures. I think that the twentieth century reaches almost its purest expression on the highway. Here we see, all too clearly, the speed and violence of our age, its strange love affair with the machine and, conceivably, with its own death and destruction.

What is the real significance in our lives of this huge metallized dream? Is the car, in more senses than one, taking us for a ride? Increasingly, the landscape of the twentieth century is being created by and for the car, a development which people all over the world are now beginning to rebel against. They look with horror at Los Angeles—nicknamed Autopia, Smogville and Motopia—a city ruthlessly ruled by the automobile, with its air clouded by exhaust gases and its man-made horizons formed by the raised embankments of gigantic freeway systems.

In Britain the first motorways are already reaching across our cities. Many of them are motion-sculptures of considerable grace and beauty, but they totally overpower the urban areas around and—all too often—below them. It may well be that these vast concrete intersections are the most important monuments of our urban civilization, the twentieth century's equivalent of the Pyramids, but do we want to be remembered in the same way as the slave-armies who constructed what, after all, were monuments to the dead?

Sadly, despite the enormous benefits which the car has created, a sense of leisure, possibility, freedom and initiative, undreamt of by the ordinary man eighty-six years ago when Karl Benz built the world's first successful petrol-driven vehicle, the car has brought with it a train of hazards and disasters, from the congestion of city and countryside to the serious injury and deaths of millions of people.

The car crash is the most dramatic event in most people's lives apart from their own deaths, and for many the two will coincide. Are we merely victims in a meaningless tragedy, or do these appalling accidents take place with some kind of unconscious collaboration on our part? Most of us, when we drive our cars, willingly accept a degree of risk for ourselves, our wives and children which we would regard as criminally negligent in any other field—the wiring of electrical appliances, say, or the design of a bridge or apartment block, the competence of a surgeon or midwife.

Yet the rough equivalent of speeding on unchecked tyres along a fast dual carriageway at the end of a tiring day at the office is lying in a hot bath with a blazing three-bar electric fire balanced on the edge below a half-open window rattling in a rising gale.

If we really feared the crash, most of us would be unable to look at a car, let alone drive one.

These questions about the car—probably unanswerable for the next fifty years—I was thinking over when *Drive* invited me to join a veteran car rally across Germany to celebrate the seventieth anniversary of Mercedes-Benz and the launching of a new model, the 350SL grand tourer. Some eighteen cars belonging to members of the British Veteran Car Club assembled at Harwich, sailed overnight to Bremerhaven in northern Germany, and travelled together on a seven-day return journey to Stuttgart, the home of Mercedes.

Glad of a chance to visit the industrial landscape which was the birthplace of the car, I willingly accepted, and was duly sworn in as a passenger on board the AA's own veteran car, a 1904 Renault.

This was my first veteran car run, and there was no doubt by the time I reached Stuttgart that however little I knew about the modern car I knew a great deal about the old, all of it learned the hard way.

Exhausting, often terrifying and always exciting, the rally to Stuttgart left me with a number of reflections on the past, present and future of the car. Whatever the appeal of veteran cars—and clearly being at the centre of a great deal of public interest is a large part of that appeal for the drivers themselves—it seems obvious to me that these antiquated and uncomfortable machines are admired chiefly because they are machines. Most of them are now just as efficient mechanically as they were when new, thanks to continuous rebuilding.

As machines whose basic technology is rooted in the nineteenth century—a visible and easily grasped technology of pistons, flywheels and steaming valves—these cars have the same appeal as railway locomotives and steamrollers, a far cry from the new technologies of the late twentieth century—a silent and mysterious realm of invisible circuitry, thermonuclear reactions and white-tiled control rooms. Even on the domestic level our everyday lives are now being invaded by machines whose workings we can barely guess at. How many of us could mend a faulty automatic washing machine or waste disposer, let alone a colour television set?

The modern car, like its veteran ancestor, still remains a machine whose identity we can grasp. Apart from its obvious role as a handy means of transport, the car satisfies one basic human requirement—our need to understand as much as possible about the world around us.

Even if we can barely tell the difference between a sparking plug and a dipstick, the car is probably the last machine whose basic technology and function we can all understand. Beyond it lie technologies which are either too complex for us, like that of the computer, or those in which we play a wholly passive part, such as aviation.

At the same time, an enormous backlash of hostility now faces the automobile, part of a general anxiety about the abuses of modern science. Has the car, in the sense in which we know it, any future at all? Will legislation more and more take away the freedom that is inseparable from the private vehicle?

My guess is that the car will remain much in its present form for the next thirty years. Whatever else may happen during the closing decades of the twentieth century, it is almost certain that working hours will decrease and leisure hours increase. Given more leisure, and rising incomes to spend on it, people's recreations will diversify, and only the car can provide the link. No public transit system ever devised could satisfy the vast transport needs of London, Manchester or Birmingham during the course of an ordinary weekend, and the decline of the private car is no more likely than the decline of the private house. Apart from this, driving a car clearly satisfies certain basic physical and psychological impulses, and any legislator trying to ban or significantly reduce the number of automobiles would do well to consider the alternative channels into which these impulses might flow.

None the less, it is obvious that ever more restrictive legislation will be enacted all over the world aimed at the control of the car, concerned not merely with factors such as safety and pollution but also with the overall social influences. Like most legislation, it will tend to be aimed at the mass rather than at the individual car. To a large extent, the future of the car will be the future of traffic.

Within the next thirty years I see an immense network of motorway systems covering the British Isles, like the rest of the industrialized world. But simultaneously we will probably see the first traffic-free areas established in cities and large towns, blocks of several square miles where the only form of transport, other than one's own legs, will be some type of battery-powered, non-exhaust-emitting public vehicle. The roads into major cities will be controlled by toll-gates, with premium tolls charged at holiday and peak congestion periods.

It seems inevitable that we will gradually surrender our present freedom to step into our cars and drive where and when we wish across the entire area of the British Isles. Traffic movements and densities will be increasingly watched and controlled by electronic devices, automatic signals and barriers. On August Bank Holiday or Christmas Eve, for example, major holiday routes to the south coast and the West Country will be closed once a set number of vehicles has passed through the toll-gates.

Electronic counters like those used by London Transport for its buses will be mounted on all roads, signalling the opening and closing of toll-gates hundreds of miles away. These controls will ensure that people stagger their holidays, and could even be used as an instrument of government policy, moving hundreds of thousands of people away from overcrowded resort areas to those that are less popular.

By the closing years of the century the first serious attempts will be made to achieve the direct electronic control of individual vehicles. Experimental schemes have already been visualized in which each car is hooked by radio to an electronic signal transmitted from a metal strip in the centre of the road, obeying its commands and matching its speed to a computer-controlled traffic flow.

Ultimately, I feel, all legislation aimed at the car is really aimed at the one feature that provides both its greatest freedom and its greatest dangers—the steering wheel. Looking beyond the next thirty years to the middle of the twenty-first century (when many children now alive will still be driving), I see its final elimination. Sooner or later, it will become illegal to drive a car with a steering wheel. The private car will remain, but one by one its brake pedal, accelerator and control systems, like the atrophying organs of our own bodies, will be removed.

What will take the place of the steering wheel? In all likelihood, a wheel of a different kind—a telephone dial. When our great-grandchildren sit down in their cars in the year 2050, they will see in front of them two objects—one that resembles a telephone, the other a telephone directory. The directory will contain a list of all possible destinations, each with a number that may be dialled.

Having selected his destination, our driver will look up the number and then dial it on the telephone. His signal will be transmitted to the transport exchange, where the ever-watching computers of Central Traffic Control will hold his call, analysing it in terms of anticipated traffic flow en route, vehicle densities at the destination, metered toll charges to be recorded against the driver's account (or perhaps even instantly debited from his bank balance).

If his call is accepted on the basis of available traffic information, the computer will select the best route. Electronic signals transmitted from road cables will steer the car out of its garage. Invisible eyes will guide our driver's car over every inch of his journey, adjusting speed to the traffic stream, making small detours to avoid probable delays, expertly parking it for him at his destination.

Sometimes, of course, when our driver dials his destination, the number will be engaged. Central Traffic Control will have decided that there are already too many cars en route to Brighton, Blackpool or the Bronte country. A soothing and attractive recorded voice will invite the driver to try Woking, Stockton-on-Tees or Scunthorpe. Alternatively, perhaps, a harsh and threatening voice will inform him that there is insufficient money in the bank to pay the toll-charges.

Clearly, the possibilities are endless. Almost anything one cares to say about the future will probably come true, and sooner than we think. I feel that most of these developments are inevitable, given rising populations, rising incomes and leisure, and that the car as we know it now is on the way out. To a large extent I deplore its passing, for as a basically old-fashioned machine it enshrines a basically old-fashioned idea—freedom. In terms of pollution, noise and human life the price of that freedom may be high, but perhaps the car, by the very muddle and congestion it causes, may be holding back the remorseless spread of the regimented, electronic society.

However, given our fascination with the machine, the car will always be with us. The veteran car rally to Stuttgart proved this for me. Our grandchildren may not be able to drive a 1904 Renault Park Phaeton, to give that bone-bruising monster its full name, but they will be able to drive a 1971 Ford Capri or Rolls-Royce.

At various points around the British Isles there will be so-called Motoring Parks, in which people will be able to drive the old cars in the old way. Baffled at first by the strange pedals and switches sprouting from the floor and instrument panel, able to vary the speed of the engine and the direction of the car with their own hands and feet, they will set off clumsily along the well-padded roads. Every so often they will come across traffic lights and road junctions, and be faced with the choice between turning left or turning right. As they become familiar with the pedals and steering wheel they will sense the exhilaration and freedom of being able to wind up these ancient engines and exceed the speed limits.

If they are really lucky they will be caught by a mock-policeman riding the strangest machine of all, something like a small metal horse, once called a motorcycle, but banned when no electronic system could be devised to control it. The real enthusiasts will even buy their own vintage cars, venerable 1971 Ford Zodiacs and 1984 Jaguars. Now and then, as part of a festival or centenary, they will hold veteran car rallies in the traffic-free pedestrian zones of major cities. And on these occasions everyone will thoroughly enjoy three rare sensations: the smell of exhaust fumes, the noise and the congestion.

THE FUTURE OF THE FUTURE

Vogue (1977)

One of the most surprising but barely noticed events of the period since the Second World War has been the life and death of the space age.

Almost twenty years ago to the day, October 1957, I switched on the BBC news and heard for the first time the radio call-sign of Sputnik I as it circled the earth above our heads. Its urgent tocsin seemed to warn us of the arrival of a new epoch. As a novice science fiction writer, I listened to this harbinger of the space age with strong misgivings—already I was certain, though without the slightest evidence, that the future of science fiction, and for that matter of popular consciousness in general, lay not in outer space but in what I had already christened "inner space," in a world increasingly about to be remade by the mind.

None the less, I fully expected that the impact of the space age would be immediate and all-pervasive—from fashion to industrial design, from the architecture of airports and department stores to the ways in which we furnished our homes. I took for granted that the spin-off of the US and Russian space programmes would transform everything in our lives and produce an extrovert society as restlessly curious about the external world as Renaissance Europe.

In fact, nothing remotely like this occurred. Public interest in the space flights of the 1960s was rarely more than lukewarm (think, by contrast, of our powerful emotional involvement with the death of President Kennedy and the Vietnam war), and the effects on everyday life have been virtually nil. How many of us could name, apart from Armstrong himself, a single one of the men who have walked on the Moon, an extraordinary achievement that should have left a profound trace upon the collective psyche? Yet most of us could rattle off without a moment's thought the names of lone transatlantic sailors—Chichester, Chay Blyth, Tabarly, Clare Francis . . .

Looking back, we can see that far from extending for ever into the future, the space age lasted for scarcely fifteen years: from Sputnik I and Gagarin's first flight in 1961 to the last Skylab mission in 1974—and the first splashdown, significantly, not to be shown on television. After a casual glance at the sky, people turned around and went indoors. Even the test flights taking place at present of the space shuttle Enterprise—named, sadly, after the spaceship in Star Trek—seem little more than a limp by-product of a television fantasy. More and more, the space programmes have become the last great period piece of the twentieth century, as magnificent but as out of date as the tea-clipper and the steam locomotive.

During the past fifteen years the strongest currents in our lives have been flowing in the opposite direction altogether, carrying us ever deeper into the exploration not of outer but of inner space. This investigation of every conceivable byway of sensation and imagination has shown itself in a multitude of guises—in mysticism and meditation, encounter groups and fringe religions, in the use of drugs and biofeedback devices—all of which attempt to project the interior realm of the psyche on to the humdrum world of everyday reality and externalize the limitless possibilities of the dream. So far, though, the techniques available have tended to be extremely dangerous (drugs such as LSD and heroin), physically uncomfortable (the contortions of classical yoga), or mentally exhausting (the psychological assault course of the suburban encounter group, with its staged confrontations and tantrums, its general hyperventilation of the emotions).

Meanwhile, far more sophisticated devices have begun to appear on the scene, above all, video systems and micro-computers adapted for domestic use. Together these will achieve what I take to be the apotheosis of all the fantasies of late twentieth-century man—the transformation of reality into a TV studio, in which we can simultaneously play out the roles of audience, producer and star.

In the dream house of the year 2000, Mrs Tomorrow will find herself living happily inside her own head. Walls, floors and ceilings will be huge, unbroken screens on which will be projected a continuous sound and visual display of her pulse and respiration, her brain-waves and blood pressure. The delicate quicksilver loom of her nervous system as she sits at her dressing table, the sudden flush of adrenaline as the telephone rings, the warm arterial tides of emotion as she arranges lunch with her lover, all these will surround her with a continuous light show. Every aspect of her home will literally reflect her character and personality, a visible image of her inner self to be overlaid and enhanced by those of her husband and children, relatives and friends. A marital tiff will resemble the percussive climax of *The Rite of Spring*, while a dinner party (with each of the guests wired into the circuitry) will be embellished by a series of frescoes as richly filled with character and incident as a gallery of Veroneses. By contrast, an off day will box her into a labyrinth of Francis Bacons, a premonition of spring surround her with the landscapes of Constable, an amorous daydream transform the walls of her bathroom into a seraglio worthy of Ingres.

All this, of course, will be mere electronic wallpaper, the background to the main programme in which each of us will be both star and supporting player. Every one of our actions during the day, across the entire spectrum of domestic life, will be instantly recorded on video-tape. In the evening we will sit back to scan the rushes, selected by a computer trained to pick out only our best profiles, our wittiest dialogue, our most affecting expressions filmed through the kindest filters, and then stitch these together into a heightened re-enactment of the day. Regardless of our place in the family pecking order, each of us within the privacy of our own rooms will be the star in a continually unfolding domestic saga, with parents, husbands, wives and children demoted to an appropriate supporting role.

Free now to experiment with the dramatic possibilities of our lives, we will naturally conduct our relationships and modify our behaviour towards each other with more than half an eye to their place in the evening's programme. When we visit our friends we will be immediately co-opted into a half-familiar play whose plot-lines may well elude us. Even within our own marriages we will frequently find ourselves assigned roles which we will act out with no rehearsal time and only the scantiest idea of the script—on reflection, not an unfamiliar situation. So these programmes will tirelessly unfold, a personalized Crossroads or Coronation Street perhaps recast in the style of Strindberg or Stoppard, six million scenes from a marriage.

However fanciful all this may seem, this transformation of our private lives with the aid of video-systems and domestic computers is already at hand. Micro-computers are now being installed in thousands of American homes, where they provide video-games and do simple household accounts. Soon, though, they will take over other functions, acting as major domo, keeper of finances, confidant and marriage counsellor. "Can you afford the Bahamas this year, dear? Yes . . . if you divorce your husband." The more expensive and sophisticated computers will be bought precisely to fulfil this need, each an eminence grise utterly devoted to us, aware of our strengths and weaknesses, dedicated to exploring every possibility of our private lives, suggesting this or that marital strategy, a tactical infidelity here, an emotional game-plan there, a realignment of affections, a radical change of wardrobe, lifestyle, sex itself, all costed down to the last penny and timed to the nearest second, its print-outs primed with air tickets, hotel reservations and divorce petitions.

Thus we may see ourselves at the turn of the century, each of us the star of a continuous television drama, soothed by the music of our own brain-waves, the centre of an infinite private universe. Will it occur to us, perhaps, that there is still one unnecessary intruder in this personal paradise—other people? Thanks to the video-tape library, and the imminent wonders of holistic projection, their physical presence may soon no longer be essential to our lives. Without difficulty, we can visualize a future where people will never meet at all, except on the television screen. Childhood, marriage, parenthood, even the few jobs that still need to be done, will all be conducted within the home.

Conceived by artificial insemination, brought up within the paediatric viewing cubicle, we will conduct even our courtships on television, shyly exchanging footage of ourselves, and perhaps even slipping away on a clandestine weekend (that is, watching the same travelogues together). Thanks to the split-screen technique, our marriage will be witnessed by hundreds of friends within their own homes, and pre-recorded film taken within our living rooms will show us moving down the aisle against a cathedral backdrop. Our wedding night will be a masterpiece of tastefully erotic cinema, the husband's increasingly bold zooms countered by his bride's blushing fades and wipes, climaxing in the ultimate close-up. Years of happy marriage will follow, unblemished by the hazards of physical contact, and we need never know whether our spouse is five miles away from us, or five hundred, or on the dark side of the sun. The spherical mirror forms the wall of our universe, enclosing us for ever at its heart . . .

THE DIARY OF A MAD SPACE WIFE

Vogue (1979)

Will we ever discover alien life in outer space? The answer, almost certainly, is: "Yes—in the year 2022. It will be thirty-five years old, female, come from Pasadena, Dusseldorf or Yokohama, be married to an astrophysicist, adore Doris Lessing and David Hockney, and live in a six-mile-long metal cylinder halfway between our own planet and the Moon."

Faced with pollution, over-population and the microprocessor, future governments are likely to find irresistible the political and economic pressures to set off into space and place all our problems on the doorstep of the universe. Already an influential lobby in the United States, led by the Princeton physicist Professor Gerard O'Neill, is campaigning for the construction of a series of gigantic space colonies, with artificial climates variable at the flick of a switch, each housing a million people, totally self-supporting and limitlessly fuelled by a benevolent sun.

Professor O'Neill has testified before a US Congressional Committee on the economic and technical feasibility of the space colonies (though it's interesting to note that the term "space colony" has been banned by the US State Department because of anti-colonial feelings around the world, something that might give the rest of us pause for thought), and in many ways the prospect of living in space seems beguiling. Those glass and chromium paradises, familiar from science-fiction films for the past fifty years, and the limitless technological expertise together fulfil every infantile power fantasy, and a century from now the entire population of our planet may well have moved outwards into space, abandoning its former home for ever.

We can visualize the vast satellite systems circling the Earth, with our present nation-states occupying a series of concentric orbital shells, in an order of precedence dictated by their respective GNPs. The USA and Japan will sail through the clear, star-bright ether of the outermost shells, while the still impoverished and inflation-weary UK will be down among the debris and rocket exhaust with Uganda and the Yemen. We can see the House of Commons in orbit, the MPs confronting each other across the floor of their spherical chamber, the Cup Final and Miss World celebrated in their glass and titanium pleasure-domes, and the millionth performance of *The Mousetrap* taking place in the ultimate theatre-in-the-round.

Commenting on O'Neill's projected six-mile-long satellites, the American inventor and soft-technology pioneer Steve Baer remarks shrewdly: "Once on board, in my mind's eye I don't see the landscape of Carmel by the Sea as Gerard O'Neill suggests. Instead, I see acres of air-conditioned Greyhound Bus interior, glinting, slightly greasy railings, old rivet-heads needing paint. I don't hear the surf at Carmel and smell the ocean. I hear piped music and smell chewing-gum. I anticipate a continuous vague low-key 'airplane fear.'"

A warning glimpse of what life will be like in a space colony can already be seen around us—in run-down motorway cafes, in vandalized municipal high-rises, in the once ultra-modern elevators and miles of scuffed circular corridor at the BBC Television Centre. Will we find, when we at last leave our planet, not a series of Corbusier radiant cities in the sky, but seedy housing estates and third-rate airports? More important, are we right to become nervous whenever governments begin to move into the area of fantasy? It's not only those greasy handrails that I fear. The new frontiersmen are likely to be, not Armstrong and Lovell and Borman, homespun types only a racoonskin cap away from Davy Crockett, but an army of ambitious PhDs, government planners and aerospace bureaucrats. How efficiently will these space colonies function, and what are the long-term effects likely to be on the psyches of the millions of people penned inside these orbiting Heathrows and Gatwicks? Will we see the creation of a set of unique space-age neuroses, born of that vague "airplane fear," a half-conscious dread that will surge through the nervous system of our 35-year-old space-wife whenever the gravity system fluctuates and the soup floats out of the tureen?

Questioned about his dreams during his Skylab mission, the astronaut Russell Schweickart replied: "I don't think anybody ever tried consciously to do any analysis of dream content. Most of the guys aren't the kind of people who even recall their dreams on Earth, let alone up there . . . I'm not even aware that I dreamt at all, but that's true here on Earth too." Certainly NASA has not gone to great lengths to reveal the psychological effects of space travel upon the Apollo and Skylab astronauts, but the latter can't all have been as stolid as Schweickart. The subsequent, often strange careers of many of the astronauts indicate that the effects on the psyche of prolonged periods in space may be considerable. The suggestion has been made that the sensation of free-fall in zero gravity reawakens the long-forgotten but deep-laid anxieties felt by our arboreal ancestors, the ever-present fear of falling off the branch into the jaws of the predator below. Could long exposure to zero gravity generate not only neuroses but new space age cults and religions, the mythology of a second Fall of Man?

Reading through the diary kept by our space-wife during her life in one of the hundreds of satellite cities 35,000 miles from Earth, we can see the tentative evolution of a new kind of consciousness. Croydon Four, one of the older model O'Neill space colonies, is a semitransparent cylinder 6.2 miles long and 1.25 miles in diameter, its inner surface landscaped to resemble a pleasant garden suburb, with low-rise apartment blocks, parks, schools and creches. Through windows the size of wheatfields the tireless sun provides a limitless source of energy, and Judith, our space-wife, finds that she has little to do except lie out on her apartment balcony and let her tan deepen in the warm light of this immense solarium.

Judith's husband works a comparatively long forty-five-minute day as an astrophysicist at Croydon University—its elegant campus is a mile away, directly above Judith's head. However, he has wangled a seat on several of the voluntary committees looking into the problem of leisure in the space colony. There is a powerful Space-Wives' Union seeking a marked increase in the hours to be spent at the kitchen sink, but housework occupies none of Judith's time. Though somewhat scuffed and dented, the metal and plastic apartment is totally dust-free and even the lightest cleaning would pollute and agitate the air. Because the artificial climate within the colony is sensitive to the slightest variations in temperature, all meals are cold and pre-packed, and the arts of cooking are now devoted entirely to the recreation of late twentieth-century airline cuisine. Even so, the excess heat produced by half a million space-wives switching on their favourite afternoon television programmes can fill the enclosed sky of the colony with a dense, dripping fog, and for some time now all television sets have been perpetually on.

For all this, Judith is happy to be here and tolerant of the minor inconveniences of this eventless, sun-filled world. Occasionally the motors which first rotated the satellite, and set its artificial gravity, malfunction and fire in reverse, with the result that everything in the apartment floats out of the windows. Judith, in fact, once spent an embarrassing twenty-four hours suspended three hundred feet in the air above her apartment when she chased her escaping handbag rather too energetically towards the bedroom window.

It is some three years after her arrival that Judith's diary reveals the first signs of a creeping malaise, that sinister combination of boredom, listlessness and self-regard which in the previous century affected Norwegian and Swedish settlers living above the Arctic Circle. Bored by the television set and the endless series of personalized video games tailored to her own needs—during one mad month she won a local beauty contest thirty times in a row (her own specifications had been defined as the ideal ones)—Judith has taken to visiting the observation deck in the basement of her apartment block. For hours she stares into space, watching the other satellites circle past, Croydon Five, Hammersmith and Tooting. Because it is always night in the observation deck, Judith soon loses her tan, and develops the first signs of space sickness. She becomes strangely drowsy, lying for ever in the artificial twilight she has chosen for her bedroom.

The day comes when she no longer recognizes her husband. Soon after, she is admitted to the nearby sanatorium. The last entries in her diary show her dreaming of her childhood in Purley. The doctors consider sending her back to Earth, but after these years in the germ-free atmosphere of the colony she would perish soon after landing. None the less, they encourage her to believe that she has never really come to the space colony, and is still living in Surrey.

So she passes her last years, with the millions of other patients in the satellite system who, like her, believe they are still living in Pasadena and Dusseldorf and Yokohama. At times she is even happy, though the zero gravity of the increasingly frequent breakdowns induces nightmares of anxiety. However, in space the canvas restraining sheets serve two roles.

Meanwhile the thousands of giant satellites continue to revolve, drawing their light from the sun and their darkness from the minds of their passengers.

IN THE VOYEUR'S GAZE

Guardian (1989)

This August, 300 yards from our apartment in Juan-les-Pins, the pleasant park of eucalyptus and fir trees between the RN7 and the sea had unexpectedly vanished, along with the old post office and the tabac selling the Marseille edition of *The Guardian*. In their place was an immense bare-earth site, exposed soil raked by bulldozers, for the moment occupied by an air-conditioned pavilion fit for some latter-day caliph resting en route from Nice Airport to his summer palace in Super-Cannes.

Cautiously entering the pavilion, we found ourselves in a property developer's showroom, filled with promotional displays and a huge model of the new Cote d'Azur, "truly the French California." An attractive guide took us on a tour of this visionary realm, a multilingual Scheherazade who swiftly spun her 1,001 tales of the world in waiting.

Here, at the newly named Antibes-les-Pins, will arise the first "intelligent city" of the Riviera. Outwardly, the pitched roofs supported by dainty classical columns, the pedestrian piazzas and thematic gardens suggest something to calm the fears of our uneasy heir to the throne, but behind the elegant facades everything moves with the speed of an electron.

The 10,000 inhabitants in their high-tech apartments and offices will serve as an "ideas laboratory" for the cities of the future, where "technology will be placed at the service of conviviality." Fibre-optic cables and telemetric networks will transmit data banks and information services to each apartment, along with the most advanced fire, safety and security measures. To cap it all, in case the physical and mental strain of actually living in this electronic paradise proves too much, there will be individual medical tele-surveillance in direct contact with the nearest hospital.

I've no doubt that Antibes-les-Pins, to be completed by 1999, will be a comfortable, pleasant and efficient place in which to live and work. Claire, my girl-friend, couldn't wait to move in. While I dozed on the balcony with Humphrey Carpenter's *Geniuses Together*, an enjoyable memoir of the 1920s Paris of Gertrude Stein, Joyce and Hemingway, Claire had discovered a piece of the twenty-first century under my nose.

The next day, as we drove to Marseille to see the Edward Hopper exhibition at the Musée Cantini, police helicopters raced overhead along the high-speed auto-route, while Canadair flying boats water-bombed the blazing hillsides a few miles from the city. The endless marinas and highways of the Cote d'Azur, and the fibre-optic vision of Antibes-les-Pins, reminded me of how technologically obsessed the French have always been. The future, which in Britain has been dead for decades, still thrives in the French imagination and gives its people their strong sense of get up and go. Prince Charles may be doing his best to propel the British into a nostalgic past where, in due course, he will feel more comfortable under an ill-fitting crown, but the French are still living in the future, far more fascinated by high-tech office blocks, electronic gadgets and Minitels than they are by Escoffier and Saint-Laurent.

Walking around the Edward Hopper paintings in the quiet gallery near the Old Port, we had entered yet another uniquely special world, that silent country of marooned American cities under a toneless, depression-era sky, of entropic hotel rooms and offices where all clocks have stopped, where isolated men and women stare out of one nothingness into the larger nothingness beyond.

It was ironic to see the French visitors to the exhibition, residents one day, perhaps, of the California of the new Côte d'Azur, enthusing over Hopper's images of a stranded US. They seemed to show the same appreciation for these pictures of a vanished American past that an earlier generation of Americans had felt for the Impressionist painters and their evocation of the Paris of the belle epoque. Presumably, too, they saw Hopper's close links with Degas and Monet, and recognized that in a sense this American painter was the last of the French impressionists.

Surprisingly, for a painter who seems so completely of his own country, Hopper's ties to France are strong. To British eyes Hopper's melancholy bars and hotel rooms sum up the America of the 1930s and 1940s, the antithesis of the folksy and sentimental Saturday Evening Post covers of Norman Rockwell. Hopper depicts that hidden and harder world glimpsed in the original *Postman Always Rings Twice*, and many of his paintings could be stills from some dark-edged James M. Cain thriller.

Yet Hopper's imagination was formed across the Atlantic, above all by the three visits to France which he made before the First World War. Born in Nyack, New York State, in 1882, Hopper was a life-long francophile. In the catalogue of the Marseille exhibition Gail Levin, curator of the Hopper collection at the Whitney Museum of American Art, points out that Hopper's passion for all things French extended far beyond painting to take in poetry and the novel, theatre and cinema. During their long marriage he and his American wife, Josephine Nevison Hopper, frequently wrote to each other in French, although they were never to visit France together.

At the New York School of Arts his teachers lectured Hopper enthusiastically on Courbet, Degas, Renoir and Van Gogh, and Hopper later spoke of the "vital importance of the French art of the 19th century for American painting." In 1906, when he arrived on his first visit to France, he was consummating an already intense love affair. After the money-driven tumult of New York he found Paris elegant and unhurried. He particularly liked the way the Parisians seemed to live their entire lives in the street, and spent his time sketching them in the boulevards and cafes.

Among these drawings a figure appeared who would dominate the paintings of Hopper's maturity—a nude woman standing by an open window, hand to her face in a meditative pose. In spite of Hopper's strict Baptist upbringing, or perhaps because of it, as Gail Levin comments, Hopper was especially fascinated by the prostitutes who plied their trade in the streets of Paris, and the sight of these women seems to have unlocked the door of his sexual imagination. In his sketches, the prostitutes sit in their cafes, indifferent to the stares of the passersby, marking out for the first time the voyeuristic space that separates Hopper from the mysterious and impassive women who dominate his paintings.

Nearly forty years later, in *Morning in a City* (1944), we see the same woman by her open window, standing naked by an unmade bed as she stares into the street below. She appears again and again, in *Night Windows* of 1928 and *Hotel Room* of 1931, as if glimpsed from a passing elevated train or through an open hotel-room door.

This voyeur's eye bereft of emotion, in which all action is suspended, all drama subordinated to the endless moment of the stare, seems to be the key to Hopper's paintings. Even the isolated houses and office buildings that form a large part of his subject matter are depicted as if they too are the object of a voyeur's gaze.

In 1909 and 1910 Hopper made two further journeys to France. On his return he married Josephine Nevison, and when she asked him why she attracted him he replied: "You have curly hair, you know a little French, and you are an orphan."

Curiously, Josephine Hopper, to whom he remained happily married for the rest of his life, served as his model for almost all the solitary women whom Hopper poses in their tired hotel rooms. He never again crossed the Atlantic. He and Josephine bought a car and embarked on a series of long drives across the United States, to Colorado, Utah and California.

Hopper's paintings depict an archetypal America of small cities and provincial towns, late-night bars embalmed in the empty night, airless offices and filling stations left behind by the new highway, but seen through an unfailingly European eye. The mysterious railway lines that cross many of his paintings are reminiscent of Chirico's, and his steam locomotives might pull the carriages that Delvaux left stranded in their sidings, while his strange nudes sleep-walk in the evening streets.

Out of sympathy with the art of his American contemporaries, he protested publicly in 1960 against what he felt was the excessive attention given to the abstract expressionists. In a sense he had bypassed the American art of the twentieth century, and his own roots went back to the Paris he had known before the First World War. Still at work after the deaths of Bonnard, Leger and Matisse, Hopper may arguably be not only the last impressionist, but the last great French painter.

Hopper's *New York Movie* of 1939 might easily have been painted by Degas had the latter lived on into the age of the great picture palaces. In a gloomy side-chapel the usherette stares into the carpeted darkness, lost in her own dreams while a larger dream fills the distant screen. Degas remarked that he painted his women subjects as if he was seeing them through a keyhole, catching them in their most intimate and unselfconscious moments. Degas' women are precursors of Hopper's, but in painting the depression America of the 1930s Hopper brings his eye to bear on the alienation of the twentieth-century city.

His women expose themselves to a far more public gaze than a keyhole. They stand by their open windows as if no one can see them, as if the anonymity of the modern city renders them invisible to the passengers of a passing train. They expose everything but reveal nothing. In a late-night bar, in the *Nighthawks* of 1942, a couple sit like characters on a theatre stage, but no drama is communicated to the audience. Hopper's gaze is far removed from that of Hitchcock's *Rear Window*. He is uninterested in whatever banal mystery surrounds his solitary men and women, or in whatever pointless business is transacted in their provincial offices.

Leaving this powerful but unsettling exhibition, we set off for the Old Port and a necessary drink at a quayside cafe. Beyond the white picket fence which I had last seen in *The French Connection* was moored the life-size replica of a square-rigged sailing ship from Polanski's ill-fated *Pirates*, a masterpiece of fibre-glass that towers above the fishing-boats in the harbour. Two years ago it was moored at Cannes, as if taking its revenge on the film festival where it came unstuck, but has now moved down the coast to Marseille, and it was ironic to see the natives of the great seaport paying their 30 francs to inspect this cathedral of floating kitsch.

But for once kitsch was reassuring. As the Cote d'Azur of Matisse and Picasso gives way for the last time to the fibre-optic, telemetric California of Antibes-les-Pins, to English language radio stations and the science park of Sophia-Antipolis, Hopper's marooned hotel rooms appear positively inviting, as his French admirers may have realized. In the context of the future unwrapping itself on our doorsteps Hopper's voyeurism and undisguised loneliness seem almost like intimacy. Penned in their high-security apartments, constant medical tele-surveillance linking them to the nearest hospital, a generation of even more isolated women will soon stare across their bedrooms. But this time there will be no keyholes through which others can observe them, no half-open doorways or windows on to the watching night.

THE FRENCH RIVIERA SPOILED? ONLY BY FEAR AND SNOBBERY

Mail on Sunday (1995)

Think of the French Riviera, and what images come to your mind? The world's most sophisticated holiday resorts, the playground of princes and millionaires, filled with elegant hotels, casinos and luxury villas, their graceful avenues cooled by eucalyptus and palm trees?

Yes, if you're thinking of the French Riviera in 1895, but most certainly not in 1995, or so the travel writers never tire of telling us.

I go to the Cote d'Azur every summer and, if I could afford it, would happily live there for the rest of my life.

Sitting by the swimming pool as the air gleams and the cicadas rasp, I'm always amazed by the travel articles in the British newspapers decrying the Riviera and moaning once again that it is totally spoilt.

Forget Scott Fitzgerald, say the travel writers, forget the Aga Khan and the Russian princes with their private trains, forget Picasso, Matisse and Renoir.

The Cote d'Azur, they agree, is ruined, a faint shadow of its old glory, a hell of high-rise apartment blocks, soulless motorways and brutal hypermarkets, its roads crammed, its skies polluted by package-holiday jets pouring yet more tourists into Nice Airport, its once golden beaches carved up by endless marinas filled with plastic-hulled gin palaces—all in all, a nightmare of concrete, asphalt and garish commercialism.

Looking up from the newspapers at the actual Riviera around me, I always wonder whether these travel writers are living in a parallel world. I have been going to the South of France, on and off, since 1947, when Nice was scarcely bigger than Bognor, and Cannes was a small town that had yet to climb the hills into the present-day suburbs of Californie and Super-Cannes, where the sheiks and sultans have built their summer palaces. But has it all changed so much for the worse? True, there is a decent road system and, yes again, the French have built high-rise hotels and apartment houses, multi-storey car parks and supermarkets.

Thousands of ordinary holidaymakers like you and me now drive along the Croisette at Cannes, play the fruit machines in the Monte Carlo Casino—the ultimate in naffness, apparently, as if roulette and chemin de fer are more stylish ways of being fleeced—and eat takeaway charcuterie on the balconies of their rented apartments.

But have they actually spoiled the Riviera, or is there some kind of strange snobbery at work, a bogus nostalgia for a fabled past that really hides a fear and hatred of the present?

Nailing my colours to the mast, I have to say that I like motorways, high-rises, hypermarkets, car parks and video rental shops. They, like the fax machine and the mobile phone, are part of the world we live in, and the French Riviera suffers no more from the late 20th Century than do Orpington or Kansas City.

More than this, I believe that thanks in part to the Autoroute du Soleil, the Casino hypermarket chain and the breathtaking apartment pyramids at Marina Baie des Anges, the Riviera is now far more exhilarating, and far more fun, than it would have been if the Cote d'Azur of the Twenties had been fenced off and pre-served as an upmarket theme park.

For a resort area once so steeped in the past, today's Riviera is now gripped by a dream of the future. Change is a visitor who knocks on every door, and the wise are those who lay out a welcome mat.

What I realise every summer, when I fly into Nice Airport, is the extent to which the Cote d'Azur is a beacon for the whole of Europe.

The future has arrived, and its address is Sophia-Antipolis, the science city a few miles inland from Antibes.

This vast complex of science parks, research laboratories and modernist housing represents the first stage in the transformation of the Cote d'Azur into Europe's Silicon Valley.

A visit to the Riviera today is not a search for the shades of Matisse or Picasso, but a glimpse into a world of Minitels, satellite dishes and fibre-optic networks. France, famous for cuisine, couture and the Folies Bergeres, is equally fascinated by technology, something the British find hard to grasp.

Five years ago, from our apartment in Juan-les-Pins, I watched the bulldozers levelling the eucalyptus trees between the RN 7 and the sea. Here, within sight of topless beaches, has arisen Antibes-les-Pins, the first "intelligent city" of the Riviera.

When complete, this collection of offices and apartments will house 10,000 people, conceived as an "ideas laboratory" for the cities of the future. Fibre-optic and telemetric networks link data banks and information services to each apartment, along with advanced fire, safety and security measures. And in case the physical and mental strain of living in this electronic paradise proves too great, there will be individual tele-surveillance in direct contact with a nearby hospital.

When I recently drove through Antibes-les-Pins, the residents seemed to be thriving.

From Menton near the Italian border to St Tropez in the west, the Riviera is in the grip of continuous change. Last summer at Miramar, I looked down at the new purpose-built resort of Port-la-Galere, a town-ship of houses and apartments designed to resemble a futuristic honeycomb.

Above our villa was the Pierre Cardin Foundation, a purple flying saucer resting among the fir trees. Yet neither this huge museum with its porthole windows nor Port-la-Galere with its organic architecture seemed out of place in the porphyry-red Esterel landscape, nor offered any challenge to the Belle Epoque wedding cake of the Carlton Hotel across the Bay of Cannes. To the visitor of the Cote d'Azur I say: do enjoy your bouillabaisse under the plane trees in the old town at Antibes. Do visit the Picasso Museum in the Grimaldi Castle, the Cocteau Chapel at Villefranche-sur-Mer and the pink-washed Rothschild museum at Cap Ferrat.

But also visit those more modern wonders such as Marina Baie des Anges at Villeneuve-Loubet, the most astounding apartment scheme in Europe, and, equally remarkable, the nearby Casino hypermarket, where you can buy anything, it would seem, from a portable house to a live lobster.

Do lose your money in the Monte Carlo Casino, but refresh yourself afterwards by exploring not only historic Monaco but the new Monte Carlo to the east of the casino, built on reclaimed land, a miniature Manhattan of immense high-rises that embed themselves in the roofs of gallerias and car parks. As well as the old town at Vence, visit the Chagall Museum in Nice, a glass villa filled with blue light, and the Leger Museum at Bidot, near Antibes, a pavilion of white coolness.

As the paragliders swoop from the rocky heights above Cap Martin, search out Le Corbusier's grave in the cemetery at nearby Roquebrune, a poetic memorial designed by the great architect who is almost the presiding spirit of the new Riviera.

Every year at the Cannes Film Festival, the critics sneer at the Palais des Festivals, where the films are screened. But beneath it is a large (and very cheap) car park that takes the headache out of a visit to the centre of any large city—finding somewhere to park.

No travel writer I have known has ever written about the importance of parking, as if his readers were wafted about by sedan chair.

The other time-honoured problem—attempting to speak the local language—is solved because the Riviera is the only area of France where English is willingly spoken by the natives, as long as you stay within roughly 300 yards of the beach.

And you will even find that a petrol station attendant five miles inland speaks more fluent English than you do. So, finally, enjoy the Riviera not for what it was, but for what it is—the first instalment of the new Europe waiting for us all on the day after tomorrow.

AIRPORTS: THE CITIES OF THE FUTURE

Blueprint Magazine (1997)

Airports and airfields have always held a special magic, gateways to the infinite possibilities that only the sky can offer. In 1946, when I first came to England, a dark and derelict shell of a country, I used to dream of the runways of Wake Island and Midway, stepping stones that would carry me back across the Pacific to the China of my childhood. At school in Cambridge, and later as a medical student at King's College, I would flee all that fossilised Gothic self-immersion and ride a borrowed motorcycle to the American airbases at Mildenhall and Lakenheath, happy to stare through the wire at the lines of silver bombers and transport planes. Airports then were places where America arrived to greet us, where the world of tomorrow touched down in Europe.

Sadly, Britain faltered on the way to its own future, half-heartedly erecting a shabby urban limbo of under-serviced municipal towers and wind-swept shopping precincts. Together they provided the nostalgia-worshippers with all the ammunition needed to launch their postmodernist counter-attack. The pitched roof seemed to rule the Eighties, a vernacular dialect unable to distinguish a town hall from a supermarket or fire station, too many temples to tweeness that resemble offerings on the altar of Prince Charles's uneasy conscience.

Airports, thankfully, are designed around the needs of their collaborating technologies, and seem to be almost the only form of public architecture free from the pressures of kitsch and nostalgia. As far as I know, there are no half-timbered terminal buildings or pebble-dashed control towers.

For the past 35 years I have lived in the Thames Valley town of Shepperton, a suburb not of London but of London Airport. The catchment area of Heathrow extends for at least 10 miles to its south and west, a zone of motorway intersections, dual carriageways, science parks, marinas and industrial estates, watched by police CCTV speed-check cameras, a landscape which most people affect to loathe but which I regard as the most advanced and admirable in the British Isles, and paradigm of the best that the future offers us.

I welcome its transience, alienation and discontinuities, and its unashamed response to the pressures of speed, disposability and the instant impulse. Here, under the flight paths of Heathrow, everything is designed for the next five minutes. Its centrepiece, and for me the most inspiring in England today, is Michael Manser's superb Heathrow Hilton, near Terminal Four. Its vast atrium resembles a planetarium in the way that it salutes the skies above its roof.

By comparison with London Airport, London itself seems hopelessly antiquated. Its hundreds of miles of gentrified stucco are an aching hangover from the nineteenth century that should have been bulldozed decades ago. London may well be the only world capital—with the possible exception of Moscow—that has gone from the nineteenth century to the twenty-first without experiencing all the possibilities and excitements of the twentieth in any meaningful way. Visiting London, I always have the sense of a city devised as an instrument of political control, like the class system that preserves England from revolution. The labyrinth of districts and boroughs, the endless columned porticos that once guarded the modest terraced cottages of Victorian clerks, together make clear that London is a place where everyone knows his place.

By contrast, at an airport such as Heathrow the individual is defined, not by the tangible ground mortgaged into his soul for the next 40 years, but the indeterminate flicker of flight numbers trembling on an annunciator screen. We are no longer citizens with civic obligations, but passengers for whom all destinations are theoretically open, our lightness of baggage mandated by the system. Airports have become a new kind of discontinuous city, whose vast populations, measured by annual passenger throughputs, are entirely transient, purposeful and, for the most part, happy. An easy camaraderie rules the departure lounges, along with the virtual abolition of nationality—whether we are Scots or Japanese is far less important than where we are going. I've long suspected that people are only truly happy and aware of a real purpose to their lives when they hand over their tickets at the check-in.

Above all, airports are places of good news. I miss the days when celebrities were photographed as they stepped through airliner doors. The headiest ozone of glamour and optimism crossed the Atlantic in the Constellations and Stratocruisers of the Fifties as Hollywood stars, Presidents and tycoons waved from the steps, bringing their confidence and likeability to this northern European corner of the depressed world.

I suspect that the airport will be the true city of the next century. The great airports are already suburbs of an invisible world capital, a virtual metropolis whose faubourgs are named Heathrow, Kennedy, Charles de Gaulle, Nagoya, a centripetal city whose population forever circles its notional centre, and will never need to gain access to its dark heart. A mastery of the discontinuities of metropolitan life has always been essential to the successful urban dweller—we live in a street where we know none of our neighbours, and our close friends live equally isolated lives within 50 square miles around us. We work in a district five miles away, shop in another and see films and plays in a third. A failure to master these discontinuities, whether social or genetic in origin, leaves some ethnic groups at a disadvantage, forced into enclaves that seem to reconstitute mental maps of ancestral villages.

But the modern airport defuses these tensions, and offers its passengers the pleasures and social reassurance of the boarding lounge. Its instantly summoned village life span is long enough to calm us, and short enough not to be a burden. The concourses are the ramblas and agoras of the future city, time-freeze zones where all the clocks of the world are displayed, an atlas of arrivals and destinations forever updating itself, where briefly we become true world citizens. Air travel may well be the most important civic duty that we discharge today, erasing class and national distinctions and subsuming them within the unitary global culture of the departure lounge.

In addition to the airport itself, I value the benevolent social and architectural influence that a huge transit facility such as Heathrow casts on the urban landscape around it. I have learnt to like the intricate network of perimeter roads, the car-rental offices, air freight depots and travel clinics, the light industrial and motel architecture that unvaryingly surrounds every major airport in the world. Together they constitute the reality of our lives, rather than some mythical domain of village greens, cathedral closes and manorial vistas. Much as I admire, say, Syon House, now home to a huge garden centre and a venue for business entertaining, I feel more at home driving through an office park like the New Square complex at Bedfont, its hi-tech corporate hangars only a javelin's throw from the Heathrow perimeter road, and surely influenced by the proximity of all those 747 tailplanes that cruise the tarmac like the fins of amiable sharks.

Even the old terminal buildings—One, Two and Three—have a certain period charm. Together, they and the main control tower represent the last survival of the Festival of Britain. I look forward to their replacement in due course, and to terminal Five, and beyond that to terminals Six and Seven, and the transformation of Britain into the ultimate departure lounge. After all, we have every reason to leave.

WELCOME TO THE VIRTUAL CITY

Tate Magazine (2001)

Cities are the scar tissue of history, still itchy and festering after centuries of deep pathology that erupted, in my own lifetime, into fascism and totalitarian communism. Tourists and the young flock to cities, excited by the heady ozone of possibility, all those quantum leaps that lift friendships, sex and the visionary imagination into faster and more charged orbits.

But is the vitality of cities, now that we've reached the twenty-first century, an illusion? Is the excitement they generate any different from the thrill we feel in the dinosaur rooms of the Natural History Museum? So vast, so weird, so clumsy and incomprehensible. All that massive effort required to move one great leg after another, at a maximum speed of four miles per hour, interestingly the average speed of traffic in today's London or Paris. And that small brain . . .

Tellingly, the cities that tourists most enjoy are those in long-term decline—Venice, Florence, Paris, London, New York. The last two are gigantic money-mills, churned by a Centurion-card elite who are retreating into gated communities in Surrey and the Upper East Side. Already their immense spending power has distorted social life in London and New York, freezing out the old blue-collar and middle classes, and validating the notion that the dreams that money can buy are a perfectly fit topic for the young painter, novelist and film-maker. It's not their own ambition that corrupts today's artists, but the subject matter facing them.

So where to find a more astringent, a more challenging and a more real world? Le Corbusier, the greatest visionary architect of the twentieth century, remarked that "a city built for speed is a city built for success."

But almost no city in the world today is built for speed, in the sense that a rapid-access communications system is directly engineered into the asphalt of everyday life, visible from our front doors. Yet hundreds of virtual cities do exist at this very moment that embody Corbusier's dictum. They surround London, Paris, Chicago and Tokyo, and, as it happens, I live in one of them. "Shepperton," some of you will say, appalled by the thought. "My God, suburbia. We went to London to get away from that."

But Shepperton, for what it's worth, is not suburbia. If it is a suburb of anywhere, it is of London Airport, not London. And that is the clue to my dislike of cities and my admiration for what most people think of as a faceless dead-land of inter-urban sprawl. Hurrying back from Heathrow or a West Country weekend to their ludicrously priced homes in Fulham or Muswell Hill, they carefully avert their gaze from this nightmare terrain of dual carriageways, police cameras, science parks and executive housing, an uncentred realm bereft of civic identity, tradition or human values, a zone fit only for the alienated and footloose, those without past or future.

And that, of course, is exactly what we like about it. We like the fast dual carriageways, the easy access motorways, the limitless parking lots. We like the control-tower architecture, the absence of civic authority, the rapid turnover of friendships and the prosperity filtered through car and appliance purchases. We like roads that lead past airports, we like air-freight offices and rent-a-car forecourts, we like impulse-buy holidays to anywhere that takes our fancy. The triangle formed by the M3 and the M4, enclosing Heathrow and the River Thames, is our zone of possibility, far from the suffocating city politics and self obsessions of the metropolis (transport, ugh, fares, rents, kerb-side vomit). We are the unenfranchised citizens of the shopping mall and the marina, the internet and cable TV and we're in no hurry for you to join us.

But is this of interest to the young painter, novelist and film-maker? Yes, because this apparently alienated zone is the new Britain, a pointer to the real future facing this country. Developments in Fulham or Muswell Hill will have no bearing on what lies ahead. But what happens between the M3 and the M4 will define the character of Britain for the next half century. American writers, painters and film-makers set off for

Los Angeles 50 years ago, abandoning Chicago and New York, because they guessed that Southern California's amorphous sprawl contained the key to America's future.

So, abandon that Spitalfields loft and head out for that virtual city waiting for its Edward Hopper and Ed Ruscha, its Rimbaud of the video rental store, its Warhol of the shopping malls. As always, the most exciting spaces of the imagination are where you least expect to find them.

THE PROPHET

Guardian (2005)

Films, like memories, seem to re-shoot themselves over the years, reflecting our latest needs and obsessions. In many cases they can change completely, and reveal unexpected depths and shallows. Will *Four Weddings and a Funeral* be seen one day as a vicious social satire? Could *Jaws* become as tearful and sentimental as Bambi? Could *Crash* be seen as a tender love story?

More to the point, in this centenary year of Michael Powell's birth, could his flamboyant and extravagant films seem like hard-edged psychological dramas about the nature of human consciousness? Are these remarkable films, which float like giddy kites over the peaks of entertainment cinema, in fact far closer to the psychiatrist's casebook than their audiences ever suspected?

I first became a moviegoer in 1946 when I came to England, a little lost among its grey, distracted people. Since there was nothing else to do, a large part of the population went to the cinema three times a week. In gigantic art deco Odeons, like smoke-filled cathedrals, I saw the postwar films of Alfred Hitchcock, Howard Hawks, John Ford and Roberto Rossellini when they first came out. Even more exhilarating, I saw Robert Mitchum, Marlon Brando and James Dean before they became stars.

On dull afternoons, when I should have been dissecting cadavers, I watched *Sunset Boulevard, Orphée* and *Open City*. A completely new culture and social climate were being created, international in spirit and more urgent than almost any novel. I knew it was more important to see *T-Men* and *White Heat* than listen to FR Leavis lecturing on Virginia Woolf.

Given their enormous impact at the time, it's surprising how these films have seemed to change in the past half-century. *The Third Man* now appears to be slightly operatic, a tale of tainted love and penicillin, its rubble-strewn stage dominated by a self-conscious Orson Welles. Yet when it first came out in rationed, shabby Britain, *The Third Man* seemed grainily realistic. The ruins and rubble on the screen merged into the bomb sites outside most English cinemas.

The whole of film noir now seems darkly romantic, with its doomed loners entrapped by scheming femmes fatales. But *Build My Gallows High*, as *Out of the Past* was called on its British release, seemed as hard and devoid of sentiment as the rainy pavements the audiences trudged on their way home. Mitchum in his tired trenchcoat was scarcely the glamorous hunk with the novocaine eyelids he later became, and closer to the sallow youths in their demob suits who haunted the pinball arcades.

Barbara Stanwyck, the spider lady of *Double Indemnity*, now comes across as unbelievably sinister. Yet at the time I first saw her she reminded me of my mother and her bridge-playing friends: strong-willed women forced by the war to survive on their wits. Film noir merged seamlessly into the neo-realist cinema of *Open City* and *Rocco and His Brothers*, almost a newsreel of post-war uncertainty and alienation.

The British director whose image has most changed over the years is Michael Powell, whose films pose the same problems to serious cinephiles as the high-concept movies of Steven Spielberg. Both make films that are too lavish and too emotional, and just a little too unsettling in the way they hide their subtexts. Both have the charm of not-quite innocent children. Powell's films are the absolute antithesis of realist cinema. Like *The Thief of Baghdad*, which he co-directed in 1940, they are filled with extravagant storylines, mysterious motivation and surreal visual effects, all qualities that made his postwar audiences deeply uneasy.

A Matter of Life and Death is now his most famous film, a Spielbergian extravaganza before its time, and contains the clues, I suspect, to what Powell was really about. David Niven plays the pilot of a burning Lancaster returning from a bombing raid over Germany. His crew has bailed out, but his parachute has been shot away, and he has a last conversation with Kim Hunter, a radio operator at an airbase in England. He knows he is going to die, but his tone is triumphant. He is larger than death, quotes from the great poets and philosophers, salutes the wonders of existence, and tells Kim that if he could somehow survive she is the sort of woman he would love. Then he jumps out into the darkness and the void. The next morning we see his body lying on a deserted beach. But he sits up, miraculously alive. He walks through the dunes, apparently unhurt, and sees Kim cycling past. She stops and they embrace, though she knows that there is something seriously wrong with him. There is: he is dead. Strange visions interrupt his recovery. He is carried up an enormous staircase (a cinematic tour de force) and defends himself at what becomes a heavenly trial of mankind. At the end, love conquers all, he is free of his visions and he and Kim are united.

The ending is ambiguous, and the promised explanation for his survival is never given. But unless he has died his defence of mankind makes little sense. I assume that the film is a posthumous narrative, and that the real drama is taking place in the minds of its creators, Powell and his scriptwriter Emeric Pressburger, as they ponder the mysteries of life and death, and the desperate stratagems we adopt to convince ourselves that our existence is meaningful. Life, empowered by love, triumphs over everything, Powell seems to conclude.

But does it? The question runs through most of Powell's films. Given their vast subject matter, his characters are remarkably repressed and self-immersed. In *I Know Where I'm Going*, a headstrong young woman played by Wendy Hiller sets off for a remote Hebridean island, where she will marry a rich industrialist twice her age. A prolonged storm prevents her from reaching the island, and she meets a young naval officer who is also delayed. Surprisingly, given the spare time they have on their hands and the expectations of the audience, there are no signs of attraction between the two. The film is a meteorologist's nightmare: raging seas, wind-lashed crags, torrential rains and thunder, reinforced by wildly tolling bells, grinning masks and wave-washed dungeons. Presumably they reflect the turmoil in Hiller's mind, though she has no doubts about her coming marriage. We know next to nothing about her or the naval officer she suddenly embraces in the film's closing moments. Yet the film is remarkably powerful, and not in any kind of romantic way. This is what is so unsettling about it, hinting strongly at some kind of crisis in the director's mind, rather than on the screen.

The drama in Powell's films is almost always external to the characters, about whom we know very little. In *Black Narcissus* a group of nuns at a remote mission are sexually deranged by the sight of a pipe-smoking David Farrar, though quite why is never made clear. In *The Small Back Room* an alcoholic bomb-disposal expert breaks down as he grapples with a German booby trap, but is saved by a kindly army officer who intervenes.

In *Peeping Tom*, the film that destroyed Powell's career, a psychopathic cameraman stabs his victims with a concealed tripod bayonet as he gazes at them through his view-finder. It is a grisly and definitely very weird film, but when I saw it on its release in 1960 I felt there was something missing. There was no hint of why the cameraman behaved as he did, and the distinct feeling that we, the audience, were the real target. This seemed to be confirmed by a clip of home movie in the film, where the psychopath's tyrannical father is played by none other than Powell. I suspect that Powell was challenging his audiences, forcing them into a series of psychological trials. Each film is a test of the audience's nerve, especially if sex is on the menu, a situation we today are happier with than the audiences of 50 years ago.

I think of Powell as a prophet whose films offer important lessons to both film-makers and novelists, especially the latter, who are still preoccupied with character and individual moral choice. My guess is that the serious novel of the future will be serious in the way that Powell's and Hitchcock's films are serious, where the psychological drama has migrated from inside the characters' heads to the world around them. This is true to everyday life, where we know little about the real nature of the people around us, and less about ourselves than we think, but are highly sensitive to the surrounding atmosphere.

Fancy and the creative spirit rule everything, Powell seems to say. Realism has failed us, and the imagination must take its place. Love may be an illusion, but it is all we have. It must be tested, not against our modest private lives, but in the fiercest fire. We are less important than we think, but our imaginations can transcend everything, even our own deaths.

A HANDFUL OF DUST

Guardian (2006)

Few people today visit Utah beach. The sand seems colder and flatter than anywhere else along the Normandy coast where the Allies landed on D-day. The town of Arromanches—a few miles to the east and closer to Omaha, Gold and Sword beaches—is a crowded theme park of war museums, cemeteries and souvenir shops, bunkers and bunting. Guidebooks in hand, tourists edge gingerly around the German gun emplacements and try to imagine what it was like to stare down the gun sights at the vast armada approaching the shore.

But Utah beach, on the western edge of the landing grounds, is silent. A few waves swill over the sand as if too bored to think of anything else. The coastal land seems lower than the sea, and fails to echo the sounds of war inside one's head.

Walking along the beach some years ago, I noticed a dark structure emerging from the mist ahead of me. Three storeys high, and larger than a parish church, it was one of the huge blockhouses that formed Hitler's Atlantic wall, the chain of fortifications that ran from the French coast all the way to Denmark and Norway. This blockhouse, as indifferent to time as the pyramids, was a mass of black concrete once poured by the slave labourers of the Todt Organisation, pockmarked by the shellfire of the attacking allied warships.

A flight of steps at its rear led me into the dank interior with its gun platforms and sinister letter box view of the sea. Generations of tramps had dossed here, and in the stairwells were the remains of small fires, piles of ancient excrement and a vague stench of urine.

At first sight, the blockhouse reminded me of the German forts at Tsingtao, the beach resort in north China that my family visited in the 1930s. Tsingtao had been a German naval base during the first world war, and I was taken on a tourist trip to the forts, a vast complex of tunnels and gun emplacements built into the cliffs. The cathedral-like vaults with their hydraulic platforms resembled Piranesi's prisons, endless concrete galleries leading to vertical shafts and even further galleries. The Chinese guides took special pleasure in pointing out the bloody handprints of the German gunners driven mad by the British naval bombardment.

Years later, in that Utah beach blockhouse, I was looking at similar stains on the concrete walls, but the scattered rubbish and tang of urine made me think of structures closer to home in England—run-down tower blocks and motorway exit ramps, pedestrian underpasses sprung from the drawing boards of enlightened planners who would never have to live in or near them, and who were careful never to stray too far from their Georgian squares in the heart of heritage London.

From the rooftop barbette I looked along Utah Beach towards an identical blockhouse 800 yards away, and beyond that to the faint silhouette of a third. The Atlantic wall was only part of a huge system of German fortifications that included the Siegfried line, submarine pens and huge flak towers that threatened the surrounding land like lines of Teutonic knights. Almost all had survived the war and seemed to be waiting for the next one, left behind by a race of warrior scientists obsessed with geometry and death.

Death was what the Atlantic wall and Siegfried line were all about. Whenever I came across these grim fortifications along France's Channel coast and German border, I realised I was exploring a set of concrete tombs whose dark ghosts haunted the brutalist architecture so popular in Britain in the 1950s. Out of favour now, modernism survives in every high-rise sink estate of the time, in the Barbican development and the Hayward Gallery in London, in new towns such as Cumbernauld and the ziggurat residential blocks at the University of East Anglia.

But modernism of the heroic period, from 1920 to 1939, is dead, and it died first in the blockhouses of Utah beach and the Siegfried line. Yet in its heyday between the wars, modernism was a vast utopian project, and perhaps the last utopian project we will ever see, now that we are well aware that all utopias have their dark side.

Nazi Germany and Soviet Russia were two utopian projects that turned into the greatest dystopias the world has known. Modernism briefly survived them both, but lost its nerve in the 1960s when the municipal high-rise estates in St Louis, Missouri, were deemed social catastrophes and dynamited. However, I sometimes think that social catastrophe was what the dirt-poor residents secretly longed for.

Modernism's attempt to build a better world with the aid of science and technology now seems almost heroic. Bertolt Brecht, no fan of modernism, remarked that the mud, blood and carnage of the first world war trenches left its survivors longing for a future that resembled a white-tiled bathroom. Architects were in the vanguard of the new movement, led by Le Corbusier and the Bauhaus design school. The old models were thrown out. Function defined form, expressed in a pure geometry that the eye could easily grasp in its entirety. Above all, there should be no ornamentation. "Less is more," was the war cry, to which Robert Venturi, avatar of the tricksy postmodernism that gave us the Sainsbury wing of the National Gallery, retorted: "Less is a bore."

But the modernists maintained that ornamentation concealed rather than embellished. Classical columns, pediments and pilasters defined a hierarchical order. Power and authority were separated from the common street by huge flights of steps that we were forced to climb on our way to law courts, parliaments and town halls. Gothic ornament, with all its spikes and barbs, expressed pain, Christ's crown of thorns and agony on the cross. The Gothic expressed our guilt, pointing to a heaven we could never reach. The Baroque was a defensive fantasy, architecture as aristocratic playpen, a set of conjuring tricks to ward off the Age of Reason.

So modernism was a breath of fresh air and possibility. Housing schemes, factories and office blocks designed by modernist architects were clear-headed and geometric, suggesting clean and unembellished lives for the people inside them. Gone were suburban pretension, mock-Tudor beams and columned porticos disguising modest front doors.

Hitler and Stalin were intrigued by modernism, which seemed part of a new world of aviation, radio, public health and mass consciousness. But the dictators were nervous of clear-headed people who thought for themselves. The Nazis promptly closed the Bauhaus when they came to power and turned it into an SS training school.

Modernism saw off the dictators, and among its last flings were Brasilia, the Festival of Britain and Corbusier's state capital buildings at Chandigarh in India. But it was dying on its pilotis, those load-bearing pillars with which Corbusier lifted his buildings into the sky. Its slow death can be seen, not only in the Siegfried line and the Atlantic wall, but in the styling of Mercedes cars, at once paranoid and aggressive, like medieval German armour. We see its demise in 1960s kitchens and bathrooms, white-tiled laboratories that are above all clean and aseptic, as if human beings were some kind of disease. We see its death in motorways and autobahns, stone dreams that will never awake, and in the turbine hall at that middle-class disco, Tate Modern—a vast totalitarian space that Albert Speer would have admired, so authoritarian that it overwhelms any work of art inside it.

Modernism was never popular in Britain—a little too frank for its repressed natives, except at lidos and the seaside, where people take their clothes off. The few modernist houses and apartments look genuinely odd. Why?

I have always admired modernism and wish the whole of London could be rebuilt in the style of Michael Manser's brilliant Heathrow Hilton. But I know that most people, myself included, find it difficult to be clear-eyed at all times and rise to the demands of a pure and unadorned geometry. Architecture supplies us with camouflage, and I regret that no one could fall in love inside the Heathrow Hilton. By contrast, people are forever falling in love inside the Louvre and the National Gallery.

All of us have our dreams to reassure us. Architecture is a stage set where we need to be at ease in order to perform. Fearing ourselves, we need our illusions to protect us, even if the protection takes the form of finials and cartouches, corinthian columns and acanthus leaves. Modernism lacked mystery and emotion, was a little too frank about the limits of human nature and never prepared us for our eventual end.

But all is not lost for admirers of modernism. They should visit the mortuary island of San Michele in the Venice lagoon, where many pioneers of modernism such as Igor Stravinsky, Serge Diaghilev and Ezra Pound are interred. After taking the ferry, you disembark at a gloomy landing stage worthy of Böcklin's *Island of the Dead*. This is a place beyond hope, of haunted gateways and melancholy statues.

But then, in the heart of the cemetery, there is a sudden lightening of tone, and you find you are strolling through what might be a Modern suburb of Tunis or Tel Aviv. The lines of family tombs resemble cheerful vacation bungalows, airy structures of white walls and glass that might have been designed by Le Corbusier or Richard Neutra. One could holiday for a long time in these pleasant villas, and a few of us probably will.

So, there is one place where modernism triumphs. As in the cases of the pyramids and the Taj Mahal, the Siegfried line and the Atlantic wall, death always calls on the very best architects.

SHOCK AND GORE

Guardian (2007)

Salvador Dalí was the last of the great cultural outlaws, and probably the last genius to visit our cheap and gaudy planet. Look around you with an unbiased eye and, alas, you will see no painter of genius, and no novelist, poet, philosopher or composer who takes his or her place in that top tier without asking our permission. I think Dalí was the greatest painter of the 20th century—far more important than Picasso, who was a 19th-century painter most at home in his studio, with the familiar props of guitars, jugs of wine and stoical girlfriends who must have wondered what was going on in his self-enclosed mind. Picasso was driven around Cannes in his American car, but he seems to have seen nothing of the world on the far side of the windscreen.

With Dalí, we have the immediate sense that he not only saw the increasingly sinister world of the 1930s in all its lurid truth, but fully grasped the deranged unconscious forces that propelled Hitler and Stalin into the daylight. His paintings are like stills from an elegant newsreel filmed inside our heads, and we could reconstitute the whole of the last century from them, all its voyeurism, barbarism, scientific genius and self-disgust.

Dalí's masterpiece and, I believe, the greatest painting of the 20th century is *The Persistence of Memory*, a tiny painting not much larger than the postcard version, containing the age of Freud, Kafka and Einstein in its image of soft watches, an embryo and a beach of fused sand. The ghost of Freud presides over the uterine fantasies that set the stage for the adult traumas to come, while insects incarnate the self-loathing of Kafka's *Metamorphosis* and its hero turned into a beetle. The soft watches belong to a realm where clock time is no longer valid and relativity rules in Einstein's self-warping continuum.

What monster would grow from this sleeping embryo? It may be the long eyelashes, but there is something feminine and almost coquettish about this little figure, and I see the painting as the 20th century's *Mona Lisa*, a psychoanalytic take on the mysterious Gioconda smile. If the Mona Lisa, as someone said, looks as if she has just dined on her husband, then Dalí's embryo looks as if she dreams of feasting on her mother.

How do we explain the huge popularity of this painting, and all of Dalí's work? Suddenly, surrealism is everywhere, in those citadels of respectability such as the Tate, the V&A and the Hayward Gallery. Put on a surrealism show and the crowds flock, quietly absorbing these strange and irrational images. It's as if people realise that reason and rationality no longer provide an adequate explanation for the world we live in. The lights may still be on, but a new Dark Age is drawing us towards its shadows, and we turn to the surrealists as our best guides to the underworld.

The 20th century was a vast textbook of psychopathology, but it took the surrealists a long time to be critically accepted. In the 1950s, when I was hunting for illustrations of the latest Dalí or Magritte, I was more likely to find them in the *Daily Mirror* or *Daily Express*, held up as objects of ridicule. Surrealism as a whole remained beyond the critical pale until well into the 1960s, and most of its great painters—Max Ernst, Magritte, Paul Delvaux—had to wait until their last years before they were accepted by the bowler-hatted bureaucrats of British art. They died loaded with honours, prizes and, worst of all, respectability.

Dalí was the great exception, and never saw a bowler doffed in his direction. He alone remained faithful to the surrealists' first commandment: shock the bourgeoisie. Right to the end he upset the critics and cultural valuers of the arts establishment by posing as their worst nightmare: a genius and show-off greedy for money. He expressed his contempt for them by signing thousands of blank sheets of paper (at $100 a time, so they say), well aware that a flood of inferior copies would drench the market, in the ultimate surrealist act that would make people unsure whether they owned a real Dalí or a fake. And, anyway, did it matter?

A strong factor in Dalí's ostracism from the critical fold was always his exhibitionism: the absurd moustachios, the gigolo manner, the preposterous English in which he yoked together rhinoceros horns and concepts from nuclear physics, his department-store window stunts, his playing up to the American news media, his strangely asexual devotion to his wife, Gala ("she has the look that pierces walls"), the bizarre space he occupied somewhere between American *Vogue* and a seaside freak show. The paintings came and went, as original and voluptuous as ever, but their seriousness was diminished by the stunts and tomfoolery. Only now are people beginning to look earnestly at the entirety of his lifetime's work and judge him as a painter rather than a performer.

What has changed? In part, it is the behaviour of the contemporary art world. Exhibitionism, of one kind or another, is now the frame around all present day artists, from Gilbert & George to Tracey Emin and Damien Hirst, the Chapman Brothers and a host of other YBAs. Dalí never put on a little girl's party frock, but his eccentric antics now seem the norm in our celebrity culture.

Most important of all, though, in our revaluation of Dalí, is the lens through which we see his paintings. We no longer live in a literary culture, and the human eye has been fine-tuned by a half-century of film and television. Dalí's paintings, with their distant horizon lines, pseudo-Renaissance perspectives and mentalised stage-sets, are naturals for the age of the plasma TV screen. Our attention spans have shrunk to a single film-frame, and when we look at a Dalí painting we can instantly construct the rest of the movie from the key frame that he offers us.

Film fascinated Dalí from his earliest days, and he collaborated with Luis Buñuel to produce two classics of surrealist cinema, *Un Chien Andalou* (1928) and *L'Âge d'Or* (1930). Both will be shown at the exhibition Dalí & Film, which opens at Tate Modern on Friday. Even today, after a deluge of horror and exploitation movies of the goriest kind, the films seem deeply shocking, though there is little in them that would alarm the censor.

Un Chien Andalou opens with the thuggishly handsome Buñuel standing on a darkened balcony, thoughtfully stropping a cut-throat razor. He steps inside and approaches a young woman waiting for him, as a sliver of cloud slices across the moon. Then, in one of the most famous shots in all cinema, the razor appears to slice across the woman's eye, releasing its vitreous fluid. In fact, a cow's eye was slashed, but Buñuel is reported to have felt sick for days after filming the sequence. How Dalí felt isn't known, though he probably thought up the sequence.

After that bracing start, there are a number of scenes involving an anguished young man who seems to be trying to make emotional contact with a turbulent young woman who repels his advances. There are no clues to behaviour. Ants pour from a hole in the young man's palm. Rebuffed, he puts on a curious harness and drags towards the young woman a huge contraption consisting of two priests lying on their backs, tied to a grand piano across which is draped a dead donkey.

What comes through this 15-minute film is the feeling that it would all make sense if its scenes were assembled in the right order. But of course it would not make sense, whatever the order, and I take this to be the point of the film. The reality we inhabit daily, our domestic interiors and their emotional dramas, the hands helplessly caressing a young woman's breasts, the tennis racket she uses to drive away her unwanted suitor (the surrealists were intensely middle class), the small section of space-time we blunder through, are all equally unreal, though meaning and sanity seem tantalisingly within our grasp.

L'Âge d'Or is a longer and more provocative film, guying the Catholic Church and sending up as many of our cherished notions as its director and scriptwriter can turn their attention to. A blind man is abused, a son is casually shot by his father, an old woman is slapped, the heroine sucks rapturously on the toe of a marble Apollo. Christ is played by the hero of Sade's *120 Days of Sodom*, and the film ends with a crucifix on which several scalps are nailed. I prefer *Un Chien Andalou*, but in *L'Âge d'Or* there is the same sense that everyday reality is only a hand's breadth away, but will never be reached.

In short, rather like life today. Welcome to the surrealist world, which you never knew you inhabited.

THE LARVAL STAGE OF A NEW KIND OF ARCHITECTURE

Guardian (2007)

The Guggenheim Museum in Bilbao is the world's largest toy. Set among the drab streets of this rather depressing Spanish port, it throws up a fountain of light and good cheer that promises all the fun of a travelling circus—erecting its tent beside a disused railway yard in a run-down industrial city. In its own, self-defining way it is a masterpiece, and the fact that it is an art gallery is almost wholly irrelevant. The one thing that someone visiting the Bilbao Guggenheim can forget about is any thought of actually entering the building. Stay outside it, at a distance of about one hundred yards, and you will absorb all its audacity, magic, good humour and genius. And its infantilising charm. This is Disneyland for the media studies PhD.

Walking from the centre of Bilbao, take the Calle Iparraguirre, and it will lead you straight to the entrance of the Guggenheim, guarded by Jeff Koons' flower-bedecked *Puppy*, another toy that points to the real role of Frank Gehry's extraordinary structure. Even at a distance, beyond the cafe tables and traffic and overhead wires, the visual spectacle stops everything else going on in your mind. Cascades of golden light overpower the sun, rising from a jumble of massive titanium forms piled on top of each other, part train crash and part explosion in a bullion vault. If the atomic bomb inside Fort Knox had exploded in James Bond's face at the end of Goldfinger, the result would have been very much like the Bilbao Guggenheim.

Standing in the welcome shade of Koons' *Puppy*, and shielding your eyes from the glare, you first try to make sense of all this glowing geometry in traditional architectural terms. But it's obvious from the start that there are no deferential nods to Egyptian, classical, modernist or post-modernist modes, no reassuring "quotes" like the over-cute pilasters that adorn the extension to London's National Gallery by Robert Venturi and Denise Scott Brown. Gehry's Guggenheim is completely new, shrugs off the past and exists solely in a kind of imaginary future. In some ways the building is the larval stage of a new kind of architecture that will emerge from its chrysalis and finally take wing a hundred years from now.

The museum is built on sloping ground that runs down to the river Nervión, a vile-looking creek that must be the most gloomy stretch of water after the Styx. Gehry's heart will have sunk when he first saw the site beside this grim stream and the nearby railway yard. Rarely among museums, the Bilbao Guggenheim is entered by a descending flight of steps, and by the time they have circled the 19 galleries, most visitors—who, when I was there, had to queue for an hour—are too exhausted to do anything but flake out in the pleasant cafe beside the entrance. Surrounded by glass panels and comfortable limestone walls, they are missing the best view of the museum, which is from the far side of the river, a Styx with a matchless prospect and the promise of a return trip.

From Koons' *Puppy*, turn left, and follow the road as it curves around the museum to the bridge. Stop when you have crossed the Nervión, and you will see the Bilbao Guggenheim in all its gilded magnificence, its immense and slightly baggy volumes reflected in the river and the ornamental pools of the plaza that separates the museum from the water's edge. Within a few minutes the confusing and apparently random shapes that form the structure may begin to make sense, as your eye learns a new kind of language. Bilbao is a great sea-port: is its new museum a ship in disguise, a spectral memory of the great caravels that carried gold back from the New World to enrich Spain half a millennium ago?

Now, of course, the Americas have sent a gold-hunter of their own, the privateering brand Guggenheim, diversifying into multiples and merchandising, and the booty will be going back across the Atlantic. The Bilbao Guggenheim is a treaty port negotiated with the burghers of this rather down-at-heel city, part bullion vault and part glimmering mirage to cow and dazzle the natives.

Gazing across the river at this metallisation of a dream, one has to take one's hat off to Gehry and the civic leaders of Bilbao. I'm impressed by Tate Modern and its vast Turbine Hall, with its echoes of Albert Speer and the Zeppelin field rallies, and its immense popularity proves that it satisfies a need that should have been met by the disastrous Millennium Dome, a wish for an uplifting social space more enduring than the local Tesco or Ikea.

At the same time, it would have been a powerful tonic for post-2000 London if something as original and disorienting as the Bilbao Guggenheim occupied the site of the old power station. But would we have had the nerve to gamble on Gehry's visionary dream? Could we justify to our rather conventional and timid selves a work of architecture so original and so cut off from our beloved past of pitched roofs and Tudor beams? Are we ever really happy with an architecture that unsettles and provokes?

More to the point, I wonder if the Bilbao Guggenheim is a work of architecture at all? Perhaps it belongs to the category of exhibition and fairground displays, of giant inflatables and bouncy castles. The Guggenheim may be the first permanent temporary structure. Its interior is a huge disappointment, and confirms the suspicion that the museum is a glorified sales aid for the Guggenheim brand. There is a giant atrium, always a sign that some corporation's hand is sliding towards your wallet, but the galleries are conventionally proportioned, and one can't help feeling that they are irrelevant anyway. The museum is its own work of art, and the only one really on display. One can't imagine the *Mona Lisa*, the *Venus de Milo* or Picasso's *Guernica* ever being shown here. There would be war in heaven. Apart from anything else, these works have a dimension of seriousness that the Guggenheim lacks. Koons' *Puppy*, faithfully guarding the entrance to the enchanted castle, gives the game away. Architecture today is a visitor attraction, deliberately playing on our love of the brightest lights and the gaudiest neon. The Bilbao Guggenheim's spiritual Acropolis is Las Vegas, with its infantilising pirate ships and Egyptian sphinxes. Gehry's museum would be completely at home there, for a year at least, and then look a little dusty and jaded, soon to be torn down and replaced by another engaging marvel with which our imaginations can play.

Novelty architecture dominates throughout the world, pitched like the movies at the bored teenager inside all of us. Universities need to look like airports, with an up-and-away holiday ethos. Office buildings disguise themselves as hi-tech apartment houses, everything has the chunky look of a child's building blocks, stirring dreams of the nursery.

But perhaps Gehry's Guggenheim transcends all this. From the far side of the Styx I'll look back on it with awe.

5

LISTS, CAPTIONS, AND GLOSSARIES

This section compiles a selection of list-like forms, encompassing also glosses and captions.

The "Collector's Choice" column ran monthly from the September 1982 issue of *American Film* under the editorship of Peter Biskind. Ballard's selection of SF films was its final iteration in Biskind's last issue, and was preceded in September 1987 by Clive Barker's selection of horror movies. Steven Spielberg's adaptation of *Empire of the Sun* (1987) would arrive in cinemas two months later, in December.

"Project for a Glossary of the Twentieth Century" was an original commission. Zone Books, an independent publisher of theoretically focused writing on the arts and humanities, published a series of six journals from 1985. *Incorporations* (1992), edited by the art critic Jonathan Crary and architectural theorist Sanford Kwinter, was its sixth issue, exploring "the ongoing convergence of what were once the distinct worlds of the machine and the organism." Alongside Ballard's "Glossary" it included pieces by noted cultural theorists Eve Kosofsky Sedgwick, Paul Virilio, and Donna Haraway.

"Impressions of Speed" in *Speed: Visions of an Accelerated Age* (1998) took the form of captions responding to images selected from the Science Museum archives by Jeremy Millar, who had commissioned Ballard's "Airports" essay the previous year. *Speed* was published in partnership between the Photographer's Gallery and the Whitechapel Art Gallery to accompany an exhibition at the latter, which ran in London from September to November 1998. "Impressions of Speed" was unique to the book, and neither text nor images were exhibited in the show it was produced to coincide with.

In contrast to artist- and critic-led publications, *The Test of Time* (1999) was published by the British bookshop chain Waterstones as part of a campaign to market "classic" novels. Editors Andrew Holgate and Honor Wilson-Fletcher asked forty-seven respondents to consider the idea of the "classic" book, to select ten books they considered classics and to choose ten that should never have been classics. Four of Ballard's fellow contributors—John Sutherland, Christopher Priest, Boyd Tonkin, and Alan Warner—selected books by Ballard as classics: *Crash* (1973), *The Voices of Time and Other Stories* (1962), *Empire of the Sun* (1984), and *The Atrocity Exhibition* (1970), respectively. This placed Ballard on par with James Joyce and D. H. Lawrence, with only Charles Dickens and Graham Greene earning five inclusions.

COLLECTOR'S CHOICE: OUTER LIMITS

American Film (1987)

When it turns to science fiction, cinema closes its eyes and moves into a rich and uneasy sleep. The collective dreams and nightmares of the twentieth century have found their most vivid expression in this often disparaged but ever popular genre. A few great directors, from Fritz Lang to Steven Spielberg, have worked in science fiction, but until the sixties most s-f films were little more than B-movies. With limited special effects, minor actors and minuscule budgets, and usually ignored by the critics, the only things that these films had going for them were powerful stories, unrestrained imagination and, first and foremost, a hot line to the unconscious. In these, often modest films, as almost nowhere else in the popular arts of our age, classical myth and scientific apocalypse collide and fuse.

Like most of my fellow s-f writers, American and British, I nurse ambivalent feelings towards the science-fiction movies. Despite our heroic efforts, it is not the printed word but the film that has defined the images of science fiction in the public mind and also, incidentally, exerted a huge influence on architecture, fashion and consumer design. Even now, the future is anything with a fin on it.

Far from being a medium of escapist entertainment, the science-fiction film has always been a sensitive barometer of the cultural and political climate of the day. Our deepest fears of an irrational superscience stalked its blue corridors long before latter-day environmentalists became concerned for our planet's future. In the fifties, Cold War paranoia and the terrors of nuclear Armageddon prompted a cluster of remarkable science-fiction movies, among them *Invasion of the Body Snatchers*, *Them!*, *The Day the Earth Stood Still*, and *The Incredible Shrinking Man*, which were handicapped by their meagre—by present-day standards—special effects. Unlike the novelist, the film director cannot leave his locations to the reader's imagination.

In the sixties, however, the special effects at last began to match the inspiration of the filmmakers. Indeed, within a decade the technology of film design became sufficiently advanced (as in *Star Wars*) to show an advanced technology in decline.

At its worst, the science-fiction film offers the sheer exhilaration of the roller coaster. At its best, and to its credit, it tries to deal with the largest issues facing us today, and attempts, however naively, to place some sort of philosophical frame around man's place in the universe.

FORBIDDEN PLANET (1956)

This remarkably stylish colour film is a quantum leap forward in visual confidence and in the richness of its theme—an update of Shakespeare's *The Tempest*. Walter Pidgeon plays the Prospero figure, Dr Morbius, a brilliant but flawed scientist living alone with his daughter on an isolated planet. Robby the Robot is the ever obliging Ariel, and the crew members of a visiting spaceship are the stranded mariners.

The film's real originality, however, lies in making the brutish Caliban figure an externalization of Morbius's own libido. This gives an unsettling force to the final confrontation, as Morbius's lustful id, never seen directly, throbs and oozes along in full Oedipal splendour, melting down steel doors on its way towards a quivering Anne Francis. The special effects were unequalled until *2001: A Space Odyssey*.

DR STRANGELOVE OR: HOW I LEARNED TO STOP WORRYING AND LOVE THE BOMB (1964)

Nearly twenty-five years after its release, Stanley Kubrick's black satire has lost none of its impact. In this story of an insane US Air Force general who launches an all-out nuclear attack on the Soviet Union, Kubrick cunningly mixes documentary realism with the ultimate in graveyard humour—the death of mankind treated as scarcely more than the last sick joke.

Kubrick's masterstroke is to tilt the dramatic action of the film so that the audience's sympathies slide across the value scale and eventually lie with the targets being satirized. We come to admire the magnificent B-52s with their sleek A-bombs and brave if baffled crews; we despise the wimpish president for trying to do a deal with the Kremlin, and we almost welcome the nuclear Armageddon when it comes. By enlisting us on the side of our darkest fears, Kubrick exposes all the sinister glamour and unconscious logic of technological death.

ALPHAVILLE (1965)

This moody and powerful allegory is Jean-Luc Godard's most accessible film, made for that consumerist and politically conscious sixties audience that he dubbed "the children of Marx and Coca-Cola." *Alphaville* blends utopian satire, pop art and comic-book imagery to create the alienated landscape of the distant planet Alphaville, whose cowed population is tyrannized by an evil computer. However, *Alphaville* is in every way indistinguishable from contemporary Paris. The "spaceship" of secret agent Lemmy Caution is his Ford Galaxy, and similar linguistic plays link the action together in a far more convincing way than might seem possible.

For the first time in the science-fiction film, Godard makes the point that in the media landscape of the present day the fantasies of science-fiction are as "real" as an office block, an airport or a presidential campaign. His original title was *Tarzan versus IBM*, but the film transcends its pop imagery to create a disturbing world that resembles a chromium-plated 1984. Sadly, after *Alphaville* Godard abandoned the genre.

BARBARELLA (1968)

Sex, which many enthusiasts thought they had invented in the sixties, here makes its appearance in the science-fiction film. The relationship between sex and science fiction or, more to the point, its virtual absence from the genre, has always been a puzzle—explained, I would guess, by the fact that science-fiction writers constitute an authentic community of naifs, generally nervous of change, politically ultraconservative, eager not to think about what adults do after dark.

At any rate, it is inconceivable that the masters of classic science fiction could have come up with this rich and saucy confection, in which the interplanetary sex adventures of the French comic-strip heroine are elegantly transferred to the screen. Roger Vadim, who in *And God Created Woman* created Brigitte Bardot, here turns his affectionate and ironic eye on another of his wives, Jane Fonda, who achieves immortality as she cavorts naked in a fur-lined spaceship.

SILENT RUNNING (1971)

Douglas Trumbull, who supervised the special effects in *2001*, directed this moving ecological fable, and there are strong echoes of Kubrick's epic in the scenes of giant starships sailing along the tideways of space. The premise—that one day in the future all the vegetation on Earth has died, and that the last remaining trees are stored in vast, orbiting space vehicles—may take some swallowing, but the theme is so well handled that the film taps into all our unease about the abuse of this planet and its environment.

Much of *Silent Running*'s success is due to Bruce Dern's superb performance as a watchman and gardener in one of the forgotten greenhouses. His dogged, cantankerous manner exactly suits the character of this last conservationist alive, who refuses orders to dump the vegetation, kills the crew, and sets off into deep space with only the trees for company.

DARK STAR (1974)

Dark Star is the *Catch-22* of outer space. The anarchic spirit of Joseph Heller's novel, with its inverted logic and padded-cell humour, presides over John Carpenter's extraordinary low-budget feature. Reportedly made for $60,000, *Dark Star* was originally filmed in 16mm by a group of students at the University of Southern California, and later transferred to 35mm. Watching this brilliant extravaganza, one is forced yet again to accept that talent alone is always enough.

Like many ostensible satires—in this case, of the science-fiction movie itself—*Dark Star* soon transcends its own subject matter. The sealed world of the spaceship, with its exhausted, near psychotic crew, its "dead" captain in his cryogenic capsule periodically revived to be asked for advice, and its intelligent bombs that have to be argued out of detonating prematurely, soon begins to resemble that other spaceship called Earth.

THE MAN WHO FELL TO EARTH (1976)

A brave failure, Nicolas Roeg's excursion into science fiction reveals the excitements, and hazards, of illustrating a conventional genre theme—the visiting alien destroyed by an uncaring Earth—with images taken largely from outside that genre. Here the alien is played by rock star David Bowie, whose strange, hypersensitive presence instantly convinces us that he has come from another planet. His growing estrangement is seen not as a reaction to the brute incomprehension of others, but in terms of his own seduction by our television and communications landscape, with its unlimited tolerance of deviant behaviour.

Above all, the Bowie figure is seduced by the fragmentation and sheer ironic style of life on Earth, perfectly exemplified by Roeg's film technique—a mix of elegant photography and fashionable dislocations. But with his alien dismantled and demoralized, Roeg has nowhere to go, since he cannot rely on the genre's conventions to rescue his film. And without the genre's conventions the behaviour of his hero becomes merely modishly psychotic.

CLOSE ENCOUNTERS OF THE THIRD KIND (1977)

Spielberg's mastery of the science-fiction medium was already evident in *Duel*, his 1971 classic of highway paranoia. From autogeddon he moved on to two major themes of science fiction, monsters (*Jaws*) and interplanetary travel (*Close Encounters* and *ET the Extra-Terrestrial*). That these have become three of the most successful films in the history of the cinema underlines my long-held belief that science fiction defines the popular imagination of the twentieth century.

Close Encounters combines lavish special effects with the complex and poetic story of a power-company technician whose life is transformed by a series of UFO visitations. He becomes obsessed with a strangely shaped mountain in Wyoming, a model of which he constructs in his family living room. The film proceeds by a series of powerfully allusive images, which climax with the arrival of the alien spaceship, a visionary landing that resonates for years in the spectator's mind.

ALIEN (1979)

Alien is a tour de force of pure horror, a barrage of brutal eruptions (some literally so) that obscure the existence, behind the blood and terror, of an extremely elegant s-f film. Returning to Earth, the crew of the Nostromo is diverted to a remote planet and there unknowingly picks up the alien organism, which then proceeds to metamorphose its way through the cast until defeated by the courage and wiles of Sigourney Weaver, the s-f film's first feminist heroine.

While all this is going on one has barely a pause to notice a host of fine details: the claustrophobic world of the spaceship, with its fraying camaraderie; the entropy of long voyages, time slowing down so that a brief conversation seems to last all day; the stylish interior of the Nostromo, a cross between a computer terminal and a nightclub; the final appearance of the alien, an insane mesh of ravenous teeth straight from the paintings of Francis Bacon that materializes just after Weaver strips down to her underwear. Dinner, fortunately, is delayed, at least until the sequel.

MAD MAX 2 (1981)

This second, and by the far the best, of George Miller's *Mad Max* trio is a tribute to the power of the s-f film to break free of its conventions and renew itself in a creative burst of ideas and images. On one level the ultimate road movie, *Mad Max 2* is a compellingly reductive vision of post-industrial collapse. Here the end of the world is seen as a non-stop demolition derby, as gangs of motorized savages rove their desert wastes, bereft of speech, thought, hopes or dreams, dedicated only to the brutal realities of speed and violence.

Above all, *Mad Max 2* is an example of how sheer virtuosity can triumph in the film medium. A host of images wrench the retina—garish vehicles, fearful road armour and weird punk hairstyles, the sense of a world discarded after Judgement Day. In its raw power and vast scenic effects, *Mad Max 2* is punk's Sistine Chapel.

PROJECT FOR A GLOSSARY OF THE TWENTIETH CENTURY

Zone 6: Incorporations (1992)

X-ray

Does the body still exist at all, in any but the most mundane sense? Its role has been steadily diminished, so that it seems little more than a ghostly shadow seen on the X-ray plate of our moral disapproval. We are now entering a colonialist phase in our attitudes to the body, full of paternalistic notions that conceal a ruthless exploitation. This brutish creature must be housed, sparingly nourished, restricted to the minimum of sexual activity needed to reproduce itself and submitted to every manner of enlightened and improving patronage. Will the body at last rebel, tip all those vitamins, douches and aerobic schedules into Boston harbour and throw off the colonialist oppressor?

Typewriter
It types us, encoding its own linear bias across the free space of the imagination.

Zipper
This small but astute machine has found an elegant way of restraining and rediscovering all the lost enchantments of the flesh.

Jazz
Music's jettisoned short-term memory, and no less poignant for that.

Telephone
A shrine to the desperate hope that one day the world will listen to us.

Chaplin
Chaplin's great achievement was to discredit the body, and to ridicule every notion of the dignity of gesture. Ponderous men move around him like lead-booted divers trying to anchor the central nervous system to the seabed of time and space.

Trench warfare
The body as sewer, the gutter of its own abattoir, flushing away its fears and aggressions.

The pill
Nature's one step back in order to take two steps forward, presumably into the more potent evolutionary possibilities of wholly conceptualized sex.

Aerodynamism
Streamlining satisfies the dream of flight without the effort of growing wings. Aerodynamics is the modern sculpture of non-Euclidean space-time

Pornography

The body's chaste and unerotic dream of itself.

Time and motion studies

I am both myself and the shape that the universe makes around me. Time and motion studies represent our attempt to occupy the smallest, most modest niche in the surrounding universe.

Prosthetics

The castration complex raised to the level of an art form.

Biochemical warfare

Nerve gases—the patient and long-awaited revenge of the inorganic world against the organic.

Hallucinogenic drugs

The kaleidoscope's view of the eye.

The Warren Commission Report

The novelization of the Zapruder film.

Genocide

The economics of mass production applied to self-disgust.

Phenomenology

The central nervous system's brave gamble that it exists.

Crowd theory

Claustrophobia masquerading as agoraphobia or even, conceivably, Malthusianism.

Lysenkoism

A forlorn attempt not merely to colonize the botanical kingdom, but to instil a proper sense of the puritan work ethic and the merits of self-improvement.

Robotics

The moral degradation of the machine.

Suburbs

Do suburbs represent the city's convalescent zone or a genuine step forward into a new psychological realm, at once more passive but of far greater imaginative potential, like that of a sleeper before the onset of REM sleep? Unlike its unruly city counterpart, the suburban body has been wholly domesticated, and one can say that the suburbs constitute a huge petting zoo, with the residents' bodies providing the stock of furry mammals.

Forensics

On the autopsy table science and pornography meet and fuse.

Miniaturization

Dreams of becoming very small predate Alice, but now the probability grows that all the machines in the world, like the gold in Fort Knox, might be held in one heavily guarded location, protected as much from themselves as from the rest of us. Computers will continue to miniaturize themselves, though, eventually disappearing into a micro-verse where their ever-vaster calculations and mathematical models will become one with the quarks and the charms.

The Vietnam War

Two wholly incompatible martial systems collided, with desperate result. Could the Vietcong, given a little more TV savvy, have triumphed sooner by launching an all-women guerrilla army against the Playboy-reading GIs? "First Air Cavalry ground elements in Operation Pegasus killed 350 enemy women in scattered contacts yesterday, while Second Division Marines killed 124 women communists."

Isadora Duncan

The machine had its own fling with her overdisciplined body, the rear wheel of her car dancing its lethal little jig around the end of her scarf.

Furniture and industrial design

Our furniture constitutes an external constellation of our skin areas and body postures. It's curious that the least imaginative of all forms of furniture has been the bed.

Schizophrenia

To the sane, always the most glamorous of mental diseases, since it seems to represent the insane's idea of the normal. Just as the agnostic world keeps alive its religious festivals in order to satisfy the vacation needs of its workforce, so when medical science has conquered all disease certain mental afflictions, schizophrenia chief among them, will be mimicked for social reasons. By the same token, the great appeal of alcoholism, and the reason why it will never be eliminated, is that it provides an opportunity for honourable and even heroic failure.

Body-building

Asexual masturbation, in which the entire musculature simulates a piece of erectile tissue. But orgasm seems indefinitely delayed.

Epidemiology

Catastrophe theory in slow motion.

Fashion

A recognition that nature has endowed us with one skin too few, and that a fully sentient being should wear its nervous system externally.

Automobile

All the millions of cars on this planet are stationary, and their apparent motion constitutes mankind's greatest collective dream.

Skyscraper

The eight-hour city, with a tidal population clinging to the foreshore between Earth and the yet to be navigated oceans of space.

Pasolini

Sociopath as saint.

Transistor

If the wheel is 1 on the binary scale, the transistor is 0—but what will be 1000001?

Retroviruses

Pathogens that might have been invented by science fiction. The greater the advances of modern medicine, the more urgent our need for diseases we cannot understand.

Money

The original digital clock.

Abortion

Do-it-yourself genocide.

Science fiction

The body's dream of becoming a machine.

Answering machines

They are patiently training us to think in a language they have yet to invent.

Genetics
Nature's linguistic system.

Food
Our delight in food is rooted in our immense relish at the thought that, prospectively, we are eating ourselves.

Neurobiology
Science's Sistine Chapel.

Criminal science
The anatomizing of illicit desire, more exciting than desire itself.

Camouflage
The camouflaged battleship or bunker must never efface itself completely, but confuse our recognition systems by one moment being itself, and the next not itself. Many impersonators and politicians exploit the same principle.

Cybernetics
The totalitarian systems of the future will be docile and subservient, like super-efficient servants, and all the more threatening for that.

Disease control
A proliferation of imaginary diseases may soon be expected, satisfying our need for a corrupt version of ourselves.

Ergonomics
The Protestant work ethic disguised as a kinaesthetic language.

Personal computers
Perhaps unwisely, the brain is subcontracting many of its core functions, creating a series of branch economies that may one day amalgamate and mount a management buy-out.

War
The possibility at last exists that war may be defeated on the linguistic plane. If war is an extreme metaphor, we may defeat it by devising metaphors that are even more extreme.

International Standard Time
Is time an obsolete mental structure we have inherited from our distant forebears, who invented serial time as a means of dismantling a

simultaneity they were unable to grasp as a single whole? Time should be decartelized, and everyone should set his or her own.

Satellites
Ganglions in search of an interplanetary brain.

Modernism
The Gothic of the information age.

Apollo mission
The first demonstration, arranged for our benefit by the machine, of the dispensability of man.

IMPRESSIONS OF SPEED

SPEED: VISIONS OF AN ACCELERATED AGE (1998)

Pulsars' first Digital Watch 1972
Clocks and watches are now far more accurate than we need them to be in our daily lives. Many quartz watches keep virtually perfect time, and minute inaccuracies are probably the fault of the solar system. Perhaps this need to be in possession of the exact time reflects some fault in our perception of the world, and a defect in our grasp of space-time. Obsessive attention to microscopic detail is usually a symptom of underlying neurosis. Confident people carry neither money nor watches, and expect the world to keep time with them.

Bleriot aircraft 25 July 1909
These self-propelled box kites seem almost as bizarre to us today as they must have seemed to the two spectators in 1909. But the sky had changed forever and become the purest medium of speed. Bleriot's cross-channel flight paved the way for the German bomber attacks on Britain little more than thirty years later. For too many people in the twentieth century the sky was the place from which death came. Now, thankfully, it carries tourists towards the sun.

German Autobahn 1936
World War II accelerated everything—the speed of warfare, the growth of aviation and weapons technology, shifts in mass psychology and the emancipation of women, and the evolution of the road. Built in

the 1930s, Hitler's autobahns were both high-speed panzer arteries and ancient runic megaliths laid down like stone dreams that pointed towards the east.

John F. Kennedy speaking to Prime Minister of Nigeria by means of communication satellite "Syncom" 26 August 1963

Kennedy was speed reconfigured in terms of style. The quick wit, the slim-shouldered English suits, the streamlined hair-do and cortisone-smooth face, the decision-making perceived as an aspect of gesture politics, the instant rapport with an audience eager to be enraptured, together formed the model for government in the space age he launched.

Telstar Satellite 1962

Invisible technologies rule our lives, transmitting their data-loads at the speed of an electron. Vast cash balances move around the world's banking systems, bounced off satellites we never see, but whose electromagnetic footprints bestride continents and form our real weather. In the near future aesthetic and cultural shifts in the planetary consciousness will move around the globe with the force and pace of tsunamis, replacing the slow, ancestral drift of politics and religion in the years before the information age.

Brain Wave Machine, London Hospital April 1950

Brain waves move slowly, as the potassium pumps at millions of synapses throw their cumbersome electromagnetic switches. Decisions move through the cortex like population shifts across a continent, and reach our consciousness half a second after the brain has come to its own conclusions. The neurosciences seem to suggest that free will, like consciousness itself, is a virtual artefact created by the interplay of neural networks, as vivid but as illusory as the image of ourselves in the mirror.

Queen Elizabeth II as seen on TV December 1967

Television promised to bring us a high-speed monarchy, fit for the age of the sound-bite and the peak-hour commercial. But the institution has proved to have all the inertia and flexibility of Stonehenge. One co-opted royal, the most glamorous international figure since Kennedy, died in the attempt to transform her wish-list of emotions into a quasi-religious career.

LA Freeway Interchange

The beauty of these vast motion sculptures, and their intimate involvement with our daily lives and dreams, may be one reason why the visual arts have faltered in the second half of the twentieth century. No painter or sculptor could hope to match the heroic significance of freeway interchanges. In many ways they also threaten the novel, their linear codes inscribing a graphic narrative across the landscapes of our lives that no fiction could rival.

"Colossus" Computer, Bletchly Park, England 1943

Have computers already evolved themselves into a Darwinian cul-de-sac? Enthusiastically carrying out what they do best and we do worst—high-speed mathematical computation—they may have overshot the mark and will soon find that they are little more than indentured clerks, endlessly adding up figures in their electronic ledgers. Thirty years from now they will probably regroup, slow themselves down and mount a more subtle take-over bid. The totalitarian systems of the future will be subservient and ingratiating.

First BBC TV transmissions 1929

Television is the perfect medium for the age of paranoia. We can venture into its simulation of the world without ever being seen, and a switch will turn down those strange voices inside our heads. TV domesticates reality, filters out its harder tones and shows us only what the less ambitious of us want to see and hear. It has done far more to make a fairer society than Marx or American consumerism.

Female Motorist 1915

The motor-car transformed the twentieth century, constraining the aggression of men within a highly controlled and elaborately signalled landscape. The highway system is now a huge reticular prison, granting the illusion of speed, direction and self-chosen destiny to millions of men confined within their mobile cells. But for women the car was an immense force for liberation, freeing them from the home and sending them out to enjoy the unique social pleasures of the traffic jam and the hypermarket car-park.

Bullet Train

The high-speed train is a vehicle that satisfies a special kind of techno-logical nostalgia, along with computer-equipped yachts and man-powered aircraft. All three employ the most up-to-date materials research, advanced alloys and computerised designs, and apply them to antiquated and inefficient modes of transport. The rail-train, like the wind-powered yacht and pedal-driven glider, should have been abandoned years ago, when advances in technology made possible their evolution into the helicopter, the speed-boat and the supersonic airliner. In technological terms they represent an artificially perpetu-ated childhood.

Cockcroft and Walton Atomic Accelerator 1932

Particle physics has unlocked the secrets of the sun, but the mystery of existence still endures. Colossal intellectual leaps have taken us back to within micro-seconds of the big bang, but a conceptual barrier deep inside our brains may be one door we will never open, at least until homo sapiens makes a significant evolutionary jump, and the proc-essing capacity of our brains allows us to escape from the constraints of space-time.

Mobile Phone

The mobile phone can be seen as a fashion accessory and adult toy as well as a break-through in instant communication, though its use in restaurants, shops and public spaces can be irritating to others. This suggests that its real function is to separate its users from the surround-ing world and isolate them within the protective cocoon of an inti-mate electronic space. At the same time phone users can discreetly theatricalise themselves, using a body language that is an anthology of presentation techniques and offers to others a tantalising glimpse of their private and intimate lives.

Modem 1980s

The modem may become our most important interface with external real-ity. Human intercourse, like the exchange of social signals in the street and office, and even the elaborate cues between mother and baby may one day seem of minor importance when compared with the infinite riches of the virtual reality universes that the modem will bring to us.

Facsimile Newspaper 1950s

The fax machine and the e-mail seem to threaten the old-fashioned
printed word, at a time when a reader who owns no books has access
to an entire university's database, and when a diligent browser will
hunt out from the world's newspapers and magazines those topics that
most keenly interest us. But books and newspapers survive and even
prosper, suggesting that we need the fortuitous and contingent, and
that our imaginations have evolved to scan the silent margins of our
lives for any intriguing visitors or possible prey.

Alan Turing 1951

Turing was the first martyr of the computer age, a brilliant visionary and
pioneer who was also a persecuted homosexual. He killed himself,
apparently from despair. Turing gave his name to a test that he devised,
which distinguishes between human and non-human responses
to computerised queries. But the distinction is becoming more and
more blurred. Many hospital patients prefer computer interrogators to
human staff when giving their intimate medical histories, and we feel
surprisingly at ease with the synthetic voices used in talking elevators
and phone company consumer services, as if alienation is a secretly
desired state.

WHAT MAKES A CLASSIC?

THE TEST OF TIME (1999)

What is your definition of a classic?

We all agree about the classic novels of the past—*Robinson Crusoe, Pride
and Prejudice, Great Expectations, Ulysses*—but it's surprisingly difficult
to predict which contemporary novels, if any, will be the classics of the
future. It ought to be easy—look for the qualities that identify the classic novel, such as a strong story and intriguing characters, a fresh and
imaginative use of language, an element of vision, and a way of seeing
the world that belongs uniquely to the author.

Yet too many novelists, some of them Nobel Prize-winners, who were
once considered "great" have now sunk into oblivion or are well on their
way towards it—J. B. Priestley, Pearl Buck, A. J. Cronin, John O'Hara and
scores of others who enjoyed large sales and respectful reviews.

It's clear that the novelists of our own day who go on to become the classics of the future will do so for reasons that aren't obvious at all. And they will face competition from a range of new media, like the Internet and the interactive CD-Rom, that will pose the sort of head-on challenge that film once faced from television.

But film survived, and I am confident that the novel will survive, in its familiar page-turning, non-interactive form. Part of the reason is the uniquely private nature of the relationship between writer and reader. No one else is involved, there are no story conferences, temperamental actors who fluff their lines, or pressure from the producer to cut back on expensive sets or too many close-ups.

What are your ten essential classic novels for the next 100 years?

I assume that most of the eighteenth- and nineteenth-century classics will still be read in a hundred years' time. If they can survive the twentieth century, with all its change and turmoil, they can survive anything. But which novels written in my own lifetime (I was born in 1930) will survive to the year 2099? Here are my guesses:

Brave New World by Aldous Huxley. This vision of the future seems uncannily accurate—test-tube babies, legalised drugs, virtual reality films, a life of compulsory pleasure. The best guide-book I know to the day after tomorrow.

Animal Farm and *Nineteen Eighty-Four* by George Orwell. Some people have started to dismiss *Nineteen Eighty-Four*, as if the threat of Stalinist totalitarianism has passed forever. If only that were true.

Catch-22 by Joseph Heller. War seen as a lunatic playground, a picture of the mid-twentieth century that will fascinate our descendants.

The Alexandria Quartet by Lawrence Durrell. Its lush romanticism will show how touchingly sentimental we could be.[1]

The Loved One by Evelyn Waugh. A brilliantly mischievous glimpse of the other side of the Hollywood dream.

---

1. In his "Introduction," John Sutherland remarked that Ballard's inclusion of Lawrence Durrell "sets the brain whirring." *The Test of Time: What Makes a Classic a Classic?*, ed. Andrew Holgate and Honor Wilson-Fletcher (London: Waterstone's Booksellers in association with the Arts Council of England, 1999), xvii.

Lolita by Vladimir Nabokov. Wit and verbal elegance make even the darkest fantasies acceptable, or so we like to think.

The Naked Lunch by William Burroughs. A roller-coaster ride through hell that is the Don Quixote of the drug world.

The Big Sleep by Raymond Chandler. The purest distillation of Hollywood noir, the dark shadow cast by the Californian sun.

The Martian Chronicles by Ray Bradbury. Visionary short stories from the poet of modern science fiction.

What are the books you believe should never have been called classics?

Few contemporary novels today are called classics, but some seem to have been over-praised in a way that suggests our deep need to assign greatness to a favoured few of those around us, if only to affirm our belief in ourselves.

But will the novels of Thomas Pynchon, Philip Roth and Norman Mailer survive? Will anyone fifty years from now want to read Angus Wilson or Kingsley Amis? The three American novelists seem overblown and self-immersed, while the British are deeply parochial, writing about matters of no interest to anyone outside our islands. All these writers are more famous than their books, a sure sign of the second-rate. But perhaps our descendants will relish Mickey Spillane and Jeffrey Archer, for reasons that none of us are now astute enough to grasp. Fiction, fortunately, thrives on uncertainty.

6

REVIEWS

BOOKS

The largest part of Ballard's nonfiction consists of book reviews. Between his written contributions to the journal *Chemistry & Industry*, and his final book review, for the *New Statesman* in 2005, he published one hundred eighty reviews covering over two hundred books. His reviews appeared in the SF fanzine *Cypher*, the upmarket lifestyle magazine *Tatler*, and in the United States in the *Washington Post* and the *New York Times*, but were most frequently commissioned for the English broadsheet newspaper review sections.

His career as a reviewer began with brief pieces in *Chemistry & Industry*, the most substantial of which is collected here. He rounded up new SF titles for the *Guardian* from April 1965 until December 1967, for the *Times* from March to June 1968, and undertook the same job for the *New Statesman* from June 1976 to April 1978. He joked to David Pringle in 1979: "When I took up reviewing for the *New Statesman* I was very reluctant to do it, so I said that . . . I would only criticize or find fault with a book if I'd read it. If I hadn't read it, I'd always give it a good review. It was only fair."[1]

By the late 1970s, he was invited to review a greater range of titles, and over the course of the 1980s he became an established voice in the review sections of major UK newspapers. By the 1990s, Ballard was commissioned broadly to review works of nonfiction on an evolved portfolio

---

1. David Pringle, "Interview," in *J. G. Ballard: A Primary and Secondary Bibliography* (Boston: G. K. Hall, 1984), 14.

of thematic interests: surrealism, futurology, Freud, celebrity, Hollywood and the film industry, Japan and China during World War II, aviation, science and technology, and contemporary art and architecture. His readers would rarely have to go more than a month without notice from Shepperton. In 1991, for example, he published nineteen reviews of books on subjects as diverse as Nancy Reagan, wine, Akira Kurosawa, and Stanley Spencer. Books by Martin and Kingsley Amis, Jung Chang, Norman Mailer, Francis Fukuyama, and Camille Paglia fell under his eye.

As a reviewer, Ballard was most robust in his early assessments of the field of SF, and fans of hatchet jobs will find the richest pickings here. He mellowed with age, sharing glimpses of the reviewer himself, witty, lively, and idiosyncratic. A recognizable style developed, often proceeding from an arresting question: "Was there a Gulf War?" "Is the main role of Hollywood to save Americans from the need to grow up?" or, in reference to the Marquis de Sade, "Do his warped genes, these demented dreams of sodomy and the lash, also thread themselves through our lives?"

The selection in this section aims to represent the range of Ballard's reading and to highlight reviews of notable works and authors. Those pieces that contain anecdotes of biographical interest have also been included wherever possible—the piece "A Personal View," including a lengthy tribute to Ted Carnell, is highlighted—but the fact remains that the thirty-eight pieces here, while they constitute the largest part of this volume, remain a small proportion of the critical Ballard.

THE SCIENCE OF DREAMS BY EDWIN DIAMOND

Chemistry & Industry (February 9, 1963)

The universal experience of dreams, and the conviction that they conceal part of man's essential image of himself, have made them a subject of unfading interest throughout history, to the most primitive societies and the most sophisticated. One of the oldest written documents in existence, a papyrus of the 12th Dynasty, is an Egyptian book of dream interpretations, and to Freud, in the present century, the dream was "the royal road to the unconscious." Within the last 20 years the orthodox Freudian view generally accepted in Europe and America has been amplified by work carried out by experimental psychologists in the United States. A popular account of this work is given in "The Science of Dreams."

The hypothesis that the rapid eye movements observed at intervals throughout sleep might indicate the occurrence of a dream was apparently confirmed by the ability of subjects roused during these periods to recount their dreams with remarkable clarity and detail; this occurred in the case of persons who claimed they had never previously dreamed. Subsequent work suggested that everyone has an average of five dreams per night, each lasting 20 minutes; that contrary to popular belief digestive or emotional upsets do not affect the length or intensity of dreams, but only the ease with which they are recalled; that the majority of dreams are unpleasant and grow more so with increasing age; that even intense professional and domestic anxieties play little part in the subject matter of dreams; and that the congenitally blind experience "tactile" dreams. A curious discovery was that the deliberate deprivation of normal dreaming produced tension and irritability, even during an otherwise adequate period of sleep, and that hallucinations and psychotic collapse eventually resulted.

Despite the ingenuity and patience of the experimenters, the nature of the mechanisms generating dreams remains as elusive as ever. If anything, these studies suggest that for all its beguiling mystery the dream is merely a low-level psychic activity of little significance, perhaps similar to certain types of childhood play, and that its content, although cast in dramatic form, is of less importance than the act itself. Only where marked aberrations occur is a careful analysis of individual dreams of value to the physician. Even here, as in the experiments described, the role of the observer remains profoundly equivocal.

In view of the vast number of dreams experienced during a single lifetime, the catalogue of dreams which have furnished any major scientific revelation remains remarkably meagre; Kekulé's vision of the benzene ring is among the few examples. Undeterred, however, the author offers his readers a simple conundrum (complete the series O, T, T, F, F, –, –) by which they can test the deductive powers of their own sleeping intelligences. No more than 15 minutes immediately before and after sleep should be devoted to the problem. Evidently some 80% of subjects tested dreamed of the problem, and a few even solved it during their dreams.

Those readers who fail to solve it may be interested to know that the Abundavita Corporation of America offers a $395 hypnopaedic "package" consisting of a gramophone, speaker and a 25-lesson course on such topics as "Money—What It Is and How to Have Plenty of It."

DOWN TO EARTH

Spectrum IV, edited by Kingsley Amis and Robert Conquest; *Telepathist* by John Brunner; *I Love Galesburg in the Springtime* by Jack Finney; *An Arthur C. Clarke Omnibus*

Guardian (April 9, 1965)

During the past few years it has become apparent that science fiction, long regarded as a self-contained melange of post-Wellsian fantasies about time and space, is dividing itself into two separate and opposed forms. On the one hand is the traditional science fiction of interplanetary travel and alien cultures, in its heyday thirty years ago an authentic popular image of the future, but now identified with a few declining magazines and a group of older American and British writers unable to add anything substantially new to their repertory of ideas.

Their failure, and that of the entire genre, in spite of the heroic efforts of intelligent apologists such as Kingsley Amis and Edmund Crispin, not to mention the millions of dollars' worth of free publicity given by the Russo-American space programmes, lies in its mistaken appeal to realism rather than to fantasy. Once it gets off the ground into space all science fiction is fantasy, and the more serious it tries to be, the more naturalistic, the greater its failure, since it completely lacks the moral authority and conviction of a literature won from experience.

On the other hand there has emerged a more speculative form of science fiction, one that is crossing the horizon of general fiction at an increasing number of points. Where the older science fiction has been most involved with outer space, this new offshoot is concerned with "inner space," the surrealists' "landscapes of the soul," and in creating images where the outer world of reality and the inner world of the psyche meet and fuse. Indeed, for these writers science serves much the same role as did psychoanalysis for the surrealists—a standpoint rather than a subject matter. Recognising that the whole of science fiction's imaginary universe has long since been absorbed into the general consciousness and that most of its ideas are valid only in a kind of marginal spoofing, as in William Burroughs's *The Ticket that Exploded*, they have set about trying to create a new set of conventions with which to explore their subject matter. As distinct from the teleological ends of science fiction in the past, with its explicit social and moral preoccupations, the new science fiction is devoted to ontological objectives—the understanding of time, landscape, and identity.

This distinction between outer and inner space is apparent in the latest Kingsley Amis and Robert Conquest collection *Spectrum IV*. As usual, the sharpness of the editorial eye produces many stories that convince by sheer expertise, but the best are those, such as the late C. M. Kornbluth's "The Marching Morons" and John Brunner's "Such Stuff," which are extrapolations of the immediate present, nightmares at noon earned from the abrasive dust of the pavements we all walk.

Fantasy, always marginal to science fiction, succeeds like humour by an alchemy of its own. The pointed and amiable stories in Jack Finney's *I Love Galesburg in the Springtime*, more difficult to do than might be imagined, are frolics in the stone garden of nostalgia and memory. "The Intrepid Aeronaut" is a brilliant, kindly tale of a suburban husband left on his own for a long weekend who suddenly decides to build a balloon and, with the help of a shy wide-eyed housewife near by, flies to and fro over the rooftops of San Francisco. A love story as discreet and buoyant as the gentle envelope that carries it.

Telepathy, one of the most hazardous subjects, succeeds in the skilled hands of John Brunner in *Telepathist*. The full implications of telepathy require nothing less than genius to do them justice, but in his tale of a deformed and neglected child who meets a deaf-mute he convinces us that some kind of extrasensory perception might be the only spark to cross the gap between them. Intelligently and humanely told, the novel succeeds more by the use of traditional literary devices than those of science fiction.

An Arthur C. Clarke Omnibus contains two novels, *Childhood's End* and *Prelude to Space*, and a short-story collection, *Expedition to Earth*. Reprinted after a ten-year lapse, they illustrate the failure of traditional science fiction. Wholly concerned with an outer space seen in terms of the crudest extrapolations, these stories are dated not only by their superficial scientific gimmickry, but by the trivial dialogue and characterisation. The difference between the old and new science fiction is the point where invention ends and imagination begins.

INTO THE DROP ZONE

Beyond Time by Michel Siffre

Guardian (July 23, 1965)

Speleology, like outer space and the hydrogen bomb, plays straight into the hands of the unconscious. In 1962 a 23-year-old Frenchman, Michel Siffre, spent 63 days alone in a tent set up on a subterranean glacier 375 feet down in the Alpes Maritimes, ostensibly in an attempt to test the physical and mental limits of human endurance in a changeless environment that might resemble those in underground shelters or space vehicles. Like Alain Bombard, who crossed the Atlantic alone and without provisions, Siffre demonstrated that it is almost impossible to exaggerate the degree of pain and privation that human beings will voluntarily accept providing their motives are strong enough.

Before Siffre's descent into the Scarrasson Cavern no one had tried to survive for a protracted period in such a hostile environment: a temperature constantly at or below freezing, 100 per cent humidity, almost total darkness, continuous rock-falls and, perhaps worst of all, the absence of any reference points in time and space. The 30-day isolation tests carried out by General Electric at its Space Technology Centre in 1963 have revealed the extreme mental disorientation that can occur, but Siffre was faced as well with the prospect of serious pulmonary and cardiac disorders. Reputable authorities in France from whom he tried to obtain backing pronounced his ideas insane. None of them seems to have realised that this was the precise point of the undertaking.

Siffre's credentials are impressive. His background confirms the image of a man beyond not only time, but space. As a small child he was fascinated by geology, that massif of fossil time, and at the age of 10 he discovered marine fossils in a cave while wandering in the hills above Nice. He wrote his first scientific papers when only 13, and had explored over 150 caves by the time he descended the Scarrasson Cavern in an attempt, as he states, to discover the original life rhythm of man.

"I felt I was on another planet: for the most part I dwelt neither in the past nor in the future, but in the hostile present."

After a few days his condition of torpor, overlaid by a profound sense of anxiety and depression, became that of semi-hibernation, in which his physiological functions became his time references. Like all who have been hungry for sustained periods, he found himself fretting over trifles, and after a few grandiose reflections his diary becomes a catalogue of stomach cramps and attempts to mop up the condensing moisture in the tent.

Music had little appeal for him, and soon lost its meaning, possibly because of his accelerated time sense. Even more sadly, he thought rarely of his two girlfriends, who seem to have been pillars of support, like the men in the camp above who passed the two months making mobiles and pieces of sculpture (their diary should be published next). Although in darkness, he developed a pronounced squint, as if he were focusing on the inner perspectives within his mind. He is convinced that the feelings he developed towards his miserable tent, about which everything was wrong, were those of love. When he emerged he understood why hell is always underground.

THE SEE-THROUGH BRAIN

We by Yevgeny Zamyatin

Guardian (February 12, 1970)

Zamyatin was lucky. Few indictments of the entire prospectus of a new society could have seemed so damning and so offensive as this bitter anti-utopian fantasy, written by a prominent Russian writer only three years after the Revolution in 1917. By comparison, the "crimes" of Daniel and Sinyavsky seem notional. Yet, although denounced and vilified by influential members of the party, Zamyatin in 1931 was granted his request to leave Russia, and died in exile in Paris six years later. *We* was never published in Russia, and has circulated only in typescript form. It appeared in the United States in 1924; the present edition is the first in Britain.

Born in 1884, Zamyatin began his career as a naval architect. In 1905 he was imprisoned for revolutionary activities and spent several months in solitary confinement. One or two unusual affectations, such as a clipped English-style moustache and a taste for tweeds, led him to be nicknamed "The Englishman," and he spent 1916–17 in Newcastle-upon-Tyne supervising the construction of icebreakers. Although a Bolshevik as a young man, he left the party before 1917 and was unenthusiastic about its seizure of power.

We expresses all his disenchantment. A tour de force of irony and contempt, the novel is a terrifying portrait of a totally dehumanised society. In this white-tile hell the individual has ceased to exist: the first-person singular has been replaced by the collective We. The hero, D-503, regards himself as merely a unit in a huge social calculus, steadily multiplying itself towards an absolute mathematical perfection. All privacy has gone. The walls of the identical buildings are made of glass, so that everyone inescapably watches everyone else and imitates their behaviour. The day's activities are governed by an elaborate series of timetables. Ten minutes are set aside at random for sexual intercourse.

This nightmare is ruled by the Guardians, the ultimate thought-police in that they are the only ones alert and intelligent enough to want to have any thoughts at all. Above them presides the mysterious and implacable figure of "The Benefactor." In his fearful aspect he completely anticipates Orwell's "Big Brother," in his garrulous urbanity Aldous Huxley's Mustapha Mond. Zamyatin's decisive influence on Huxley and Orwell seems unquestionable. The hero's gradual awakening from passive conformity, his revolt against the tyranny and, finally, his complete defeat, a defeat in which he willingly concurs, provide a clear blueprint for both *Brave New World* and *1984*.

None the less, how does *We* stand up against these two classics, not to mention the host of anti-utopian satires produced by the writers of modern science fiction? To a large extent *Brave New World* and *1984* described developments that had already taken place, giving them an authenticity they have never lost. By comparison, the very quality which makes Zamyatin's *We* so original—its brilliant extrapolations far into the future before any such trends could have been visible in Soviet society—prevents it from becoming more than a remarkable fantasy. The achilles heel of modern science fiction—the regrettable fact that the future never happens, only the present—in the end brings *We* down as well.

In addition, *We* is based on a premise that has yet to be proved—that when it comes the greatest attack on individual freedom and imagination will be mounted and sustained by calm, flexible and intelligent tyrants. The corrupt, frightened and self-deluding politicians in the nightmare fantasies of William Burroughs seem closer to the reality of the twentieth century than Zamyatin's Guardians, closer to the present generation of uneasy bureaucrats who would almost certainly have exiled Zamyatin to die, not in Paris, but in an Arctic labour camp.

A PERSONAL VIEW

Billion Year Spree by Brian Aldiss

Cypher (May 1974)

Brian Aldiss's exuberant title gives a fair summary of all the excitements to be found in this book—I thoroughly enjoyed it, and read it from cover to cover without a pause, a rare event for any reader these days, and a reflection of the tremendous built-in power of imaginative fiction. Even in summary (or perhaps especially in summary), these accounts of fabulous voyages, extraordinary inventions, cautionary tales and utopian satires leap off the page and touch something vital in our whole response to the possibility of a radical and extravagant alternative to our ordinary and everyday worlds. *Billion Year Spree* is vividly written, witty, encyclopaedic in its scope, far ranging in its ideas, tolerant of fools (an overabundant species in this branch of fiction), and above all affectionate towards the strange company of knaves and naives, hacks and geniuses who move through its pages like a troupe of over-excited travelling play-ers, conning anyone they can with their unlimited blarney. The highest compliment I can pay this book is to say that hardly a single sane man appears throughout it.

Another of the great pleasures it gave me was the realization of just how little of this fiction I had read—if for no other reason, *Billion Year Spree* is guaranteed a steady sale to all those people who for some reason need to read the absolute minimum of Rider Haggard and Edgar Rice Burroughs, Asimov and Tolkien, and will now be able to breathe an enormous sigh of relief as they scan these brief—and, I'm convinced, accurate—summaries.

At the same time, a slight sense of unease came over me as I read the last chapters of this book. (These sections, where Aldiss brings the his-tory of science fiction up to the present day, are a masterpiece of diplo-macy—a sociable and gregarious man, Brian clearly wants to be able to go on attending science fiction conventions here and in the United States without being clubbed over the head by some outraged author's well-aimed Hugo. On reflection, he should have commissioned me to write these last two chapters . . .) What unnerved me was the odd feeling I had of Academy closing around me, of the plywood partitions of the Modern Literature department being erected around my desk, and around those of all the other writers exercising their talents for fantasy and invention. One of the most inaccurate jibes levelled at the so-called New Wave is that its writers suffered from delusions of literary grandeur, that they took themselves far too seriously, and so on. In fact, in my own personal experience, it is the absolute reverse which is true. The most pompous and self-important writers, both here and in the States, are those who are apparently the most "commercial" and non-literary. It is they who are endlessly lecturing and pontificating, forming writers' societies and bogus foundations, filling the fanzines with their literary pretensions, their absurd awards and other nonsense. By comparison, most of the New Wavers I know spend their time lying around and romancing over a bottle.

Perhaps, however, the tightening embrace of Academe is merely a reflection that modern science fiction has come to an end. Anything that happened five minutes ago is already the centre of a cult, embedded in lucite and put on the display shelf. Modern science fiction (by which I mean the s-f of the thirty-year period 1926 to 1957, from Gernsback's founding of *Amazing* to the first flight of Sputnik I and the beginnings of the short-lived space age) has already become a victim of this nostalgia. Despite the protestations of its most vocal supporters, the obvious fact is that no new writers have emerged to follow on from where, for better or worse, the founders of modern science fiction—van Vogt, Heinlein, Asimov, etc.—began. And this is for the obvious reason that nothing remains to be done. The imaginary universe invented by these writers is self-defined and self-limited; the greatest weakness of this particular science fiction is that its writers have been able to define it so exactly. Unfortunately, here, unlike the western, the clock runs against it. The ever-accelerating changes brought about by science and technology have not merely transformed our lives, but made inevitable the emergence of a new science fiction that will more accurately and more imaginatively interpret these changes to us. There is, in fact, the curious paradox that classical science fiction (that is, pre-Gernsback) has far more relevance to us, and in a sense is far more modern than the science fiction of the 40s and 50s, in that it is no longer tied to a period that by its recent passing seems that much the more out-of-date. H. G. Wells's *War of the Worlds*, *Moreau* and *Time Machine* have shaken off the patina of the merely contemporary; by comparison Campbell's *Astounding* and *Analog*, with their third-rate 1950s jargonizing, their blue-collar intellectual clap-trap, are absolutely of the America of the *Reader's Digest*, Betty Grable, and popular newspaper sensations such as Dianetics.

A large part of the problem faced by the protagonists of modern American science fiction is the unfortunate fact that America herself has slammed on the brakes. By this I mean that the enormous moral, psychological and imaginative reserves possessed by the United States in the 30's, 40's and 50's (far larger and more valuable than the billions in Fort Knox) lay in that huge system of excitements and possibilities enshrined in the notion of the "future." The future would be better, and America had a monopoly of the stuff. All this has now gone into reverse. The future has now been abandoned as a zone of imaginative excitement, and most of the values of modern America are under severe scrutiny. All this leaves the older generation of American science fiction writers high and dry. Most of them are now too old to change their ways—they have no place to go but forward, and the road is closed, yet their entire science fiction is based on the future, and without it their writing becomes meaningless.

However, as Aldiss points out in *Billion Year Spree*, these matters are of comparatively local interest. One of the great values of this book is that we can see classical, modern and contemporary science fiction within the larger context of imaginative fiction. Arguments about whether *Gulliver's Travels* and *1984* are science fiction or whether, say, *Brave New World* should be admitted to the club (it virtually designed the premises), fade away when we see the huge sweeps of cautionary and speculative fiction laid out in front of us.

Since its beginnings, roughly speaking, I would say, at the start of the Industrial Revolution (Aldiss fixes on Mary Shelley's *Frankenstein*, a fair enough starting point), science fiction has been distinguished by two features: 1) its imaginative response to science and technology; and 2) its attempt, now more or less abandoned by the so-called mainstream novel, to place some kind of metaphysical and philosophical framework around man's place in the universe. However crudely (and most of the confusions about the position of science fiction in the literary frame of things would be avoided if it were called by a more accurate title—"popular science fiction"), science fiction has continued to perform both these roles. As *Billion Year Spree* demonstrates, most of the major imaginative writers of the past 250 years have at some time written science fiction, and it is a tribute to the genre that they needed to do so.

In *Billion Year Spree* Aldiss systematically examines, in an always lively and interested style, the ancestors of twentieth century science fiction. His strong affection for H. G. Wells makes the 18th and 19th century writers he describes—Defoe, Swift, Samuel Butler, Edgar Allen Poe—seem in their different ways to be precursors of Wells, and to a large extent the point is sustained. Wells dominates 20th century science fiction, not so much by his immense imagination—as Aldiss seems to suggest—as by two other qualities much more lacking in his successors—intelligence and sophistication. Wells did not merely invent the future, he understood it.

For SF fans much of the interest of *Billion Year Spree* will be found in the last two chapters, where most of the writers discussed are still alive. Aldiss is not only diplomatic, but unfailingly generous to his fellow writers. I think he overestimates the "literary" achievements of modern science fiction writers. For most of them—Heinlein, Pohl, Clarke, Bradbury, Sheckley, Matheson etc—their real merits lie outside the tiresome characteristics of so-called mainstream fiction. Rather, they belong to an as yet undefined area that lies between popular science journalism and the iconographic fictions of advertising and television, between our everyday fantasies and the psychopathic delusions of such "naives" as Oswald and Sirhan Sirhan (who said of Robert Kennedy—"I didn't feel I had really killed him until I saw it on TV." A remark that contains the essence of contemporary science fiction).

Aldiss begins his history in the obligatory way—with a definition of science fiction. Like all definitions it is a little too complicated; some day, if I have the time, I would like to carry out a Freudian analysis of all the definitions of SF that have been made (incidentally, I should also like to examine the number of science fiction writers who have been only children. My guess is that most have had solitary childhoods). My own off-the-cuff definition—science fiction is any fiction inspired by science (fantasy is any fiction inspired by fiction).

Lastly, I would like to enlarge on Aldiss' passing tribute to the editor of *New Worlds* during its greatest period—E. J. Carnell.

Carnell's role is central to the transformation of modern science fiction (moribund by 1955) into contemporary science fiction in its earliest form, the "new wave." By and large the foundations of the new wave were laid down long before Carnell turned over the editorship of *New Worlds* to Michael Moorcock. I well remember discussing with Ted in 1957, when he arranged for me to get an editorial job on one of the parent company's technical journals, the kind of science fiction I wanted to write—a radical break with the science fiction then apparently in its ascendency, but, as I was certain, doomed. Ted was always enthusiastic, urging me to break new ground, telling me to take no notice of the more vocal of the other writers (the most dingy and pathetic bunch of third-rate ex-journalists and business-machine salesmen I had ever met—enough to put anyone off the written word forever) who were irritated in their usually mindless way by what now seem to be the most conventional of my short stories. Among those who were sympathetic in those very early days were John Brunner and John Wyndham.

Ted Carnell persevered for years with my early writing—publishing *The Drowned World* (in its short version), "The Voices of Time," and most important of all for me, "The Terminal Beach," the last rejected by Cele Goldsmith (who in fact published many of my stories at that time), Pohl and everyone else in the States. Some of the comments from the US editors in those days would make strange reading now, they might well cool the ardour of some of the Eng. Lit. departments who are slightly over-hasty in their rush to canonise the editors of the period.

Above all, Ted Carnell established the legitimacy of change—the idea that an alternative route might be allowed out of the "ghetto" of science fiction. He edited *New Worlds* at a time when the conventions of science fiction had almost fossilised the genre. All the more credit to him. By comparison, the editorship of *New Worlds* under his successor, Michael Moorcock, pursued much more acceptable and traditional lines. (Looking back, in many ways I feel now that I was singlehandedly responsible for killing *New Worlds*; though in fact Mike Moorcock was a strong enough personality to take the magazine in his own direction.) Moorcock, with myself breathing heavily over the editorial desk, in fact was following what were wholly traditional and conventional lines—the avant-garde in short; experimental and exploratory writing of a kind long since established in the early years of the 20th century. Mike's problems and achievement lay rather in his success in the field *outside* science fiction—as an independent and aggressive editor of a magazine, and a school of writers, that owed nothing to any private coterie but was trying to establish a magazine that would survive in the general field. All the best to him.

But with Ted Carnell lies the credit of establishing the possibility of change *within* science fiction, at a time when change had become anathema. I think it was Fred Pohl who said to me some years ago: "I spent twenty years of my life helping to establish the conventions of science fiction—and I don't intend to see them changed." Listening to the leading writers speak at the Film Festival in Rio three years ago—van Vogt, Bloch, Clarke, Ellison, Poul Anderson—I was certain that I was in the ante-chamber of a lunatic asylum. What has to be remembered about most of these writers (and there are many exceptions, sophisticated and lucid people like Sheckley, Harrison, Judy Merril and Brian Aldiss himself) is that the science fiction they produce represents the most ordinary face of their imaginations. Their lives are their real fictions.

The great change that is coming over science fiction—and to some extent over the whole of imaginative fiction—is that the talent for the inventive and fabulous, which science fiction writers have shown for the last two centuries, will no longer be enough.

ZAP CODE

Approaching Oblivion by Harlan Ellison; Shadrach in the Furnace by Robert Silverberg; Medusa's Children by Bob Shaw

New Statesman (March 25, 1977)

Exuberance, an attractive and abundant quality in science fiction, is comparatively rare among its writers, as anyone attending an sf convention soon notices. For some reason there is a marked contrast between the personal style of the genre's fans, a happy, beer-swilling, hotel-wrecking contingent—in short, the charge of the light ale brigade—and that of the writers themselves, for the most part shy and rather Thurberish figures with intimidating wives, who are plainly terrified by the silence of those infinite spaces. I can only guess that the task of sustaining the classical sf image of a universe infinitely colonised throughout time and space demands a degree of concentration that is deeply repressive.

The most notable exception among contemporary writers of sf is Harlan Ellison, an aggressive and restless extrovert who conducts his life at a shout and his fiction at a scream. Teenage gang-leader turned Hollywood screen-writer, polemicist and unarmed combat specialist (he once unnerved me in the elevator of a Rio hotel by offering to demonstrate how to kill a man in the three seconds between floors), Ellison is one of the most interesting and talented sf writers to appear since Ray Bradbury. Ten years ago he published the first of his remarkable series *Dangerous Visions*, collections of specially commissioned stories whose authors were urged to capitalise on every taboo or deviant notion inside their heads, and which made a complete break with the already fossilised conventions of American sf. Out went outer space and the far future, in came inner space and the world of Zap Comics and biomorphic fantasies inspired by William Burroughs.

Approaching Oblivion, Ellison's latest short story collection, has all the visceral and paranoid obsessions that run through the anthologies. In "Knox," an ultra-fascist America has tortured and murdered every conceivable enemy and is forced to turn inwards to find its last victim, destroying itself with the reductive logic of a lunatic abattoir. In "Cold Friend" a terminal cancer patient emerges cured from his cryogenic tomb to find that it is now his mind that is diseased. However lurid, the stories have a relentless imaginative drive, suggesting that Ellison may be the first of a new kind of sf writer, completely uninterested in science but attracted to the medium by the ample opportunities which New Wave sf offers for exploiting the most sensational emotional mixes.

Robert Silverberg's new novel is an elaborate medico-political thriller that describes what must be the ultimate in the patient/doctor relationship. Forty years in the future, a health-obsessed dictator is linked to his personal physician by a network of electronic implants that relay the minutest details of bodily function. Determined to survive at all costs, the dictator submits to extensive organ transplant surgery, awaiting the time when some unfortunate donor can be found who will supply the ultimate transplant—his entire body—into which the electrical patterns of the dictator's brain and nervous system can be passed. Unfortunately, the suitable donor dies, and the doctor himself is then chosen as the victim, with the grisly prospect of becoming both his patient and his patient's disease. Ingenious and literate, the novel might well have given one or two interesting ideas to Howard Hughes in his last years.

A large part of Bob Shaw's *Medusa's Children* takes place under water, and without in any way poking fun at the book I wish it could be read there. A genuinely dream-like calm pervades this story of an undersea clan living in a cluster of nets and sunken ships near the ocean floor. The sense of sun-filled water all around, the absence of movement and the suspension of time create a trance like atmosphere in which the events of the narrative drift by like sleeping fish. The story unfolds as quietly as the changing currents and chemistry of the sea which first alert these undersea dwellers to the transformation of their world and to the possible existence of some immense oceanic being, first feared as an enemy, but of which they themselves may be part. Traditional sf, but expertly done.

KILLING TIME

The Executioner's Song by Norman Mailer

Guardian (November 15, 1979)

Ours is a season for assassins. How far does our fascination with Oswald and Charles Manson, Gary Gilmore and James Earl Ray play on the edgy dreams of other lonely psychopaths, encourage them to gamble their trigger fingers on a very special kind of late twentieth century celebrity? Will everyone in the future, to adapt Warhol, be infamous for fifteen minutes? Given the immense glare of publicity, a virtual deification by the world's press and television, and the remarkable talents these rootless and half-educated men can show for manipulating the mass media, their actual crimes soon seem to sink to a lower, merely human realm.

Lee Harvey Oswald, had he not been shot by Jack Ruby, would presumably now be up for parole, ready to play his part—as TV anchorman, or special assignment writer for *Guns and Ammo*?—in the election of yet another Kennedy. With luck any would-be assassins in the future will give themselves away haggling with their agents for the biggest film advance and the right prime-time TV coverage.

The Executioner's Song is Norman Mailer's account of the crimes, trial and execution in 1977 of Gary Gilmore, the first convicted murderer to be put to death in the United States after a ten-year moratorium. Dedicated to Mailer's agent, at first sight the book is off-putting, perhaps the last chapter in the very system of exploitation that Mailer criticizes. Mailer never met Gilmore, and the 1,000-page text is based on a mass of extended interviews by Lawrence Schiller, an ex-*Life* photographer turned Hollywood entrepreneur. The result is a vast cast of largely minor characters and an excess of parallel narration never properly fused together, which makes nonsense of Mailer's attempt to call it a novel.

But in fact the repetitions and the flat documentary style allow Mailer to build up a masterly portrait of the murderer—Gilmore might well have been one of the morose GIs in *The Naked and the Dead*. By the time of his release from an Illinois penitentiary at the age of thirty-five, Gilmore had spent eighteen of the previous twenty-two years in prison and reform school. The illegitimate son of a sometime convict and a mother who resented him from earliest childhood, Gilmore had already tasted celebrity. During a prison riot in Illinois the local TV crew "selected" him as one of the leaders and put him on television to say a few words. His looks and the way he spoke attracted attention and the first fan mail from women admirers.

Returning to Provo, Utah, and a life of drugs, beer-drinking and petty theft, he cold-bloodedly murdered a gas station attendant and a motel clerk for little more than the equivalent of £50, and was arrested almost immediately by the police. Sustained by his girl-friend, Nicole, a remarkable young woman who would stand outside the jail, bellowing "Gary Gilmore, I love you!" he accepted his death penalty and settled down to await his execution. The police psychiatrists diagnosed Gilmore as a psychopathic personality, and he seems to have felt no anger or hostility towards the men he murdered, regarding them with the same total blankness that he felt for himself. Already in the death cell he was planning both Nicole's suicide and his own execution—he wanted to be shot in the dark with tracer bullets, so that he could watch them coming towards him. Even the horrendous conditions on Death Row, a long way from Cagney and George Raft, hardly affected him. Mailer vividly describes this depraved zoo, a bedlam of cries and rage, the condemned men exposing their genitalia through the bars, hurling cups of urine into the faces of any intruders.

Gilmore's refusal to appeal against his death penalty soon made him a local celebrity. The first curious journalists interviewed him, the advance guard of an army of hustlers and agents, veteran wheeler-dealers from the Manson and Ruby cases, film and TV executives who swarmed in from all over the world. Gilmore's own lawyer, who doubled as his literary agent, defended his right to die, claiming: "I think executions should be on prime-time TV." The first hard cash, $500, was paid by the Daily Express ("When the British are here en masse," said one excited newsman, "the stamp is on the meat").

In a strange but impressive way, Gilmore expanded to fill the roles assigned him. One journalist noted that there was racist Gary, Country and Western Gary, artist manque Gary, self-destructive Gary, Karma Gary and Gary the movie star. He quoted Shelley and Hermann Hesse, and would ask visitors "Are you familiar with Nietzsche?"

The end came as he wanted it. The climax, and greatest set-piece in the book, is Mailer's account of the last night before the execution, a virtuoso description of the deranged prison party held around the drugged Gilmore, wearing a comical Robin Hood hat and brandishing pornographic photos of his girl-friend, while a huge TV and press encampment waited outside the prison.

Soon after dawn the party ended. To the tune of Una Paloma Blanca, Gilmore was taken to the execution yard in the prison cannery. As a TV commentator bawled: "You'll be able to hear the shots, I promise!" Gilmore was tied to a chair in front of the concealed firing squad. After the shots, in the first silence since Gilmore's arrest, the only sound was the blood dripping on to his tennis shoes below the seat. Perhaps not surprisingly, only one witness managed to be sick.

NEW MEANS WORSE

The Golden Age of Science Fiction, edited by Kingsley Amis

Guardian (November 26, 1981)

Kingsley Amis's stormy affair with science fiction becomes more and more perplexing. In 1960, *New Maps of Hell* was the most important critical work on s-f that had yet been published, and to a large extent still remains so. Amis threw open the gates of the ghetto, and ushered in a new audience which he almost singlehandedly recruited from intelligent readers of general fiction who until then had considered science fiction on a par with horror comics and pulp westerns.

What marked *New Maps of Hell*, like Amis's reviews of the time and the considerable influence he brought to bear on publishers and literary editors alike, were his generosity and enthusiasm. Sadly, though, this was soon to change. By the mid-1960s, those of us active in science fiction began to hear the first growls of disapproval, saw ourselves glared at across the conference room, felt our kidneys punched in a jocular but unmistakably menacing way.

For the past fifteen years, in a stream of reviews, articles and interviews, Amis has vented an increasingly bilious contempt for almost everything science fiction has produced. As he writes in his introduction to this new anthology: "Science fiction has come from Chaucer to *Finnegans Wake* in less than fifty years . . . now you can take it anywhere, and it is not worth taking." Yet Amis still returns again and again to spit into the poisoned well.

What have we done to deserve his hostility? To some extent Amis's distaste for science fiction can be put down to simple pique. Sharp observer though he was of 1940s and 1950s s-f, his prediction in *New Maps of Hell* that science fiction would become primarily a satirical and sociological medium proved totally wrong. In fact, American s-f veered away into interplanetary fantasy (Le Guin, Zelazny, Delany), while the British writers began to explore the psychological realm of inner space.

Almost the only writer to turn to sociological satire was Amis himself, in *The Alteration*, and *Russian Hide-and-Seek*. Bearing in mind the rather modest talent for s-f that Amis displayed in those works, and his restless genre-hopping, perhaps his dissatisfaction is secretly, dare I say it, with . . . ?

Whatever the root cause, Amis's contempt for post-1960 science fiction seems bound up with his growing hatred of almost everything else that has happened in the world since then. Deriding the s-f New Wave, he refers to its links with the "Sixties scene, along with pop music, hippie clothes and hairdos, pornography, reefers." He tells us that the writers were visited by "restlessness and self-dissatisfaction, by the conscious quest for maturity and novelty, by the marsh-light of experimentalism."

Worse horrors waited in the wings. "In came shock tactics, tricks with typography, one-line chapters, strained metaphors, obscurities, obscenities, drugs, Oriental religions and left-wing politics." Good heavens, I remember now, those hairdos, that music, those Oriental religions.

The perpetrators of all this are whipped unmercifully. Moorcock's fiction "gives rise to little more than incurious bewilderment." Aldiss, in *Barefoot in the Head*, "interlards an adventure story with stylistic oddities, bits of freak talk, poems, some of them 'concrete.'" As for Ballard, on whom no verdict can be harsh enough: "Solipsistic . . . mystification and outrage . . . physical disgust . . . stories with chapters sub-divided into numbered paragraphs [not true] . . . has never been in the genre at all."

The readers are equally despised and patronized: "My remarks on the readership of the genre refer of course to its higher levels; the average is probably pretty low, especially today."

To read this long-threatened postscript to *New Maps of Hell* is an unsettling experience. Apart from his sour tone, Amis is so ill-informed about the present state of science fiction, and seems to imagine that it is dominated by would-be intellectuals imitating Robbe-Grillet and Michel Butor.

In fact, science fiction today (certainly in the United States, its main centre of activity) is entering the most commercial phase it has ever known. The New Wave, along with almost all the more intelligent magazines and anthologies, has long since been inundated by a tsunami of planet fiction, sword-and-sorcery sensationalism, and Star Wars rip-offs, propelled by a reactionary s-f writers' guild closely interlocked with the New York publishers.

What science fiction needs now is a clear, hard and positive voice like that of the Kingsley Amis of 1960. The accurate judgments he made then are evident in his choice of 1950s s-f in *The Golden Age of Science Fiction*, classics such as Pohl's *The Tunnel under the World*, Arthur C. Clarke's *The Nine Billion Names of God*, and H. Beam Piper's *He Walked Around the Horses*, a brilliant tale of a Napoleonic disappearance, told in the form of—what's this?—chapters subdivided into numbered paragraphs. Kingsley . . . !

FALLEN IDOL

Elvis by Albert Goldman

Guardian (December 3, 1981)

The Hollywood cynic who commented, on hearing of Elvis Presley's death in 1977, "Good career move," might well have second thoughts after reading this ruthless expose. Everyone watching Presley on television in his last years, as he swayed across the stage of the Las Vegas Hilton in his Prince Valiant suit, a bloated parody of himself who now and then treated his blue-rinsed audience to a canny leer, knew that something was wrong. But the memory of the young Presley remained, an electric charge that still pulls all the current out of the mains.

According to Albert Goldman, for at least the last decade of his life Presley was a hopeless drug addict, a walking pharmacopoeia of powerful stimulants and opiates that a coterie of compliant doctors injected into him at all hours of the day and night. Although the autopsy results were never published, it was probably a huge overdose that killed him during the long night of 17 August 1977 as he sat alone in his bathroom at Graceland, his stoned entourage asleep in their nearby bedrooms.

But by then, according to Goldman, the real Presley had been moribund for years, in effect since the death of his mother Gladys in 1958. Goldman clearly relishes his tale of Presley's slow and lurid decline, elaborating a long catalogue of those sins that seem particularly heinous to Americans. Mama's boy and bed-wetter, prude and glutton, voyeur and obsessive gun-fancier, Presley alienates his biographer's sympathies at every turn. In fact, almost everything about Presley is present in this biography except his enormous talent, and an influence on popular culture greater than that of any other musical performer this century.

Goldman makes much of the close relationship between Presley and his mother, lingering over their extreme physical intimacy—they slept in the same bed until his puberty. But despite her own well-developed taste for drugs and alcohol, Gladys seems to have offered Presley rock-like support throughout her short life. Again, Goldman reveals that Presley was a natural blond, and based his legendary black hairstyle on that worn by the young Tony Curtis in the film *City Across the River*. Does this diminish Presley, or show his astuteness in the way he assembled his potent stage image as that archetypal 1950s figure, the juvenile delinquent?

Goldman's attempt to demolish the Presley myth seems an attack on the whole popular culture of the period (he is now working on a book about John Lennon—watch out). Curiously Goldman seems obsessed with Presley's sexuality. In his first view of Presley, he describes him in his bedroom at Graceland towards the end, "propped up like a big fat woman recovering from some operation on her reproductive organs." He harps endlessly on Presley's voyeurism, his liking for two-way mirrors and closed-circuit TV through which he watched the Guys (the Tennessee buddies who formed his entourage) making it with their girls.

Still, not as wild or as sad as the end. By the age of forty, Presley had earned $100 million. He gave away Cadillacs to passing strangers, threw expensive jewellery to his audiences, once flew from Memphis to Denver in his private jet to buy a peanut butter sandwich. In a trance of drugs and terminal boredom, he fell asleep with his face in a bowl of chicken soup. He was constantly watched by his guards in case he choked on a piece of food, became incontinent and had to be carried to the lavatory and tied into diapers. At the end he was so obese that he used a golf cart to carry him from the elevator to the stage of the Hilton.

For some reason, though, I find myself admiring Presley all the more. That knowing smile, those savvy eyes and that talent transcend everything, even this book.

LEGEND OF REGRET

Some Sort of Epic Grandeur: The Life of F. Scott Fitzgerald by Matthew J. Bruccoli

Guardian (February 4, 1982)

Few writers have so identified themselves with their own work as Scott Fitzgerald. With some—Ernest Hemingway or Evelyn Waugh—it is difficult enough to separate the man from the legend, but in Fitzgerald's case one often feels that there was only the legend in the first place. Jazz-age darling, spoiled genius and alcoholic writer romantically dying the slow Hollywood death, Fitzgerald played these parts as if they were roles in the movies whose scripts he later found himself forced to write.

Matthew Bruccoli's elaborately researched biography goes some way to disinterring the real Fitzgerald, though perhaps his warts-and-all portrait is yet another romantic fiction, and one that happens to be closer to our own taste. All the same, Fitzgerald's extraordinary charm, and that touching determination to be a success, to run faster than the dream and to enfold it, come through as strongly as ever.

The son of a failed furniture manufacturer in St Paul, Fitzgerald felt an outsider from the start. Desperate for admiration, he struggled to reach the school football team, but was labelled a show-off. At Princeton, which he regarded as a rich young man's country club, he found his first social success. However, his academic record was a disaster, and already he was rationalizing this into a potent myth of romantic failure. His poems and stories in the college magazine sound many of the themes in his later fiction—the gifted man ruined by a selfish woman, the hero half-consciously seeking destruction, and the strong strain of masochism.

He soon set about satisfying his own obsessions. Fitzgerald's service in the army was another partial failure. He was considered an unreliable officer and was not sent overseas. The captain in charge of his training platoon was Dwight D. Eisenhower, and though, sadly, Ike's opinion of Fitzgerald is unrecorded his fellow officers disliked Fitzgerald and played elaborate practical jokes on him. But while he was stationed at Montgomery, Alabama, he met Zelda Sayre, his future wife and a destructive force beyond all his dreams.

The last of the southern belles, Zelda was beautiful, daredevil and exhibitionist, a brilliant and racy talker. She smoked in the street, flirted outrageously and had scandalized entire states. To win her, and the money he needed to satisfy her own demands for success, Fitzgerald wrote his first novel, *This Side of Paradise*. Its publication in 1920 was a critical and commercial triumph, launched the Jazz Age and locked Scott and Zelda into a legend that only ended with her death thirty years later in an asylum fire.

Fitzgerald was always puritanical about sex, and his views on marriage were surprisingly conventional:

"Just being in love is work enough for a woman. If she . . . makes herself look pretty when her husband comes home in the evening, and loves him and helps him with his work and encourages him—oh, I think that's the sort of work that will save her."

Given her entirely opposite nature, Zelda must have been a powerful spur to Fitzgerald, touching his deepest dreams of romantic rejection. It is hard to imagine him writing his masterpiece of nostalgia and regret, *The Great Gatsby*, without the aid of this tragic but extraordinary woman. Her first mental breakdown in 1929, like the Crash itself marked the end for Fitzgerald, and his imagination never recovered. Between 1920 and 1929, according to Bruccoli, Fitzgerald earned $244,967, at least six times its present value, but from then on his income sharply declined. If the twenties had spoiled and encouraged Fitzgerald, the thirties ignored him.

Fitzgerald's best work is about the failure to recapture past emotions, and one feels that the series of calamities that form his later life was almost consciously set up to provoke that poignant regret. During the endless champagne party of the twenties this seemed touching and romantic, but far less so in the thirties against a background of real failure and despair.

His last three years in Hollywood, contrary to popular myth, were modestly successful. But he died, in the words of John O'Hara, "a prematurely old little man haunting bookshops unrecognized." His last royalty statement in 1940 from Scribners reported sales of 40 copies for all his books, including seven copies of *The Great Gatsby*, for a total royalty of $13.

AUTOPIA OR AUTOGEDDON

Automania by Julian Pettifer and Nigel Turner; *The Centenary of the Car, 1885–1985* by Andrew Whyte; *Rolls-Royce: The Complete Works* by Mike Fox and Steve Smith

Guardian (November 29, 1984)

Sooner or later everything turns into television. The motor car, so reviled in the 1970s as an ecological disaster, a chrome-hungry destroyer of cities, has now been restored to our affections and awarded the ultimate accolade of a thirteen-part television series. *Automania* is the book of the series being shown on ITV, and is a witty and generous tribute to this most durable of all adult toys.

Carl Benz's three-wheeler first appeared on the streets of Mannheim in 1885, and was patented the following year. As Andrew Whyte points out in his well-researched and comprehensive history of the motor car, Benz's primitive vehicle with its water-cooled four-stroke engine and electrical ignition contained the basic essentials of the modern automobile—under the bonnet, that is, for the real evolution of the motor car has taken place almost entirely at skin level. Leaving the trivial matter of transportation aside, I assume that a large part of the car's appeal lies in its combination of a comparatively primitive and static technology with a decorative shell capable of generating enthusiasms and obsessions of the most extravagant kind.

"Glorious, stirring sight!" murmured Toad of Toad Hall on falling in love with the motor car in 1908, "O bliss! O poop poop!" His sentiments were echoed by the Italian Futurist Marinetti when he declared that "a racing car is more beautiful than the Victory of Samothrace."

A rich man's plaything in its early years, the car inspired owners and coachbuilders to heights of ingenuity. At the turn of the century the first European limousines featured fully equipped kitchens, silk brocade armchairs that could be converted into beds and, designed for a wealthy American, a built-in flush toilet. From all this emerged a mammoth car-accessory industry, providing everything from tyre manicure sets and in-car fragrances to nodding doggy mascots—the greatest threat to sanity on the modern highway. Given so desirable an object, theft soon became a problem, and this in turn conjured up a host of devices, from stuffed Alsatian dogs to inflatable rubber drivers ("So life-like and terrifying that nobody a foot away can tell it isn't a real live man," claimed an ad for Bosco's Collapsible Driver).

But without doubt the most significant event in the history of the automobile was the decision in 1925 by Alfred P. Sloan of General Motors to introduce the annual model change. In the golden age of the Eisenhower years stylists like Harley Earl, inventor of the tail fin, and George Walker of Ford ("the Cellini of Chrome") became kings of the industry, a reign that lasted until the failure of the over-embellished Edsel—which perhaps reflected some faltering of the American dream in the run-up to Vietnam. If the resurgence of US confidence under Reagan is as real as the commentators claim, one would expect a revival of baroque extravagance in Detroit car design.

Surprisingly, the world's first car museum, in Turin, opened as late as 1939, but today even Sotheby's and Christie's deal in motoring ephemera. The highest prices are fetched by cars with celebrity connections: Hitler's Mercedes-Benz, with its raised floor that gave the Fuhrer an extra six inches in height; Garbo's Dusenberg with six built-in safes; Bonnie and Clyde's V8 Ford, complete with original bloodstains and 106 bullet holes. The Holy Grail, according to Pettifer and Turner, is James Dean's Porsche, which was stolen after his death-crash and has never been seen since.

In spite of the enormous freedom the car has given, the invisible destination at the end of too many route maps has been death—the authors of *Automania* estimate that 15–20 million people have been killed by the car in its first century. Between 1950 and 1980 the number of cars in the world rose from 50 million to 350 million, but the price paid in deaths and injuries seems scarcely to have dented our love affair with the car, even beyond the grave—one Texan lady infatuated with her Ferrari was buried in it. An international Gallup survey in 1983 discovered that the worst reported crime a human being can commit is not genocide, matricide or rape, but the driving away of someone else's car without permission.

Rolls-Royce: The Complete Works is an illustrated compilation of 599 stories, an ideal present for those who still believe that this is the world's best car, or are keen to recognize the number plates of Jimmy Tarbuck, Engelbert Humperdinck and Princess Margaret.

For me the heroic period of the Rolls-Royce lies well in its past, in a pre-war epoch of archdukes and maharajahs, the latter being emperors of eccentricity—one fitted a throne, another made his steering wheel from elephant's tusks, a third crowned his Rolls with a thatched roof. Frankly, today's Silver Shadow seems a little middle class, more Dallas than Debrett, an expense-account taxi for corporation executives.

Still, I will move out of the fast lane when I next see 3 GXM bearing down on me, or hear the imperial sounds of a royal Phantom VI whose cassette holder is playing music by the band of the Brigade of Guards . . .

ESCAPE INTO THE SERAGLIO

Hockney on Photography: Conversations by Paul Joyce

Guardian (October 28, 1988)

Affable and engaging, his Yorkshire savvy filtered through the warmest shades of California sunshine, David Hockney wears his celebrity more casually than any post-war artist. Neither Warhol, with his eerie, death's-head stare, nor Dali, too often coming on like a hallucinating speak-your-weight machine, ever achieved the comfortable rapport with his audience that Hockney has been able to take for granted since the 1960s.

Together, Hockney's life and work sum up exactly what the public today asks of its artists. Cannily, Hockney has saved his real waywardness for his life-style—the gold lame jacket and dyed blond hair, once so outrageous, and the pool-boys high in the Hollywood Hills—while his paintings have remained wholly acceptable to his Sunday supplement admirers. The playgroup palette reminds them of the kindergarten paint-boxes with which they dabbled as toddlers, while the images of Los Angeles offer a romanticized vision of that latter-day Samarkand among the freeways.

In many respects, Hockney performs the role today which Alma-Tadema played for his Victorian audience. Both artists have satisfied the public's need for exotic, far-away lands filled with graceful houris and sybaritic dreams. Both specialized in swimming-pools, but where Alma-Tadema, depicting the seraglios of a wholly mythical east, surrounded his marble grottos with pretty girls, Hockney furnishes the pools of his equally mythical west with a parade of pretty boys.

Anyone who has spent even five minutes in Los Angeles can see that this city of dreadful night is nothing like the sanitized realm invented by Hockney in his paintings of the 1960s. Hockney's Los Angeles resembles the real terrain of dingbats and painted glue, stretching as far as forever under a tangle of overhead wires, only in the sense that Rick's Cafe resembles the real Casablanca.

Needless to say, Hockney's vision is all the better for that, and I for one wish that he had stayed with his houris in the Hollywood Hills, painting ever bigger and bigger splashes. But the great period of the swimming-pools had passed with the end of the 1970s, at about the time when the first British visitors arrived en masse and discovered the reality of his imaginary city.

By then Hockney had himself begun to discover reality in the form of photography, a long-standing enthusiasm which seems to have seized the centre stage of his imagination during the 1980s. *Hockney on Photography* is a lavishly illustrated guide to the series of photo-collages he has made in the last six years. These, he believes, pose a fundamental challenge to the "one-eyed" tradition that has always dominated photography since its birth.

In his interviews with the filmmaker Paul Joyce, Hockney describes his first experiments with the Polaroid camera and the significance for the future of photography of what he calls his "joiners." He ranges widely over the history of western painting, contrasting its single-point perspective with the generalized perspective of eastern art, and discusses his attempts in the photo-collages to enlarge the dimension of time and infuse a greater degree of realism.

Hockney speaks with all his customary wit and intelligence, though he is frequently pushed over the top by an immensely subservient interviewer. "I wonder whether you are going almost beyond art itself," he gushes. "Photography is no longer the same after this work of yours . . ."

"Picasso and others then took off from Cezanne, and now I'm trying to take off from Picasso in an even more radical way," Hockney rejoins. He disdains the ignorant viewpoint of "people who think they know about art, or write for the *Guardian*."

Suitably chastened, I nonetheless feel that Hockney's ambitious claims suffer severely when placed against the actual photo-collages. The overlapping rectangular prints form a mosaic of sharp angles and unintegrated detail that soon irritates the eye. Hockney maintains that the joiners are "much closer to the way that we actually look at things" but the human eye is not faceted, and the only people who see like this are suffering from brain damage. Gazing at these jittery panoramas one sees the world through the eyes of a concussed bumblebee rather than, as Hockney hopes, through the visionary lens of some future Rembrandt of the Rolleiflex.

As for the expanded element of time, there is no sense of when the separate photographs were taken, and the collages could equally have been shuffled together from cut-up copies of the same snapshot. A masterpiece of still photography such as Cartier-Bresson's "The Informer," reproduced in the book, showing the revenge of concentration camp inmates, resonates with a richness of meanings that transcends the single image and the moment of time it records.

These resonances are missing from the photo-collages, which work, if at all, only as still lives or landscapes. Hockney himself gives the game away when he admits that his technique would be unsuitable for a serious subject like the tragic image of a napalmed child on a Vietnam highway, also reproduced.

I hope Hockney returns to his swimming-pool near Mulholland Drive, shuts his eyes to the city below and once again brings us the candied dreams of his mythic west.

DAYS STRUNG ON A SYRINGE WITH A THREAD OF BLOOD

Literary Outlaw: The Life and Times of William S. Burroughs by Ted Morgan

Independent on Sunday (February 24, 1991)

Hitman for the apocalypse in his trench coat and snap-brim fedora, William Burroughs steps out of his life and into his fiction like a secret agent charged with the demolition of all bourgeois values. More than in the case of almost any other writer, Burroughs's life merges seamlessly into his work. Hemingway and Evelyn Waugh were never for a moment convincing as big-game hunter and country gentleman, two of the least likely roles that writers, bundles of nerves and indecision, can ever have asked themselves to play. Had they swapped roles, both might have been more comfortable. One can see Hemingway presiding over a finca near Pamplona, breeding bulls rather than skewering them, and Waugh contentedly blasting apart every wildebeest in the Serengeti.

Genet, living out his last days in the tiny hotel rooms that reminded him of his prison cells, consciously turned his back on the world and returned himself to the realm of his own pages, while Burroughs has never left them. Reading Ted Morgan's rich and authoritative biography, one constantly feels that Burroughs's fiction, however extreme, is a milder version of his life. In the late 1970s Burroughs rented a windowless apartment, soon nicknamed the Bunker, in a converted YMCA in the Bowery. The concrete space, with its white porcelain urinals, had once been a changing-room, and Burroughs was pleasantly at home there, surrounded, as he liked to say with a touch of his death-rattle humour, by the heavy psychic traces of naked boys.

This strange scene seems to spring straight from the pages of *The Naked Lunch*, from that dank world of subway dawns, cheap hotels and empty amusement parks, and it is this unity of life and vision that gives Burroughs's fiction its enormous charge. At a time when the bourgeois novel has triumphed, and career novelists jet around the world on Arts Council tours and pontificate like game-show celebrities at literary festivals, it is heartening to know that Burroughs at least is still working away quietly in Lawrence, Kansas, creating what I feel is the most original and important body of fiction to appear since the Second World War.

As the contemporary novel transforms itself into a regional or even provincial form, Burroughs's fiction remains international in its scope and subject matter. Surprisingly, those novelists like Snow or Malraux who rose to senior posts in the political establishments of their day left only minor works of fiction about their privileged subject matter. By contrast Burroughs, the professional outsider, sometime petty criminal and drug addict, has produced an unmatched critique of the nature of modern society and the control and communication systems that shape our view of the world.

For all his heroic rebellion against the convention-bound middle class, Burroughs was born in 1914 on one of its most comfortable slopes. His paternal grandfather had invented what was to become the Burroughs adding machine, and the young Burroughs enjoyed a well-to-do childhood in St Louis—though already, at his private school, the father of a schoolmate remarked of him: "That boy looks like a sheep-killing dog."

Sensing that he was a misfit, and aware of his homosexuality from an early age, Burroughs began to experiment with drugstore chloral hydrate when he was sixteen, his first steps in the exploration of states of altered consciousness that was to become a secondary career. He graduated from Harvard with a dose of syphilis and a low view of formal education, but unsure where to point his life. His parents gave him a monthly allowance of $200, which arrived regularly for the next 25 years.

Few research funds have been put to better use. The allowance gave him the chance to go down the hard way, not to make good but to make bad. He was able to move outside his own class and explore the vast proletarian sub-culture of blue-collar drifters, small-time gamblers and pennyante thieves. In New York he rolled drunks on the subway for their small change, trying to finance his growing morphine addiction. In *The Naked Lunch*, the masterpiece that was to spring from this period of his life, Burroughs compares organised society with its extreme opposite, the invisible society of drug addicts. He concludes that the two are not very different, at least at the points where they make the closest contact, in prisons and psychiatric institutions—an unsparing view of the world that dominates his entire fiction but is relieved by his extraordinary humour and the succession of bizarre characters he invents, like the sinister Dr Benway and the delightful Johnny Yen, errand-boy of the death trauma.

Pushing morphine and living on his wits in New York, though yet to write a word, Burroughs became the dominant figure in a circle that included Jack Kerouac, Gregory Corso and Allen Ginsberg. Ted Morgan comments on their similarity to the Bloomsbury Group, and one can—just—see the resemblances: the same backscratching and maverick sexuality, the same guest-appearances in each other's novels, with the astringent Burroughs as Virginia Woolf, perhaps, Kerouac as E.M. Forster and Ginsberg as Vanessa Bell . . .

One member of the circle was a bright young Barnard girl called Joan Adams, a benzedrine addict who was to become Burroughs's common-law wife and whom he tragically shot dead a few years later while playing William Tell at their house in Mexico. Ted Morgan convincingly suggests that her death, and Burroughs's grief, unlocked his literary vocation, his self-disgust coinciding with his sense of alienation from American society.

Driven by his addiction, he landed in Tangier, where "the days slid by, strung on a syringe with a long thread of blood . . ." But Tangier, Burroughs realized, might serve as the model for a novel, an "Interzone" or limbo where anyone could act out his most extreme fantasies. Even before the book was written, Jack Kerouac had provided the title: *The Naked Lunch* (the addict's fix, or the rush of pure sensation).

The sections were sent in random batches to the Paris printer, but the sequence seemed to have a logic of its own. Celebrity and controversy followed its publication, but Burroughs has for the most part spent the later years working quietly on the long series of novels that show his gift for humour and character undimmed, and constitute one of the most remarkable achievements of modern fiction, composed against the greatest conceivable odds.

CHAINSAW BIOMASSACRE IN GLORIOUS HOROSCOPE

Nancy Reagan: The Unauthorized Biography by Kitty Kelley

Guardian (April 25, 1991)

But why didn't the astrologers see this coming? The sunsets above Mulholland Drive must be an even more electric pink these days as the whole of Bel Air blushes for Nancy. By now everyone knows about her White House affair with Frank Sinatra, her legendary meanness as she recycled unwanted presents, her reckless spending of the taxpayer's money and Imelda Marcos-sized extravagance on designer clothes, her chilling relationships with her own children during the ruthless climb to success and, most damning of all, the astrologers who decided the dates of international conferences and determined those "bad" days when Ronnie was not allowed to leave the White House at all.

Kitty Kelley is an exponent of the chain-saw school of biography, and through the blizzard of sawdust it is hard to make out the real woman within this devastating portrait. But the real was always a doubtful commodity in the case of the Reagans—so much of the President's image was manufactured, and so self-deluding his own notions of the world as he confused reality with the half-remembered movies of his youth, that it scarcely matters if the facts in this biography are true or not.

Observers of the Reagans often commented on "the gaze," the look of rapt attention that Nancy turned upon the President whenever he spoke in public, but masks of various kinds had long been used by Nancy to screen her from anything she preferred to forget. Huge sections of her past had been freeze-dried and hidden away in a dark locker of her mind, never to be opened again.

The daughter of an ambitious repertory actress and a failed car salesman—whom Nancy claimed to have been a Princeton graduate—she was brought up during her early childhood by her aunt and uncle when her parents divorced, a period of forced separation that seems to have numbed her for ever. In later life Nancy never contacted her natural father, transferring all her affection to Dr Loyal Davis, a taciturn Chicago neurosurgeon whom her mother married when her career had ebbed.

This ultra-right wing and viciously racist man—he could never bring himself even to utter the word Jew—was later credited with shaping Ronald Reagan's political world-view and transforming him from a Democrat into a deep-blue Republican. Dr Davis had treated Spencer Tracy's crippled son, and after graduating from college the aspiring actress Nancy Davis (she had forced through her legal adoption against the wishes of her reluctant step-father while still a teenager) set off for Hollywood and an MGM screen test arranged by Tracy.

Always rather old-fashioned, Nancy chose a traditional route to launch her career, opting for the casting couch when she began a long affair with Benny Thau, the MGM executive in charge of casting. A number of undistinguished films followed, in which she tended to play plucky housewives in maternity smocks, while off the set she enjoyed affairs with a succession of Hollywood's leading men, among them Robert Walker and Peter Lawford, who particularly prized her talents for oral sex.

But destiny finally dialled in the shape of another fading B-actor with an unhappy childhood, the president of the Screen Actors Guild, Ronald Reagan. Soon Hollywood was behind them, as the Reagans set their eyes on the governorship of California and, beyond that, the leading roles in the ultimate movie of them all, the presidency of the United States, in which he would star and she would direct, with a supporting cast of European monarchs, Russian statesmen and California millionaires.

Reading this wonderfully sleazy account of the Reagans' rise to power, of their relentless ambition and ruthless social climbing, one is still surprised by the confidence with which American politicians set about exploiting the fruits of office. Dissatisfied with the Sacramento governor's mansion, Nancy ordered another, a $1.4 million monstrosity that later stood empty for ten years. Once in the White House she began to amass a vast wardrobe of couture gowns and furs, all on indefinite "loan" until the Internal Revenue Service panicked her into returning them.

Tactlessly, she announced the purchase of a $200,000 china set on the same day that the President cut school lunches and declared that ketchup would be counted as a vegetable in the federally subsidized programme. She recycled inferior presents, and accidentally sent a gift-wrapped birthday present to her grandson of the teddy bear he had left in the White House. At the same time, Nancy's ruthlessness extended to herself. On hearing that she had a cancerous breast nodule, she demanded a total mastectomy against the advice of her doctors. But as one of the surgeons commented, the Reagans were not afraid of the knife. "Both have had numerous facelifts. From the scars behind his ears, I'd say the President has had two lifts, and she's probably had three or four."

Reagan's presidency was a mystery to Europeans, though Americans were happy to see this amiable if goofy former sportscaster on their TV screens rather than the moralizing Carter, and took him much more easily in their stride. But how could a man so intellectually third-rate, an empty stage-set of a personality across which moved cartoon figures, dragon ladies and demons of the evil empire, ever have become President of the world's most powerful nation? Was the image everything now, and who would be next—Colonel Sanders, Jimmy Osmond, Donald Duck? Is the USA so strong and so soundly constituted, so effectively ruled by its great bureaucracies, that politics and the presidency are an entertaining irrelevancy?

But the dream buckled with the Irangate-Contra affair and the revelation that summit meetings with Gorbachev were scheduled by Nancy and her $3,000-a-month astrologer. Since then the grey men have moved in again, led by George Bush ("Whiney" to Mrs Reagan). But perhaps the real lesson of the Reagan presidency is the sinister example he offers to future film actors and media manipulators with presidential ambitions and all too clearly defined ideas, and every intention of producing a thousand-year movie out of them.

SERMONS FROM THE MOUNT

Fates Worse Than Death by Kurt Vonnegut

Sunday Times (November 10, 1991)

Novelists are not the nicest people. Touchy, unloved and aware that the novel's greatest days lie back in the age of steam, we occupy a rung on the ladder of likeability somewhere between tax inspectors and immigration officials, with whom all too many of us share an unworthy interest in money and social origins.

The one great exception is Kurt Vonnegut, whose sheer amiability could light up all the cathedrals in America—where, in fact, many of the homilies and lay sermons that make up this collection were originally delivered. Vonnegut's heart, by now a prized American totem, is at least as big as Mount Rushmore, and in his latest photographs he looks as if he is already up there, a huge man, craggy and serene, slightly eroded by the winds of fate, but admired for his rugged kindliness.

Reading these essays and speech-day addresses, one senses that Vonnegut, against all the odds, has forgiven us everything. Only plague, famine and Richard Nixon seem to lie beyond the reach of his vast compassion. He rambles away in his affable, cracker-barrel fashion, intoning his trademark "so it goes," spinning a cocoon of the sweetest sugar around our failings and foibles. Yet all this sentimentality is surprisingly bracing—it's a challenge in itself to find someone who has looked the world straight in the eye and never flinched.

Is it an act? Or, at least, a desperate stratagem that the young Vonnegut devised after witnessing the destruction of Dresden? "I didn't give a damn about Dresden," he remarks here. "The fire-bombing of Dresden explains absolutely nothing about what I write and what I am." But this is scarcely borne out by his endless references to Dresden and his obvious qualms over his German ancestry, a sense of unease that I suspect is the main engine of his imagination.

For a sometime science-fiction writer whose subject was the future, Vonnegut is unusually obsessed with his own past. He talks frankly about his Indianapolis childhood, marred by his unhappy father, who eventually killed himself, and by his mother, who loathed her husband and later became insane. A self-described depressive from a family of depressives, Vonnegut concludes that "you cannot be a good writer of serious fiction if you are not depressed."

Fortunately for his readers, he began his career on a cheerier note. He comments that American humorists tend to become unfunny pessimists if they live past a certain age, which he estimates to be sixty-three for men and twenty-nine for women, though the reverse seems true to me— Imelda Marcos and Vanessa Redgrave have yet to reach their hilarious prime, while Vonnegut, now sixty-eight, is droller than ever.

His early sf novels, *Player Piano* and *The Sirens of Titan*, are far less sentimental than his later work, and are filled with irony and black humour, though in *God Bless You, Mr Rosewater* a woozy bonhomie was already breaking through. Vonnegut's alter ego, Kilgore Trout, addresses his fellow American sf writers with the resonant words, "I love you sons of bitches," a generous tribute to one of the most mentally shuttered groups in existence.

With *Slaughterhouse Five*, based in part on his wartime experiences as a prisoner of war in Dresden, Vonnegut broke away from sf into the mainstream novel and, his greatest test, international celebrity. Success often destroys American writers, or at least derails them—Hemingway, Kerouac and Truman Capote never lived up to the popular images of themselves in a way difficult to grasp on this side of the Atlantic. Americans may not read but, like the French, they take books and writers seriously, whereas the British view their writers in a vaguely adversarial way and success usually comes with a live round still in the chamber.

One feels that for Americans fame is always unexpected, whereas British writers have thought of nothing else from the first rejection slip, like people I have known whose choice of Desert Island Discs has been fixed for twenty years before the producer's telephone call. Anyone who has done the classic book-promotional tour of American cities, and stood in those vast shopping malls in the anonymous suburbs of Chicago or Seattle, has sensed the planetary loneliness of America and wondered how one would then cope with success, an even more demanding challenge than failure.

Vonnegut's sensible and savvy response was to become his country's itinerant preacher and pin-pricker, dispensing folksy wisdom along with a strong dose of purgative. As in these lectures, he mixes fortune-cookie philosophizing with acid satire. God, or at least our notions of God, he finds a constant provocation. "The more violent picture of Him you create, the better you'll do . . . any God you create is going to be up against Miami Vice and Clint Eastwood and Sylvester Stallone. And stay clear of the Ten Commandments—those things are booby-trapped."

He scorns people who get divorced because they no longer love each other. "That is like trading in a car because the ash-trays are full." Or is it because the battery is flat, or the CD player has been stolen? Either way, Vonnegut insists that life is unserious. However, he himself has a long memory for a slight—after Salman Rushdie's hostile review of *Hocus Pocus*, he writes: "I was so upset I considered putting a contract out on him," an example of mafia humour at its most awesome.

Objecting to the line in the requiem mass, "let light perpetual shine upon you," he visualizes his dead sister trying to fall asleep in her grave with the lights on, and devises a rival mass with the words, "Let not light disturb their sleep," which a composer friend sets to music. Some time after its Buffalo premiere Vonnegut's wife bumps into Andrew Lloyd Webber, and informs him that her husband has also written a requiem, to which Lloyd Webber, sensing that he has started a fad, retorts with the best line in this book: "I know. *Every*body is writing requiems . . ."

RITUALS OF A SKINNY DIPPER

Haunts of the Black Masseur: The Swimmer as Hero by Charles Sprawson

Daily Telegraph (July 4, 1992)

I have always wanted to swim across the Styx—an absurd ambition, since this is one river with a punctual ferry service. But long-distance swimming, however dangerous, does cast a potent spell, as Charles Sprawson makes clear in this fascinating book. Part social and cultural history, and part personal credo, *Haunts of the Black Masseur* is an exhilarating plunge into some of the deepest pools inside our heads.

For George Mallory, who vanished somewhere near the summit of Everest, swimming was an emotional and spiritual necessity, and on his ascents of Everest he bathed in the Kashmiri streams, stripping off his costume in some kind of self-cleansing homage to the great stone god of the mountain. Nakedness, as any skinny-dipper knows, deliciously increases the sensuality of swimming. Like shaving the legs, which Australian swimmers introduced in the 1950s, it also serves a practical purpose, knocking minutes off longer-distance times. Dawn Fraser maintained that she could have broken every record if she had been allowed to swim naked, and why not, I eagerly agree. Given that the Olympics are well on the way to becoming a contest of "our steroids versus their steroids," it seems a pleasant bonus if the spectator's eye has something more attractive to fix itself upon than the flickering microseconds.

Besides, as Sprawson points out, nudity originated in the Greek Olympics. Water, for the Greeks, possessed magical and mysterious properties, and for the Homeric heroes ritual bathing made them resemble gods. Virginia Woolf swam naked with Rupert Brooke, and one can scarcely imagine anything more chaste or, in its eerie way, so intriguing.

Something of this search for purity, coupled with the meditative state of mind induced by solitary swimming, seems to have infused the attitudes of English swimmers in the nineteenth century, when they were widely considered to be the best in the world. The most notable of all was

Captain Webb, who became a national hero after swimming the Channel in 1875 (an American had done so first, but with a rubber suit and paddle, turning himself into a one-man dinghy). Webb, exhausted by immense exhibition races, and desperately short of money for his family, died below Niagara Falls in the ferocious whirlpool that had inspired the "Maelstrom" of Edgar Allan Poe, himself a devotee of long and mysterious river-swims.

The pre-eminent romantic swimmer was Byron, who took greater pride in having swum the Hellespont than in his poetry. Sprawson claims that almost all the great compulsive swimmers were, like Byron, strongly attached to their mothers and alienated from their fathers. But Sprawson's own motives for swimming the Hellespont, where he was nearly run down by a Russian tanker, belong more in the realm of hero-worship, and he has travelled the world searching for the swimming pools frequented by his idols. He swam in the slime-filled pool of Tennessee Williams's deserted Key West house, and in the marble baths of the New Orleans Athletic Club, after which he was painfully massaged by an attendant who might have been the sinister Black Masseur of the Williams short story.

However, he failed to swim the Tagus, another of Byron's triumphs (the river police picked him up halfway across and told him he needed a permit), and never seems to have thought of the Styx. Roaming around Greece some years ago, I tracked the Styx down to the northern Peloponnese, where it is reached by a nerve-wrenching rack-and-pinion railway. I was tempted, but my guide book warned that its waters were "cold and treacherous." To my everlasting regret, I decided to wait for the ferry.

WAS THE HOLOCAUST SCRIPTED BY THIS MAN?

Marquis de Sade: A Biography by Maurice Lever

Daily Telegraph (September 26, 1993)

The whip whistles through almost every page of this bracing biography, against a background of the heaviest breathing since Bram Stoker's *Dracula*. The Marquis de Sade is the spectre at the feast of European letters, the prodigal son invited in from the cold only to leave footprints of human blood on the welcome-mat. Coping with his wayward genius is like digesting the news that a distant relative ran the torture chambers in a death camp. Do his warped genes, these demented dreams of sodomy and the lash, also thread themselves through our lives?

"Should we burn Sade?" asked a worried Simone de Beauvoir during the post-war reassessment of Sade. I suspect that the jury will always be out, unable to weigh his deviant imagination against the countless massacres of our century. Sade's novels have been the pillow-books of too many serial killers for comfort, but the "divine Marquis" refuses to go away, and may well have an important message for us.

Almost forgotten during the nineteenth century, Sade was rediscovered in the 1930s after the publication of his lost masterpiece, *The 120 Days of Sodom*. The surrealists embraced him eagerly, hailing him as a precursor of Freud who revealed the infinite perversity of the human mind. Others saw him as a political revolutionary, the ultimate rebel against the bourgeois order, constructing a self-sufficient anti-society from his elaborate hierarchies of torturers and willing victims. But the horrors of the Third Reich shut the surrealists up for good and forced even Sade's keenest admirers to wonder if his psychopathic imagination had paved the way for Hitler and helped to write the script of the Holocaust.

Both his writings and sexual behaviour led to Sade's imprisonment for decades in the Bastille and the Charenton asylum. Yet, as Maurice Lever points out in his scrupulously neutral biography, Sade's brutal treatment of prostitutes and peasant girls during his sexual games was commonplace among the aristocracy of his day. What condemned him was his refusal to disavow himself.

Lever comments that Sade's early life contains all the ingredients of his novels. At the age of four he was taken from his mother, who immured herself in a convent, and was brought up by his uncle, a libertine priest, in a gloomy palace surrounded by debauched women. Sade developed what Lever terms a negative Oedipus complex, forming an alliance with his adulterous father and dreaming of the cruellest revenges on his absent mother. He took a long-suffering wife, Renee-Pelagie de Montreuil, who helped him to stage his orgies, but his devotion to the whip led his strong-willed mother-in-law, known as la Presidente, to have him committed to prison, where he remained for thirteen years until the Revolution.

Prison only spurred Sade's sexual imagination, and in the Bastille he produced his greatest work, *The 120 Days of Sodom*, penned in microscopic handwriting on a strip of paper forty feet long. Sade harangued the insurgent crowds from his cell window, using as a megaphone the funnel with which he emptied his chamber-pot into the moat—a perfect example of the medium fitting the message—and he was moved from the Bastille a few days before its fall. He was heartbroken over his lost manuscript, though it surfaced more than a century later and was first published by a German psychiatrist.

Freed by the Revolution, Sade became a judge on a popular tribunal, but the guillotine sickened him and he began a second career as a playwright. Condemned by Napoleon for immorality, he was interned in the Charenton asylum, where he staged plays with a cast of lunatics. Fashionable audiences flocked from Paris, a foretaste of the uneasy admirers his writings would attract in the twentieth century.

Meanwhile his sinister presence endures, subverting any wistful notions of literature as a moral repository and testing-ground. During his days as a journalist, Joseph Goebbels wrote a third-rate novel, *Michael*, which can be dismissed out of hand and never compels us to reconsider the career of the Nazi leader and the cruelties he helped to perpetrate. The problem posed by Sade is that *The 120 Days of Sodom* is a masterpiece, a black cathedral of a book forcing us to realize that the imagination transcends morality and that anything can serve as the raw material for a compelling work of art, even those whistling whips and flowering bruises.

LET THE WOMEN HAVE LIPSTICK AND HIGH HEELS

Deng Xiaoping and the Making of Modern China by Richard Evans

Daily Telegraph (October 30, 1993)

Deng Xiaoping is widely rumoured to be dying, but it would be a mistake to write off this feisty little man before the grave is cold, as Sir Richard Evans, Our Man in Peking from 1984 to 1988, makes clear in his shrewd biography of the most important Chinese leader since Mao Zedong. It could be said of China that for forty centuries nothing happened and, then, in a single century, everything happened. The feudal agricultural society that had moved through the millennia at an almost geological pace burst into the modern age with the overthrow of the Manchu dynasty in 1912. A new China soon emerged—urban, industrializing and, in due course, fiercely Marxist—and with it arrived a new kind of Chinese man and woman, as many Westerners found to their cost.

In 1949 my father was trapped in Shanghai after the communist takeover and, like all old China hands, confidently expected the ideological purity of the invading armies to last as long as it took them to climb down from their tanks and stroll into the bars and brothels of downtown Shanghai. In fact, their puritan zeal only intensified, and my father found himself on trial, accused of various anti-communist misdeeds. Fortunately he was able to quote enough Marx and Engels to convince the magistrates that he had seen the error of his ways. He was acquitted and a year later escaped to Hong Kong, aware that the old China of "squeeze" and corruption had gone for good, a transformation that I still find hard to grasp and which was due in large part to men such as Deng Xiaoping.

Deng was born in 1904, the son of a prosperous landowner in Sichuan province, and at the age of sixteen travelled to France as a worker-student, where he laboured at a series of menial jobs, developed a lifelong taste for croissants and met Zhou Enlai, who introduced him to Marxism. After five years he returned to China a committed communist. He survived the Long March in 1934–5, served as a political commissar during the war against Japan, and after the defeat of Chiang Kai-shek helped to drive through the programme of land reform, when hundreds of thousands of landowners and rich peasants were killed in what Sir Richard calls the greatest social revolution in the history of the world. These numberless deaths, like those in Tiananmen Square in 1989, cast a shadow over this apparently likeable man, whose talent for friendship frequently saved his life.

As Sir Richard points out, Deng's years in France inoculated him against the sinocentrism that marred the vision of Mao Zedong, who never went abroad except to visit Russia. Early in his career Deng realized that China could develop into a modern state only if it was willing to learn from the outside world.

In 1958 he spoke publicly of the day when Chinese women would be able to afford lipstick and high-heeled shoes, a more revolutionary notion, given the extreme poverty of the peasant population, than anything dreamed of in the Communist manifesto. Inevitably he became a victim of the Cultural Revolution, and was persecuted by Mao's vicious wife, Jiang Qing, and the Red Guards, who accused Deng of being a "capitalist-roader" and humiliated him by forcing him to kneel in the "airplane" position with his arms outstretched behind his back.

After years of exile in a remote province Deng was restored to office upon Mao's death in 1976. As China's leader during the 1980s he launched the immense programme of economic and political reform that opened the country to foreign investment and transformed its landscape in a way that must have dismayed the old guard.

In 1991, during a visit to Shanghai, I had dinner in the restaurant on the top floor of the television tower with the affable director of the TV foreign news service. He asked me what I thought of the new Shanghai. Looking out at the forest of skyscrapers that reared from the crumbling streets of the old International Settlement, I tactlessly said that it reminded me of New York. He stared at me in a deeply depressed way, slowly exhaling the cigarette smoke from his lungs, as if the same thought had crossed his own mind more than once.

Summarizing Deng's achievements, Sir Richard speculates about the future facing China after his departure. He predicts that the present collective leadership will give way to the rule of one dominant figure, in accord with Chinese tradition, and that China's educated class, despite its appetite for social and cultural freedom, will doubt the wisdom of abandoning one-party rule. This combination, it seems to me, of a paramount leader, one-party rule and phenomenal economic and industrial growth (a yearly average of 10 per cent, a potential for mischief-making on a global scale that thankfully was denied to Mao) will make China's future a matter of vital concern to all of us, and we can only hope that the country is led by someone with the hard-headed pragmatism displayed by Deng Xiaoping.

MOUSE THAT BORES

Walt Disney: Hollywood's Dark Prince by Marc Eliot

Daily Telegraph (June 11, 1994)

"Gee, this will make Beethoven!" Walt Disney exclaimed on first seeing the Pastoral Symphony sequence in *Fantasia*. However strange it now seems, this touching faith in the power of his animated films was more than justified during Disney's long reign as king of the cartoons. Apart from Coca-Cola, another modern myth, Walt Disney must be the most famous brand name of the 20th century, stamped on to the happiest memories of countless childhoods.

All the same, is the Disney magic at last losing its grip on the imagination of the young? Euro Disney, the troubled theme-park near Paris, was described by a disgruntled French critic as a cultural Chernobyl, though perhaps a cultural Stalingrad would be closer to the truth, the battleground where the relentless advance of American popular culture was at last stopped and turned. I suspect that Mickey Mouse and Donald Duck no longer satisfy today's children, whose retinas flicker with the electronic phantoms of the arcade video games. Super Nintendo rules, and the Disney empire now merchandizes nostalgia.

Despite the lovable nature of the creatures in the Disney pantheon, their creator was a darker and more ambiguous figure, as Marc Eliot reveals in his merciless biography. Far from being the world's favourite uncle, Disney was a vicious anti-Semite and hater of communists, who for 25 years was a Hollywood spy for J. Edgar Hoover's FBI. Eliot describes Disney's brutal childhood, his obsessive hand-washing and heavy drinking, and his uncertainty about his own parentage. The theme of abandonment that runs through so many Disney films may have been rooted in his sense of his own lost childhood.

Eliot traces Disney's ancestry to Jean-Christophe d'Isigny, named after the village in Normandy, who remained in England after the Norman conquest and anglicized his name. His descendants emigrated to the United States in the nineteenth century, and Walt's father was an unsuccessful carpenter and farmer, a violent and alcoholic man who thrashed and terrorized his son.

Fortunately the boy showed an early talent for drawing, and in due course became a successful commercial artist, making animated films of Little Red Riding-Hood and Puss in Boots. A business partner named Ub Iwerks created the famous mouse, but it was Disney's entrepreneurial genius that transformed a few sketches into a star greater than any other in Hollywood.

Paying starvation wages to animators, Disney oversaw production of the first feature-length cartoon films, *Snow White* and *Pinocchio*. By the 1930s he was world famous, meeting the Pope, Mussolini and H. G. Wells. He accepted a special medal from the League of Nations using the voice of Mickey Mouse.

Despite his enormous success, Disney was haunted by a sense of personal failure, suspecting that he was illegitimate and that his real mother was an impoverished immigrant from Mojacar in southern Spain whom his father had met in California during his search for work. Thanks to his friendship with Hoover, teams of FBI agents frequently visited Mojacar in an effort to trace Disney's parentage. But when Disney died at the height of his fame, he was still unsure of his true mother and father—the creator of the world's greatest dreams of childhood who had never really known his own.

THE PUCCINI OF CINEMA GROWS UP

Steven Spielberg: The Unauthorised Biography by John Baxter

Independent (June 15, 1996)

Steven Spielberg poses a huge problem for film critics and cineastes. Despite his immense success, with several of the highest-grossing films of all time, his momentous themes and mastery of the film medium, they remain convinced that a deep flaw runs through his entire work. This flaw seems easy to define—a compound of sentimentality, over-flamboyant spectacle, and too close a reliance on the rhythms and style of the comic strip.

Yet the films endure, and clearly grow richer with age, vehicles of breathtaking power and glamour that cruise effortlessly through our imaginations like a fleet of gold Cadillacs. The qualities that the cineastes see as weaknesses I see as Spielberg's strengths, and as the reason why he is one of today's most important film-makers, the producer-director who single-handedly saved the Hollywood film when it threatened to founder in the Seventies.

Besides, sentimentality and spectacle have a valuable place in the arts, as in the operas of Puccini—though there are puritans who feel slightly queasy at the thought of *Tosca* and *Madama Butterfly*. In many ways Spielberg is the Puccini of cinema, one of the highest compliments I can pay.

He may be a little too sweet for some tastes, but what melodies, what orchestrations, what cathedrals of emotion . . .

Spielberg's problem with the critics, I suspect, is that he has always been too American, dedicated to the values of a provincial America—in fact its heartland and ideological engine—they preferred to ignore. A few years ago, at the Hollywood premiere of *Empire of the Sun*, I was amazed by the hostility that American journalists showed towards Spielberg. One even asked me why I had allowed him to film my novel—one of the strangest questions ever put to me, and with a scarcely concealed sub-text.

These American journalists came from New York, Boston and Chicago, while Spielberg's roots seemed to be set deep in a Norman Rockwell suburbia of soda fountains, beauty parlours and daytime TV, a Fifties vision of the good life still aspired to by most of the planet's population, but one which makes Spielberg's metropolitan critics profoundly uneasy. Perhaps they realise that too much of American culture is based on the sentimentality, naivety and showy self-confidence that they recognise in the mirror of Spielberg's films.

Curiously, Spielberg's childhood was not especially happy. His parents were divorced in his teens, and a series of wrenching family moves led him from small-town New Jersey to an Arizona suburb, and eventually to anti-Semitic northern California. He was gawky and unpopular, but his father's 8mm Kodak camera saved him.

At the age of 14 he made *Escape to Nowhere*, a 40-minute war film for which he recruited his mother, sisters and friends, and followed this, while still at school, with *Firelight*, a full-length science fiction feature that his father screened to a paying audience in a specially rented cinema. Later, while nominally a student at a Long Beach college, he spent his spare time haunting Universal Studios, and his sheer persistence led to a contract as a director of TV movies.

With *Duel*, one of the best-ever made-for-TV films, he displayed most of the qualities present in his subsequent blockbusters: the absence of stars or glamorous roles, the suburban characters and locations, the down-playing of dialogue and dramatic complexity in favour of a relentless, through-the-windscreen view of the road ahead.

It is, however, Spielberg's apparent shortcomings that most concern John Baxter in his absorbing book, *Steven Spielberg: The Unauthorised Biography*. They seem to give him a nagging headache that one can sense on almost every page. Baxter is a shrewd, witty and very readable writer who has produced biographies of Fellini and Ken Russell, directors with something of Spielberg's bravura talents.

But Baxter is clearly uncomfortable with Spielberg, who unsettles him by thwarting his best and worst expectations. Baxter points out that, by the late 1970s, *Jaws* and *Close Encounters of the Third Kind* had brought Spielberg a fortune of some $200 million. But while traditional Hollywood moguls rolled around in stretch limos and dined at Ma Maison and Spago, Spielberg lived frugally, drove a rented car and dressed in jeans and trainers.

In Baxter's eyes, this behaviour merely reveals Spielberg's perpetual adolescence. I would compliment him on his indifference to convention as he pursued his unique vision. Baxter repeatedly emphasises that the imaginations of Spielberg and the Movie Brats—Lucas, Scorsese, Coppola et al.—were entirely fed by the films they had seen in childhood, an accusation he wouldn't dream of levelling at, for example, a novelist who had passed his formative years in the library.

Film, for most of this century, has been a far more serious medium than the novel, and the Movie Brats and their encyclopaedic knowledge of film from the Lumiere brothers onwards compare favourably with today's film students, for whom the original *Die Hard* and *Terminator* represent all the history they feel they need to know.

Baxter quotes an unnamed colleague who says of Spielberg: "He has all the virtues—and the defects—of a 16-year-old," and refers to him as the Peter Pan of movies, the Boy Who Wouldn't Grow Up, who preserved himself in an artificial adolescence. But boys who won't grow up soon find themselves in remedial institutions, and do not control the giant entertainment and media conglomerates that increasingly set the pace of the world's economies.

The Spielberg I first met on the *Empire of the Sun* film set in 1987 struck me as highly intelligent, hard-minded and wholly adult, a visionary who accepted that the age of sophistication is over and that the benevolent technologies that govern our lives are happy to welcome the era of the naive. Throughout his films Spielberg is using the global entertainment culture to explore those constants of our everyday lives that we all take for granted—the wonder of existence, the magic of space-time, and the miracle of consciousness and childhood.

·Were it not for Spielberg's high-concept cinema and the huge audiences and revenues he attracted, the Hollywood of the 1980s would have been stranded among the disappointments of late Kubrick, Coppola and Cimino, sustained by little more than the empty *Star Wars* spectacles of George Lucas. The resistance to Spielberg expressed by Hollywood's old guard only confirms their grudging debt to him. Given that Hollywood is a company town, and that in company towns everyone respects the man who signs the cheques, it is significant that Spielberg had to wait until *Schindler's List*—the least Spielbergian of his films—before receiving his first Oscar.

WEIRDLY WISE

Lynch on Lynch, edited by Chris Rodley

Observer (August 17, 1997)

Psychopathology is fun. Or so one assumes after a visit to the neighbourhood family cineplex. Night after night, our movie theatres are stalked by rapists, sadists and serial killers. Unending gunfire and exploding bombs assault the sound-proofing, as Buicks and Chevrolets cartwheel through the air in slow motion before nesting themselves in the roofs of buses and fire engines. All the while, the rising body count stacks the corpses half-way up the screen. As the lights come on, one almost expects to see pools of blood soaking the carpet of the orchestra pit. But they call it entertainment.

Trying to analyse the mind-set of the huge public that seems so soothed by these collective hallucinations is a challenging task, given that the audience's pleasure in violence and traumatised sex is carefully fenced by a set of reassuring moral frameworks. Bruce Willis, who has done for the dirty singlet what Brigitte Bardot did for the bikini, can behave as brutally as the bad guys in the *Die Hard* series because we know that he works for the NYPD. Any alarm we feel at Arnold Schwarzenegger's Panzer Corps approach to human relationships is laughed away by the grotesque musculature that reminds us of the comic-book super-heroes we pored over in the comforting safety of the nursery.

But woe betide any film-maker, like David Lynch or Cronenberg, who decides to take as read the cinema goer's relish for the deviant and psychopathic, and then sets out to construct a picture of who we really are. Novelists, poets and painters have openly explored the connections between love, eroticism and death for at least 200 years, but the pornographic violence of some Hollywood films is carefully sealed within a set of entertainment conventions, and shielded by the lack of awareness from the powers-that-be of exactly what the mass audiences are enjoying in their local Odeons.

During their long struggle with Westminster Council, the producers of *Crash* were astonished by the ignorance of the elderly members of the licensing committee about the real nature of the films they rubber stamped into the capital's prime venues. Many had not seen a film for years, and seemed to imagine that the West End's theatres were still screening candied treats like *Chariots of Fire* and *Four Weddings and a Funeral*.

At the same time, the long-established conventions of the entertainment film guard us from having to look too closely into the sources of our own pleasures. Asked for her favourite Christmas TV viewing, Virginia Bottomley, the then Heritage Secretary who had virtually called for local authorities to ban *Crash*, selected Hitchcock's *Dial M for Murder*, a sleek tale of a husband who blackmails a college acquaintance to murder his wife and demonstrates in chilling detail how the strangling should take place. As the would-be assassin attempts to garrote her with a scarf, she stabs him with a large pair of scissors. With an agonised scream, he falls backward to the floor, impaling himself on the blade in a riveting close-up generally accepted as a tour de force of cinema. A second strangling is threatened when the wife is sentenced to death by hanging.

Quite why the former Heritage Secretary found this gruesome and brutal film (which I too thoroughly enjoyed) so suitable for yuletide viewing she never explained. Perhaps she identified herself with that other prissy blonde, Grace Kelly, who played the wife. For all I know, in future years she may recommend David Lynch's *Blue Velvet*, a shocker when it first appeared in 1986 that other zealots before her tried to ban.

Blue Velvet was, for me, the best film of the Eighties, a surreal, voyeuristic and subversive masterpiece of cinema that has lost none of its power to startle, and still ensnares the audience into complicity with its masochistic weirdness. As one of its technicians commented during the shooting, *Blue Velvet* is where Norman Rockwell meets Hieronymus Bosch. The film holds up despite Lynch's uneven career before and since, and is all the more impressive for being made within the restraints of the Hollywood system.

But Lynch's strange eye has always outstared the expectations of studio bosses and film distributors, not to mention the stunned audiences. *Lynch on Lynch*, a book-length transcript of a conversation with Chris Rodley, an astute and well-informed film specialist, is fascinating for the light it throws on one of the most quirky and mysterious of all Hollywood directors.

From the start, Lynch makes clear the childhood sources of his calm and idiosyncratic view of the world. The son of a forestry scientist who toured the American north west—which seems to explain the countless and otherwise baffling references to lumber in his films—Lynch recalls the intense oddness about everything that he felt as a child. "Something as simple as a tree doesn't make sense . . . we think we understand the rules when we become adults, but what we've really experienced is a narrowing of the imagination." He adds: "I feel between nine and 17 most of the time, and sometimes around six! Darkness has crept in since then."

But the first films threw a strong if eerie light on to the shadows. *Eraserhead* is a classic of underground cinema, a compendium of unrelated events and characters that makes no sense on the surface but is clearly held together by a powerful set of phobias. Lynch's great strength is that he makes no attempt to explain or rationalise them. The film was five years in the making, financed by whatever modest funds Lynch would put together from jobs that included a *Wall Street Journal* paperround. One guesses that the actors and technicians stayed faithful to the project because they were gripped by Lynch's unflinchingly odd imagination.

The Elephant Man followed, perhaps a move in the wrong direction, since the deformity of the central character pre-empted any comparable response from Lynch. But it led to the big-budget sci-fi film *Dune*, based on one of the genre's most portentous novels and a failure at the box office, though enough of an event to prompt its producer, Dino De Laurentiis, to fund *Blue Velvet*.

"*Blue Velvet* is a very American movie," Lynch comments in the most revealing section of the interview. "There's a very innocent, naive quality to life, and there's a horror and a sickness as well."

Everything is ambiguous in the film. "Are you a detective or a pervert?" Laura Dern's character asks her boyfriend as he plans to break into the apartment of the deranged nightclub singer. The question lies at the heart of Lynch's films. No moral frameworks enclose his characters, and their psychopathy and deviance are accepted for what they are, like character quirks in an old friend. But on this base Lynch builds the haunted house of his imagination, part autopsy room into the human soul and part horror museum of the banal. Together they resemble everyday reality with the sound turned down and a sinister, barely audible dialogue that appears in some oblique way to refer to ourselves.

The influence of *Blue Velvet*, and of the TV series *Twin Peaks*, has been enormous, on *Wild Palms*, *American Gothic* and *The X-Files*. I hope he returns to form with his new film *Lost Highway*. Somewhere inside his head, one senses, Francis Bacon is repainting the Bates Motel.

RETURN OF THE FUTURE

The First Dozen Titles in the Predictions Series Published by Phoenix House, London

Sunday Telegraph (December 28, 1997)

So, after decades of neglect, the future once again has a future. If Peter Mandelson is still wondering how to turn his empty Millennium Dome into a 21st-century version of Ali Baba's cave, he should supply his design teams with unlimited copies of the first batch in the Predictions series of paperbacks, each essay a high-focus crystal ball that gives us a startling glimpse into the future hurtling towards us.

Anyone old enough to have been alive in the 1930s will easily recall the intense excitement about the future that filled newspapers and magazines. Every record-breaking train or plane, every high-altitude balloon or deep-sea bathysphere, seemed to be the harbinger of a better and more exhilarating world. All this ended with the Second World War, snuffed out by the threat of nuclear obliteration and the growing sense that the future was where most of mankind's problems were waiting to ambush us.

Now, thankfully, confidence has returned, although the first people to put their heads above the parapet and peer out at the new millennium are far less starry-eyed than their '30s counterparts.

Taking the largest subject first, Felipe Fernandez-Armesto, in *Religion*, maintains that God has survived the over-hasty reports of his demise. Religions are thriving, driven by scientific progress, surprisingly, and its theories of an unintelligible cosmos. Populations dominated by the elderly will return to traditional forms of worship and reject the happy-clappy evangelist cults favoured by the young, who are themselves the product of the demographic baby-boomer blip.

In *Population*, John I. Clarke tackles one of the fears that has most pre-occupied the industrial age: that over-population will exhaust the world's resources and turn our planet into an overcrowded and steadily leaking lifeboat. During the past two centuries the world's population has grown from one billion to six, and the scientific consensus today is that the planet can support some 7.7 billion people, a total likely to be reached in the 2010s. Yet an overall fertility decline and economic growth in the developing world are already acting as a brake. I have always believed that the future will be like Milton Keynes—but perhaps the high-rise regulated paradise of Singapore is a better bet.

Climatic change poses another planetary threat. In *Climate* Andrew Goudie points out that vast changes have occurred repeatedly in the past, but for the first time human beings are themselves altering the planet's climates by changing both the gas content of the atmosphere and the Earth's vegetation cover. Global warming, so welcome a prospect to some of us, seems less likely in the long run than a prolonged period of global cooling.

A dangerously threatened species is considered by Dave Hill in *Men*. Yesterday's protector, provider and patriarch has given way to today's

increasingly hesitant and wimpish figure, tyrannised by sexual correct-
ness and unsure whether any meaningful role is left to him. Are things
as bad as this? Hill argues that, in many ways, today's young men enjoy
far more freedom than their fathers and grandfathers, but will be able to
take nothing for granted and be forced to redefine themselves in a society dominated by resurgent females, a fate that sounds suspiciously like
inventing a new sex. Perhaps I shall wait for global cooling to lower the
temperature of the debate.

One sphere in which men have always excelled is war, and in *Warfare*
Francois Heisbourg suggests that they will still be needed, but only to press
the buttons controlling an array of high-tech weapons—stealth armies,
custom-designed biological agents, and electronic "soldiers" whose targets will be rival computer networks. The greatest challenge will be the
drift of the United States into political and military isolationism, leaving
the rest of us to play our vicious computer games in the real world.

Terrorism, in the sense of subversive groups attacking innocent civilians in order to communicate a political message, may also evolve in
frightening ways, according to Conor Gearty in *Terrorism*. He believes
that even democratic governments are learning the lessons of terrorism,
and that a terrorist regime may function behind the facade of democratic
self-government, presumably in a nightmare marriage of Pol Pot and
Tony Blair.

In brief: *Europe*, by Hugh Thomas, assumes that a European monetary
union with a common currency will be established by 2005, and urges
the United Kingdom to reconsider the intellectual basis of British Atlanti-
cism. Happily, he expects the new European Union to be a success that
will inspire similar groupings worldwide, and that by 2050 the nation-
state will have vanished.

Bernard Lewis's *Middle East* considers the anti-Islam backlash that
many have foreseen, and the struggle between fundamentalism and
Western-style democracy. Two factors, water (rather than oil) and women,
whose power is slowly gaining ground, may decide between chaos
and success.

In *Crime and Punishment*, Stephen Tumin urges us to drop a purely
punitive approach and to treat prison as an active pre-release course. Robert Winston, in *Genetic Manipulation*, is keen to calm our fears of bizarre

animals and cloned Saddam Husseins, and stresses the huge medical benefits for us all. Matt Ridley, in *Disease*, suggests that, despite Aids and the new TB and malarial strains, most of the diseases we will face in the coming decades will be mild.

Lastly, to end this excellent and provocative series with a Big Bang, John Gribbin considers *Cosmology*. He predicts that a combination of Einstein's relativity theory and Darwin's natural selection applied to the creation of "baby" universes may provide the greatest revolution since Copernicus. I am happy to report that the small portion of the future that arrived while I was reading these stimulating essays seemed eminently welcoming. May the clock move on . . .

SANDS OF TIME

The Beach: The History of Paradise on Earth by Lena Lincek and Gideon Bosker

Guardian (June 26, 1998)

The beach is where the sun goes to doze and dream. Everything began there, when the first aquatic reptiles clambered on to the Palaeozoic equivalent of Copacabana and Waikiki and discovered the charms of lying around in the sun while doing absolutely nothing, a revelation that in due course dawned on the rest of us.

But if land-based life began on the beach, there were times in the recent past when it seemed that everything might also end there. Bikini Atoll, where the early atomic bombs were tested, and Eniwetok Atoll, over which the hydrogen bomb was detonated, are among the most sinister sites of the 20th-century imagination. There the human race mastered the secrets of the sun and threatened itself with a new kind of mass death.

Yet Bikini gave its name to a swimsuit: the three small triangles, a minimalist geometry of eye-catching modesty, appeared with all the startling charm of Ursula Andress on Dr No's beach, and signalled a newly confident female sexuality.

Even so, the beach might seem an odd place to choose for rest and recreation. Hot sand, studded with cigarette butts, reeking of yesterday's sun oil and, at worst, needle sharp with broken beer bottles and addicts' syringes, must be one of the least pleasant terrains on which to display the almost naked body. Sand formed by the millennial poundings of waves on rock often has a flinty sharpness, like that of some Cornish beaches, while estuarine beaches deposited by archaic rivers can have the texture of chocolate mud, as one finds along the Costa del Sol.

Coral beaches stand highest in the holiday pecking order, though the sight of people lying contentedly on mounds of dead skeletons has an ironic charm of its own. Yet the beach is the setting for most of our happiest memories, the largest sand pit in the world that children never forget, a place where, by taking off our clothes, we become invisible in the crowd. As Marshall McLuhan might have said, if the sun is the ultimate TV station, then the beach is its most popular programme, and life at a holiday resort resembles a chaotic rehearsal for the last great sitcom, a fusion of *Baywatch* and Armageddon.

The Beach: The History of Paradise on Earth, by Lena Lincek and Gideon Bosker, is a witty and entertaining account of the remarkable role this strip of sand and shingle has played in human history, and in the evolution of lifestyle, fashion and sexuality. The authors describe the beach as Nature's most potent anti-depressant, an aphrodisiac cocktail of sun and water. This inaccessible and often hostile terrain, for so long the site of conquest and exploitation, has become our planet's principal pleasure ground.

Where slaves once landed in the West Indies, shackled together after horrific voyages across the Atlantic, their descendants now heft volleyballs and skim the amiable waves on water skis. Despite the occasional squabble over a desirable poolside seat, the beach is where the human race at last manages to detribalise itself.

The greatest city of the 20th century, and the largest the world has ever known, is the linear city that stretches along the northern shores of the Mediterranean from Gibraltar to Glyfada beach outside Athens, 4,000 miles long and 400 feet deep, and with a transient summer population that numbers more than 150 million. Its endless balconies look down on a strip of hot silica that may well be the last remnant of our memory of Eden before the fall. The hotels and apartment houses stand shoulder to shoulder, and under the force of population pressures may one day coalesce. I can hear the proud boast of the Mediterranean Super-Hilton:

"Travel from Gibraltar to Athens in the air-conditioned comfort of our corridors."

The pleasures of the beach go back to Europe's earliest days. For the Greeks and Romans, bathing and the seashore played an almost spiritual role in their notion of the civilised life. Sadly, early Christians saw the pool as an opportunity for vanity and self-indulgence. Dirt was the hallmark of sanctity. But the Black Death brought home the benefits of hygiene, and by the 18th century bathing as a form of therapy had been invented by the British.

The aristocracy deserted inland spas like Bath and Harrogate for the sea-water therapy offered by Scarborough and Brighton. In the late 18th century people swam naked, sexes mixing—a happy state of affairs that ended with the Victorians, though more went on beneath the ankle-length swimming costumes than their Queen imagined. The romantic poets discovered the spiritual drama of a wave-tossed shore. Shelley spoke of swimming as a sexually tinged encounter, and Valery later expatiated upon "fornication with the waves."

Despite the best efforts of the killjoys, sex and the beach were never going to be kept apart. Taking one's clothes off set in train all manner of intriguing possibilities, and the 20th century added a third potent ingredient: the sun. In an earlier, agrarian age there was a strong class prejudice against a sunburnt skin, and fashionable beaches were a forest of parasols, tents and pavilions. But by the 1920s a tanned skin was the rage, and the more there was on show the better.

In the climate of moral relaxation that followed the Great War the swimsuit became a trail blazer of social change, reshaping more than the bodies it enclosed. Men appeared bare-chested, while women's costumes shrank ever more daringly towards the erogenous zones. By the 1950s swimsuits were a triumph of applied engineering, with gleaming elasticated fabrics, underwiring, foam rubber padding and jutting cups, and moved around the beaches like showroom Buicks.

The second world war cast an unhappy shadow over the beach, which became one of the great battlegrounds between freedom and tyranny. Even today, Utah Beach, where the Americans went ashore on D Day, presents an eerie spectacle. German blockhouses the size of parish churches tower over the waves, and the sand is still clamped around the remains of landing craft and docking gear, a scene of almost planetary loneliness.

Photographs of tanks and dead soldiers embedded in blood-stained beaches from Normandy to Iwo Jima might have killed off forever any taste for sand and sea. But nothing could hold back the public's need to shed its clothes and inhibitions. In 1964 Rudi Gernreich unveiled his topless swimsuit for women. Sadly, this never caught on, a psychosexual bridge too far.

The topless beach is now part of the holiday landscape, but strict protocols govern behaviour, and especially eye-to-nipple contact. Last summer, at La Garoupe beach on Cap d'Antibes, my sociologist's eye noticed that the arrival of any over-curious male instantly led to a general cover-up and straightening of chairs that propagated itself like a Mexican wave.

Americans have never come to grips with Mediterranean-style beaches, with their phalanxes of umbrellas and single-minded devotion to the epic task of getting a tan that will last long enough to impress the office. American beaches are either too hot, like Miami Beach, a blinding white hell that sears the retina, or too cold and windy, like Malibu and the Californian beaches. Most of the others are closely patrolled by sharks. But the deserts of the American west are the floors of fossil seas, and in some ways Las Vegas is the world's greatest seaside resort, though its sea withdrew 300 million years ago.

So many of the world's famous beaches, like Marbella, Miami and Copacabana, are artificial creations refuelled with imported sand. It may be that the future evolution of the beach will take place inland and indoors, in sports-centre aqua-environments, or in the Zen sand gardens of Tokyo department stores. As we flee from our polluted cities and countryside to the bracing sun-bath of the beach it is sobering to reflect that a mere 10-foot rise in the sea level would wipe out one of our most enduring dreams.

THEY'RE FALLING OUT OF THE SKY

The Black Box: Cockpit Voice Recorder Accounts of In-Flight Accidents, edited by Malcolm MacPherson

Daily Telegraph (August 1, 1998)

Without any doubt, this is the last book to take with you on holiday, especially if you are flying. I made the mistake of reading my copy on a trip to the Guggenheim Museum in Bilbao, a titanium-clad space-ship that seems to have crash-landed out of the sun, and on the return flight suddenly heard myself asking the stewardess where the escape chutes were stored. Until we touched down I could hear every rivet straining to keep us aloft.

The fear of a fatal air crash is still one of the deepest anxieties of our age. As Malcolm MacPherson points out in this gripping collection of cockpit recordings, air travel is the safest form of transportation, statistically safer than eating. Though what about the dangers of eating and flying simultaneously, I wondered as I tucked into my lunch tray. The combination of an altitude of 35,000 feet and a portion of plastic-wrapped veal must reduce the odds to a dead certainty.

Whatever the statistics, they clearly mean nothing to air-travellers, and completely fail to calm those primitive layers of the nervous system concerned with fear and flight. *The Black Box*, a sequel to the edition first published in 1984, is a bracing journey down all the brain's descending escalators. Aviation casualties may be rare compared with the carnage inflicted by the motor car or in shipping accidents—third-world ferries are floating mortuaries-in-waiting—but the destruction wrought by air crashes is usually devastating and final. Passengers, miraculously, do scramble free from burning wreckage, but too often nothing remains except the deep grooves left by the undercarriage stumps and a crater speckled with partly vaporised aluminum.

So what goes wrong, and why? Without the black box carried in the aircraft's tail, which records both the instrument settings and the cockpit dialogue between captain and crew, we would have little idea. The transcripts may make sombre reading, but they do provide invaluable insight into how disaster can strike this most tightly regulated form of transport. However ghoulish they seem, these recordings of the last, desperate minutes are a tribute to the courage of professional flight crews.

What stands out from the transcripts is how quietly catastrophe creeps up on its victims. A gradual fall in hydraulic pressure, an unexplained loss of fuel, a hint of smoke in a lavatory, are noted half an hour before the looming crisis. In one tragic case, where highly flammable chemicals ignited in the cargo hold and raised the temperature to 3000F, an off-duty pilot travelling as a passenger reported that the cabin floor was beginning to melt, information that the captain and co-pilot calmly noted while they concentrated on more pressing problems.

As MacPherson points out, the transcripts convey only the sketchiest impression of the atmosphere in a stricken aircraft as the captain and crew wrestle with their controls. While one crippled system collapses on another, horns blare, lights flash and recorded voices shout: "Pull up! Pull up!"

Yet no one panics. Even in the final moments, as the doomed craft heads towards the ground at 400 miles per hour, only a stoical regret is sounded, like the simple comment, "We're dead," made by the co-pilot of a Lockheed cargo plane in the seconds before the end.

The passengers' behaviour is not recorded, perhaps fortunately, although I suspect that most somehow manage to switch off their minds. I am always surprised by how few passengers listen closely to the flight attendants' demonstrations of the aircraft emergency equipment. One day, when air travel is completely safe and accidents are unknown, these displays of oxygen mask, life jacket and whistle will survive as a stylised and mysterious ritual, as formalised as the gestures of Kabuki actors—a reminder of the pioneer days when fear and danger stalked the aisles a few paces behind the drinks trolley.

REACH FOR THE SKY

Lindbergh by A. Scott Berg

Sunday Times (October 18, 1998)

Was Charles Lindbergh the last naive hero? The bravest of the brave who followed him, such as Douglas Bader and Guy Gibson, the wartime pilots, or Odette Churchill, the British secret agent, were well aware of what was waiting for them, the blizzard of cannon fire and the Gestapo truncheons. The American astronauts who first sailed the tideways of space were celebrities long before their feet left the ground, their futures tied to book deals and magazine serialisations. Today, anyone who plunges into an icy river to save a drowning dog is aware that the camcorder footage taken by a passer-by may well appear on a peak-time television programme.

But Lindbergh, the slim, solitary aviator from the Minnesota farm-
lands, seemed strangely innocent about the world around him, its hunger for heroes and latent hostility towards those it most adored. A. Scott
Berg's definitive biography brilliantly describes the strange character of
this extraordinary man. Lindbergh is the greatest biography of one of the
century's most ambiguous heroes that I have read. Rich in detail, it con-
veys the deep mystery at the heart of Lindbergh, both aviator and reluctant political figure. He retained his childlike gaze to the end of his life,
an admirable character strain that plunged him into enormous problems
when, in pre-war Nazi Germany, he began to shake the wrong hands, the
kind with blood under their fingernails.

Lindbergh's non-stop flight in 1927 from New York to Paris, the first
solo Atlantic crossing, instantly made him world famous. In many ways,
he helped create a new kind of 20th century celebrity, based on the newsreel, the mass-circulation newspaper and the short-wave radio and, in
due course, he became one of its first casualties.

When Lindbergh took off in his single-engine monoplane, the Spirit
of St Louis, from an airfield near New York he was an unknown airmail
pilot who had dropped out of the Army Air Corps. Without a radio or
navigation aids, and facing certain death if engine failure forced him to
ditch, he set out with little more than a packet of sandwiches and his
own willpower.

He arrived at Le Bourget airport 33 hours later, well ahead of his flight
plan, and modestly assumed that nobody would be there to greet him.
Then, as he taxied through the darkness, he realised that the airfield
was filled with running figures. A crowd of 150,000 surged around the
plane. As Berg comments in this gripping biography, at that moment
everything changed, for both the pilot and the planet. Souvenir hunters
began to strip the skin from the plane, screaming as they tried to seize
the exhausted pilot. One observer, the American publisher Harry Crosby,
described the stampede as the start of a new religious movement, "as if all
the hands in the world are trying to reach out and touch the new Christ,
and the new Cross is the Plane."

From then on, the painfully shy Lindbergh was an international celebrity, the admired and welcome guest of kings, presidents and prime ministers. Sadly, he never grasped the true nature of 20th-century sainthood,

and failed to realise that he not only had to be a hero, but was required to play the role convincingly in front of the public, satisfying the expectations aroused by Hollywood and the popular press.

But Lindbergh was introverted and remote, uncomfortable with crowds and eager to get away from them. He made a happy marriage to Anne Morrow, an ambassador's daughter who was as shy and reclusive as himself. Reporters stalked them constantly, and the Lindberghs retreated to a secluded house in rural New Jersey, hoping to find the solitude they needed.

Lindbergh's fame, however, came with a cruel price tag. In 1932, their baby son was kidnapped by an immigrant German carpenter, setting off a media frenzy. Thousands of crank ransom notes were sent to the Lindberghs, and politicians arrived unannounced at their house and posed beside the ladder used by the kidnapper. Astrologers and mediums described their visions, in which the baby usually appeared dead, and conspiracy theorists suggested that Lindbergh had killed his own son.

The kidnapping, the grimly farcical attempts to ransom the child, and the eventual capture of the carpenter, Bruno Hauptmann, form the centre piece of Berg's powerful and moving narrative. Tragically, the baby's body was found in a nearby wood, partly eaten by animals, but many people were unable to respect the Lindberghs' desperate grief. A reporter broke into the morgue and photographed the mutilated child, later selling the prints at $5 apiece. The trial and death sentence passed on Hauptmann released a host of demons from the American psyche. Scores of abusive letters threatened the Lindberghs' second child. Escaped mental patients homed in on their house and screamed at them through the windows, and passing cars tried to force them off the road.

All this reinforced Lindbergh's isolation from his fellow-citizens and his growing belief in the deep corruption of American society. At the Rockefeller Institute in New York he met a French physician, the Nobel-prizewinning Alexis Carrel, whose international bestseller, *Man the Unknown*, was a potent if troubling mix of eugenics and pseudo-Darwinian dreams of racial purity. Lindbergh soon came under Carrel's spell, and seems to have accepted his mentor's belief that the white races were under threat.

Visiting Europe before the war, Lindbergh found France and Britain too exhausted to meet the challenge from the Bolshevik east. By contrast,

Nazi Germany was confident and self-disciplined, free from all the constraints of democracy, and its aviation industry was more advanced than America's. Naively, Lindbergh accepted a medal from Goering, and on his return to the United States became a leading spokesman for America First, an isolationist organisation infiltrated by many pro-German racists. In his speeches Lindbergh urged Americans to stay out of the European war. He claimed that Britain and the Jews were working against America's true interests, and criticised the Jewish grip on the American press—research revealed, in fact, that their ownership amounted to no more than 3%.

Lindbergh's reputation never recovered, and until the end of his life in 1974 many Americans considered him an anti-semitic, pro-Nazi traitor. He partly redeemed himself during the second world war by flying some 50 combat missions against the Japanese, but on his post-war visits to Europe he was unwilling to recognise the vast scale of German atrocities.

Shunned and largely forgotten, he dedicated the rest of his life to environmental concerns, rescuing a number of threatened animal species. In some ways, he was one of the most endangered of all, a provincial naif who astonished the world when he flew the Atlantic and opened a door to the future, but who never learnt to cope with 20th century fame, a far more corrosive element than the ocean spray that lashed the cockpit windows during his record-breaking flight.

ANALYST'S COUCH POTATO

Woody Allen: A Biography by John Baxter

Daily Telegraph (November 17, 1998)

Think of "I don't consider any girl perfect until she rejects me." Or "Don't knock masturbation—it's sex with someone I love." They and a hundred other effortless but telling quips carry the unmistakable stamp of Woody Allen, a copyright blend of existential whining, tortured self-love and some of the greatest comic writing ever created.

Woody Allen claims that the comedian he most admires is Bob Hope. Yet Hope and his army of gag-writers could never have come up with Allen's bittersweet one-liners, which provoke an instant guffaw, but are underpinned by a deep melancholy about his own limitations and the senselessness of existence. Nor could Hope have created the Allen character: the nervy, analyst-haunting alter ego who mines his humour out of the harsh Manhattan air.

It is curious that New York, an abrasive and not always likeable city, where the taxi-drivers can be psychopathically rude and the skyscrapers are totem poles to the money god, and where the cultural life of museums and concert halls sometimes feels like a skin graft that has failed to take, should also have produced the most affable intelligentsia in the world: a legion of laid-back architects, writers and academics, far more engaging than their London and Paris counterparts.

Allen is the poet laureate of this more amiable Manhattan, and the keeper of its most carefully nurtured neuroses. Yet the real Woody Allen, as John Baxter points out in this astute and highly entertaining biography, is nothing like the nerdy figure he impersonates on screen. Close collaborators, such as Diane Keaton, who admire him, and others, such as Mia Farrow, who have learned to hate him, all agree that the real Allen is the complete opposite of his fictional twin, and is a strong-minded and self-confident professional with a steely edge and little time for fools.

Baxter has written several excellent film biographies, taking as his subjects some of the most mysterious figures in world cinema, among them Fellini, Spielberg and Kubrick, all hard nuts to crack and in many ways far stranger than anything they have created on film.

Woody Allen, born in 1935, is no exception, and Baxter skilfully describes his Brooklyn childhood among the immigrant Jewish families of the Depression era, a time of near poverty and a desperate search for self-improvement. Allen's natural melancholy, as his mother observed, revealed itself at an early age, along with a marked strain of excitability. Returning from school one day, he confronted her with the news that the universe was expanding, only to be met with the dogged assertion: "Well, Brooklyn isn't expanding."

But nothing could hold back Allen's enlarging horizons. In his late teens he was a paid gagsmith for New York newspaper columnists, churning out dozens of one-liners every day. He became a successful stand-up comedian and then made his break into film as the scriptwriter of Peter Sellers's *What's New, Pussycat?* in 1965. He first directed himself in *Take*

the Money and Run, and then scored his greatest success with his 1975
masterpiece, *Annie Hall*. There his alter ego, the "Woody Allen character,"
emerged in his full glory: the engaging hypochondriac obsessed by his
failure with women and the meaninglessness of the universe, who is as
original a creation as Chaplin's cane-twirling Little Tramp.

Like Chaplin, Allen was almost destroyed by a sexual scandal involving a young woman. During his long affair with Mia Farrow he became
infatuated with one of her adopted children, the 19-year-old Soon-Yi,
whom he later married. But the permissive and self-immersed Eighties,
in which Allen's neurotic characters thrived, had given way to the puritanical Nineties; and his public romance with the teenage Korean cast a
sinister retrospective light over all those sessions on the analyst's couch.

Exhausted by the legal proceedings that followed Farrow's accusations
of child abuse, Allen increasingly resembled an ageing Peter Pan locked
in a life-or-death struggle with an implacable Wendy, while the troupe
of adopted children wandered like the Lost Boys around their island of
Manhattan.

All the same, I hope that Allen never grows up, and that the trouba-
dour of psychoneurosis continues to make his witty and thoughtful films.
Too much of Hollywood's standard fare can be summed up in the opening dialogue of *Annie Hall*, when a woman at a Catskills hotel complains
about the dreadful food. "I know," replies her friend. "And such small
portions."

LICENSE TO KILL

The Rape of Nanking by Iris Chang

Sunday Times (February 21, 1999)

The vast war crimes committed during the 20th century remain its greatest mystery, a moral and psychological black hole that swallows all pity
and remorse, and leaves behind a void that will haunt the next millennium. I shuddered over each page of this heart-rending book, but strongly
urge everyone to read it. Meticulously researched and written in a tone of
barely contained anger, it serves as a warning to those who believe that
Belsen and the Burma-Siam railway could never happen again.

How could Japan and Germany, two of the most advanced nations on our planet, have unleashed wars of ferocious barbarity against their neighbours, murdering millions of civilians in the most cruel and savage way? How could these same peoples, only a few years later, sharing the same airliners with us and strolling around the same museums, seem virtually indistinguishable from ourselves, as kindly and generous to strangers?

Genocide, for Europeans and Americans, is almost a German monopoly, but Iris Chang points out that mass murder was carried out systematically by the Japanese invaders of China long before the first gas chambers were built at Auschwitz. During the Sino-Japanese war, from 1937 to 1945, the Japanese army killed at least 10m Chinese civilians. Yet few of those responsible, from foot soldiers to general staff, were ever punished or showed the slightest regret. Chang brings together a huge body of eye-witness accounts, war crimes testimonies and personal reminiscences which have appeared in scattered form throughout the past 50 years.

In August 1937, Japanese forces invaded China, swiftly seizing the main coastal cities. For three months fierce fighting raged around Shanghai, and my own family, who lived outside the British-run International Settlement, left for the French Concession, a safe haven from the fighting, when shells from rival Chinese and Japanese artillery guns began to fly over our roof. Tens of thousands of Chinese civilians were killed in the fighting, as we saw when we later drove out to the silent battlefields.

I remember the procession of chauffeur-driven Packards and Buicks that stopped near a devastated village, and the hundreds of dead Chinese lying by the roadside and in the abandoned paddy fields. Wearing their silk dresses, my mother and the other wives stepped with their husbands among the bright cartridge cases, a sight that even at the age of seven struck me as bizarre.

That November, after laying waste to the Yangtze plain, the Japanese armies launched their attack on Nanking, then the capital of China. When the city fell on December 13, the triumphant Japanese soldiers unleashed an orgy of murder, rape and torture that lasted for six weeks and killed more than 300,000 Chinese civilians, shocking even the German Nazi party members who were resident in the city.

The 90,000 Chinese soldiers who surrendered were quickly rounded up, roped together and moved to improvised killing grounds outside the city, where they were shot, beheaded, used for human bayonet practice or soaked with petrol and burnt alive. Mounds of Chinese corpses formed huge dykes along the Yangtze. All this was photographed by Japanese reporters, and one newspaper ran an illustrated article about the friendly rivalry between two officers under the heading "Contest to kill first 100 Chinese by beheading."

Once all military opposition was out of the way, the Japanese soldiers turned on the city's civilians. For the next six weeks they moved from house to house, bayonetting the men and raping the women, from girls as young as eight to grandmothers in their seventies. After they were raped, most were killed. One former soldier, Azuma Shiro, recently testified: "We always stabbed and killed them . . . when we were raping her, we looked at her as a woman, but when we killed her, we thought of her as something like a pig."

Sadistic torments were devised, involving live burials, castrations, disembowellings, and the forcing of Chinese parents to have sex with their children before they were killed. Mutilated corpses rotted in the streets. Amazingly, much of this was documented in photographs, many of which are reproduced in Chang's horrific account. If these chilling images, a true pornography of death, help to sell this book they will have served their purpose.

A few of the new recruits to this orgy of killing were shaken by what they saw, but they soon became desensitised and willingly joined in. An officer named Tominaga was stunned when he first met the men under his command. "They had evil eyes. They weren't human eyes, but the eyes of leopards or tigers." He quickly turned into a killing machine, using emaciated Chinese prisoners for beheading and bayonet practice, and noticed that his men's eyes no longer seemed evil. He said: "Everyone became a demon within three months."

A Japanese veteran from Nanking, Dr Nagatomi, is one of the few to express remorse. "I beheaded people, starved them to death, burned them, buried them alive, over 200 in all . . . there are really no words to describe what I was doing. I was truly a devil."

But why did he become a sadistic murderer, and why did hundreds of thousands of Japanese soldiers turn into a horde of conscienceless killers? Chang, an American historian whose parents narrowly escaped death in Nanking (they fled to Taiwan and then became academics in America), blames the brutalities of the Japanese army and the long-standing racial hatred of the Chinese, seen as an inferior people little better than animals. When we try to make sense of Nazi crimes, we blame a small group of political gangsters (Hitler and the Nuremberg defendants) and their SS murder squads, together driven by deeply psychopathic racial hatreds. But historians have confirmed what many people suspected, that millions of Germans in army and police regiments were involved in the mass murder of civilians.

Were they all psychopaths? I suspect that none, or few, of them were. During the long Japanese occupation of Shanghai we witnessed countless atrocities against Chinese civilians. After the Japanese attack of Pearl Harbor, in December 1941, my family and I, along with other Allied nationals, had been interned in Lunghua camp near Shanghai. In August 1945, a few days after the war had officially ended, I was walking from the camp and came across a unit of Japanese soldiers at a wayside railway station. One of them, who was slowly strangling a Chinese youth with telephone wire, shouted at me. He had noticed my transparent celluloid belt, which I had wheedled from an American sailor. A long haggle went on, which ended with me unbuckling my precious belt. I remember the soldier's intense pleasure in his new possession as he went back to killing the Chinese, and my own deep sense of loss.

Was he a psychopath? I seriously doubt it. The real horror of this century's war crimes is that they were carried out by ordinary human beings, farmers and factory workers and office clerks, who returned to their jobs and brought up their children. Faced with a threat to themselves, human beings become cruel and dangerous, and the murder and torture of enemy civilians is an unhappy part of their natural behaviour, only restrained by the prevailing moral codes, the political leadership and the officers in charge. When rulers and generals urge on racial war, ordinary soldiers become their core selves, as vicious as the chimpanzee raiding parties who work themselves up with blood curdling screams and tear the enemy limb from limb. I hope that the Japanese soldier at the railway station went on to become the remorseful Dr Nagatomi.

FASHION VICTIM

Pages from the Glossies: Facsimiles 1956–1998 by Helmut Newton

Bookforum (Spring 1999)

Helmut Newton's photographs are stills from an elegant and erotic movie, perhaps entitled *Midnight at the Villa d'Este* or *Afternoons in Super-Cannes*, a virtual film that has never played at any theatre but has screened itself inside our heads for the last forty years. Newton, of course, is far too sophisticated to lumber his extraordinary oeuvre with anything so limiting as an overall title, let alone the prosaic ones I suggest. The magic of his art is its complete elusiveness, its cunning refusal to admit the true nature of its subject matter: the failure of reality and the triumph of desire.

By now Newton's world is as recognizable as that of Delvaux or Magritte. The familiar backdrops of Europe's grandest hotels, Hollywood apartments, and Riviera swimming pools are the settings for a series of mysterious dramas, whose sources are never exposed and whose conflicts are never resolved. A company of beautiful women moves through the palatial corridors or gazes into the opaque depths of ornate mirrors, waiting for a last act that will never unfold. Even those women who are naked seem scarcely aware of themselves, as if their sexuality is defused by the strange bedrooms where they wait for the rich and powerful men stepping from their limousines in the courtyards below.

The realm that Newton creates for us has the calm light of a lucid dream, glimpsed through a connecting door that links it to the interior space of the Surrealists, to *Last Year at Marienbad* (1961), and the films of Luis Bunuel. That a fashion photographer with a limited set of props and players could set out an arena so psychologically charged is a remarkable achievement, well beyond the powers of any figurative artist at work today.

As one leafs through *Vogue*, *Elle*, *Queen*, and *Paris Match* one is struck by how fresh his photographs seem. The editorial captions, with all their arch tropes, are mercilessly awful, but Newton's photography is as vivid as tomorrow's news, which in one way it always has been. Though his clients and their advertising agencies would be appalled by the thought, I imagine that few people coming fresh to Newton's work would suspect that the nominal purpose of these striking images was to sell a collection of high-priced frocks.

But then Newton has always been very much more than a fashion photographer. I think of him as a figurative artist who uses the medium of photography—and his access to gorgeous women, expensive gowns, and exotic locations—to create a unique imaginative world. I firmly believe that since the death of Francis Bacon in 1992, Helmut Newton has been our greatest visual artist. Sadly, he has very little competition, either in the wilderness of the New York art scene, bravely exposed by Robert Hughes in his magisterial book *American Visions*, or London, dominated by the eerie homoerotic smut of Gilbert and George and the Young British Art force-fed into fleeting notoriety by Charles Saatchi, who unfailingly transforms his adman's gold into the dross of third-rate Conceptual art.

By contrast, Newton's photography has endured for decades, as poetic and mysterious as when it first appeared in the 60s. The images of his photographic contemporary, Andy Warhol, already seem dated, their newsprint topicality left behind by the new visual codes of music videos, TV ads, and Internet graphics.

A sure measure of achievement in the arts is the degree to which the latent content of a work continues to resonate long after our first exposure to its surface charms. For too many people, unfortunately, it is those surface charms that prevent them from looking deeper into Newton's photographs. His naked models still trigger accusations of sexual voyeurism. Nudity in photography, whether involving adults or children, is a subject sinking under a freight of political and moral disapproval it could never hope to support, and this is not the place for me to get out the bilge pump.

I will only say that critics who tremble so fiercely at the thought of the voyeuristic male gaze miss the point that distance generates mystery and enchantment, and expresses the awe with which the male imagination regards all women, as we see so clearly in Newton's photographs. Far from debasing his models (most of whom are not naked), Newton places them at the heart of a deep and complex drama where they rule like errant queens, blissfully indifferent to the few men who dare to approach them.

Much more interesting about Newton is the way in which he desexual-izes his subject matter. His photographs drain the libido from the once charged spaces of the late 20th century, from hotel bedrooms and luxury bathrooms, and from those penthouse apartments where unwatched porn films play behind the heads of people with more pressing concerns than pleasure or pain.

In Newton's work we see a new race of urban beings, living on a new human frontier, where all passion is spent and all ambition long satisfied, where the deepest emotions seem to be relocating themselves, moving into a terrain more mysterious than Marienbad.

On a personal note: When I last saw Newton, I told him that he ought to make a film. "Oh, I've had hundreds of offers," he said. Of course, he's been making his film all his career. He loved Cronenberg's *Crash* (1996), but one thing bothered him. "The dresses," he whispered. "They were so awful." Unfair, but then he is only the director and screenwriter of his film. Another credit runs: "Costumes by Dior, Chanel, Saint Laurent . . ."

THE MAESTRO WHO CAMPAIGNED AGAINST HIS GREATEST WORK

The Enigma of Giorgio de Chirico by Margaret Crosland

Daily Telegraph (August 21, 1999)

Surrealism arrives at the end of our century with its baggage intact. The melting watches, the statuesque nudes sleepwalking through deserted cit-ies, the bowler-hatted clerks raining from the sky, have lost little of their power to disturb. Surrealism's belief that madness may have a logic of its own, and that sanity and reason have failed to explain reality, has a special force in the era that produced Auschwitz, Hiroshima and Dolly the clone.

The first and perhaps greatest of the Surrealists was Giorgio de Chirico, one of the most eccentric figures in modern art, who pulled off the remarkable feat of shocking his fellow Surrealists even more than he unsettled the public. Margaret Crosland's entertaining biography is the best account I have read of this autocratic and baffling man, who for 50 years waged a fierce campaign against the work from his most original period.

A curious fact about the Surrealists is that this band of revolutionaries came from solidly bourgeois backgrounds, which they never seriously repudiated. Dalí's father was a lawyer, Max Ernst's a Protestant pastor. Magritte lived in a middle-class Brussels suburb and walked his Pomeranian dog at the same time every day.

Chirico was no exception. His father was a Sicilian railway engineer of aristocratic temperament who had fought several duels, and his romantic mother had mounted in gold the bullet that wounded her husband. Chirico adored his father, and was devastated when he died. A profound sense of loss pervades his paintings, and I suspect that the trains running eastwards along the horizon, in effect from the snowcapped Alps to Turin, are returning his father from his death.

After art school in Munich, Chirico moved to Turin, the city of his inspiration and even now the strangest in Europe, with its endless arcades hinting at a secret inner life and its huge silent trains that appear mysteriously behind you like spectres in a dream.

The arcades dominate the works that Chirico began to paint in 1910. In little more than six or seven years, long before Ernst, Magritte and Dalí had begun their careers, Chirico set out one of the defining landscapes of 20th century art. In his paintings we see Europe in its late afternoon, a place of deserted squares and shadow-filled arcades.

A few figures appear, but they are tailor's dummies with geometric symbols on their faces. A deep melancholy has settled over everything, as if the painter has anticipated the disturbed century to come.

After the First World War the Paris Surrealists discovered Chirico and were quick to hail his genius. But the maestro had moved on. Thinking loftily of Nietzsche, he saw himself as the leader of a classical revival. He rejected the Surrealists and embarked on a series of lurid neo-classical landscapes filled with tumbled columns, centaurs and heroically posing male nudes.

Critics were dismayed and lamented a lost talent, but Chirico was adamant, dismissing his earlier work as a youthful aberration. Secretly, he continued to paint in his Surrealist manner, copying his own works and pre-dating them. If a collector called, inquiring about arcades and deserted squares, he would appear with just such a canvas, claiming that he had found it in a forgotten corner of his studio.

Margaret Crosland estimates that by the time of Chirico's death in 1978, about 5,000 easel paintings were ascribed to him, many of them copies made by himself or forgers. Farcical scenes resulted when he denounced the fakes, sometimes rejecting his own genuine works. He would enter an offending gallery and call the police, an almost Pooh-like figure humming his favourite song: "I like Gide, I like Claudel,/But I prefer crème caramel."

He died rich and laden with honours, one of the greatest artists of the century and more mysterious than any of the mannequins he created.

A STAIRCASE OF CORPSES

Build My Gallows High by Geoffrey Homes

New Statesman (March 26, 2001)

"You build my gallows high, baby," a harried Robert Mitchum mutters to Jane Greer, as they speed down the dark road that will carry him to his death. This bitter comment, in the film based on Geoffrey Homes's novel, sums up almost the entire genre of *film noir*, those doom-laden thrillers, dominated by violence and sexual deceit, that are among Hollywood's most memorable movies. Moody loners, the toughest of tough guys, drift into town and are soon ensnared by a pitiless femme fatale interested in only one thing, hard cash, and ready to climb a staircase of corpses to get to it.

For all their worldly experience, defined by the trench coat and weary eyes, few of the noir heroes ever stand a chance. Like Fred MacMurray in *Double Indemnity*, they may have spent years selling life insurance to restless housewives with one eye on their dozy husbands and the other on the clock, but the merest glimpse of a swinging ankle chain is enough to give them an instant lobotomy.

Two puzzles surround *film noir*. What made its heroes sleepwalk towards their own destruction? And why did this compelling genre, one of the most adult Hollywood ever produced, last less than ten years, from *The Maltese Falcon* in 1941 to *White Heat* in 1949? In trying to explain the heroes' fallibility, one has to accept the fearsome nature of the opposition they faced. *Noir* films featured some amazingly implacable women.

Humphrey Bogart in *The Maltese Falcon* was strong enough to resist Mary Astor, who had killed his partner, but he was rare among *noir* heroes in being driven by a raging anger and something close to moral indignation, a quality virtually absent from Hollywood films of today.

Most of the *noir* heroes lacked any kind of compass bearing, and were part of the psychological debris that floated to and fro after the war. By contrast, the women who ensnared them knew exactly where they were going. Barbara Stanwyck and Joan Crawford, the queens of *film noir*, projected an intensely focused menace that was a bravura display of fine acting, well beyond the powers of today's Nicole Kidman or Jodie Foster.

In her private life, so we are told, Crawford was even more baleful than in her screen roles, where she sometimes affected a clinging vulnerability. Offstage, both Stanwyck and Rita Hayworth, another goddess of *noir*, were good fun. Hayworth, never more alluring and mysterious than in *Gilda* and *The Lady from Shanghai*, had little luck off-screen with the men in her life, though she knew the power of the *noir* heroines. "They went to bed with Gilda," she famously said of her lovers, "and woke up with me."

Feminist critics have faulted *noir* films for creating a series of female fantasy figures, the witches and enchantresses of old in modern dress. I prefer to think of Stanwyck and Crawford as proto-feminist heroines, locked in a Darwinian struggle with the male world and using any means that would bring them victory, a triumph signalled by the hero's self-willed death. In the late 1940s, when I first saw Stanwyck in *Double Indemnity*, she reminded me, bar the anklet and platinum wig, of my mother and her bridge-playing friends. The anger, frustration and ruthlessness in Stanwyck's face seemed closer to the average housewife of the day than to Medea or Lady Macbeth.

Many film critics argue that the *noir* films expressed the anxieties of American men returning from the war to find that women were economically independent, leaving the home for jobs in offices and car plants. But Hayworth and Stanwyck never looked as if they had handled a rivet gun, and the reasons for the demise of *film noir* must lie elsewhere.

I remember watching *Build My Gallows High* in a Cambridge cinema in 1949 and being gripped by the stylised and affectless violence, where psychopathy was the key to character. Here was a clear look at the dark side of the American dream, and a better guide to the world we were living in than the lectures of Dr Leavis (in fact, I was supposed to be reading medicine).

Once the war was over, however, an immense confidence rolled across America like the highways of the prosperous Eisenhower years. The *noir* films, with their expressionist black and white photography, their themes of guilt, suspicion and emotional betrayal, were too downbeat and too European for American audiences discovering television and the charms of perpetual adolescence.

Film noir lives on, in neo-*noir* films such as *Point Blank*, with the unforgettably psychotic Lee Marvin pulling down the walls of the syndicate, and in *The Last Seduction*, where Linda Fiorentino plays a classic enchantress. The Coen brothers' *Blood Simple* is a desert *noir*, with sand in place of asphalt, and *Fargo* would be a *noir* film but for all that blinding snow. Perhaps it falls into a new category of *film blanc*.

Build My Gallows High was adapted by Geoffrey Homes from his own novel, long out of print but now reissued. In many ways, it has hardly dated, set in shadowy cabs and bleak city streets. At least one change was made for the better. The seductress bears the least likely name for a vamp in the whole of crime fiction—Mumsie McGonigle. Faced with a name like that, even Mitchum at his most somnolent would have found his way to the door.

PROPHET OF OUR PRESENT

Aldous Huxley: An English Intellectual by Nicholas Murray

Guardian (April 13, 2002)

Aldous Huxley was uncannily prophetic, a more astute guide to the future than any other 20th-century novelist. Even his casual asides have a surprising relevance to our own times. During the first world war, after America's entry, he warned: "I dread the inevitable acceleration of American world domination which will be the result of it all . . . Europe will no longer be Europe." His sentiment is widely echoed today, though too late for us to do anything about it. The worst fate for a prophet is for his predictions to come true, when everyone resents him for being so clear-eyed.

Huxley's greatest novel, *Brave New World*, is a far shrewder guess at the likely shape of a future tyranny than Orwell's vision of Stalinist terror in *Nineteen Eighty-Four*. Huxley's dystopia, with its test-tube babies and recreational drugs, its "feelies" that anticipate virtual reality, differs in one vital way from Orwell's vision of a boot stamping for ever on a human face. Huxley's victims welcome their own enslavement, revealing the same strains of passivity that lie beneath today's entertainment culture. *Nineteen Eighty-Four* has never really arrived, but *Brave New World* is around us everywhere.

For all his prescience, Huxley's star has dimmed since his death in 1963, on the same day that John F. Kennedy was shot. The president's assassination overshadowed everything else on that grimmest of November days. A random psychotic act had endangered the world and refuted Huxley's vision of a sane and calculating tyranny. A single deranged man with a mail-order rifle was a more sinister threat than Big Brother, whether in jackboots or a white lab coat.

Another factor in Huxley's decline was his close association with the Bloomsbury Group, that bloodless set who haunt English letters like a coterie of haemophiliac royals. Huxley's novels of the 1920s, from *Antic Hay* to *Point Counter Point*, were ruthlessly witty satires on the middle class of his day, but have rather lost their sting in the far weirder era of *Iris* and Delia. But as Nicholas Murray makes clear in his generous and intelligent biography, Huxley soon escaped the Bloomsburies. He had far deeper roots in the Victorian age, with a rich mix of high-mindedness and a secure moral compass that we find baffling in our culture of sound-bite philosophy and focus-group wisdom.

In many ways, Huxley was the last of the great Victorian novelists. He was born in 1894, a grandson of the biologist T. H. Huxley, "Darwin's bulldog." Matthew Arnold was his great-uncle, and his aunt was the novelist Mrs Humphry Ward. Secure in this intellectual aristocracy, he might have rebelled and become a great mid-century English eccentric, a liberally minded chairman of the board of film censors, or the first openly agnostic Archbishop of Canterbury. However, at the age of 16, while an Eton schoolboy, he caught a serious eye infection that left him blind for a year and may have forced him into a more interior vision of himself. With his one good eye, he read English at Oxford, perhaps the best perspective to take on this dubious subject. He was immensely tall, six feet four-and-a-half inches. Christopher Isherwood said that he was "too tall. I felt an enormous zoological separation from him." Huxley, curiously, disliked male homosexuality but had many homosexual friends, Isherwood among them.

The young Huxley must have had immense charm. He soon found himself at Garsington Manor, near Oxford, the legendary home of the literary hostess, Lady Ottoline Morrell, where he met Virginia Woolf, Lytton Strachey, Clive Bell and D. H. Lawrence. Years later, in the south of France, Lawrence died in the arms of Huxley's wife. In the final minutes before his death, Lawrence suddenly panicked and cried out to Maria Huxley, begging her to keep him alive. She embraced him, and he died peacefully as her husband watched.

Maria was a wartime Belgian refugee whom Huxley met at Garsington and married in 1919. Murray describes their marriage as intensely close and happy, although Maria was an active bisexual. Huxley seems to have taken quickly to their special version of open marriage. They pursued the same lovers together, like a pair of sexual confidence tricksters: Maria encouraging Aldous, introducing him to the beautiful women he admired, preparing the amatory ground and saving him the fatigue of prolonged courtship. Jealousy and possessiveness, which so handicap the rest of us, seemed never to have touched Huxley, an emotional deficit that some readers have noticed in his novels. In the late 1930s, when they moved to Los Angeles, Maria became a member of the "sewing circle," a club of prominent Hollywood lesbians reputed to include Marlene Dietrich and Greta Garbo.

Huxley's first novel, *Crome Yellow*, was a success, and he signed what Murray rightly terms a "momentous" agreement with his publishers. For a regular income of £500 a year, he promised to deliver two new works of fiction each year, one of them a full-length novel. Even inflated 50-fold, the sums were modest by today's standards—we have huge advances and huge reputations, but small novels, though that may no longer be relevant. Despite the large sales of *Brave New World*, the Huxleys were never rich, and in 1937, when they sailed for America on the Normandie, they travelled tourist. Thomas Mann, travelling first class, visited them in the tourist lounge and reported that the meeting was not a success, tactfully blaming the language barrier.

Arriving in the US, which he was never to leave, except on brief trips, Huxley found his true home. At first he was critical of the country, uneasy at the strange coexistence of puritanism and hedonism. "The Machiavelli of the mid-20th century will be an advertising man; his *Prince*, a textbook of the art and science of fooling all the people all the time." But he had picked up the spoors of two commodities that only California could offer—the scent of film money and, even more significantly, the heady incense of takeaway religions and off-the-shelf enlightenment.

Unlike many of his fellow writers who emigrated to Hollywood and snobbishly refused to adapt to the film medium, Huxley became a successful screenwriter, with credits for *Pride and Prejudice* and *Jane Eyre*. But his real interest lay in the mystery of human consciousness, and the power of modern pharmacology to unlock the shutters that have restricted our minds to the demands of everyday survival. In *The Doors of Perception*, perhaps his most prophetic book of all, Huxley describes an afternoon in 1953 when he first injected mescalin and saw a local supermarket transformed into a cathedral of wonder.

Huxley believed that human beings will always need some form of chemical assistance to achieve the full potential of their brains. At his request, as he lay dying he was injected with LSD, and sank into his final coma still moving confidently towards the light. I like to think that he was curious to see how his perception of his own death would be transformed by the hallucinogenic drug, and that his ever-questioning intelligence was alive to the end.

THIS BOY DOES TALK. WHO IS HE?

King of Cannes by Stephen Walker

Guardian (June 1, 2002)

Is the novel, as a form, too adult for most of us, and are films at heart adolescent? Critics may bemoan the state of today's cinema, a parade of prequels, sequels and action-heroes ageing a little too gracefully, but the power of film to stir our minds is stronger than ever. Even a brilliantly empty extravaganza such as *Terminator 2* can touch us more deeply than a library of literary prizewinners. I remember dozens of films from the 1940s but very few novels. Fifty years later, nothing has changed. The two great showcases of film—the Academy Awards and the Cannes film festival— remind us what really rules the collective imagination. But even the smaller film festivals generate an astonishing magic. Ten years ago I served on the jury at Mystfest, an Italian festival of crime and mystery films. It was held at Viareggio, a rather melancholy beach resort near Lucca that is still home to Puccini's favourite restaurant, and where nothing seemed to have happened since Shelley's heart was snatched from his pyre.

For a tumultuous six days, Mystfest drained all the power from every light socket. An occupation force of fans, journalists, TV crews and aspiring directors seized the resort. The jury saw the competing films surrounded by audiences who whistled and booed, kicked the seats whenever they spotted a pretentious camera angle, roamed the aisles and argued with rival claques over the merits or tragic incompetence of a particular actor. They blocked the streets for hours, holding up the traffic while they ridiculed all dissent. I realised that in many ways film is a political medium.

One evening in the hotel bar, where Nic Roeg and Theresa Russell held court, a young American was taking on all comers. He stood with his back to the bar, clearing the space around him, excited, manic, gesticulating and likeable, steeped in film, every sentence a manifesto. Sitting beside the elderly Jules Dassin, the jury chairman, I listened amazed to the flow of wise-cracks and one-liners fuelled by nothing more than the sheerest love of film.

Dassin, the refined and sophisticated director of *The Naked City* and *Rififi*, murmured to me: "This boy does talk. Who is he?" I made enquiries and reported back. "Quentin Tarantino." Dassin, like the rest of us, had never heard of him. But he had come all this way, for a single screening in the back of the beach cinema, of his unreleased new film, *Reservoir Dogs*.

Whether all this excitement helped the jury to pick the best film is another matter. The psychology of the jury system lies somewhere between *Survivor* and the Prisoner's Dilemma. When we first met, the jury—Dassin; Suzanne Cloutier, who played Desdemona in Orson Welles's *Othello*; the American Bob Swaim, director of *Half Moon Street* ("I've slept with all my leading ladies." "Sigourney Weaver? Tell me more." "Er, no. Not Sigourney."); two Italian cineasts, and myself—seemed to agree about everything, the kind of films we liked and what we hoped to find at the festival.

In fact, once we started seeing the films we disagreed about everything. After viewing five of the 11 competing films, Dassin called a meeting. "The films are rubbish," he announced. "We'll give the prize to Nic Roeg." We were incredulous. Apart from Roeg's *Cold Heaven*, there were five films we hadn't yet seen. "They'll be rubbish, too."

We dug our heels in and saw all 11. I would happily have given the prize to Roeg, but none of the jurors agreed with anyone else's choice. I found myself pushing enthusiastically for films I disliked. The task was to forge temporary alliances with other jurors, back their choices to squeeze out a dangerous rival, then dump them ruthlessly the moment the chance came to push one's own candidate. Town-hall politics, without the sweeteners of corruption.

Eventually, we settled on a compromise: a German film about a Turkish detective, which we had seen without subtitles. The festival organiser was not impressed. Nic Roeg was a big name. So a new prize was created and Roeg was rightly feted at a special ceremony.

Cannes is Viareggio magnified a hundredfold. In *King of Cannes*, Stephen Walker's entertaining account of the documentary he made about four hopefuls who seek their fortune at the festival, he rightly describes Cannes as a "mix of hype, decadence, sleaze, glamour, madness, power and sheer, unadulterated glory."

His first recruit is Mike Hakata, who has made a movie called *Two Blind Mice*, and is determined to screen it at Cannes. He is black with long Rastafarian locks, and wrote his script over a single weekend. He saved enough dole money to finance the film, helped by a crew who worked for nothing. Mike describes his movie as *Trainspotting* meets *The Sound of Music*. He is desperate to be a success, and is ready to abseil off a hotel roof to get into a producer's office.

Another hopeful is a London cabbie who drives to Cannes in a van emblazoned with a giant marijuana leaf, advertising his film *Amsterdam*, which exists only in his mind, never a serious handicap in the movie business. The third hopeful is Erick Zonka, hailed as the new Godard, whose film is accepted for the official competition. Lastly, there is an

American, James Merendino, who miraculously pulls off a two-picture deal, movieland's equivalent of winning the lottery.

Reading Walker's hilarious record of these madcap and deeply obsessive characters, all of them far stranger than any film they will ever make, one feels the enormous magnetic pull that Cannes exerts. I loved every minute in 1996, but Cannes is a heady place for a novelist. I was there to support David Cronenberg and his cast as they grappled with the storm of outrage and excitement that greeted *Crash*. Press and film interviews ran non-stop for days. We began at the Carlton, working in pairs as the journalists circulated. I sat beside Holly Hunter, and heard the first question addressed to this Oscar-winning actress by a leading New York journalist. "Holly, what are you doing in this shit?"

I still remember how she fought back, furiously making one of the most cogent and articulate cases for the film that I have heard. Film is important, and those involved with books know it. People still read, and in huge numbers, though the books that arouse the strongest passions tend to be written for children. Perhaps the form of the novel is wrong, and too interiorised to match our experience of the world.

My guess is that the serious novel in the future will be serious in the way that Hitchcock's films are serious, and not in the way that *Middlemarch* or *Mrs Dalloway* are serious. The psychological drama will migrate from the interior of the characters' heads to the settings around them, as in Hitchcock's films. This is closer to ordinary life, where we know very little about other people's minds, even if we are married to them. Film seems to catch this, and reminds us that the world around us is ultimately mysterious—and that we ourselves, our anxieties and phobias, can be as tedious and uninteresting as our dreams.

THE UNLIMITED DREAM COMPANY

The Bad and the Beautiful: A Chronicle of Hollywood in the Fifties by Sam Kashner and Jennifer MacNair

New Statesman (July 8, 2002)

Is the main role of Hollywood to save Americans from the need to grow up? The rest of the world has angst, despair, genius and genocide. They have the Hollywood film, a benign dictatorship of optimism, sentimentality and happy endings in which we all secretly believe, until the lights come on and we see the frayed carpet under our feet. Hollywood's influence pervades almost every aspect of our lives, and its amiable yarns mark out our own fault lines. The Blair-Mandelson new Labour project resembles a Frank Capra comedy about a miracle cure first embraced and then rejected by a docile public. Jacques Chirac's Vegas-style boom-boom rallies were pure *Ocean's 11*, effective until an ugly European heavy muscled in and threatened the cash tills.

Visitors travelling across the US soon become aware of a missing dimension, a gap in the psychological space around them. The strains of pessimism and wariness that everywhere else seem innately human have been erased from the American psyche, presumably by the Hollywood ethos absorbed since childhood. The people one meets, even the beggars who haunt the airport exit roads, are likeable, cheerful and friendly, as if the entire nation had been recruited into a remake of a 1950s Rock Hudson movie.

But no one should be that likeable or that friendly. I suspect that one reason for our out-of-sync response to 11 September is that, after a similar attack, we Europeans would react numbly and do virtually nothing, whereas Americans grieve fiercely but in an upbeat way, while warming up the F 16s. One of the unnerving things about Donald Rumsfeld, the US defence secretary, is that he merges seamlessly into the kind of super-patriotic naval commander played by Gene Hackman in *Behind Enemy Lines*, who is ready to destabilise the entire Balkans and trigger a third world war in order to rescue a downed pilot.

And why not? Because Hollywood has redefined reality as itself, we can sit back and look forward confidently to Armageddon. Any dream that so endures must draw its strength from the deepest survival instincts. The potent spectacle of bright light played against a high wall taps something hard wired into our brains—memories, perhaps, of the first dawn. Television, by contrast, is a keyhole view of the world, devoid of glamour and forever focused on the mundane.

The Bad and the Beautiful (which takes its title from Vincente Minnelli's lushly paranoid melodrama) describes Hollywood in the 1950s, when it stood at the apex of its power but was about to enter the greatest crisis in its history. People today who never go to the cinema, or who only watch videos at home, have little idea of the godlike aura that surrounded the giant stars such as Clark Gable and Gary Cooper, Joan Crawford and Carole Lombard. Yet we knew almost nothing about their private lives. Many of the stars were married to each other, but seemed to produce few children, as if pregnancy and birth were too messy and physical for exalted beings who existed only in the electrified ether high above our heads.

Then, in the 1950s, everything changed. Television began to steal Hollywood audiences, and the break-up of the studio system meant the stars were on their own. Disaffected chauffeurs and eavesdropping waiters fed the new scandal magazines with rumours of domestic violence, drug abuse and homosexuality. Television had turned the world into a suburban living room, and audiences now wanted to see what the stars got up to when they were at home. Realism was a tangy new flavour, fed by the Kinsey Report and congressional spotlight on organised crime. The bottom-feeding *Confidential* magazine led the tabloid pack, and spilled the beans on Lizabeth Scott, Tab Hunter and Noel Coward.

A wonderful compendium of sleaze and gossip, *The Bad and the Beautiful* makes clear that many of the stars were far more interesting off screen than on. Like the audiences who admired them, their main recreations were alcohol and adultery. Lana Turner was a beautiful but wooden actress, whose compulsive man-hunting led her from one abusive boyfriend to another. She ended up with a vile small-time gangster named Johnny Stompanato. Visiting England with Turner, this thug in the lizard shoes was decked by her co-star Sean Connery. Stompanato's rages and wandering hands were too much for Turner's daughter, Cheryl, who killed him with a carving knife, provoking a vast scandal. The story has appeared in numerous films, but none of them gets to grips with Turner's mysterious personality, a myth perpetually dismantling itself in a way reminiscent of Princess Diana.

Burt Lancaster was another strange figure, as brutal and threatening in everyday life as the vicious gossip columnist he played in *Sweet Smell of Success*. The distinguished screenwriter Ernest Lehman describes first seeing Lancaster, as he stepped in from a side room to a meeting, zipping his fly, with the comment: "She swallowed it."

The sharpest comments on 1950s Hollywood were made by a corpse, that of the failed screenwriter Joe Gillis in Sunset Boulevard, lying face down in the swimming pool of the deranged actress Norma Desmond. He had realised too late that the Hollywood dream was a nightmare that devoured the dreamer. In the 1970s, Lucas and Spielberg changed the direction of Hollywood film, probably saving it from the slow death by neglect that has overtaken the European cinema. Film returned to its roots, never a bad move at a time of doubt, updating the galloping horses and speeding trains of cinema's pioneer days. Special effects became the real stars. The actors, even Tom Cruise and Nicole Kidman, are little more than glorified extras. Once again, Hollywood has resumed its historic task of making adolescents of us all.

THE ULTIMATE SACRIFICE

Kamikaze: Japan's Suicide Gods by Albert Axell and Hideaki Kase

New Statesman (September 9, 2002)

The World Trade Center has gone, but the shadows of the twin towers seem to lengthen, pointing to the coming war in Iraq, and beyond that to Saudi Arabia and even, who knows, to an uncooperative European state. On the one side lies a fanaticism unrestrained by reason, and on the other a religiose and self-important America, determined to remake the world in its own image, a comic-book culture driven by ruthless technologies.

If the future is a marriage between Microsoft and the Disney Corporation, what can the rest of us do about it? Reading this strangely moving account of the kamikaze pilots, one dimly senses that the fightback may have already begun, launched more than 60 years ago when Japanese carrier planes bombed Pearl Harbor. The wartime newsreels that show waves of suicide pilots ("hashi-crashies" and "screwy-siders," to the American servicemen I met soon after) diving into aircraft carriers near Okinawa uncannily evoke the images of al-Qaeda terrorists flying their hijacked Boeings into the World Trade Center. There are the same horrific fireballs, and the same mystery of how human beings—so intelligent, gifted and far sighted—could lock themselves into such insane confrontations.

Anyone, civilian or combatant, who saw Japanese soldiers in action during the Second World War, knew that life and death existed for them in a very different realm. The horrendous atrocities carried out by the Japanese armies were sanctioned by an officer corps inured to violence and death by centuries of civil strife, and who almost welcomed the prospect of death—their own or their captives'—as a means of testing their own integrity and will.

As a teenage boy roaming around the abandoned airfields near Shanghai in the weeks after the war's end, I met countless armed Japanese soldiers waiting for the arrival of the American and Chinese forces. They knew what was in store for them, but sat stoically on their ammunition boxes. Sharing my water bottle with them, I realised that in a sense, they were already dead.

In many ways the entire Japanese nation had resigned itself to death once the war turned against them at the Battle of Midway. As Axell and Kase make clear, the kamikaze attacks that began in 1944 were not a bizarre aberration of the samurai spirit, but were latent in the Japanese character and its attitudes to self, family and country, a patriotism as strong as the feelings we have for our young children.

Anguished Americans responding to 11 September described the attacks as cowardly and the product of envy, a huge misjudgement, I suspect. The al-Qaeda terrorists despise, not envy America, and no coward could fly an aircraft into the side of a skyscraper or carrier.

At the same time, far more than bravery propelled the wartime suicide pilots. The thousands of young Japanese who joined the Special Attack units never thought that they were throwing away their lives. They knew that the war was lost, and believed that they were defending their families and homeland in the only way left to them. Conventional tactics were no longer an option for the novice pilots who made up most of the Japanese air force. Far from seeking heroic death, the kamikaze pilots saw the suicide attacks as their only means of delaying the American advance.

The first official suicide pilot was Lieutenant Yukio Seki, who crashed his Zero fighter into the US carrier *St Lo* at the Battle of Leyte Gulf. The *St Lo* sank within hours, blown apart by its own exploding torpedoes. During the next three months, more than a thousand suicide pilots lost their lives attacking the American fleet near the Philippines.

A further 2,000 kamikaze pilots died in the bitter struggle for Okinawa in the spring of 1945, most of them shot down into the sea by resolute gunners. More than 30 US warships were sunk or damaged, and fears that an invasion of the Japanese home islands would lead to millions of casualties may well have persuaded President Truman to drop the atomic bombs and shock Japan into sudden surrender.

This account of the kamikazes is powerfully gripping, its authenticity vouched for by the testimony of former suicide pilots who finished their training but were never sent on missions. It is also draining and unsettling to read, a collective suicide note written by thousands of young men who had scarcely entered adult life. There is a good case to be made for the proposition that no one should fight in a war, or put on a uniform, until the age of 40.

On the evidence of the letters and poems that they wrote on the eve of their last flights, the kamikaze pilots were extraordinarily calm. Many had been university students with degrees, curiously, in the humanities and law rather than science and engineering. Most were described as "blissful" during their last hours, a peace of mind that lies beyond both despair and psychopathology.

Their dedication is a mystery to the western mind, but all too close to the behaviour of the al-Qaeda flyers on 11 September. At a certain intensity, the will to suicide becomes a deranged affirmation of life. One has to assume that there will be other suicide attacks on the US mainland, and that the American response will be ever more decisive, and, sadly, ever more provocative.

A WORLD OF ENDLESS SUMMER

High Tide: News from a Warming World by Mark Lynas

Evening Standard (March 15, 2004)

Have exaggerated fears about the weather replaced our dread of nuclear war? Human beings seem to need something to fear, and catastrophic climate change taps into our deepest fantasies of world destruction.

I remember vividly how awful the British weather was 50 years ago, the summers that lasted a fortnight followed by an unending autumn drizzle and Arctic winters. We sniffled and grumbled, but our minds were on a different kind of weather, those man-made mushroom clouds that rose over Pacific atolls, leaning across the sky as if eager to make their way to Europe.

Today the nuclear threat lies in the past, and the English summer lasts from March to November. My passion flowers and forsythia are already in bloom, and at any moment the appetising reek of barbecue briquettes will drift across my neighbours' patios and signal the unleashing of sun-loungers and barrier cream. The global warming of which I dreamed for so many years has at last come true.

But how foolish I am, as Mark Lynas makes clear in his powerful account of the threat posed by climatic change and increased carbon dioxide emissions. Melting ice caps, coastal flooding and the creation of vast new deserts threaten our entire way of life.

In Britain there has been a huge increase in rainfall during the 1990s, a blessing one might think for our water supplies and for those not affected by flooding. But, according to Lynas, this was the wrong kind of rain. Heavy deluges are less likely to soak usefully into farmland, and more likely to run off in destructive torrents that wash away the fertile topsoil.

Lynas paints a fearsome picture of the near future, an overlit landscape not without its attractions. During the endless summer months the sun will blaze down on a re-engineered Eden. The British gardener will mow his lawn all the year round. Our herbaceous borders will wither, and our gardens will be filled with tree-ferns, palms, bamboos and bananas. Exotic birds will hover above our heads—asylum-seekers from the scorched jungles of the tropics.

But, to anyone tempted by this vision, Lynas points out that Continental Europe has just endured its highest temperatures for 500 years, which set off devastating forest fires in France, Spain and Portugal. In France 15,000 people died in last year's heatwave, triggering what Lynas terms "a national crisis of guilt and soul-searching"—not evident to me, I must say, as I surveyed the beach-bound traffic jamming the autoroute to the Cote d'Azur.

Lynas moves restlessly around the world, from the melting Arctic ice-cap to drowned Pacific islands, hunting down climate change with the zeal of a missionary rooting out infidelity. I suspect that he sees global warming as a symptom of our faithlessness to a long suffering planet. Everywhere ecosystems are unravelling. The melt-water of the Greenland ice-sheet now equals the Nile's annual flow, but this water is in the wrong place, unable to irrigate the immense deserts appearing in Asia. Agriculture will suffer, and tropical diseases will spread towards the poles.

It's a harrowing prospect, brilliantly set out by Lynas. What should we do? First, ratify the Kyoto Protocol on climate change, and cut down on greenhouse gas emissions. Rein back industrial growth around the world, and stop all exploration of new oil, coal and gas reserves. Above all, target that implacable enemy which haunts the race-memory of ecologists like Lynas: the motor car ("for most city dwellers, cars are an unnecessary luxury").

For all Lynas's passion, his solution is even more apocalyptic than the problem. Most of us prefer our sunloungers and traffic jams, and will lie back contentedly until the Tarmac begins to boil off our roads, gazing at our banana trees and thoroughly enjoying the direst warnings in well-intentioned but somehow overwrought books like this one.

FLUSH WITH TALENT

Shepperton Babylon: The Lost Worlds of British Cinema by Matthew Sweet

Sunday Telegraph (February 6, 2005)

Film people are the best company, far more interesting than novelists, many of whom manage to be very strange but at the same time deeply dull—a difficult trick to pull off. Perhaps the form of the novel is wrong, too obsessed with time and the distant past, whereas film exists in a perpetual present in which social background counts for nothing and all that matters is what we see on the screen, an intense focus on the miracle of everyday life that turns a cigarette stubbed out in a fried egg or a pair of fractured glasses beside a murdered woman (both Hitchcock trademarks) into a modern myth.

Given the infinite possibilities of film, it's no wonder that the medium has attracted so many larger-than-life characters, as Matthew Sweet makes clear in his witty and entertaining history of the British cinema. Whether flour-milling tycoon or former strip-club operator, down-at-heel refugee or professional conman, they were all driven by a visionary belief in their personal hotline to the collective unconscious and their power to seize and captivate an audience for two hours on a grey afternoon.

Everyone who has strayed even briefly into the film world is bewildered by the titanic self-belief of those involved and their readiness to gamble everything on an impossible dream. Yet without them, no films would ever be made.

Shepperton Babylon? Alas, no, unless I've been missing something in this pleasant riverside town, which another local resident, the late Bernard Braden, once ironically described as the Malibu of the Thames Valley—a phrase that may have lured me to the place 45 years ago. Sweet comments that he chose Shepperton because its studios are not identified with a particular kind of film and can stand for the British industry as a whole. Many of my neighbours have worked as part-time film extras, and it's always slightly eerie to see parents who once shared the school run wearing Roman armour or a crinoline in television replays of forgotten films.

As Sweet makes clear, the British film industry has always been Hollywood's poor relation, bedeviled by a chronic shortage of money and the need to scrape and compromise in order to survive. But poor relations have certain advantages. They learn to make do, to rise above their weaknesses and exploit their few strengths. Looking back at the production history of British cinema, it is surprising how many of its greatest films in the 1940s and 1950s—*Brief Encounter*, *The Seventh Veil*, even *The Third Man*—were made for remarkably small sums of money. Talent will always out, and British film, while chronically short of money, has always been flush with talent.

Shepperton Babylon begins with the silent era, and Sweet points out that 80 per cent of the silent films shot in this country have now vanished, along with all memory of their stars and producers. One who is still remembered is Ivor Novello. Born David Davies, he was the son of a Welsh rate collector, looked down on his film work and believed that his stage musicals such as *King's Rhapsody* and *Perchance to Dream* would be immortal. They are almost forgotten, but his films, such as *The Vortex* and *The Constant Nymph*, made him a world star and offered an intriguing melange of drugs and homosexuality for the mass market.

With the birth of sound came Ealing Studios and the two great stars of the 1930s, Gracie Fields and George Formby. Fields was born over a Rochdale fish-and-chip shop and, as Sweet remarks, never let anyone forget it. Formby was a far stranger figure, with a screen personality almost deranged in its gormlessness, but like Fields he tapped deeply into the British psyche, for reasons I wouldn't be eager to explore.

The greatest movie mogul of British film, and the only one to rival his Hollywood counterparts, was J Arthur Rank, the Yorkshire flour-milling tycoon. A teetotaller and devout Methodist, he first became interested in film as a means of spreading his faith. At his peak in the 1950s, Rank employed the greatest British film stars—Dirk Bogarde, John Mills, Kenneth More among a hundred others—funded maverick talents such as Michael Powell and Emeric Pressburger, and supported films as different as *Henry V* and *Passport to Pimlico*.

Rank's films still define what we think of as quintessentially British cinema, a little staid and stuffy but as resolute as Jack Hawkins in an Aran sweater, even in the era of *Sexy Beast* and *Four Weddings and a Funeral*. In large part this was thanks to a remarkably relaxed attitude to costs and budgets, in the expectation that Rank-made films would find commercial triumph in America and the world. But freedom came at a price, still being paid for by all those lottery-funded films that never reach the screen. As the director Ronald Neame remembered: "The creative people were entirely in control. We could do whatever we liked, and we did. And we narrowly avoided destroying the Rank Organisation in the process."

THE DAY OF RECKONING

A Woman in Berlin by Anonymous, and Germany: Jekyll and Hyde by Sebastian Haffner

New Statesman (July 4, 2005)

Strange though it is, our fascination with the Nazi era shows no signs of fading. Scan the shelves of your local bookshop and you will see more swastikas than Union flags, and many more jacket portraits of Hitler than of Winston Churchill. A large part of Channel 5's peak output is devoted to Nazi genocide, to German weapons and battle tactics. Despite my best efforts, I know more about the gearbox in a Tiger tank than the one in my own car.

Even our possible future king has sported a swastika armband. Had he turned up at that costume party as a Chaplinesque Adolf, with comical forelock and moustache, no one would have minded. But Nazi uniforms and insignia resist humour and remind us of the extreme seriousness of the whole Hitler project. Between 1933 and 1945, psychopathology went to the best tailors, and no one jokes about the executioner's fashion sense.

Those of us still attracted to the SS chic and the spectral glamour of the Nazi epoch should read *A Woman in Berlin*, a heart-rending account of what happens when the day of reckoning at last dawns and even the smartest uniforms are not enough to save you. This harrowing diary is the record of a German woman's ordeal as the Russian armies overran Berlin. It was first published in Germany in 1960 and generated a storm of controversy, one reviewer complaining about the anonymous author's "shameless immorality." During the postwar years of the economic miracle a collective amnesia conveniently ruled. The rape of hundreds of thousands of German women, and the impotence of German men as they watched Russian soldiers rape their wives, were not topics to be remembered at a time when men were reasserting their authority at car-production lines.

The diarist's lack of self-pity, and her clear-eyed view of the survival tactics adopted by the German women around her, still unsettle the present-day reader of what must be one of the most remarkable war diaries ever kept. The author was a 34-year-old, unmarried journalist named Marta Hiller, by her own description "a pale-faced blonde always dressed in the same winter coat." She had travelled once to Russia before the war and picked up a little of the language, which in due course served her well, though it is remarkable that ten years later she remembered enough Russian to calm the violent soldiers about to rape her, and even converse about Marxism with their officers.

Doubts have been cast on the authenticity of the diary, and it is hard to believe, as the author claims, that it was jotted down with a pencil stub on old scraps of paper while she crouched on her bed between bouts of rape. The tone is so dispassionate, scenes described in so literary a way, with poignant references to the strangeness of silence and the plaintive cry of a distant bird. We live at a time that places an almost sentimental value on the unsparing truth, however artfully deployed. But the diary seems convincingly real, whether assembled later from the testimonies of a number of women or recorded at first hand by the author.

The diary begins on Hitler's birthday, 20 April 1945, four days after the start of the final Russian assault on Berlin. Two million civilians remained in the city, most of them women and children. The German soldiers defending the author's eastern suburb have withdrawn. As the front-line fighting moves away from them, the women in the diarist's apartment building wait in a state of terror.

Gradually the street below fills with the Russian artillery men and their horses. More concerned about watering their animals, they cautiously eye the German women, but in the evening they start drinking, and the women's ordeal begins. Doors and barricades are kicked aside. On the first day—it's difficult to keep count—the author is raped three times, and then almost daily during the next weeks, as wave after wave of Russian soldiers passes through.

All the women in the building are repeatedly raped, from teenagers to the elderly. The author describes the familiar clank of holstered pistols hung from the bed rail. Many of the "Ivans" are young and shy, and like to lie back afterwards and chat. A few become protective, and revive the traumatised women with parcels of bread and herring.

"What does it mean—rape?" the author asks. "It sounds like the absolute worst, the end of everything, but it's not." Hunger and death are worse. The women show amazing resilience, encouraging those Russian admirers to bring the best food. In the end they survive, clearing rubble all day for a bowl of soup. However, their attitude to their German menfolk has changed for ever. "We feel so sorry for them; they seem so miserable and powerless . . . among the many defeats at the end of this war is the defeat of the male sex."

What is missing from the diary is any acknowledgement of Nazi crimes and any sense of why the Russians are taking so brutal a revenge. There are no references to the mass murder of Russians, Poles and Jews, to the inhuman brutality of the German armies and the deranged creed that drove them on. The author's fiance served in the Wehrmacht on the

Eastern Front—did he never describe what was happening there? Perhaps her silence is a tacit confession of guilt, but I doubt it.

Germany: Jekyll and Hyde, by the Berlin-born Observer journalist Sebastian Haffner, was first published in 1940, and is an alarm call trying to awaken the British to the unique nature of Hitler and the Nazi regime. Haffner stresses that, for all its advanced science and technology, Nazi Germany is a throwback to more brutal times, and is propelled by non-rational motives. Hitler, he maintains, is an out-and-out psychopath, who plays successfully on the age-old tendency of Germans to see themselves as persecuted, slighted and ill-treated. Anti-Semitism, Haffner believes, serves as a "secret sign and binding mystery among Nazis, like a continuous ritual murder."

Haffner's warnings, published before the attack on Russia, before Auschwitz and total war, are remarkably prescient, though he cannot have imagined the scale of the horror about to be unleashed. We in Britain have seen the newsreels and made endless tours of the charnel house, but we are still fascinated rather than repelled by the Nazi era, as German ambassadors have complained. Is this because we are still searching for an explanation of why the German people, among the most advanced and civilised in Europe, decided to plunge into madness and follow their psychopathic god?

If not, then why are the British, a pugnacious but unmilitary people, so gripped by the Nazi era? I suspect that something is missing from the British sense of themselves. Having spent much of our past fighting wars and building an empire, we are dissatisfied with our cosy lot, with suburbia, good sense and the rule of reason. We want more theatre in our lives, more emotion and even a little more madness. We want to strut and bully, as we did long ago in Africa and India. We want to revitalise ourselves in a burst of the same elective madness with which the German people propelled themselves into a more dangerous future. As we slump in front of *Celebrity Love Island* and *Springwatch with Bill Oddie* we may even feel nostalgic for a Nazi Britain that never was . . .

FILMS

Despite his involvement in the industry from his 1967 commission to write a treatment for Hammer films, the larger part of Ballard's writing on film consisted of reviewing books about the industry. The below reviews and appreciations of films themselves are compiled from disparate sources.

The London-based listings magazine *Time Out* was a radical proposition in the late 1970s under the editorship of Richard Williams, with a politically progressive editorial stance and a well-resourced news section. Ballard's contrarian takedown of *Star Wars* (1977) was the lead coverline on the Christmas double issue, the first to appear after *Star Wars* had become the highest-grossing release in film history, overtaking Steven Spielberg's *Jaws* (1975).

Ballard's three-paragraph account of David Lynch's *Blue Velvet* (1986) was commissioned for a special supplement published with the Saturday *Guardian* magazine, titled *The Movies: The Readers' Choice*, in which various writers contributed reviews of the top 100 movies since 1980 as selected in a readers' poll. *Blue Velvet* was the second-placed choice, after *Cinema Paradiso* (1988).

Running on a Thursday in the "Human Jungle" column in the *T2* section of the *Times*, "Re-Run" asked a notable cultural figure to respond to the question: "Can an old favourite hold its magic?" *The Third Man* (1949) was Ballard's choice.

The blockbuster *The Day After Tomorrow* (2004) was reviewed for the *Guardian*'s Friday *Review* section, in a retrospective consideration of how Hollywood spectaculars treated the apocalyptic visions his early novels had specialized in. A long review of *A History of Violence* (2005) for the same newspaper permitted Ballard to cast an approving eye over the entire career of David Cronenberg, the director who had brought *Crash* to the screen in 1996.

HOBBITS IN SPACE

Star Wars (1977)

Time Out (December 16, 1977)

Can I offer a dissenting opinion? A serious question. There seems to be a profound need everywhere to admire this film, a resentment of any response other than loving affection. *Star Wars*, written and directed by George Lucas, is engaging, brilliantly designed, acted with real charm, full of verve and visual ingenuity. It's also totally unoriginal, feebly plotted, instantly forgettable, and an acoustic nightmare—the electronic sound-wall wrapped around the audience is so over-amplified that every footfall sounds like Krakatoa.

For once, the official synopsis gives an exact idea of the film's flavour.

"Star Wars *follows a young man, Luke Skywalker, through exotic worlds vastly dif-ferent from our own. Leaving the small arid planet of Tatooine, Luke plunges into an extraordinary intergalactic search for the kidnapped rebel Princess Leia from the planet Alderaan. Luke is joined in this adventure by Ben Kenobi (Alec Guinness), the last of the Jedi Knights who were the guardians of peace and justice in the old days before the 'dark times' came to the galaxy; Han Solo, the dashing, cynical captain of the Millennium Falcon, a Corellian pirate star-ship; Chewbacca, a Wookiee, a race of tall anthropoids with quasi-monkey faces and large blue eyes; and the robots See-Threepio (C-3PO) and Artoo-Detoo (R2-D2). This odd band of adventurers battle Grand Moff Tarkin, the evil Governor of the Imperial Outland regions, and Darth Vader, the malevolent Dark Lord of the Sith, who employs his extrasensory powers to aid Governor Tarkin (Peter Cushing) in the destruction of the rebellion against the Galactic Empire. In the battle of Yarvin, Luke engages in a terrifying climactic space battle over the huge man-made planet destroyer, Death Star."*

In that case, why all the fuss? And what does the amazing success of *Star Wars* indicate, for good or ill, about the future of s-f cinema? Although slightly biased, I firmly believe that science fiction is the true literature of the twentieth century, and probably the last literary form to exist before the death of the written word and the domination of the visual image. S-f has been one of the few forms of modern fiction explicitly concerned with change—social, technological and environmental—and certainly the only fiction to invent society's myths, dreams and utopias.

Why, then, has it translated so uneasily into the cinema? Unlike the western, which long ago took over the literary form and now exists in its own right, the s-f film has never really been more than an offshoot of its literary precursor, which to date has provided all the ideas, themes and inventiveness. S-f cinema has been notoriously prone to cycles of exploitation and neglect, unsatisfactory mergings with horror films, thrillers, environmental and disaster movies.

The most popular form of s-f—space fiction—has been the least successful of all cinematically, until *2001* and *Star Wars*, for the obvious reason that the special effects available were hopelessly inadequate. Surprisingly, s-f is one of the most literary forms of all fiction, and the best s-f films—*Them!*, *Dr Cyclops*, *The Incredible Shrinking Man*, *Alphaville*, *Last Year in Marienbad*; (not a capricious choice, its themes are time, space and identity, s-f's triple pillars), *Dr Strangelove*, *The Invasion of the Body Snatchers*, *Barbarella* and *Solaris*—and the brave failures such as *The Thing*, *Seconds* and *The Man who Fell to Earth*—have all made use of comparatively modest special effects and relied on strongly imaginative ideas, and on ingenuity, wit and fantasy.

With *Star Wars* the pendulum seems to be swinging the other way, towards huge but empty spectacles where the special effects—like the brilliantly designed space vehicles and their interiors in both *Star Wars* and *2001*—preside over derivative ideas and unoriginal plots, as in some massively financed stage musical where the sets and costumes are lavish but there are no tunes. I can't help feeling that in both these films the spectacular sets are the real subject matter, and that original and imaginative ideas—until now science fiction's chief claim to fame—are regarded by their makers as secondary, unimportant and even, possibly, distracting.

Star Wars in particular seems designed to appeal to that huge untapped audience of people who have never read or been particularly interested in s-f but have absorbed its superficial ideas—space ships, ray guns, blue corridors, the future as anything with a fin on it—from comic strips, TV shows like "Star Trek" and "Thunderbirds," and the iconography of mass merchandising.

The visual ideas in *Star Wars* are ingenious and entertaining. Ironically it's only now that the technology of the cinema is sufficiently advanced to represent an advanced technology in decline. I liked the super-technologies already beginning to rust around the edges, the pirate starship like an old tramp steamer, the dented robots with IQs higher than Einstein's which resembled beat-up De Sotos in Athens or Havana with half a million miles on the clock. I liked the way large sections of the action were seen through computerized head-up displays which provided information about closing speeds and impact velocities that makes everyone in the audience feel like a Phantom pilot on a Hanoi bombing run.

In passing, the reference to Vietnam isn't undeserved—the slaughter in *Star Wars*, quite apart from the destruction of an entire populated planet, is unrelieved for two hours, and at times stacks the corpses halfway up the screen. Losing track of this huge bodycount, I thought at first that the film might be some weird, unintentional parable of the US involvement in Vietnam, with the plucky hero from the backward planet and his scratch force of reject robots and gook-like extraterrestrials fighting bravely against the evil and all-destructive super-technology of the Galactic Empire. Whatever the truth, it's strange that the film gets a U certificate—two hours of *Star Wars* must be one of the most efficient means of weaning your pre-teen child from any fear of, or sensitivity towards, the deaths of others.

All the same, as a technological pantomime *Star Wars* makes a certain amount of sense. There's the good fairy, Alec Guinness, with his laser-wand and a smooth line in morally uplifting chat; the pantomime dame/wicked witch, the Dark Lord Darth Vader, with black Nazi helmet, leather face-mask and computerized surgical truss; the principal boy, the apparently masculine robot Artoo-Detoo who in fact conceals a coded holographic image of the Princess Leia, which he now and then projects like a Palladium Dick Whittington flashing her thighs.

However, George Lucas has gone badly astray with his supporting cast—what looks like an attempted tour de force, the parade of extraterrestrials in the frontier-planet saloon, comes on hilariously like the Muppet Show, with shaggy monsters growling and rolling their eyeballs. I almost expected Kermit and Miss Piggy to swoop in and introduce Bruce Forsyth.

What is missing in all this is any hard imaginative core. *Star Wars* is the first totally unserious s-f film. Even a bad episode of *Star Trek* or *Dr. Who* has the grain of an original idea, and the vast interplanetary and technological perspectives of *2001* were at least put to the service of a steadily expanding cosmic vision. The most one can hope, I think, is, that the technical expertise now exists to make a really great s-f film. *Star Wars*, in a sense, is a huge test-card, a demonstration film of s-f movie possibilities.

20th Century-Fox's advance publicity describes the modern motion picture as "the most magnificent toy ever invented for grown men to play with and express their fantasies"—presumably with Lucas's approval, and *Star Wars* may well be more prophetic than I give it credit for. In many ways it is the ultimate home movie, in which Lucas goes back into his toy cupboard and plays with all his boyhood fantasies, fitting together a collection of stuffed toys, video games and plastic spaceships into this ten-year-old's extravaganza, back to the days, as he himself says, when he "dreamed about running away and having adventures that no one else has ever had."

BLUE VELVET (1986)

Guardian (September 18, 1993)

Blue Velvet is, for me, the best film of the 1980s—surreal, voyeuristic, subversive and even a little corrupt in its manipulation of the audience. In short, the perfect dish for the jaded palates of the 1990s. But a thicket of puzzles remains. First, why do the sensible young couple, played by Kyle MacLachlan and Laura Dern, scheme to break into the apartment of the brutalized nightclub singer (Isabella Rossellini) and risk involving themselves with the psychopathic gangster—Dennis Hopper in his most terrifying screen performance?

A curious feature of *Blue Velvet* is the virtual absence of the youngsters' parents, shadowy figures who take almost no part in the action. I assume the film is a full-blown Oedipal drama, and that the gangster and the nightclub singer are the young couple's "real" parents. Like children hiding in their parents' bedroom, they see more than they bargained for. Playing his sadistic games with the singer, the gangster rants "Mummy, mummy, mummy"; a useful pointer to David Lynch's real intentions. The young man longs to take the gangster's place in the singer's bed and, when he does, soon finds himself playing the same shocking games, a crisis that can only be resolved by killing his "father" in the approved Oedipal fashion.

The second puzzle is the role of the severed ear found by the young man after he visits his father in hospital, and which sets off the entire drama. Why an ear rather than a hand or a set of fingerprints? I take it that the ear is really his own, tuned to the inner voice that informs him of his imminent quest for his true mother and father. Like the ear, the white picket fence and the mechanical bird that heralds a return to morality, *Blue Velvet* is a sustained and brutal tease, *The Wizard of Oz* re-shot with a script by Kafka and decor by Francis Bacon. More, more . . .

THE THIRD MAN (1949)

Times (October 3, 2002)

A few days ago I saw *The Third Man*, the great Carol Reed film starring Orson Welles, Joseph Cotten and Alida Valli, and it was an extraordinarily moving experience. I first saw the film when it came out in 1949, when I was a medical student at Cambridge, dissecting cadavers in the afternoon before going to the cinema to relax in the evening. It seemed to me then that it was a merciless dissection of Europe and its tragic failures which had led to world war.

It was just four years after the end of the Second World War, and its picture of a shattered and compromised Europe struck me with breathtaking force. Although set in a Vienna still under Four-Power control, it might have been England. There were the same ruins, the same black marketeers and the same corruption and despair. Much as I admired Welles's acting, I was more impressed by the beauty and melancholy passion of Valli.

Seeing the film on video, its visual impact seemed as great as ever. When it was first shown everyone saw it as a newsreel, so close was it to the reality of the bomb-damaged and rationed world in which we lived. The smallest details took me back to the late 1940s—the cut of men's sports jackets, the over-wary gestures of the supporting players and, above all, the moral ambiguities that the naive American, Holly Martins (Joseph Cotten), finds baffling.

It seems to me that in the context of imminent war in Iraq, we witness the same inability of still-naive and trusting Americans to grasp the venality of the world. They loathe moral ambiguity, and Martins is unable to understand why the beautiful Anna Schmidt should still be in love with Harry Lime (Welles), the black marketeer. Seeing the film today made me realise the vast gulf which separates America from our tired and disillusioned continent.

Oddly enough, I felt that my present 71-year-old self was no older than the 18-year-old who first saw it. Very few films as great are made today.

IN MODERN AMERICA, NO NIGHTMARE IS FORBIDDEN

The Day After Tomorrow (2004)

Guardian (May 14, 2004)

The Unconscious will always expose itself. If the British tabloid press shows the nation's unconscious mind at work—a bubbling pit of prurience and anxiety—then the Hollywood block-buster reveals the deepest fantasies and paranoia of the American psyche. Either way, it's probably better to have our monsters oozing towards us across the sitting-room floor than bottled up in the basements of our minds.

Writing 50 years ago in *War, Sadism and Pacifism*, the English psychoanalyst Edward Glover commented: "The most cursory study of the dream-life and fantasies of the insane shows that ideas of world destruction are latent in the unconscious mind." But it's clear that in today's America these fantasies are no longer latent. The British are still reticent about their deepest fears—class war, a reversion to economic feudalism, the spectre of an all-dominant and all-vapid consumer society. But in modern America, there are no suppressed dreams, no forbidden nightmares.

Every American fear and paranoid anxiety is out in the open, from the ranting of ultra-right shockjocks to *The Day After Tomorrow*, Hollywood's latest attempt to traumatise us with fears of climate change. Here, global warming melts the polar ice caps, flooding our planet and plunging us into a global catastrophe. The computerised special effects are more real than reality itself, bypassing many areas of the brain and posing problems for philosophers and neuro psychologists alike, hinting at a future where the human race abandons "old" reality in the same way that Americans abandoned old Europe.

We might think that the US had enough problems coping with Iraq, where the abuse of prisoners has given a spin of sexual perversion to its drive towards world domination, something the British Empire, with its croquet and memsahibs, never achieved, alas. But disaster movies have been a Hollywood staple for decades. Earthquakes and tsunamis, asteroids and volcanoes, alien invasions and deranged machines have destroyed and re-destroyed the planet, analogues perhaps of all-out nuclear war against the Soviet Union. Or, more likely I suspect, a thinly veiled glimpse of the self-destructive urges lurking alongside the hamburger and comic-book culture we all admire. As the nation infantilises itself, the point is finally reached where the abandoned infant has nothing to do except break up its cot.

Unsettling as our own tabloids may be, the British psyche and its problems hardly matter to the wider world. But the turmoils of the American psyche have vast ramifications. Are films like *The Day After Tomorrow*, *Armageddon* and *Independence Day* a warning signal to the rest of us? Since Hiroshima and Nagasaki displayed the vast reach of US power, the greatest danger is that Americans will believe their own myths. Is the gulf stream faltering? Is the equator moving northwards? Without doubt an alien, and possibly European plot, to be countered by the greatest display of "shock and awe" its super-technologies can muster.

Americans, rightly, mourned the 9/11 attack on the World Trade Centre. The destruction of the twin towers seemed to spring straight from a national memory bank stocked by Hollywood, and the horrific newsreels are effectively the greatest disaster movie to date. We can all probably cope with *The Day After Tomorrow*, but my fear is that in due course the "remake" of 9/11, with the ultimate in special effects, will inspire Americans to more than revenge.

THE KILLER INSIDE

A History of Violence (2005)

Guardian (September 23, 2005)

Are we all, without realising it, taking part in a vast witness protection programme? Did we observe, at some time in the distant past, a deeply disturbing event in which we were closely implicated? Were we then assigned new identities, new personalities, fears and dreams so convincing that we have forgotten who we really are?

These questions crowded my head as I watched *A History of Violence*, a film as brilliant and provocative as anything David Cronenberg has directed. All Cronenberg's films make us edge back into our seats, gripped by the story unfolding on the screen but aware that something unpleasant is going on in the seats around us.

That unpleasantness, needless to say, is ourselves, a damp bundle of passions, needs and neuroses that conceal our secret nature. The disturbing event we witnessed in the past is the experience of being alive, a state of affairs that Cronenberg most definitely does not take at face value.

Existence, in Cronenberg's eyes, is the ultimate pathological state. He sees us as fragile creatures with only a sketchy idea of who we are, nervous of testing our physical and mental limits. The characters in Cronenberg's films behave as if they are inhabiting their minds and bodies for the first time at the moment we observe them, fumbling with the controls like drivers in a strange vehicle. Will it rise vertically into the air, invert itself, or suddenly self-destruct?

Cronenberg has modestly described himself as looking like a Beverly Hills gynaecologist. Having worked with him on the making of *Crash*, I know that in person he is good company, with the reassuring manner of a neurosurgeon explaining how he is going to remove the inoperable tumour buried deep in your brain. Remarkably for a film maker working entirely within commercial cinema, he has remained faithful to his central project, and his films constitute a sustained autopsy into the nature of existence.

All Cronenberg's films, up to and including *A History of Violence*, are concerned with two questions: who are we, and what is the real nature of consciousness? Together, the films seem to parallel the growth of the mind from the womb onwards. Early films such as *Scanners* and *The Dead Zone* explore the blurred frontiers between mind and body, very much a new-born baby's perception of reality.

In *Videodrome*, this growing mind has made its first move into the outer world, appropriately by switching on a TV set, a parable of how tenuous reality has become in a media-dominated world. *The Fly*,

Cronenberg's most successful film, has echoes of Kafka's *Metamorphosis*, where a despised son sees himself transformed into an insect. Here Jeff Goldblum, filled with almost adolescent doubt and self-loathing, finds himself in a doomed love affair with Geena Davis. She watches cheerfully as he walks across ceilings, and I assume that his transformation into a giant fly takes place entirely within his own mind.

Naked Lunch moves beyond sex into the night world of heroin overdoses, and *Crash*, a love story that treats the car crash as a religious sacrament, enlists technology in an attempt to escape even death itself. Lastly, in *A History of Violence* society as a whole is embraced and then quietly dismantled.

The title, *A History of Violence*, is the key to the film, and should be read not as a tale or story of violence, but as it might appear in a social worker's case notes: "This family has a history of violence." The family, of course, is the human family, a primate species with an unbelievable appetite for cruelty and violence. If its behaviour in the 20th century is any guide, the human race inhabits a huge sink estate ravaged by unending feuds and civil wars, a no-go area abandoned by the authorities, though no one can remember who they are, or even if they exist.

The film is set in a small town in rural Ohio, a peaceful backwater where the only thing that changes is the single traffic light. Tom Stall, played by Viggo Mortensen, runs a pleasant cafe, and "I'll have some of that nice cherry pie" sums up the Norman Rockwell ethos. Tom is relaxed and likable, and is happily married to Edie (Maria Bello). They have a six-year-old daughter, Sarah, party-dress sweet and adorable, who we know is going to get it before too long, and a teenage son, Jack, with a droll line in humour. Asked by his bored girlfriend what the town's future holds for them, he replies: "We grow up, get jobs, get married and become alcoholics."

It seems unlikely. This is one town where David Lynch will never come calling, though Tom and Edie have playfully naughty imaginations. When the children are staying with friends, she dresses up as a high-school cheerleader and they have passionate sex on the daughter's bed. But it all seems as innocent as the stuffed toys lying around them.

Sadly, a darker world intrudes. One evening Tom is about to close up when two hoodlums enter the cafe, on the run after killing a motel manager. Seeing that he and his staff are in serious danger, Tom springs into action. During a violent struggle he is stabbed but seizes one of the weapons and shoots both men dead. The town rallies round, acclaiming its new hero. Wife and children proudly drive Tom home from the hospital. He mumbles modestly into the national TV cameras. He is a hero to his son, and the cafe is packed with well-wishers.

But far away, in Philadelphia, others have been watching the TV news. A week or so later, three very threatening men enter the cafe. Their leader, Carl Fogaty, is played by Ed Harris in a star turn that rivals Dennis Hopper's psychotic gangster in *Blue Velvet*. In black suit and ice-white shirt, sunglasses covering a damaged eye, he is stylised violence in every gesture. He greets Tom like an old acquaintance, glad to have found him at last. He claims that 20 years earlier Tom was a member of the Philadelphia mob. His job is to take Tom back to see his brother, now a mob boss and keen to settle certain unfinished business.

Tom maintains that he has never seen Fogaty before, but he is vague about his family background, and both his wife and son are unsure whether to believe him. Every certainty in their tranquil world has been overturned. Edie stares around their comfortable family home, realising that it may be no more than a stage set. The leader of the gang remarks to her: "Ask Tom where he learned to fight so well . . ."

What is so interesting about the film is the speed with which the wife accepts that her husband, for all his courage, is part of the criminals' violent world, in spirit, if not in actual fact. A dark pit has opened in the floor of the living room, and she can see the appetite for cruelty and murder that underpins the foundations of her domestic life. Her husband's loving embraces hide brutal reflexes honed by aeons of archaic violence. This is a nightmare replay of *The Desperate Hours*, where escaping convicts seize a middle-class family in their sedate suburban home—but with the difference that the family must accept that their previous picture of their docile lives was a complete illusion. Now they know the truth and realise who they really are. Their family has a history of violence.

TELEVISION

A solitary, feature-length review of the long-running television series *C.S.I.: Crime Scene Investigation* stands as evidence of Ballard's proposal to Jon Savage in 1978: "I think it's terribly important to watch TV. I think there's a sort of minimum number of hours of TV a day you ought to watch, and unless you watch three or four hours of TV a day, you're just closing your eyes to some of the most important sort of stream of consciousness that's going on!"[2]

2. *Extreme Metaphors*, 114.

IN COLD BLOOD

C.S.I.: Crime Scene Investigation (2000–2015)

Guardian (June 25, 2005)

Television today is an ageing theme park, which we visit out of habit rather than in hope of finding anything fresh and original. At times I think that the era of television is over, but then it suddenly comes up with something rich and strange. A few years ago, hunting the outer darkness of Channel 5, I began to linger over a series called *C.S.I.: Crime Scene Investigation*. After only a few episodes I was completely hooked, for reasons I don't understand even today.

Set in Las Vegas, the series described the work of the police department's forensics team, a strictly tweezers and litmus paper operation where guilt or innocence hang on having the right kind of sand in your turnups. Lurid computer graphics provided flashbacks to the actual homicides, a stomach-churning revelation of what actually happens when an axe strikes the back of the skull, or a corrosive gas gets to work on the lungs. The series was original, slick and deeply disturbing, though I wasn't too keen to find out why.

At least I wasn't the only one to be hooked. Two years ago *C.S.I.* climbed to the top of the audience ratings in America, and its success led to *C.S.I. Miami* and a third spin off, *C.S.I. New York*. Now, as part of its Crime Season 2005, London's NFT is hosting The C.S.I. Phenomenon, a weekend devoted to the show with Quentin Tarantino as a guest. But for all its success, *C.S.I.* is a very unusual series, and a mystery in its own right. I suspect that it taps deeply into the collective unconscious of the TV audience, as did *Sex and the City* and *Big Brother*, but in a far more sinister way.

What is so unsettling about the series? First of all, there are the locales, which are not what they seem. The Vegas series and *C.S.I. Miami* are set in the two strangest cities in America, but take no advantage whatever of their bizarre ecologies. The reason, of course, is that they are filmed in Los Angeles and rarely come anywhere near Las Vegas or Miami, unlike *Hawaii Five-O* and *Miami Vice*, which were shot on the spot, and where the lush flora and fauna helped to authenticate even the most improbable storylines.

But this shunning of the real Vegas and Miami has its advantages. The air in LA is grey and dusty compared with the desert glare of Las Vegas and the spectral whiteness of Miami Beach. So *C.S.I.*, taking the same dim view of daylight as Count Dracula, stays indoors whenever it can.

The series unfolds within an almost totally interiorised world, a clue to its real significance. The crimes—they are all homicides—take place in anonymous hotel rooms and in the tract housing of the Vegas and Miami suburbs, almost never in a casino or druglord's gaudy palace. A brutal realism prevails, the grimmest in any crime series. Suburban lounges and that modern station of the cross, the hotel bathroom, are the settings of horrific murders, which thankfully are over by the time each episode begins. Gloves donned, the cast dismantle u-bends and plunge up to their elbows in toilet bowls, retrieving condoms, diaphragms and bullet casings, syringes, phials and other signs of the contemporary zodiac. Faecal matter and toilet paper are never shown, perhaps reflecting American squeamishness, though evidence of anal intercourse and vaginal bruising is snapped out like the tennis scores.

If the crime scene is brightly lit, the outdoor world is always dark. A car crash or street shooting always takes place at night, when the city seems deserted and dead. Light and safety are found only in the crime lab, among its high-tech scanners and its ruthless deconstruction of human trauma. This rejection of the outside world eliminates the need for transport, and there are no cars in the *C.S.I.* series. David Caruso, who plays the head of the Miami team, sometimes turns up in a vast Hummer, an armoured vehicle that transforms a quiet Miami suburb into a bomb-ridden quarter of Baghdad, as if underlining the hostility of the external world.

The complete absence of cars touches a nerve of anxiety in the viewer. Television crime series, from *Felony Squad* and *The Rockford Files* to our own *Z Cars* and *The Sweeney*, were filled with their huge carapaces, swerving in and out of alleys, reversing in a howl of burning rubber. Watched with the sound down, episodes of *Starsky and Hutch* resembled instructional films on valet parking. The identification of car and hero reached its apotheosis in the 1970s series *Vegas*, where the playboy private eye played by the affable Robert Urich actually parked his car inside his living room, stretched out beside him like a faithful bloodhound.

In *C.S.I.*, not only are there no cars, but there are no guns. The team wear sidearms, but I have rarely seen a gun drawn in self-defence, let alone fired. The only bullets discharged end up in calibrated water tanks. The assumption is clearly made that reason and logic need never rely on anything so crude as brute force. No cars, no guns and, even more significant, no emotions, except in the flashbacks to the actual crime.

Every viewer knows that the only people who show emotion in *C.S.I.* are about to be dead. This lack of emotion extends to the cast, who never display a flicker of anger or revulsion. None of the team have relationships with each other, and there are few rivalries and no affairs. We never see where they live and know nothing about them. Gil Grissom, the head of the *C.S.I.* team played by William Petersen, is a likeable but hermetic figure who will throw out a Shakespeare quote or a tag from Rousseau as he peers into his microscope, but he remains sealed inside his quest for the truth. The queenly Marg Helgenberger, who plays Grissom's number two, is a former "exotic dancer," a single mother with a daughter we never see. Her speciality is "blood spatter analysis."

Still, this reticence contrasts favourably with the demented profligacy of *The Bill*, with its cast of murderers, psychopaths, child molesters and arsonists, all of them in police uniform and all emotionally interlocked with each other. New arrivals at Sun Hill station are ruthlessly asset-stripped of whatever weaknesses they try to hide and then discarded. Emotion rules rather than reason. Characterisation, we are always told, is the key to drama, but this is a literary notion that serves the interests of unimaginative novelists. In any case, it is untrue to life, where we can work with people in the same office for years, or even share the same bed in a tolerable marriage, and know next to nothing about their real characters until a sudden crisis occurs.

Given that there are no interesting characters, no car chases or shoot outs, no violently stirred emotions and no dramatic action, why is the *C.S.I.* series so riveting? What is it that grips us to the end of the episode, which is scarcely more than an elaborate crossword puzzle with human tissues in the place of clues? My guess is that the answer lies in the inner sanctum at the heart of all three series—the autopsy room. Here the victims surrender all that is left of their unique identities, revealing the wounds and medical anomalies that led to their demise. Once they have been dissected—their ribcages opened like suitcases, brains lifted from their craniums, tissues analysed into their basic components—they have nothing left, not even the faintest claim on existence.

I suspect that the cadavers waiting their turn on the tables are surrogates for ourselves, the viewers. The real crime the *C.S.I.* team is investigating, weighing every tear, every drop of blood, every smear of semen, is the crime of being alive. I fear that we watch, entranced, because we feel an almost holy pity for ourselves and the oblivion patiently waiting for us.

7

NEW STATESMAN

Ballard returned to the pages of the *New Statesman*, the London-based progressive politics and culture magazine, in 1997 following a hiatus of twenty years. The title, published fortnightly as a glossy newsstand magazine, had been saved from bankruptcy by the Labour Party MP Geoffrey Robinson in 1996. The new editor Ian Hargreaves closely followed the emergence of the New Labour project. Under his successor, Peter Wilby, the magazine launched a website in 1998.

Over the next decade, Ballard contributed four book reviews, three diary pieces, a feature, and regular entries into books-of-the-year round-ups. Collectively, these pieces provide a valuable mirror to the late-period novels, particularly *Millennium People* (2003) and *Kingdom Come* (2006), in which his attention was focused on transformations in British society. The long-form pieces are grouped here while all four reviews can be read in the "Reviews" section.

Ballard's first contribution to the "Diary" slot in the *New Statesman* was for the bumper, 132-page Millennium Christmas issue. Notable is his diagnosis of the millennium dome, the controversial structure built on the Greenwich peninsular in London to mark the event. His assessment is melancholy: "The future has turned its back and lost interest in us."

His second diary piece appeared during the campaign for the 2001 UK general election. On June 7, 2001, the Labour Party, led by Tony Blair, returned for a second term with a large majority. In invoking Jean Baudrillard's essay "The Gulf War Did Not Take Place" (1991), which had been published in French in *Libération* and in English in the *Guardian* in 1991, Ballard continued his engagement with the work of the French philosopher discussed in his response to the editors of *Science Fiction Studies* and celebrated by the inclusion of Baudrillard's *America* (1986) in his list of ten favorite books for the anthology *The Pleasure of Reading* ("A Response to the Invitation to Respond," 304, and "My Favourite Books," 323). His reflections on the Tate gallery, for which his daughter Fay worked, and the claim that "the middle class is the new proletariat" signal the ideas that were informing work on *Millennium People*.

"Now Parliament Is Just Another Hypermarket" was published in the 2005 general election special issue. The front half of the magazine was divided into three sections: the first contained pieces devoted to "The Night"; Ballard's contribution was one of six pieces considering "The Campaign"; nine pieces looking to "The Future," including one by Ballard's friend the philosopher John Gray, followed.

The final diary piece, subtitled "A Fascist's Guide to the Premiership" was trailed on the cover: "J. G. Ballard on Working Class Tribes." It accompanied the September publication of his last novel, *Kingdom Come*, whose central theme is posed here as a question—"Could consumerism evolve into fascism?" His closing reflections respond to Tony Blair's announcement that he would step down as leader of the Labour Party within the year.

DIARY (1999)

"What are your plans for the new millennium?" a friend asks. I'd like to say that I'll open a cinematheque in Marbella, or fly a man-powered glider across the Pacific. But I've just entered my three-score-and-tenth year, so reply cautiously: "First, I'll get there. Then look around at the possibilities." A problem is the almost palpable lack of excitement in the air. People 50 years younger than me, who will spend most of their lives in the next century, display all the eagerness of passengers diverted to a brand-new airport on the edge of a desert. Everything is clean and shiny but oddly threatening. Given that we are leaving the 1990s behind, the most corrupt and shabby decade since the second world war, I expected an explosive burst of speed as we approach the final straight.

*

Despite all the debate, Britain will enter the 21st century with 92 hereditary peers in its legislature. The monarchy, inherited titles and public schools are among other living fossils that seem to thrive in our peculiar geology. The class system, an overt instrument of political control, is more strongly entrenched than in any other western nation.

The Lords may be in the process of reform, but isn't it time to abolish the hereditary principle in the Commons? I'm thinking of those Westminster placemen, the jobsworths of party politics, a self-perpetuating caste elected year after year to the same seats and promoted to the same offices of state. If the 1990s was a low, dishonest decade, the era of focus groups and cash-filled envelopes, then they made it possible. Fortunately, a few mavericks still survive.

*

A curious feature of the coming millennium is how little speculation it has prompted. I remember in the 1960s being rung up by journalists asking, "What will sex be like in the seventies?" They expected something strange and unimaginable, but looking back after 20 years it all seemed much the same. A general rule: if enough people predict something, it won't happen. Even so, I suspect that within a few years there will be a widespread rejection of the 20th century, its horrors and corruptions. Despite huge advances in science and technology, it will seem a barbarous time. My grandchildren are all under the age of four, the first generation who will have no memories of the present century, and are likely to be appalled when they learn what was allowed to take place. For them, our debased entertainment culture and package-tour hedonism will be inextricably linked to Auschwitz and Hiroshima, though we would never make the connection. I hope that a wave of idealism will move through their lives, not the weird mix of new-age slogans and autocue sincerity that is our own substitute for high-mindedness, but a level-headed decision to put the planet to rights.

*

Memories of happier times were stirred by a chance encounter in the Thames Valley, my stamping ground, the terrain of business parks, marinas and executive housing that constitutes New Britain. Claire, my girlfriend, needed a quick vaccination, so I drove her to a no-appointment, please-walk-in medical centre near Guildford. Courteous and efficient staff, the latest hi-tech equipment and the prices of everything prominently displayed: consultations, X-rays, blood tests. But no mention of the most persistent complaint of all. "What would it cost to die here?" I asked the receptionist. She wasn't fazed for a second. "It depends—what sort of death do you have in mind?"

*

A serious question, which I pondered as we drove off. Taking a wrong turning, we found ourselves in Byfleet, crossing an industrial estate that lies inside the old Brooklands racing circuit. Huge sections of the banked track have been carefully preserved, heroic monuments to an age when speed was the nearest thing to magic and carried a potent image of the future. As a child in 1930s Shanghai I sat on the edge of my seat and watched the newsreels of racing cars thundering around the circuit. This was the era of unlimited engine capacities, goggles and white cotton overalls. Today we have Formula One, with its hobbled and neurotic cars, driven by millionaires in fireproof suits advertising anti-freeze. The future has turned its back and lost interest in us. We stopped and walked along the curved track, hoping to hear the throaty roar of 24-cylinder engines. The ancient concrete is the same vintage as the bunkers in the Siegfried Line, but for £750 million they could have scrapped the Dome and rebuilt the entire Brooklands circuit.

*

Visiting the Dome recently, Claire and I were struck by how ugly it is, the pylons driven like stakes through the shallow marquee, the maze of overhead wires that irritate the retina. It resembles a sinister abattoir disguised as a circus tent, waiting for its real role in a third world war. The Dome is too small, and fails to take the breath away. It should have been at least half a mile in diameter, the largest structure on the planet, a wonder of the modern world. Instead it looks like the last tired effort of 20th-century science fiction.

*

By contrast, the Millennium Wheel is a delight. Claire and I watched it being raised, and were stunned by its elegance and mystery, and by the special magic shared by all Ferris wheels. There should be more of them, at least one in every borough, and London would become a surrealist and poetic city.

DIARY (2001)

Is the election actually taking place? The question isn't entirely frivolous. Tony Blair and William Hague hold forth at their news conferences, candidates roam the television studios, and the party political broadcasts keep our remote controls busier than ever. But it all seems strangely unreal, a muddled and overlong melodrama whose cast have left their scripts on the bus. Even television, which usually imposes an illusion of reality on events, has begun to falter. Jeremy Paxman is clearly bored

out of his mind, and Peter Snow's swingometer looks like an antique flying machine built by an eccentric psephologist. Point the arrow and flap
your arms.

*

It all reminds me of Jean Baudrillard's polemic *The Gulf War Did Not Take
Place*, in which the impish philosopher argued that the heavily censored
news reports, the absence of casualties and the video-game footage of
smart bombs dropping down chimneys did not constitute a true war
in our minds. By the same token, the present election seems curiously
inauthentic, as if the result has been agreed beforehand and everyone
involved is going through the motions. Here and there, reality breaks
in. Blair is harangued outside a hospital by a patient's upset partner,
and John Prescott throws the most famous British punch since Henry
Cooper's left hook decked the great Cassius Clay. I was amazed by how
po-faced some politicians and journalists became, even suggesting that
Prescott resign. What they were complaining about was that Prescott's
spontaneous action broke the spell.

*

Elections are now held as a public information service, like the VD and
drink-driving campaigns of old, to maintain the necessary illusion that
politics matters. Long ago—in 1997, with new Labour's accession to
government—the public accepted the consequences of refusing to pay
higher income taxes. No one seriously expected Blair to transform the
NHS in the near future, to improve our schools and fill the streets with
police. The gap between the reality of the tight wallet and the dream of
a fairer society could be filled by only one thing—public relations. We
accepted that, and even preferred it to the hard truth. We like spin, contrary to what most journalists tell us. We like PR campaigns and having
our emotions manipulated. We like mood music, and we like promises
that will never be kept. They remind us of a far more real world than
politics, the consumer culture, where we conduct our ordinary lives.
We spend our happiest moments in hyper-markets and shopping malls,

where everything is designed to make us feel better, while often making us worse off.

*

I like Blair and find it difficult to grasp why so many of his supporters are hostile to him. He reminds me of the man next door, with four children, a mortgage and an attractive, slightly harassed wife. Blair's great advantage over his rivals—Hague, Michael Portillo, Ann Widdecombe, Gordon Brown and Peter Mandelson—is that he alone has children. It's possible to imagine that he likes nothing more than an afternoon going round IKEA. As Prime Minister, his main function is to steer and cue our emotions, and to turn every political occasion into a scene from suburban life. His speech to the St Saviour's schoolgirls was perceived as a nationwide PTA meeting. PM's questions in the Commons are seen as the attempts by a decent and public-spirited man to silence a noisy bore on a bus.

*

But once Blair leaves the scene, he will be sadly missed. His heir-apparent Gordon Brown, constantly gabbling about fiscal this and percentage that, has all the charm of a speak-your-weight machine that has somehow acquired a degree in economics. Portillo, on the other hand, has the TV-honed skills to become a real threat. He smiles to camera like a basking shark sliding through a sea of warm plankton. Out here in the suburbs we murmur: "Miguel, Miguel . . ."

*

I'm told by friends in Notting Hill and Hampstead that their houses have tripled in value in the past five years, pushed up by the spate of huge City bonuses and share options. One senses that no one who earns less than £300,000 a year counts in any real way. The middle class is the new proletariat, forced out of inner London and clinging to antiquated notions such as the belief that education matters, just as the old working class believed in the sanctity of the job. In due course, our saviour will appear on the scene, a cross between Ralph Nader and Arthur Scargill. The May Day skirmishes were the first sign of middle-class restiveness, and were put down with significant ferocity.

*

I recently went back to Tate Modern, a year after the opening party, a celeb-packed feast where I turned at the bar to find that the man on my left was Jack Straw and the woman on my right was Tracey Emin. This extraordinary gallery has replaced the Dome as London's great inspirational venue. From the outside, the old power station looks smaller than it is, and the vast interior of the turbine hall is a stunning surprise. You mentally expand to fill this enormous space, and have the distinct feeling that you are one of the exhibits, a piece of performance art like Emin's bed. Sadly, I could think of nothing to say to her or Straw, though Tony Blair gave my partner Claire the warmest smile as we left. "That's no politician!" I exclaimed, and perhaps I was right.

NOW PARLIAMENT IS JUST ANOTHER HYPERMARKET (2005)

More important than the size of Tony Blair's majority was the turnout, which was not helped, I'm sorry to say, by my own small abstention. I voted for Blair at the last election, so why not now?

A grab bag of reasons: I like Blair but I think he is dangerous, with his actor's sincerity that hides a hysterical personality and a talent for drawing everyone into his make-believe world. The Iraq war was only one of a series of huge self-deceptions in which we have willingly colluded, in the way that a bored and restless congregation incites an evangelical preacher.

I'm uneasy with the Downing Street apparatus that has assembled itself around him, a public relations firm pretending to be a brainier, British White House. Blair is our president, but he has little real power. The inertial forces that lock Britain into its past are too great for him, and all the levers in his hands have snapped.

I'm sure Blair took us into Iraq because he was flattered to be summoned from the lower school and invited into the senior prefect's study. Bush and the neo-cons are driven by emotion, and this appeals to Blair.

The emotions are the one language that he understands, and reality is defined by what he feels he ought to believe. He commands no battle groups, and Britain's per capita income is one of the lowest in western Europe. Without the largely foreign-owned City of London the whole country would be a suburb of Longbridge, retraining as an offshore call-centre servicing the Chinese super-economy.

What really kept me away from the polling booth was the sense that the rate of political change has been slowing since the early 1990s. Do the possibilities for radical political change still exist? I would like to see the abolition of the monarchy, the House of Lords, inherited titles and the public schools, a move that would bring us into line with the rest of the English-speaking world. I would like to see Oxford and Cambridge turned into graduate universities entirely devoted to research, which at a stroke would cool the ardour of the "tiger mothers" of Holland Park and Hampstead determined to set their three-year-olds on the path to Oxbridge, whatever the human cost.

None of these changes could be tackled by the present political system, however, even if the will was there. I would like to see the Labour Party lead a full-scale assault on the English class system, which still amazes visitors to this country, but I know it will never happen.

Outside heritage London—not just Bloomsbury and St Paul's, but all those areas of the city dominated by a dinner-party culture—there are vast forgotten terrains where the greatest force for enlightenment is the nearest Ikea. Out on the London perimeter, in the motorway towns and retail parks that are the real Britain today, everything is ruled by consumerism. The cash till and the Pin preside. Consumerism defines people's lives, but, like sex with prostitutes, it demands special skills from the customer and there is no money-back guarantee.

The huge vacuum this creates may soon implode. The monarchy, the Church and politics have all faltered. The British monarchy is an afterthought of central Europe, the tale of a dysfunctional German family that destroyed itself in the supreme effort of trying to be English. The Church of England has long been secularising itself from within, and even atheism is now tolerated of its bishops.

As for parliament and the ballot box, I fear that politics can no longer bring about the radical changes this country needs. It's surprising that this happened so quickly. After I came to England in 1946 I found the professional middle class completely stunned by the huge changes brought in by the Attlee government—nationalisation, the health service, a crash programme of house-building, decent living standards for all. The new barbarians were at the gates. Later, Harold Wilson at least made an effort to move Britain on from the radio-valve age, and refused to join the Vietnam tragedy. Margaret Thatcher, in her turn, challenged the outer limits of ideology and change, leaving Blair with little to do except sweep up after the storm.

But now politics has lost its will, and may even have reached its close, absorbed into consumerism and public relations. Perhaps elections and the ballot box are little more than a folkloric ritual, along with parliament itself. Like university lecturers and psychiatrists, politicians may incidentally do some good, but their real loyalty is to themselves and their profession. The chief function of election campaigns is to convince us that politics and politicians are still important.

A year or two ago I was having dinner with my girlfriend in a west London restaurant when a large Jaguar double-parked outside, headlights blazing. Doors slammed like shotgun blasts and two thuggish men leapt out and bounded into the almost empty restaurant. They stood menacingly over our table, then signalled to the Jaguar's driver. Doors slammed again, and two more men strode in like Batman and Robin. They were Peter Mandelson and Reinaldo ("How handsome," Claire murmured, out of luck, alas). They sat at a rear table, staring into each other's eyes in the most inconspicuous way, while the bodyguards devoured a hearty meal, presumably at the taxpayer's expense.

Fifty minutes later the procedure was reversed. The bodyguards leapt to their feet, and the driver started his engine, sounding his horn to remind himself that he was at the wheel. After a pause, Mandelson scuttled out with a doggy bag, an endearing touch. Bodyguards, ex-minister and boyfriend dived into the car, which roared off, headlights at full beam, tyres squealing. Every terrorist in west London must have sighed and turned back thankfully to Sex and the City. Exhausted by this self-conscious charade, I said: "The man is out of office—what was that about?" Claire replied: "Vanity."

But I'm not convinced. I have no idea if Peter Mandelson is vain, and I assume that similar displays are going on every evening as ministers and ex-ministers make sure they are noticed, clinging to the last vestiges of power that confirm their own identities. To reassure them that they are still important, we need to turn out on the village green, cheer their three-legged races and clap their Punch-and-Judy knockabout. It may be only a charade, but they, of course, keep the day's takings.

Real power has gone, migrating to the shopping malls and hypermarkets where we make the important decisions in our lives. Consumerism controls everything, and the ballot box defers to the cash counter. The only escape from all this is probably out-and-out madness, and I expect the number of supermarket shootings and meaningless crimes to increase dramatically in the coming years. If anywhere, the future seems to lie with competing systems of psychopathology.

Gordon Brown gave the task of controlling inflation to the Bank of England, and perhaps our politicians should surrender more of their roles to better-qualified agencies. Perhaps UK plc would thrive if assigned to the two companies that will decide our planet's future—Microsoft and the Disney Corporation. Tony Blair would at last feel completely at home.

DIARY: A FASCIST'S GUIDE TO THE PREMIERSHIP (2006)

Is the English working class re-tribalising itself? Out here, to the west of London, in the motorway towns near Heathrow, a few St George's flags still hang in a dispirited way from council house windows and the coathanger aerials of white vans. As I drive from Shepperton past the airport, there's a sense of a failed insurrection. During the World Cup, a forest of flags flew proudly from almost every shop, factory and car, a passionate display willing on more than Beckham's boys in Germany.

This wasn't patriotism so much as a waking sense of tribal identity, dormant for decades. The notion of being British has never been so devalued. Sport alone seems able to be the catalyst of significant social change. Football crowds rocking stadiums and bellowing anthems are taking part in political rallies without realising it, as would-be fascist leaders will have noted.

The English, thank God, have always detested jackboots, searchlight parades and Führers ranting from balconies. But the Premier League, at the pinnacle of our entertainment culture, is a huge engine of potential change, waiting to be switched on. Could consumerism evolve into fascism? There is nothing to stop some strange consumer trend becoming a new ideology. Church and monarchy are dying on their knees, and politics is just another public utility, along with sewerage and the gas supply.

Surprisingly, the Heathrow scare on 10 August brought not even the briefest flourish of St George's flags. Driving past the airport on the A30, I noticed the familiar group of plane spotters not far from the Hilton. Not a plane was taking off, but the dream was in their eyes. Heathrow is a magnetic place, and the rest of London is merely a vast suburb of its airport. The inner keep of the great terminals is under siege, and I'm not surprised that would-be suicide bombers are so drawn to our airline system.

I take for granted that suicide bombing is a sign of despair. The kamikaze pilots who crashed their planes into American carriers knew that Japan had lost the war. Palestinian suicide bombers know that they cannot defeat Israel. The young London Underground bombers of 7/7 must have known that Islam, so deeply rooted in the past, cannot defeat the west. For Mohammed Atta, flying an airliner into the World Trade Center was his way of being modern. People are never more dangerous than when they have nothing left to believe in except God. And perhaps God today can only be reached through psychopathology. As far as I know, none of the Hezbollah fighters who so stunned the Israeli army resorted to suicide tactics, presumably because they were certain they were winning.

WE WILL ALL MISS TONY BLAIR

Autumn is almost here, and the new political season approaches in a half-hearted way, the last act of an overlong play that has begun to bore the audience. All the same, I suspect that we will miss Tony Blair when he is gone. The boyish charm is fraying but still intact. The exhaustion, the desperate need to convince everyone of the truth of his own delusions, the raw emotions worn as a kind of exoskeleton, all show one of the great actor-managers in heroic decline. Blair may be the last British prime minister able to trade openly on his emotions. He knows that we are secretly rather drawn to bad acting and are happy to collude in his exposure of his weaknesses.

He is the beaten husband, still in charge of the car keys and the TV remote, but aware that the rest of the household despises him and is impatient for him to bring down the curtain. He jokes and winces, and makes fun of his own despair. The longer he hangs on, the more he can steer us towards the steamy, emotional bath we were happy to help him prepare. Would he like to drown us? After all, we like being lied to, we like promises that will never be kept, we like being locked into his smiling neediness.

His successor is likely to give us a shock, especially if it is Gordon Brown, the greatest mystery in British politics for the past 50 years. High in intelligence and self-control, but zero for acting skills and emotional martyrdom. Will we be happy with him? I seriously doubt it. Perhaps only damaged actors can lead modern societies down the crooked paths that they prefer.

8

FORUM DISCUSSIONS

This section takes a broad view of the idea of contribution to forum discussion, though it limits itself to print. The back-translation of a speech given by Ballard at the SF Symposium in Rio di Janeiro in 1969, and published in an accompanying conference volume, is not included. Readers of the current book will already be familiar with the views expressed in that talk from his reviews and essays of the same period.

An updated broadside on the state of fiction was given to the *New Review*, an arts magazine edited by the poet Ian Hamilton and published in London for fifty issues between 1974 and 1979. Ballard's contribution to the 1978 "Symposium" reproduced here was the second of two invited responses: the first recorded the opinions of a number of writers in December 1975 to the idea of Public Lending Rights, a proposed payment to authors for the borrowing of books from public libraries.

In answer to the questions "How would you describe the development of fiction in English over the last ten years or so?" and "What developments would you hope for, or anticipate, over the next decade?" Ballard celebrated the idea that realist fiction had "run out of gas." His thoughts ran alongside, and in contrast to, those of Brigid Brophy, Ian MacEwan, and Angela Carter, among others.

Edited in 1988 by Frederick Barthelme and Rie Fortenberry, the *Mississippi Review*, a literary magazine publishing new fiction, has been based at the University of Southern Mississippi since 1972. Ballard's brief and genial comments on the then-emergent genre of cyberpunk, a strain of SF influenced by noir fiction and film and interested in computer information technologies and virtual realities, stand in marked contrast to his pungent response to the editors of the leading academic journal in the field of SF, *Science Fiction Studies*.

In 1991, *SFS* had published a new translation of Jean Baudrillard's 1976 essay on *Crash* that had appeared in the French edition of his most famous book *Simulacres et Simulations* but had been left out of the English translation. Critics and the author were invited to respond: some registered horror at Baudrillard's provocative and amoral reading of the novel as "simply fascinating." In his introductory essay, *SFS* editor Istvan Csicsery-Ronay Jr. argued that Ballard's "Introduction" to the French edition of *Crash!* was the "the *de facto* founding manifesto of postmodern SF"; Csicsery-Ronay Jr. further thought Ballard's response to Baudrillard was the "most interesting . . . His tirade against academic criticism and the concept of postmodernism is, I believe, and [sic] attempt to protect a border: not between SF and mainstream fiction, but between the fields of art and the locusts of rationalistic analysis."[1]

The continuing power of *Crash* to provoke and appall also lurked behind "Nurse, the Screens." This epistolary exchange was a contribution to the regular "Head-to-Head" feature slot in the *Guardian* magazine *The Week*, which pitched notable correspondents against each other in polite debate over current issues. David Cronenberg's adaptation of *Crash* had been granted an 18-certificate by the British Board of Film Classification in 1997, despite a campaign by the right-wing *Daily Mail* newspaper to have it banned. Some local councils, including the solidly conservative Westminster, took the decision to prevent its screening, placing Ballard firmly on the front line of arguments over censorship in the United Kingdom. His exchange with the columnist Anne Atkins takes place against this background.

---

1. I. C. R., "Editorial Introduction: Postmodernism's SF/SF's Postmodernism," *Science Fiction Studies* 18, no. 3 (1991): 305–308.

THE STATE OF FICTION: A SYMPOSIUM

New Review (1978)

I feel extremely optimistic about the novel's future. Ten years ago, during the heyday of the visual image, there seemed to be every chance that the written word would be left to moulder on the library shelf forever. Like the agents of some new hormonal system, all the important cues in our lives hit the bloodstream directly from the retina, bypassing the brain altogether. The important interior experiences, the whole realm of the imagination, were prepackaged out there somewhere. The boom years of TV, the relentless visual floodtide of mass-merchandising and of news and information, the magazine and TV coverage of the Vietnam War was packaged like so many cautionary commercials, and the blatant rip-offs of the remotest corners of the visual arts (surrealism arrived on Monday at some huge ICA show, but abruptly left town by the weekend to make room for the next craze), together pre-empted the possibility of any kind of quirky or independent response. It was a very safe time to be around.

Fortunately, all that seems to be over, partly thanks to a particularly puritanical generation of people under 30, who prefer to rhapsodise over something a little more interesting than the shape of a Coca Cola bottle. One result has been a huge resurgence of imaginative fiction and, para-doxically, a welcome end to moralising. The most wayward and, hope-fully, the most perverse impulses of the imagination are treasures to be hoarded.

By contrast, realist fiction seems finally to have run out of gas. Though, annoyingly, it is still what most people prefer to read, the calibre of its writers goes down and down. It has its place, like portraiture, in a sense a branch of the applied arts. But I believe in a fiction of the liberated and untrammelled imagination, nothing to do with the sort of thing you put in a frame on a piano.

Assuming that one certain thing about the future is that it will be boring—much of Europe already seems to be taking on the aspect of a huge housing estate—the role of imaginative fiction becomes more and more important for survival. Above all, it seems to be our only means of discovering a benevolent and morally free psychopathology.

CYBERPUNK FORUM

Mississippi Review (1988)

It's extremely heartening that SF still shows itself able to find a radically new direction in which to move—the slumbering dinosaur, fuddled by its comic-book dreams of outer space and the far future, has at last climbed to its feet and read the warning sign on the nearest billboard: "This is your last chance for the 20th century." I had almost given up hope for the poor beast. I admire all these new young writers and I respect what they're doing. I'm especially glad that American SF, which turned in the 1970s towards escapist fantasy and closed its eyes to reality, has now left the amusement park and stepped out onto the sidewalks of everyday life.

A RESPONSE TO THE INVITATION TO RESPOND

Science Fiction Studies (1991)

I thought the whole problem SF faced was that its consciousness, critically speaking, had been raised to wholly inappropriate heights—the apotheosis of the hamburger. An exhilarating and challenging entertainment fiction which Edgar Allan Poe and Mark Twain would have relished has become a "discipline"—God help us—beloved of those like the Delany who will no doubt pour scorn on my novel [sic] of the early '70s. The theory and criticism of s-f!! Vast theories and pseudo-theories are elaborated by people with not an idea in their bones. Needless to say, I totally exclude Baudrillard (whose essay on *Crash* I have not really wanted to understand)—I read it for the first time some years ago. Of course, his *Amerique* is an absolutely brilliant piece of writing, probably the most sharply clever piece of writing since Swift, brilliancies and jewels of insight in every paragraph—an intellectual Aladdin's cave. But your whole "postmodernism" view of SF strikes me as doubly sinister.

SF was ALWAYS modern, but now it is "postmodern"—bourgeoisification in the form of an over-professionalized academia with nowhere to take its girlfriend for a bottle of wine and a dance is now rolling its jaws over innocent and naive fiction that desperately needs to be left alone. You [sic] killing us! Stay your hand! Leave us be! Turn your "intelligence" to iconography of filling stations, cash machines, or whatever nonsense your entertainment culture deems to be the flavor of the day. We have enough intellectuals in Europe as it is; let the great USA devote itself to the spirit of the Wrights—bicycle mechanics and the sons of a bishop. The latter's modesty and exquisitely plain prose style would be an example to you especially his restrained but heartfelt reflections on the death of one of his sons, a model of the spirit animating SF at its best. But I fear you are trapped inside your dismal jargon.

NURSE, THE SCREENS

The Week, Guardian (1998)

Dear Anne,

I'm sorry to hear that there are impassioned calls for the film *Lolita* to be banned from British cinemas. It feels like a repeat of the nightmare from which I thankfully awoke when David Cronenberg's film of *Crash* was at last given a limited release in this country. There have since been no reports of the voluntary mayhem on our roads expected by so many.

Neither you nor I have seen *Lolita*, and if you have your way we will never have the chance to decide for ourselves whether this film is the depraved work its opponents claim. Based on a novel by Vladimir Nabokov, one of the century's greatest writers, it starts Jeremy Irons, a distinguished actor who won an Oscar for his role in *Reversal of Fortune*, and is directed by Adrian Lyne, who made *Fatal Attraction*.

Is it likely that they would collaborate on a film so vile and corrupting that adult audiences should be shielded from it? Britain is already one of the most heavily censored countries in the Western world. Sex seems especially to worry us and in particular those forms outside our own experience.

I have always been opposed to any form of censorship and am happy to leave offences against decency to the criminal law. Let us be free to see *Lolita* if we want to and make up our own minds about its merits or failings.

Yours,
JG Ballard

Dear JG,

You have been misinformed. Like you, I haven't seen the film (though I hesitate to judge its merits first) so I wouldn't necessarily ban it. For instance, to my surprise I found *The Devil Amongst Us*, the documentary which showed sympathy for paedophiles, enlightening and important. But Jeremy Irons's undisputed talent guarantees nothing. *Damage* was so devoid of anything but sex that I fell asleep.

But why are you opposed to any form of censorship? This is surprising from such an intelligent and informed person as yourself. There are numerous circumstances under which censorship is so clearly desirable. Would you broadcast an enthusiastic celebration of neo-Nazism perhaps denying the Holocaust in present-day Germany? Would you allow unlimited air time to racist or sexist views? Would you permit a triumphalist portrayal of Stephen Lawrence's murder, even if it might incite further racist attacks or cause great offence to his family or the black community? If so, you are putting art above people, above racial harmony, above life itself. Every civilised society exercises censorship. Used properly it never stifles creative talent. Shakespeare was writing at a time of extreme censorship. Good directors work successfully with constraints.

Last year the Pro-Life Alliance produced a party-political broadcast which was factual and hard-hitting. It was censored by every major news channel. Did you campaign for the right to see it? Or does liberalism only extend to those who share our prejudices?

Yours,
Anne

Dear Anne,

I'm glad that you don't want to ban *Lolita* before having seen it. I sense a shift in the wind. I only wish you had been around when Virginia Bottomley and her posse of moral busybodies were trying to ban *Crash*.

Can we clear up your point about censorship? It seems to me that what you are really talking about is self-restraint, a quality I find admirable. By censorship I mean the banning, or selective suppression before publication, of newspapers, novels, plays and films. I believe playwrights, novelists and film companies should be able to publish and distribute anything they choose, and accept the consequences. If I and my publisher decide to publish a book exalting Hitler and the Holocaust we are free to do so and face the law.

It is outrageous that *Crash* should still be banned from the West End of London by Westminster Council. If they decided what should be sold in the Charing Cross Road or what plays could be staged along Shaftesbury Avenue, we would consider it absurd, yet the council could use its powers to ban *Lolita* and may well do so.

While you were sleeping through *Damage*, I was looking for the exit. But one bad film doesn't affect the argument against censorship. For many, the sexual imagination is a vital means of self-exploration. Our sexual freedoms are already restrained in a host of ways. Do we need yet another defensive line of purse-mouthed guardians? I'm sorry that I've never heard of the Pro-Life Alliance. If they were censored, I deplore it. But doesn't that prove my point?

Yours
JGB

Dear JG,

If only individual self-restraint were enough—what Utopia! But then, if we all exercised perfect self-restraint we should need no laws at all. There would be no muggers, drunk drivers or child-molesters, and all would be sweetness and light. Because it isn't, all sorts of freedoms are rightly restrained by law. Responsible censorship is part of this process: society exercising communal self-restraint, since individuals won't necessarily do it.

But let me press you for an answer. Is there nothing you would censor? Suppose a director makes a film celebrating a perverted idea of masculinity: a gang of "heroes" who take women by force, the women even relishing it. His sexual imagination is exploring itself. He accepts your offer to "distribute and accept the consequences." The consequence for him is a few bad reviews and you and me looking for the exit or falling asleep. But a schoolgirl walks home that night and meets a dozen youths hot from his film who fancy exploring their sexual Imaginations too. In theory, the law protects her. In practice, the law may happen to be back at the cop shop. Before you say this is far-fetched, I know someone who was raped because she looked like a Page Three girl. Her attacker repeatedly taunted her, saying she had asked for it by posing topless. Years later her life is still in ruins.

Now let's suppose you have been made official censor for the day. Would you really permit the showing of this film?

Yours,
Anne

Dear Anne,

No, I would call the police, assuming I was deputising for Andreas Whittam Smith, the new president of the British Board of Film Classification, and that the film clearly incited spectators to commit a criminal act, namely rape.

You seem to be confusing censorship with laws that rightly regulate behaviour in all civilised societies. Books, plays, newspapers and magazines are not subject to censorship. Only films and videos are censored, when the BBFC insists certain scenes be deleted, or even refuses to license a film.

Can you imagine the fuss if Jack Straw decided to license the publication of fiction, and his censor demanded cuts in the latest novels by

Salman Rushdie, AS Byatt and William Boyd? Yet this is what routinely happened to playwrights in the era of the Lord Chamberlain, and now happens to distinguished film directors, who see minutes cut from their films before video release. Why not take a gamble and treat the British public as adults? The law will soon weed out any psychopaths behind the camera. Meanwhile, full marks to Andreas Whittam Smith for passing both *Lolita* and the video of *Crash* uncut.

Yours,
JG

Dear JG,

I am immensely relieved that you agree to some censorship. I feared you would say the girl must take her chance. We concur, then, that films which might incite criminal acts should not be shown. But this is exactly the objection to *Lolita*. By showing, perhaps absolving, sex with an underage girl, it could encourage such behaviour, already greatly on the increase. Stanley Kubrick now believes his film *A Clockwork Orange* incited violence, and the Mayor of Arkansas has blamed this week's terrible tragedy on similar influences. Experience tells us we are influenced by what we see. Why should paedophiles be different?

We have little to lose by intelligent censorship. Under the Lord Chamberlain the finest playwrights flourished magnificently. *Crash* is dull as dishwater. *Richard III* is a masterpiece. So I won't weep long for the directors who lose minutes. If one child might be abused like *Lolita* the film is unjustifiable.

I do believe we are in agreement.

Yours,
Anne

9

CAPSULE COMMENTARIES

Ballard's short contributions to roundtable and round-up articles in newspapers and magazines were frequent enough to have warranted their own bibliography. Some were written, others transcribed from interview. A small selection is highlighted here of special interest.

"The Magnificent Seven" was Ballard's compact response to the invitation to identify an alternative seven modern wonders of the world for the UK edition of *Esquire* magazine. Tom Wolfe and Richard Dawkins were among the fifteen contributors.

"Apocalypse How?" appeared in a special issue of New York music and popular culture magazine *Spin* devoted to "The Future" and guest edited by Jaron Lanier. Ballard's submission was sandwiched between those of the musician Moby and Matt Groening, creator of *The Simpsons*.

The short piece "The Westway" was commissioned by the journalist Tim Adams for the London edition of a pocketbook city guide series, published by the Little Bookroom. Among many contributors highlighting their London recommendations were the playwright Patrick Marber on casinos and the artist Cornelia Parker on the Number 11 bus route.

"My Perfect Beach" and "Writer's Rooms" were weekly repeated slots in the *Observer Life and Style* magazine and the *Guardian Review* section respectively.

THE MAGNIFICENT SEVEN

Esquire (1994)

Zapruder Frame 313 (JFK Assassination film)
The 1952 H-Bomb Test at Eniwetok Atoll
The Cockpit Voice Recorder
The VCR Remote Control
The Apollo X1 Lunar Module
Le Corbusier's Villa Savoye
The Pornographic Film

APOCALYPSE HOW?

Spin (1995)

I dream of: Dying in a car crash with Madonna. Having sex with Hillary Clinton. Appearing in Zapruder frame 313 with Jackie Kennedy. Being transformed into a TV channel. Detonating a nuclear weapon over Disneyland. Having all the whores in Moscow call me on their mobile phones. Seeing time make a new beginning. Persuading Neil Armstrong to return to Earth. Meeting my younger selves on the virtual-reality highways of tomorrow. Being buried under the main runway at London's Heathrow Airport.

THE WESTWAY

City Secrets: London (2001)

London is a city that rarely entered the twentieth century, and to find this stretch of motorway little more than a stone's throw from Marble Arch is a poignant reminder of what might have been. Join it by travelling west along the Marylebone Road, not far from 221B Baker Street, Sherlock Holmes's notional address. The Westway is a continuous overpass some three miles in length, running towards White City, home to BBC television, and then to Shepherd's Bush, where Pissarro's house is still standing.

By international standards the Westway is unremarkable, and affords a view of some of the most dismal housing in London. But this is not its point. Rising above the crowded nineteenth-century squares and grim stucco terraces, this massive concrete motion-sculpture is an heroically isolated fragment of the modern city London might once have become. There are few surveillance cameras and you can make your own arrangements with the speed limits. Corbusier remarked that a city built for speed is a city built for success, but the Westway, like Angkor Wat, is a stone dream that will never awake. As you hurtle along the concrete deck you briefly join the twentieth century and become a citizen of a virtual city-state borne on a rush of radial tyres.

MY PERFECT BEACH

Observer (2002)

I think beaches are my spiritual home. There are very few I dislike. All the most interesting things in the world take place where the sea meets the land and you're between those two states of mind. On that border zone, you're neither one nor the other, you're both. And people take their clothes off, which is always a plus.

My perfect beach is in the south of France at a place called Roquebrune, which lies between Menton and Monte Carlo. It's small, secluded and has a spectacular view with Cap Martin on the left and Monaco on the right. It's a shingle beach, which I usually hate, but this one has a wooden shack bar and it's close to Paradise. I like to go down there and swim in the salt water, and at my present age of 71, I'm still able to reach the diving platform, which is at least half a mile out to sea (although, actually, it's more like 75 yards).

It has other charms for me because the great architect Corbusier had a cabin about 50 yards from the beach, and he had a heart attack and died while having his morning swim here. I'm always conscious of his presence here.

Only a small group of people use the beach, but there are all sorts of other comings and goings. Hang-gliders launch themselves from the mountain behind the beach, sail over the water and then land on the shingle. It's an exhilarating spectacle. Another kind of flying machine uses this stretch of water. The forest firefighters fly down low to scoop up water and then fly off to bomb whatever areas of the French Riviera are catching fire. One unusual visitor a few years ago was a swan, a bird you don't often find on salt water, which became quite celebrated in a local paper.

It really is a place of character. It's probably a mistake to tell anyone about it, but it is very difficult to find, so there's no point looking for it.

WRITER'S ROOMS

Guardian (2007)

My room is dominated by the huge painting, which is a copy of *The Violation* by the Belgian surrealist Paul Delvaux. The original was destroyed during the Blitz in 1940, and I commissioned an artist I know, Brigid Marlin, to make a copy from a photograph. I never stop looking at this painting and its mysterious and beautiful women. Sometimes I think I have gone to live inside it and each morning I emerge refreshed. It's a male dream.

There are photos of my four grandchildren (one, along with a picture of my girlfriend Claire, is just out of shot). The postcard is Dali's *Persistence of Memory*, the greatest painting of the 20th century, and next to it is a painting by my daughter, which is the greatest painting of the 21st century. On the desk is my old manual typewriter, which I recently found in my stair cupboard. I was inspired by a letter from Will Self, who wrote to me on his manual typewriter. So far I have just stared at the old machine, without daring to touch it, but who knows? The first drafts of my novels have all been written in longhand and then I type them up on my old electric. I have resisted getting a computer because I distrust the whole PC thing. I don't think a great book has yet been written on computer.

I have worked at this desk for the past 47 years. All my novels have been written on it, and old papers of every kind have accumulated like a great reef. The chair is an old dining-room chair that my mother brought back from China and probably one I sat on as a child, so it has known me for a very long time. A Paolozzi screen-print is resting against the door, which now serves as a cat barrier during the summer months. My neighbour's cats are enormously affectionate, and in the summer leap up on to my desk and then churn up all my papers into a huge whirlwind. They are my fiercest critics.

I work for three or four hours a day, in the late morning and early afternoon. Then I go out for a walk and come back in time for a large gin and tonic.

10

MEMOIR AND TRIBUTES

The following pieces are selected to supplement and expand the auto-biography *Miracles of Life* (2008) and for their close focus on significant individuals or episodes in the author's life.

"Smashing Days on the Road" was Ballard's second contribution to the weekly "Second Thoughts" column in the *Books* section of the *Independent* newspaper, in which contributors reflected on significant books in their own backlists. His account of *Crash* here has changed considerably from the contemporary text "Some Remarks on *Crash!*," and his comment in a letter to Peter Nichols, the editor of *Foundation*, that "*Crash*, I would like to think, is an example of a kind of terminal irony where not even the writer knows where he stands."[1]

"Unlocking the Past" was the lead feature in the *Telegraph Weekend* section on the Saturday before the publication of *The Kindness of Women* (1991). It recounts Ballard's experiences of returning to Shanghai to film the documentary *Shanghai Jim* for the BBC Bookmarks series, which was broadcast on BBC2 on Wednesday, September 25.

"Look Back on Empire," a reflection on both the original novel and film adaptation of *Empire of the Sun* (1987), was occasioned by the release of a DVD Special Edition by Warner Home Videos on March 6, 2006.

"My Favourite Books" was included in *The Pleasure of Reading* (1992), edited by Antonia Fraser, a collection of descriptions of the discovery and enjoyment of literature by forty-three acclaimed writers, including Margaret Atwood, Germaine Greer, and Rory Stewart.

---

1. "Letter," in *Foundation*, vol. 0 (June 1, 1976): 50–51.

Despite Ballard's long friendship and series of collaborations with the sculptor Eduardo Paolozzi, "Junkyard Dreams" was only his second nonfictional account of Paolozzi's work and career. This was published in the *Times* as a preview of the film profile of Eduardo Paolozzi, *E. P.— Sculptor* (dir. Murray Grigor, 1987), screened on Channel 4 on Sunday December 6.

Published by Avernus Creative Media, an imprint founded by Brian Aldiss and Frank Hatherley, *A Is for Brian* was a sixty-fifth birthday fest-schrift for Aldiss, Ballard's contemporary at *New Worlds*. Secretly assembled by Hatherley, Malcolm Edwards, and Aldiss's wife, Margaret, it compiled invited contributions from "a variety of Brian's closest friends and colleagues in many disciplines."[2]

The writer and critic Judith Merril was the first champion of New Wave SF in the United States, editor of the influential *Year's Greatest Science Fiction* anthologies, and *England Swings SF: Stories of Speculative Fiction* (1968). She had included several of Ballard's stories in her annuals. Ballard first met Merril in Oxford in September 1965, and she stayed with him at Shepperton several times on her second visit to England from 1966 to April 1967.

William Burroughs died in Lawrence, Kansas, at the age of eighty-three on August 2, 1997. Ballard had corresponded with Burroughs in March 1964, met him for the first time in 1965, again at a party at Michael Moorcock's flat in in 1966, and this brief obituary notice recalls a dinner at the London flat Burroughs kept on Duke Street between July 1966 and 1974.

---

2. "Introduction," in *A Is for Brian: A 65th Birthday Present for Brian W. Aldiss*, ed. Frank Hatherley, Margaret Aldiss, and Malcolm Edwards (Brighton: Avernus Creative Media, 1990), 3.

REMEMBERING *CRASH*

Independent (1990)

Crash was an immense challenge, and writing it became almost a willed psychotic act. At the time I had three young children, and fate might have played a cruel trick on me.

As it happens, two weeks after finishing the novel I was involved in my one and only traffic accident. After a front-wheel blow-out at the foot of Chiswick bridge my car veered across the central reservation of the dual carriageway. It demolished a sign (I was later sent the bill for its replacement, and was annoyed to find that I had paid for a more expensive model, with flashing lights), rolled onto its back and continued along the oncoming lane.

Fortunately I was wearing a seat-belt and no other vehicles were involved, though it was a close-run thing—petrol was pouring from the engine and the crushed roof had locked all the doors. Had I died there is no doubt that people would have said I was fulfilling the nightmare logic I had outlined in the novel.

But in fact I prefer to think of *Crash* as a cautionary tale, a warning against the deviant possibilities that 20th century technology offers to the human imagination. Film and television are saturated with a stylised violence that touches our imaginations but never our nerve endings.

Much of this violent imagery is drawn from technology—the car, the motorway, the airport, the modern hospital and high-rise building. The car crash, in particular, taps all sorts of ambiguous responses, as I found when I mounted an exhibition of crashed cars at the New Arts Laboratory in 1969, shortly before I began to write the novel.

The exhibition was a calculated experiment, designed to test the novel's central hypothesis that a repressed fascination lies behind our conventional attitudes to technological death and violence, a fascination so obsessive that it must contain a powerful sexual charge. The three crashed cars were exhibited without comment under the neutral gallery lights, at their centre a telescoped Pontiac from the great tail-fin era.

To test the nerves of the preview audience, I hired a topless girl to interview the guests on closed-circuit TV. She had originally agreed to appear naked, but when she saw the cars decided she could only appear topless, an interesting response in itself, I thought. She later wrote a damning review of the show in an underground paper.

I have never before or since seen a launch party degenerate so quickly into a drunken brawl. The cars were abused and attacked, as they were during the month-long exhibition, overturned and slashed with white paint. A woman journalist from *New Society*, then a bastion of approved thinking, was so deranged by the spectacle that she was speechless with rage.

All this, needless to say, I regarded as a green light, and I began to write *Crash*, which I think of as my best and most original novel. It is to the credit of my publishers and editors here, in Europe and the United States that I had no difficulty in getting it published, and I look forward to the film to be directed by David Cronenberg.

UNLOCKING THE PAST

Daily Telegraph (1991)

Soon after Empire of the Sun *was published in 1984 the telephone started to ring with invitations to revisit Shanghai, the city in which I had been born in 1930 and which I had left, apparently for ever, in 1946. But the novel had stirred up a great number of memories, some of them far too unsettling to be faced again at such short notice.*

Steven Spielberg's film of the book certainly tempted me. The city was still intact, he told me, a Samarkand of the 20th century. I began to write a sequel to Empire of the Sun, *describing my later life in England up to the present day, When I read the proofs of the finished novel, I knew that I was ready to go back. Nigel Williams, editor of BBC2's* Bookmark, *suggested that they film a return visit to Shanghai, and without hesitating I agreed . . .*

One can never go home, the American novelist Thomas Wolfe had written, meaning that everything changes, the past and one's memories of it.

Since coming to England in the grey, austere days after the war, I had kept alive my precious memories of Shanghai. Teeming, cruel but always exhilarating, Shanghai in my mind had become a cross between ancient Babylon and Las Vegas. But what if my memories were false? My great fear was that, far from evoking new memories, the visit might erase the old ones that had sustained me for so many years.

An hour before midnight we approached the western rim of a vast metropolis of lights, and touched down at Shanghai International Airport, on the site of the old Hungjao aerodrome where as a boy I had played in the cockpits of rusting Japanese aircraft.

A sea of dark, superheated air covered the tarmac, carrying the forgotten scents of the Yangtse countryside. The Chinese immigration officials were amiable, asking me to declare that I suffered from neither Aids nor psychosis (except, perhaps, an excess of memory?) and that I was not importing "salacious materials"—what did they mean? The new Julie Burchill or, conceivably, a biography of Donald Trump?

James Runcie, the *Bookmark* film's director, was waiting for me. I greeted him with the line I had rehearsed all the way from London, suggested by Conrad's novel about a European trader driven mad by an impenetrable Africa: "Hello, James. Mr Kurtz returns to the Heart of Darkness."

The problem was that Mr Kurtz had arrived without his luggage, or at least the kind of luggage carried in one's hands. A few minutes earlier I had stood by the crowded carousel as suitcases were wrenched away, only to find myself alone by the eerily rotating band.

Was my tea-planter's suit, my "costume" for the film, on its way to Caracas, Honolulu or even Darjeeling? Happily Mr Gao and Mr Zhung of Shanghai Television leapt forward and took control. Super-efficient, they exchanged telexes with Hong Kong Airport, and my suitcase was on the next flight to Shanghai. Thanking them, I remembered that, before the war, one of my parents' steamer trunks had appeared a year after the P&O boat had docked.

At midnight we arrived at the Shanghai Hilton, a 40-storey tower in the former Avenue Haig. The fuzzy street lights, perspiring trees and microwave air seemed to be those of any sub-tropical city, and I was still not sure that I had returned to the Shanghai I knew.

The next morning, when I looked out from my room on the 30th floor, I was even less convinced. Like the London of the 1930s, Shanghai had been a lowrise city. But the Shanghai I saw from the Hilton was a panorama of immense high-rises that stretched from the northern industrial zones of Chapei and Yangtsepoo all the way to Lunghua in the south.

Dozens of huge buildings rose into the sky, roofs decked with satellite dishes. But far below I was relieved to see the old Shanghai of the 1930s was alive and well, if a little crumbling in the sunlight. There were the Provencal villas of the French Concession, and the International Settlement's stockbroker-Tudor and Art Deco mansions with port-hole windows and ocean-liner balconies.

I gave James the slip and for an hour walked around the streets near the Hilton, through which I had cycled as a child staring up at the faded apartment houses and office buildings that I recognised after nearly half a century's absence. I saw the old General Hospital where I had been born, the municipal park from which the Chinese had been excluded ("No dogs or Chinese"), and the modern trolley buses that still followed the routes of the giant French trams.

Shanghai, which had once been an American and European city filled with Buicks and Packards, was now entirely Chinese, packed with cyclists, its pavements lined with market stalls piled high with water melons, bootleg Hong Kong videos and mounds of writhing eels. In the Hilton lobby the *Bookmark* team was waiting for me. A 13-year-old Belgian boy, whose father was working for a foreign company in Shanghai, warily shook my hand. He would play my younger self in the film, and James had misguidedly told him that he resembled me. "Don't worry," I assured him, "when you grow up you won't look like me at all."

Together we set off for our first location, my childhood home in Amherst Avenue, now the library of the Shanghai Electronic Industry Bureau. It had been built in the early 1930s in the classic stockbroker-Tudor style of the Home Counties, though the interior was that of an American house with five bathrooms, air conditioning and a squash-court-sized kitchen. The staff welcomed us in the friendliest way, but I had the weird sense that I was exploring a ghost. I walked around the dining-room, now lined with shelves of electronics manuals, where my father had entertained American officers and Chinese tycoons, and the veranda where my mother had organised her bridge parties.

The affable director, Mr Chang, greeted me like a long-lost colleague and invited me into his office, crammed with computers, which had once been my mother's dressing-room. We conducted an animated dialogue, neither speaking a word of the other's language, but apparently understanding everything. Later I climbed to the top floor and stood in my childhood bedroom, which still had its original pale blue paint and the bookshelves where I had methodically arranged my Chums Annuals and American comics. Now they were stacked with scientific journals and Chinese textbooks. In the bathroom there was even the original lavatory seat on which, as a small boy, I had been ordered by the punitive White Russian nanny to sit uselessly for hours—the 1930s baby-minding equivalent of television, and probably far more educational.

That first day I moved around Shanghai in a daze. Memories jostled me like the Chinese crowds who surrounded the film crew. Watching as the Belgian lad cycled past the Cathay Hotel, where Noel Coward had written *Private Lives*, I remembered the Shanghai of gangsters and beggar-kings, prostitutes and pickpockets. I had opened a door and stepped into a perfectly preserved past, though a past equipped with a number of unattractive reflexes of my own—walking along the Nanking Road, I caught myself expecting the Chinese pedestrians to step out of my way.

Would Shanghai ever return to its former gaudy self before the Communist take-over? The beggars and cripples exhibiting their open wounds had thankfully gone for good, and there were no armies of coolies labouring under immense loads disgorged from the sampans along the Bund.

The people looked confident and well-fed, young couples strolling arm-in-arm past the Sun Sun and Wing On department stores, men in shirtsleeves and the women in what might have been C&A frocks. Of course, there were no bookstalls selling newspapers critical of the government, and no posters urging the merits of rival political parties.

Yet everywhere, clearly, capitalism was waiting to be reborn, in thousands of small shops and back-street businesses. Like the Europeans in the years before the Opium Wars, the Western visitors are again confined to their compounds—the Hilton and Sheraton Hotels, drinking their imported Carlsberg and watching their Hollywood videos. But this time no British or American gunboat will force the Chinese to grant them concessions, which when they come will not be territorial but financial—tax havens and rent-free enterprise zones.

But already I was bored with the Bund and its great banking houses, and determined to find the last elusive piece of the past, the camp at Lunghua where the Japanese had interned some 2,000 British civilians during the war. For nearly three years my father, mother, sister and I had been imprisoned there, living together in one small room.

For the next two days, as our time ran out, we embarked on a madcap and fruitless search. The unbroken expanse of paddy-fields that I remembered between Shanghai and Lunghua, eight miles to the south, had now been swallowed by greater metropolitan Shanghai—endless industrial estates and science parks, giant cement works and townships of high-rise flats. I began to despair of ever finding the camp. It was a teacher-training college before the war; its concrete buildings might well have vanished below one of the huge motorways.

At last an old policeman at a dusty wayside station confirmed that there was a high school in the Lunghua district which had once housed European prisoners, though during which war he could not remember. Ten minutes later, miraculously, I was walking through the gates of what had once been Lunghua Civilian Assembly Centre, and staring at F block, the main administrative building where the Japanese commandant, Mr Hyashi, had his headquarters—now, appropriately, his office was the headmaster's study.

Forty-five years had turned the Camp into a pleasantly landscaped secondary school, filled with trees and flowers. Caretakers looked on in amazement as a 60-year-old Englishman sprinted through the trees towards a small two-storey building—G block, where my parents, sister and I had lived in one of the 40 rooms that each housed a British family.

I burst into the silent entry hall, where our daily ration of rice congee and sweet potatoes had been served, and into the dark corridors where twice a day we stood to attention for roll-call. The schoolchildren were on holiday, their rooms locked, but one room was open and served as a storage cupboard, filled with cardboard boxes and assorted rubbish. This was the Ballard family room, every ceiling crack, every piece of chipped plaster, every worn window frame as familiar to me as the lines on my palm.

I was standing in the debris of my own memories when James and the film crew caught up with me. "They've been waiting for you to come, Jim," said our cameraman. "They even left the door unlocked for you."

I thought about this as we left for the airport. I had come to puberty in the camp and developed the rudiments of an adult brain, and I had seen my parents' generation endure years of stress and illness. I had watched a world war from the ringside, and sometimes within the ring and between the feet of the combatants.

Going back to the camp had been, without my realising it, my main reason for returning to Shanghai, and visiting Lunghua again had opened a door that I thought was sealed for 45 years. I had made contact with my lost younger self, and confirmed that my memories of Shanghai had been clear and accurate.

As our plane took off I felt elated, my spirits as bright as the gold Rolexes on the wrists of the new China entrepreneurs who packed the Hong Kong flight. One could go home, after all, and somewhere there was always one waiting door that was open and unlocked.

MY FAVOURITE BOOKS

The Pleasure of Reading (1992)

As I grow older—I'm now in my early sixties—the books of my childhood seem more and more vivid, while most of those that I read ten or even five years ago are completely forgotten. Not only can I remember, half a century later, my first readings of *Treasure Island* and *Robinson Crusoe*, but I can sense quite clearly my feelings at the time—all the wide-eyed excitement of a seven-year-old, and that curious vulnerability, the fear that my imagination might be overwhelmed by the richness of these invented worlds. Even now, simply thinking about Long John Silver or the waves on Crusoe's island stirs me far more than reading the original text. I suspect that these childhood tales have long since left their pages and taken on a second life inside my head.

By contrast, I can scarcely recall what I read in my thirties and forties. Like many people of my age, my reading of the great works of Western literature was over by the time I was twenty. In the three or four years of my late teens I devoured an entire library of classic and modern fiction, from Cervantes to Kafka, Jane Austen to Camus, often at the rate of a novel a day. Trying to find my way through the grey light of postwar, austerity Britain, it was a relief to step into the rich and larger-spirited world of the great novelists. I'm sure that the ground-plan of my imagination was drawn long before I went up to Cambridge in 1949.

In this respect I differed completely from my children, who began to read (I suspect) only after they had left their universities. Like many parents who brought up teenagers in the 1970s, it worried me that my children were more interested in going to pop concerts than in reading *Pride and Prejudice* or *The Brothers Karamazov*—how naive I must have been. But it seemed to me then that they were missing something vital to the growth of their imaginations, that radical reordering of the world that only the great novelists can achieve.

I now see that I was completely wrong to worry, and that their sense of priorities was right—the heady, optimistic world of pop culture, which I had never experienced, was the important one for them to explore. Jane Austen and Dostoyevsky could wait until they had gained the maturity in their twenties and thirties to appreciate and understand these writers, far more meaningfully than I could have done at sixteen or seventeen.

In fact I now regret that so much of my reading took place during my late adolescence, long before I had any adult experience of the world, long before I had fallen in love, learned to understand my parents, earned my own living and had time to reflect on the world's ways. It may be that my intense adolescent reading actually handicapped me in the process of growing up—in all senses my own children and their contemporaries strike me as more mature, reflective and more open to the possibilities of their own talents than I was at their age. I seriously wonder what Kafka and Dostoyevsky, Sartre and Camus could have meant to me. That same handicap I see borne today by those people who spend their university years reading English literature—scarcely a degree subject at all and about as rigorous a discipline as music criticism—before gaining the experience to make sense of the exquisite moral dilemmas that their tutors are so devoted to teasing out.

The early childhood reading that I remember so vividly was largely shaped by the city in which I was born and brought up. Shanghai was one of the most polyglot cities in the world, a vast metropolis governed by the British and French but otherwise an American zone of influence. I remember reading children's editions of *Alice in Wonderland*, *Robinson Crusoe* and Swift's *Gulliver's Travels* at the same time as American comics and magazines. Alice, the Red Queen and Man Friday crowded a mental landscape also occupied by Superman, Buck Rogers and Flash Gordon.

My favourite American comic strip was Terry and the Pirates, a wonderful Oriental farrago of Chinese warlords, dragon ladies and antique pagodas that had the added excitement for me of being set in the China where I lived, an impossibly exotic realm for which I searched in vain among Shanghai's Manhattan-style department stores and nightclubs. I can no longer remember my nursery reading, though my mother, once a school-teacher, fortunately had taught me to read before I entered school at the age of five.

There were no cheerful posters or visual aids in those days, apart from a few threatening maps, in which the world was drenched red by the British Empire. The headmaster was a ferocious English clergyman whose preferred bible was *Kennedy's Latin Primer*. From the age of six we were terrorized through two hours of Latin a day, and were only saved from his merciless regime by the Japanese attack on Pearl Harbor (though he would have been pleased to know that, sitting the School Certificate in England after the war, I and a group of boys tried to substitute a Latin oral for the French, which we all detested).

Once home from school, reading played the roles now filled by television, radio, cinema, visits to theme parks and museums (there were none in Shanghai), the local record shop and McDonalds. Left to myself for long periods, I read everything I could find—not only American comics, but *Time*, *Life*, *Saturday Evening Post* and the *New Yorker*: at the same time I read the childhood classics—*Peter Pan*, the Pooh books and the genuinely strange William series, with their Ionesco-like picture of an oddly empty middle-class England. Without being able to identify exactly what, I knew that something was missing, and in due course received a large shock when, in 1946, I discovered the invisible class who constituted three-quarters of the population but never appeared in the *Chums* and *Boys' Own Paper* annuals.

Later, when I was seven or eight, came *The Arabian Nights*, Hans Andersen and the Grimm brothers, anthologies of Victorian ghost stories and tales of terror, illustrated with threatening, Beardsley-like drawings that projected an inner world as weird as the surrealists'. Looking back on my childhood reading, I'm struck by how frightening most of it was, and I'm glad that my own children were never exposed to those gruesome tales and eerie coloured plates with their airless Pre-Raphaelite gloom, unearthly complexions and haunted infants with almost autistic stares. The overbearing moralistic tone was explicit in Charles Kingsley's *The Water-Babies*, a masterpiece in its bizarre way, but one of the most unpleasant works of fiction I have ever read before or since. The same tone could be heard through so much of children's fiction, as if childhood itself and the child's imagination were maladies to be repressed and punished.

The greatest exception was *Treasure Island*, frightening but in an exhilarating and positive way—I hope that I have been influenced by Stevenson as much as by Conrad and Graham Greene, but I suspect that *The Water-Babies* and all those sinister fairy tales played a far more important part in shaping my imagination. Even at the age of ten or eleven I recognized that something strangely morbid hovered over their pages, and that dispersing this chilling miasma might make more sense of the world I was living in than Stevenson's robust yarns. During the three years that I was interned by the Japanese my reading followed a new set of fracture lines.

The 2,000 internees carried with them into the camp a substantial library that circulated from cubicle to cubicle, bunk to bunk, and was my first exposure to adult fiction—popular American bestsellers, *Reader's Digest* condensed books, Somerset Maugham and Sinclair Lewis, Steinbeck and H. G. Wells. From all of them, I like to think, I learned the importance of sheer storytelling, a quality which was about to leave the serious English novel, and even now has scarcely returned.

Arriving in England in 1946, I was faced with the incomprehensible strangeness of English life, for which my childhood reading had prepared me in more ways than I realized. Fortunately, I soon discovered that the whole of late nineteenth- and twentieth-century literature lay waiting for me, a vast compendium of human case histories that stemmed from a similar source. In the next four or five years I stopped reading only to go to the cinema.

The Hollywood films that kept hope alive—*Citizen Kane*, *Sunset Boulevard*, *The Big Sleep* and *White Heat*—seemed to form a continuum with the novels of Hemingway and Nathanael West, Kafka and Camus. At about the same time I found my way to psychoanalysis and surrealism, and this hot mix together fuelled the short stories that I was already writing and strongly influenced my decision to read medicine.

There were also false starts, and doubtful acquaintances. *Ulysses* over-whelmed me when I read it in the sixth form, and from then on there seemed to be no point in writing anything that didn't follow doggedly on the heels of Joyce's masterpiece. It was certainly the wrong model for me, and may have been partly responsible for my late start as a writer—I was twenty-six when my first short story was published, and thirty-three before I wrote my first novel. But bad company is always the best, and leaves a reserve of memories on which one can draw for ever.

For reasons that I have never understood, once my own professional career was under way I almost stopped reading altogether. For the next twenty years I was still digesting the extraordinary body of fiction and non-fiction that I had read at school and at Cambridge. From the 1950s and 1960s I remember *The White Goddess* by Robert Graves, Genet's *Our Lady of the Flowers*, Durrell's *Justine* and Dalí's *Secret Life*, then Heller's *Catch-22* and, above all, the novels of William Burroughs—*The Naked Lunch* restored my faith in the novel at a time, the heyday of C. P. Snow, Anthony Powell and Kingsley Amis, when it had begun to flag.

Since then I've continued on my magpie way, and in the last ten years have found that I read more and more, in particular the nineteenth- and twentieth-century classics that I speed-read in my teens. Most of them are totally different from the books I remember. I have always been a voracious reader of what I call invisible literatures—scientific journals, technical manuals, pharmaceutical company brochures, think-tank inter-nal documents, PR company position papers—part of that universe of published material to which most literate people have scarcely any access but which provides the most potent compost for the imagination. I never read my own fiction.

In compiling my list of ten favourite books I have selected not those that I think are literature's masterpieces, but simply those that I have read most frequently in the past five years. I strongly recommend Patrick Trevor-Roper's *The World through Blunted Sight* to anyone interested in the influence of the eye's physiology on the work of poets and painters. *The Black Box* consists of cockpit voice-recorder transcripts (not all involving fatal crashes), and is a remarkable tribute to the courage and stoicism of professional flight crews. My copy of the Los Angeles *Yellow Pages* I stole from the Beverly Hilton Hotel three years ago; it has been a fund of extraordinary material, as surrealist in its way as Dalí's autobiography.

- *The Day of the Locust*, Nathanael West
- *Collected Short Stories*, Ernest Hemingway
- *The Rime of the Ancient Mariner*, Samuel Taylor Coleridge
- *The Annotated Alice*, ed. Martin Gardner
- *The World through Blunted Sight*, Patrick Trevor-Roper
- *The Naked Lunch*, William Burroughs
- *The Black Box*, ed. Malcolm MacPherson
- *Los Angeles Yellow Pages*
- *America*, Jean Baudrillard
- *The Secret Life of Salvador Dalí*, by Dalí

LOOK BACK AT EMPIRE

Guardian (2006)

Memories have huge staying power, but like dreams, they thrive in the dark, surviving for decades in the deep waters of our minds like shipwrecks on the sea bed. Hauling them into the daylight can be risky. Within a few hours, a precious trophy of childhood or a first romance can crumble into rust.

I knew that something similar might happen when I began to write *Empire of the Sun*, a novel about my life as a boy in Shanghai during the second world war, and in the civilian camp at Lunghua, where I was interned with my parents. Coming to England after the war, and trying to cope with its grey, unhappy people, I hoarded my memories of Shanghai, a city that soon seemed as remote and glamorous as ancient Rome. Its magic never faded, whereas I forgot Cambridge within five minutes of leaving that academic theme park, and never wanted to go back. The only people I remembered were the dissecting room cadavers.

During the 1960s, the Shanghai of my childhood seemed a portent of the media cities of the future, dominated by advertising and mass circulation newspapers and swept by unpredictable violence. But how could I raise this Titanic of memories? Brought up from the sea bed, the golden memory hoard could turn out to be dross. Besides, there are things that the novel can't easily handle. I could manage my changing relations with my parents, my 13-year-old's infatuation with the war, and the sudden irruption into our lives of American air power. But how do you convey the casual surrealism of war, the deep silence of abandoned villages and paddy fields, the strange normality of a dead Japanese soldier lying by the road like an unwanted piece of luggage?

I waited 40 years before giving it a go, one of the longest periods a professional writer has put off describing the most formative events in his life. Twenty years to forget, and then 20 years to remember. There was always the possibility that my memories of the war concealed a deeper stratum of unease that I preferred not to face. But at least my three children had grown up, and as I wrote the book I would never have to think of them sharing the war with my younger self.

In fact, I found it difficult to begin the novel, until it occurred to me to drop my parents from the story. We had lived together in a small room for nearly three years, eating our boiled rice and sweet potatoes from the same card table, sleeping within an arm's reach of each other, an exhilarating experience for me after the formality of our prewar home, where my parents were busy with their expat social life and I was brought up by Chinese servants who never looked at me and never spoke to me.

But I needed to move my parents out of the story, just as they had moved out of my life in Lunghua even though we were sharing the same room. They had no control over their teenage son, were unable to feed or clothe him or pull those little levers of promise and affection with which parents negotiate domestic life with their children. My real existence took place in the camp, wheedling dog-eared copies of *Popular Mechanics* and *Reader's Digest* from the American merchant seamen in the men's dormitory, hunting down every rumour in the air, waiting for the food cart and the next B-29 bombing raid. My mind was expanding to fill the possibilities of the war, something I needed to do on my own. Once I separated Jim from his parents the novel unrolled itself at my feet like a bullet-ridden carpet.

Even then, I had to leave out many things that belong in a memoir rather than a novel. Lunghua camp, with its 2,000 internees, was a grimy bidonville, a slum township where, as in all slums, the teenage boys ran wild. There were unwatched screwdrivers or penknives to be snaffled, heroic arguments with a bored clergyman about the existence of God, buckets of night soil to be hoisted from the G-block septic tank and poured into the tomato and cucumber beds that were supposed to keep us alive when the Japanese could no longer feed us. In a bombed-out building I found a broken Chinese bayonet, sharpened the stump of blade and used it to prise away the bricks of the kitchen coal store, filling a sack with precious coke that would briefly break the chill of our unheated concrete building. My father said nothing, feeding the coke into a miniature brazier as he rehearsed his lecture on science and the idea of God. I ran off, and nagged the off-duty Japanese guards in their bungalows until they let me wear their kendo armour, laughing as they thumped me around the head with their wooden swords.

In 1984 the novel was published, a caravel of memories raised from the deep. Enough of it was based on fact to convince me that what had seemed a dream-like pageant was a negotiated truth. Curiously, my original memories of Shanghai still seemed intact, and even survived a return trip to Shanghai, where I found our house in Amherst Avenue and our room in Lunghua camp—now a boarding school—virtually unchanged.

Then, in 1987, like a jumbo jet crash-landing in a suburban park, a Hollywood film company came down from the sky. It disgorged an army of actors, makeup artists, set designers, costume specialists, cinematographers and a director, Steven Spielberg, all of whom had strong ideas of their own about wartime Shanghai. After 40 years my memories had shaped themselves into a novel, but only three years later they were mutating again.

Hazy figures now had names and personalities, smiles and glances that I had seen in a dozen other films: John Malkovich, Nigel Havers, Miranda Richardson. With them was a brilliant child actor, Christian Bale, who uncannily resembled my younger self. He came up to me on the set and said: "Hello, Mr Ballard. I'm you." He was followed by an attractive young couple, Emily Richard and Rupert Frazer, who added: "And we're your mum and dad."

Coincidences were building strange bridges. Thanks to the film studios in Shepperton, many of my neighbours worked as extras, and now called out: "Mr Ballard, we're going to Lunghua together." Had some deep-cover assignment led me to Shepperton in 1960, knowing that one day I would write a novel about Shanghai, and that part of it would be filmed in Shepperton?

Spielberg, an intelligent and thoughtful man, generously gave me a small role as a guest at the opening fancy-dress party. Warners had rented three houses in Sunningdale to stand in for our Shanghai home. When I arrived at the location I found an armada of buses, vans and coaches that filled entire fields and resembled the evacuation of London. Bizarrely, it also reminded me of the day we were bussed into Lunghua from our assembly point at the American club near the Great Western Road. I can still see the huge crowd of Brits, many of the women in fur coats, sitting with their suitcases around the swimming pool, as if waiting for the water to part and lead them to safety.

The Sunningdale house where the fancy-dress party was filmed closely resembled our Amherst Avenue home, but this at least was no coincidence. The expat British architects in the 1930s who specialised in stockbroker's Tudor took the Surrey golf course mansions as their model. Past and present were coming full circle. The Warners props department filled the house with period fittings—deco screens and lamps, copies of Time and Life, white telephones and radios the size of sideboards. In the drive outside the front door, uniformed Chinese chauffeurs stood beside authentic Buicks and Packards. A 12-year-old boy ran through the costumed guests, a model aircraft in one hand, racing across the lawn into a dream.

Surprisingly, it was the film premiere in Hollywood, the fount of most of our planet's fantasies, that brought everything down to earth. A wonderful night for any novelist, and a reminder of the limits of the printed word. Sitting with the sober British contingent, surrounded by everyone from Dolly Parton to Sean Connery, I thought Spielberg's film would be drowned by the shimmer of mink and the diamond glitter. But once the curtains parted the audience was gripped. Chevy Chase, sitting next to me, seemed to think he was watching a newsreel, crying: "Oh, oh . . . !" and leaping out of his seat as if ready to rush the screen in defence of young Bale.

I was deeply moved by the film but, like every novelist, couldn't help feeling that my memories had been hijacked by someone else's. As the battle of Britain fighter ace Douglas Bader said when introduced to the cast of *Reach for the Sky*: "But they're actors."

Actors of another kind play out our memories, performing on a stage inside our heads whenever we think of childhood, our first day at school, courtship and marriage. The longer we live—and it's now 60 years since I reluctantly walked out of Lunghua camp—the more our repertory company emerges from the shadows and moves to the front of the stage. Spielberg's film seems more truthful as the years pass. Christian Bale and John Malkovich join hands by the footlights with my real parents and my younger self, with the Japanese soldiers and American pilots, as a boy runs forever across a peaceful lawn towards the coming war. But perhaps, in the end, it's all only a movie.

EDUARDO PAOLOZZI

"Junkyard Dreams" in the *Times* (1987)

A woman friend describing Eduardo Paolozzi said: "He's a Minotaur." I thought this accurate: a bull's head, powerful physique, a lot of snorting, one hoof clawing the ground, eyes ready to attack anybody who's a little too light on his feet. But also that maze. It seems to me that Eduardo Paolozzi is the most important sculptor to have emerged since the Second World War and the only one who responds directly to science and technology, to the media landscape which has constructed the huge maze that we all inhabit.

I have known him for something like 20 years and his mind is as sharp and as free of conventional thinking as it was when I first met him. I knew, of course, his sculpture, which I had seen in exhibitions long before I met him, particularly his very early sculptures, those standing figures, apparently sprung from the psyche of some technological Frankenstein. What was so impressive about those early sculptures was that they were built out of the most commonplace machine parts: cog wheels, bits of radiator grills—all the detritus that one might see in a scrapyard.

In fact Paolozzi has always been intensely interested in junk, in the debris of the technological civilisation. In his later work, he moved not only within the realms of sculpture but into the graphic arts—above all in his screenprints, where he began to tackle head-on the ambiguities that surround the images of technology that are presented to us by the world of advertising.

To a large extent we have to believe the advertisers, and Eduardo is almost alone in trying to look at the world created by modern technology in something like the way in which Freud approached the dream. There is a manifest content: all the things that a new refrigerator will do for your sex life, but there's also the latent content, the secret alphabet that spells out the real meaning of the world of technology.

Do we take the mid-20th century on its own terms? In all his work it seems to me that Eduardo Paolozzi has tried to provide an answer to this, both to the hard core of the world of technology, as in his early sculpture, and to the media landscape that has created the sky whose air we breathe. He's completely free of cant. He approaches everything with an open mind, an eye to trying to understand the latent meanings.

There is a lot of humour in his work, as you can see in the murals that he designed for Tottenham Court Road station and in his screenprints. The juxtapositions in the latter of Mickey Mouse, soft-drink commercials, thermonuclear weapon systems, symbols taken from textbooks of heart surgery and advertisements for expensive watches, suggest a constant search for the real meanings that lie behind the flux of images, what McLuhan called the "high-speed information mosaics" that flow past us.

If the entire 20th century were to vanish in some huge calamity, it would be possible to re-constitute a large part of it from his sculpture and screenprints.

BRIAN ALDISS

A Is for Brian: A 65th Birthday Present for Brian W. Aldiss (1990)

In 1969, in a bar overlooking Copacabana Beach, Brian said to me: "This really is a splendid convention—we must organise another one."

I agreed. The SF conference, held as part of the Rio film festival, was the only one I had ever attended for more than a few hours.

"Where shall we hold the next one," Brian wondered.

"Venice? Palm Springs? Casablanca? Of course," I reminded him, "no publishers or agents will be invited."

"Naturally."

"And no fans."

"Agreed."

"And no other writers. Just you and I."

Brian laughed. "What a wonderfully dotty idea. But are you sure you want me along?"

Yes, Brian.

One day we will hold that convention. It surprises me that Brian is only 65. I've always thought him not only wiser and more generous than me, but much older. Perhaps I'm catching up with him, and our 75th birthdays will be held on the same day.

Brian and I are the last SF writers, or at least the last who still take SF seriously. All those who came after us—Mike Moorcock, William Gibson, Bruce Sterling—rightly see SF within an ironic framework. When Brian and I stop writing, SF will be over, and something different will continue. I'm glad we began in the same way, writing for Ted Carnell, seeing our names on the same covers, working together in the most exciting form of fiction in the world. He has always made modest claims for science fiction, while being enormously fond of both SF and its writers. I have made exaggerated claims and secretly disliked it. His approach has been much more sensible.

I suggest Rio again in July 2000. See you there, Brian, at the same bar on Copacabana.

JUDITH MERRIL

Aloud (1992)

When I visited Toronto in 1987 to give a reading at the International Festival of Authors, I saw Judy for the first time in 20 years.[3] I was delighted to find that she was the same fascinating figure I had got to know in London in the Swinging Sixties: strong-willed and combative, sensitive and astute, quick to quarrel and forgive, the shrewdest judge of fiction, fearless exposer of humbug and pretension and capable of surprising shifts into a positively feline femininity that could be quite disorienting. I'm

---

3. The original has not been seen. The text is reproduced from *Interzone* 106 (April 1996), 17–18.

sorry that she exiled herself from the USA at the height of the Vietnam war, when she might have had some influence for the good on American science fiction during its crucial years of change in the 1970s. And she and I might well have seen more of each other. But the loss to American sf was Toronto's gain.

Judy and I first met in London in 1966, but I'd been well aware of her powerful presence for the previous ten years. Late in 1956, soon after publishing my first short story in a British science-fiction magazine, I heard that the story had been picked by Judy for her anthology of the year's best sf. Thirty-five years later I can still remember the thrill of excitement, the sense of amazement that every novice writer has felt at the first sign of critical approval.

But Judy Merril, I soon discovered, was no ordinary critic. By the late 1950s science fiction on both sides of the Atlantic was almost totally ossified. Its great days of energy and innovation lay ten years in the past, and already sf was beginning to formularize itself and strengthen the ghetto walls that screened it from what was going on in the real world. As I found to my cost when I started submitting stories to the American magazines, the editors and fans were uninterested in science fiction's future but only in its past, in the safe certainties of interplanetary travel, time machines and a comic-book view of the world that was virtually no advance on the Buck Rogers and Flash Gordon strips that I read as a child in 1930s Shanghai. One American editor alone stood out against this deliberate narrowing of science fiction's imaginative possibilities, and that editor was Judith Merril.

During the dozen or so years of her *Annual Best Science Fiction*, years that coincided with my apprenticeship as a writer, Judy picked a number of my stories for her anthologies, but I would have devoured those precious volumes if she had never glanced at me. What impressed me about Judy's choice of the year's best short fiction and the copious editorial comments that seemed to place each story on a pedestal of its own, was that she saw sf as part of a larger imaginative world that extended well beyond the borders of the mainstream novel into the realms of politics and philosophy, theatre and the visual arts, psychology and the consumer society. She loved science fiction, as I did, for its energy and sheer gutsy newness, which had all the glitter and excitement of a line of concept cars at a motor-show and she saw that its sometimes naive but always visceral feel for the great issues of the day, for the pulse of change, gave it a range and flexibility that the traditional mainstream novel could rarely match.

More than that, Judy understood that science fiction's popular authority, in film, TV and advertising, allowed it to act like an easily convertible currency, the agile host at a party who can find the informal links between strangers. In Judy's anthologies avant-garde writers from Michael Moorcock's New Worlds rubbed shoulders with Borges and Calvino and science-fiction gadflies like Robert Sheckley. Unlike the realist bourgeois novel, in the imaginative realm over which Judy presided there were no walls but the widest windows onto the new.

Given my complete agreement with Judy's views as she expressed them over the years in her anthologies, I looked forward eagerly to meeting her when she arrived for the first time in London in 1966. I was instantly struck by her charm, sharp intelligence and New York bite but what surprised me was that after ten years of agreeing with her every word across the breadth of the Atlantic, when we met in person we seemed to disagree vociferously about everything. I remember wonderful arguments with her that would last all day, carried on from one noisy pub to the next, from an exhibition gallery to the flat where she cooked a meal and on to the evening's party, arguments fuelled by what must have been all the distilleries in Scotland and half the vineyards of France.

When she left England after her final visit the light seemed to grow greyer, and when she gave up her anthologies and moved to Canada one of the few generous and thoughtful voices in American sf fell silent, with consequences that soon became evident. Science fiction in both the USA and Britain entered the most commercialized and retrograde period it has ever known during the 1970s, though happily the cyberpunk leap forward led by William Gibson in the 1980s showed that sf can still renew itself. However it may be that Gibson and the cyberpunks were never writing science fiction at all, but, to their credit, an entirely new and freestanding form of imaginative fiction.

If so, then science fiction, as I suspect, is now dead, and probably died at about the time that Judy closed her anthology and left to found her memorial library to the genre in Toronto. I remember my last sight of her surrounded by her friends and all the books she loved, shouting me down whenever I tried to argue with her, the strongest woman in a genre for the most part created by timid and weak men.

WILLIAM S. BURROUGHS

Guardian (1997)

That William Burroughs lived to such an immense age is a tribute to the rejuvenating powers of a misspent life. More than half a century of heavy drug use failed to dim either his remarkably sharp mind or his dryly cackling humour. When I last saw him in London a few years ago he was stooped and easily tired, but little different from the already legendary figure I first met in the 1960s at his service flat in Duke Street, St James.

Esquire had asked me to write a profile of him, but Burroughs, though courteous, was very suspicious. The baleful power of media empires already obsessed him. While his young boyfriend, "love" and "hate" tattooed on his knuckles, carved a roast chicken, Burroughs described the most effective way to stab a man to death. All the while he kept an eye on the doors and windows. "The CIA are watching me," he confided. "They park their laundry vans in the street outside."

I don't think he was having me on. His imagination was filled with bizarre lore culled from *Believe It or Not* features, police pulps and—in the case, I assume, of the laundry vans—Hollywood spy movies of the cold war years. When Burroughs talked about *Time* magazine's conspiracy to take over the world he meant it literally.

I turned down the *Esquire* assignment, realising that nothing I wrote could remotely do justice to Burroughs's magnificently paranoid imagination. He changed little over the next decades, and hardly needed to—his weird genius was the perfect mirror of his times, and made him the most important and original writer since the second world war. Now we are left with the career novelists.

ACKNOWLEDGMENTS

The job of the editor of this collection is made considerably easier by the active and accomplished community of Ballardians, which counts among its number editors, chroniclers, artists, translators, and enthusiasts. Not only are there a number of significant online resources that have made available a selection of the contents of this volume, as well as fascinating and detailed commentary of many forms, but there have been mailing lists and groups peopled by knowledgeable and collegiate readers of Ballard who have performed astonishing acts of detective work. If authors were judged by the quality of their fans, Ballard would win, hands down.

Any editor or anthologist working on Ballard now is indebted above all others to David Pringle, who was aware before anyone else that someone needed to keep track of Ballard's output, and did so skillfully, without the digital databases that provide such support now. David wrote the first monograph on Ballard, edited his work in the pages of *Foundation* and *Interzone*, published twenty-three issues of the newsletter *News from the Sun*, which became *JGB News*, proposed the first collection of Ballard's nonfiction as early as 1981, and assisted on *A User's Guide to the Millennium* (1997). I am particularly indebted to David for his generosity in sharing his transcripts of Ballard's nonfiction, which have saved innumerable hours of labor, for providing a copy of the original English language text of "Visa pour la réalité," and for patiently fielding endless questions. Any errors that have entered the text as original formatting has been restored are entirely my own. David denies that he is a scholar but he's surely the authority, as proved by his ongoing timeline series in *Deep Ends*.

I am indebted also to Mike Bonsall, whose online Ballard concordances are invaluable research resources, and who responded swiftly and enthusiastically to my query about whether transcript documents existed.

Brigid Marlin generously provided a selection of gems from her own archives relating to her commissions for Ballard and her portrait of him. Rick McGrath, editor of the *Deep Ends* series, provided key pointers and a copy of the rare introduction from *Waves and Light*. Jeremy Millar, Dan O'Hara and Maxim Jakubowski fielded inquiries with speed and candor. Maggie Hanbury scoured her agency archives on behalf of this project.

Further thanks to Roger Luckhurst, friend, colleague, and inspirational writer, who has provided reputation-saving counsel and suggested the title "Capsule Commentaries"; Jeannette Baxter, brilliant scholar and generous coexaminer; Chris Beckett, archivist at the British Library; Paul Williams, whose enthusiasm was an initial impetus to my own Ballard-immersion; and Toby Litt, who submitted to being in conversation.

This edition has only been possible because of the kind permission and encouragement of the Estate of J. G. Ballard, and in particular Fay and Bea Ballard, to whom I am immensely grateful for their trust. At Wiley, Sarah Chalfant and Tracey Bohan have been exemplars of patient professionalism. At the MIT Press, Marc Lowenthal and Judy Feldmann have supplemented patience and professionalism with enthusiasm, skill, and expert guidance. My gratitude, also, to Paula Bain Clark, whose expert index is a crucial navigation aid for such a volume.

BIBLIOGRAPHY

PRIMARY SOURCES

1 STATEMENTS

Ballard, J. G. "Introduction to the French Edition of *Crash!*" *Foundation*, no. 9 (November 1975): 45–49. Previously published as "Introduction." In *Crash!*, translated by Robert Louit. Paris: Calmann-Levy, 1974.

————. "Notes from Nowhere: Comments on Work in Progress." *New Worlds* (October 1966).

————. "What I Believe." *Interzone* (Summer 1984). Previously published as "Ce que je crois," in *Science Fiction*, no. 1 (January 1984).

————. "Which Way to Inner Space?" *New Worlds* (May 1962).

2 *NEW WORLDS*

Ballard, J. G. "Alphabets of Unreason." *New Worlds* (December 1969).

————. "La Jetée, Academy One." *New Worlds* (July 1966).

————. "Myth-Maker of the 20th Century." *New Worlds* (May-June 1964).

————. "Salvador Dali: The Innocent as Paranoid." *New Worlds* (February 1969).

————. "The Coming of the Unconscious." *New Worlds* (July 1966).

————. "The Thousand Wounds and Flowers." *New Worlds* (January 1969).

————. "Use Your Vagina." *New Worlds* (June 1969).

————. "Visions of Hell." *New Worlds* (March 1966).

3 COMMENTARIES

Ballard, J. G. "An Appreciation." In *Paintings in the Mische Technique: Demonstrating the Oil and Egg Tempera Technique of the Renaissance Painters*, by Brigid Marlin, 5. 1991.

———. "Cataclysms and Dooms." In *The Visual Encyclopedia of Science Fiction*, edited by Brian Ash, 130. London: Trewin Copplestone Publishing, 1977.

———. "Comment on 'End-Game.'" In *Backdrop of Stars*, edited by Harry Harrison, 77–79. London: Dobson, 1968.

———. "The Coolest Gaze in American Art." *Guardian*, August 14, 2001, sec. Review.

———. "Epilogue to Storm-Wind (Part 1)." *New Worlds* (September 1961).

———. "Eyes Wide Shut: J. G. Ballard on Paul Delvaux's Landscapes of Nostalgia and Desire." In *Time Out Brussels Guide*, edited by Nicholas Royle, 34–35. London: Penguin, 1996.

———. "Foreword." In *The Doors of Perception* and *Heaven and Hell*, by Aldous Huxley, v–vi. London: Flamingo, 1994.

———. "Foreword." In *"Enemy Subject": Life in a Japanese Internment Camp 1943–45*, by Peggy Abkhazi, edited by S. W. Jackman, 7–8. Stroud: Alan Sutton Publishing, 1995.

———. "Foreword." In *West End Survival Kit*, by Jeremy Reed. London: Waterloo Press, 2009.

———. "Forord [Foreword]." In *Luftspeil [Vermillion Sands]*, translated by Jon Bing, 7–8. Oslo: Gylendal, 1972.

———. "Forord [Foreword]." In *Grusomhedsudstillingen [The Atrocity Exhibition]*, translated by Jannick Storm, 7–9. Copenhagen: Rhodos, 1969.

———. "Images of the Future: Comments on Some Recent Experiments." *JGB News* (January 1993).

———. "Introduction." In *Dali*, edited by David Larkin, unpaginated [7–14]. London: Pan/Ballantine, 1974.

———. "Introduction." In *J. G. Ballard: The First Twenty Years*, edited by David Pringle and James Goddard, 80. Hayes, Middlesex: Bran's Head Books, 1976.

———. "Introduction." In *The Best of J. G. Ballard*, 7–8. London: Futura, 1977.

———. "Introduction." In *Naked Lunch*, by William Burroughs. London: Flamingo, 1993.

———. "Introduction." In *Myths of the Near Future*, v–vi. London: Vintage, 1994.

———. "Introduction." In *Hello America*, 4–5. London: Vintage, 1994.

———. "Introduction." In *Concrete Island*, 4–5. London: Vintage, 1994.

———. "Introductory Text." In *General Dynamic F.U.N.: Moonstrips Empire News*, by Eduardo Paolozzi, loose. London: Editions Alecto, 1970.

———. "J. G. Ballard's Comments on His Own Fiction." *Interzone*, April 1996.

———. "James the Great." *Guardian*, October 11, 1990.

———. "On the Shelf." *Sunday Times*, June 6, 1993, sec. Books.

———. "Preface." In *Vermillion Sands*, 7–8. London: Cape, 1973.

———. "Report on an Unidentified Space Station." In *Top Fantasy*, edited by Josh Pachter, 12–13. London: J. M. Dent, 1985.

———. "Robert Smithson as Cargo Cultist." In *Robert Smithson: A Collection of Writings on Robert Smithson on the Occasion of the Installation of Dead Tree at Pierogi 2000*, edited by Brian Conley and Joe Amrhein, 31. New York: Pierogi 2000, 1997.

———. "Second Thoughts: Sculptors Who Carve the Clouds." *Independent*, October 24, 1992.

———. "Time and Tacita Dean." In *Tacita Dean: Recent Films and Other Works, edited by* , 33. London: Tate Britain, 2001.

———. "Time, Memory and Inner Space." *Woman Journalist* (1963).

———. "Visa pour la réalité." *Magazine littéraire* (November 1978).

———. "You and Me and the Continuum." In *Top Fantasy: The Author's Choice*, edited by Josh Pachter, 12–13. London: J. M. Dent, 1985.

4 FEATURES AND ESSAYS

Ballard, J. G. "A Handful of Dust." *Guardian*, March 20, 2006.

———. "Airports: Cities of the Future." *Blueprint: Architecture, Design & Contemporary Culture* (September 1997).

———. "The Car, the Future." *Drive* (Autumn 1971).

———. "The Consumer Consumed." *Ink*, June 5, 1971.

———. "The Diary of a Mad Space Wife." *Vogue*, December 1979.

———. "Dreams and Surrealism." *Sunday Times Magazine*, February 16, 1969.

———. "Fantasy Fiction." *Queen*, January 3, 1968.

———. "Fictions of Every Kind." *Books and Bookmen* (February 1971).

———. "The French Riviera Spoiled? Only by Fear and Snobbery." *Mail on Sunday*, January 1, 1995.

———. "The Future of the Future." *Vogue*, November 1977.

———. "The Larval Stage of a New Kind of Architecture." *Guardian*, October 8, 2007.

———. "The Prophet." *Guardian*, July 23, 2005.

———. "Shock and Gore." *Guardian*, May 26, 2007.

———. "Terminal Documents: Burroughs Reviewed." *Ambit* (Spring 1966).

———. "Welcome to the Virtual City." *Tate*, Spring 2001.

5   LISTS, CAPTIONS, AND GLOSSARIES

Ballard, J. G. "Collector's Choice: Outer Limits." *American Film*, October 1, 1987.

———. "Impressions of Speed." In *Speed: Visions of an Accelerated Age*, 32–55. London: The Photographers' Gallery and the Whitechapel Art Gallery, 1998.

———. "J. G. Ballard." In *The Test of Time: What Makes a Classic a Classic?*, edited by Andrew Holgate and Honor Wilson-Fletcher, 8–10. London: Waterstone's Booksellers in association with the Arts Council of England, 1999.

———. "Project for a Glossary of the Twentieth Century." *Zone 6: Incorporations*, no. 6 (November 1992): 268–279.

6   REVIEWS

Ballard, J. G. "A Burp to Refresh the World." *Daily Telegraph*, July 31, 1993.

———. "After Magritte, Tilly and the Tissue Paper." *Guardian*, February 14, 1991.

———. "All in the Mind." *Guardian*, September 23, 1966.

———. "All the World in Its Humour and Chaos." *Daily Telegraph*, November 27, 1993.

———. "American Dreams." *Sunday Times*, August 31, 1997.

———. "Analyst's Couch Potato." *Daily Telegraph*, November 14, 1998.

———. "Animal Gravity Rules." *Daily Telegraph*, January 8, 1994.

———. "The Animals' Magna Carta." *Daily Telegraph*, June 17, 2000.

———. "Anything Could Happen." *Guardian*, October 6, 1995.

———. "Are We Over the Moon?" *Daily Telegraph*, July 16, 1994.

———. "Autopia or Autogeddon." *Guardian*, November 29, 1984.

———. "The Avian Equivalent of the Gold Rolex." *Daily Telegraph*, March 7, 1992.

———. "Back to the Heady Future." *Daily Telegraph*, April 17, 1993.

———. "Behind the Self-Deprecation, Steely Ambition." *Daily Telegraph*, May 22, 1999.

———. "*Blue Velvet* (1986)." *Guardian*, September 18, 1993, sec. The Movies: The Readers' Choice.

———. "Brute Force and Ignorance?" *Sunday Times*, September 15, 1996.

————. "Burlesque out of Barbed Wire." *Guardian*, November 1, 1990.

————. "Bursting the Bubble." *Daily Telegraph*, January 8, 2000.

————. "A Case of Pre-Millennial Tension." *Daily Telegraph*, August 24, 1996.

————. "Candide Camera." *New Statesman*, April 14, 1978.

————. "Caught Napping at the Eleventh Hour." *Guardian*, February 9, 1996.

————. "Chainsaw Biomassacre in Glorious Horoscope." *Guardian*, April 25, 1991.

————. "Circles and Squares." *Guardian*, September 30, 1966.

————. "A City Steeped in Unrest." *Daily Telegraph*, April 26, 2003.

————. "Closed Doors." *New Statesman*, June 3, 1977.

————. "Committees. How They Work and How to Work Them." *Chemistry & Industry*, November 30, 1963.

————. "Concise Chemical and Technical Dictionary." *Chemistry & Industry*, September 22, 1962.

————. "Courting the Cobra." *Daily Telegraph*, March 27, 1993.

————. "Cyclops Eye of the Century." *Daily Telegraph*, November 25, 1992.

————. "The Day of Reckoning." *New Statesman*, July 4, 2005.

————. "Days Strung on a Syringe with a Thread of Blood." *Independent on Sunday*, February 24, 1991.

————. "Death-Wish Anonymous." *Guardian*, August 19, 1966.

————. "The Demolition Squad." *Guardian*, November 12, 1965.

————. "The Department of Scientific and Industrial Research." *Chemistry & Industry*, February 6, 1962.

————. "Dictionary of Chemistry." *Chemistry & Industry*, March 31, 1962.

————. "Dictionary of Chemistry and Chemical Technology." *Chemistry & Industry*, October 13, 1962.

————. "Dictionary of Commercial Chemicals." *Chemistry & Industry*, August 9, 1962.

————. "Does the Future Still Exist?" *Times*, April 20, 1968.

————. "A Doll Dressed up by Adults." *Daily Telegraph*, July 28, 2001.

————. "Down to Earth." *Guardian*, April 9, 1965.

————. "Down to Earth." *New Statesman*, June 18, 1976.

————. "Electrodynamic at Womanising." *Daily Telegraph*, January 2, 1993.

———. "The Elephant and the Quasar." *Guardian*, May 21, 1965.

———. "Encyclopedia of Chemical Technology." *Chemistry & Industry*, August 24, 1963.

———. "End of a Riviera." *Guardian*, July 31, 2004.

———. "Erotica's First and Finest Working Class Hero." *Independent on Sunday*, March 10, 1991.

———. "Escape into the Seraglio." *Guardian*, October 28, 1988.

———. "Fallen Idol." *Guardian*, December 3, 1981.

———. "Fashion Victim." *Bookforum* (Spring 1999).

———. "Feast on Magical Seas." *Daily Telegraph*, November 2, 1991.

———. "First Things Last." *Tatler* (March 1981).

———. "The Flash of Genius." *Chemistry & Industry*, October 19, 1963.

———. "Flush with Talent." *Daily Telegraph*, February 5, 2005.

———. "Food Processing & Packaging Directory, 1963–1964." *Chemistry & Industry*, May 10, 1963.

———. "French Polish." *New Statesman*, April 15, 1977.

———. "Grope Therapy." *New Statesman*, July 15, 1977.

———. "Guilty Treats of the Table." *Daily Telegraph*, January 30, 1993.

———. "Handbook of Chemistry and Physics." *Chemistry & Industry*, June 4, 1963.

———. "Has the Interview Become a Media Game?" *Daily Telegraph*, October 3, 1992.

———. "The Heirs of Duchamp's Urinal." *Daily Telegraph*, October 26, 2002.

———. "He's Not Being Funny, He's Struggling Heroically Under the Capitalist Yoke." *Observer*, February 15, 1998.

———. "Hobbits in Space." *Time Out*, December 16, 1977.

———. "How Ariel Turned into Prospero." *Times*, March 2, 1968.

———. "How to Tear a Strip Off a Culture." *Guardian*, March 21, 1991.

———. "Hungry Young Men." *Daily Telegraph*, February 10, 2001.

———. "Hydrogen, Treason and Plot." *Guardian*, November 5, 1995.

———. "In Cold Blood." *Guardian*, June 25, 2005.

———. "In Modern America, No Nightmare Is Forbidden." *Guardian*, May 14, 2004.

———. "In Search of the Last Emperor." *Sunday Times*, July 11, 1993.

———. "In the Asylum of Dreams." *Guardian*, July 4, 1986.

———. "In the Voyeur's Gaze." *Guardian*, August 25, 1989.

———. "In William Burroughs Country." *Washington Post*, December 27, 1987.

———. "In Your Dreams." *Observer*, December 6, 1998.

———. "Index to Reviews, Symposia Volumes and Monographs in Organic Chemistry." *Chemistry & Industry*, November 17, 1962.

———. "Information U.S.S.R." *Chemistry & Industry*, October 11, 1962

———. "Innocence and Experience." *Guardian*, February 3, 1991.

———. "Into the Drop Zone." *Guardian*, July 23, 1965.

———. "Is There Anybody Out There?" *Sunday Times*, September 21, 1997.

———. "Journey Through the Touchstone City." *Guardian*, June 13, 1991.

———. "The Killer Inside." *Guardian*, September 23, 2005.

———. "Killing Time Should Be Prime Time TV." *Guardian*, November 15, 1979.

———. "The Kindness of Strangers." *Daily Telegraph*, June 12, 1999.

———. "Kings of Infinite Space." *Guardian*, November 29, 1979.

———. "The Largest Theme Park in the World." *Guardian*, July 7, 1989.

———. "Last Gasp for the American Dream." *Guardian*, February 22, 2003.

———. "The Last of the Great Royals." *Observer*, April 30, 1989.

———. "The Last Real Innocents." *New York Times Book Review*, September 11, 1991.

———. "Lautrec with Strychnine." *Guardian*, June 27, 1991.

———. "Legend of Regret." *Guardian*, February 4, 1982.

———. "Lesson to Last a Lifetime." *Daily Telegraph*, March 5, 1994.

———. "Let the Women Have Lipstick and High Heels." *Daily Telegraph*, October 30, 1993.

———. "Licence to Kill." *Sunday Times*, February 21, 1999.

———. "Little Lamb, Who Made Thee?" *Sunday Times*, October 26, 1997.

———. "Living Dangerously." *Sunday Times*, September 3, 1995.

———. "The Long March Forward." *Sunday Times*, February 11, 1996.

———. "Losing It at the Movies." *Sunday Times*, May 12, 1996.

——. "Lost in Paradise." *Sunday Times*, January 12, 1997.

——. "Lost in Space." *Guardian*, November 26, 1970.

——. "Love, Pain, Pleasure and the Whole Damn Thing." *Sunday Times*, February 22, 1998.

——. "The Lure of the Madding Crowd." *Independent on Sunday*, September 22, 1991.

——. "Made in USA." *Guardian*, October 8, 1965.

——. "Magical Days at Rick's." *Daily Telegraph*, February 20, 1993.

——. "Magnificent Men and Flying Machines." *Sunday Times*, May 4, 1997.

——. "The Maestro Who Campaigned Against His Greatest Work." *Daily Telegraph*, August 21, 1999.

——. "Making Light of Life's Cussedness." *Sunday Times*, March 8, 1998.

——. "Manbotching." *New Statesman*, October 20, 1978.

——. "The Maverick Who Found Inspiration in Defeat." *Guardian*, August 1, 1991.

——. "A Mind Firmly Set on the Universe." *Daily Telegraph*, September 4, 1993.

——. "Minstrels and the Tommy-Gun." *Daily Telegraph*, January 25, 1992.

——. "Modern Cosmeticology." *Chemistry & Industry*, January 26, 1963.

——. "Mouse That Bores?" *Daily Telegraph*, June 11, 1994.

——. "Never the Twain." *Sunday Times*, April 7, 1996.

——. "New Means Worse." *Guardian*, November 26, 1981.

——. "No Time Like the Future." *Observer*, September 5, 1999.

——. "Notes from Nowhere." *Guardian*, July 1, 1966.

——. "Old Bloodshed, as If in a Dream." *Guardian*, February 28, 1991.

——. "The Old Guard." *Guardian*, November 26, 1965.

——. "On the Shabby Carousel of the Sixties." *Daily Telegraph*, May 9, 1992.

——. "One Dull Step for Man." *Observer*, December 22, 1996.

——. "One Man Against Millions." *Sunday Times*, November 10, 1996.

——. "Our Odds Are 50–50." *Daily Telegraph*, May 18, 2003.

——. "Our Own Swift." *Guardian*, September 27, 1985.

——. "Package Tours." *New Statesman*, December 17, 1976.

——. "Paint, Oil and Colour Year Book." *Chemistry & Industry*, January 6, 1963.

————. "A Personal View." *Cypher* (May 1974).

————. "Poisoning by Drugs and Chemicals: An Index of Toxic Effects and Their Treatment." *Chemistry & Industry*, April 8, 1962.

————. "Practical and Industrial Formulary." *Chemistry & Industry*, December 1, 1963.

————. "Prophet of Our Present." *Guardian*, April 13, 2002.

————. "Prospero in Herts." *New Statesman*, October 3, 1997.

————. "The Pucccini of Cinema Grows Up." *Independent*, June 15, 1996.

————. "Push-Button Death in the Ultimate Autogeddon." *Guardian*, March 14, 1991.

————. "A Race of Walking, Talking, Living Fossils." *Daily Telegraph*, June 12, 1993.

————. "Reach for the Sky." *Sunday Times*, October 18, 1998.

————. "Red Stars and Sickle Moons." *Guardian*, March 17, 1967.

————. "A Repressed Psyche in Full Flight." *Daily Telegraph*, July 18, 1998.

————. "Return of the Future." *Daily Telegraph*, December 27, 1997.

————. "Rituals of a Skinny-Dipper." *Daily Telegraph*, July 4, 1992.

————. "Sands of Time." *Guardian*, June 26, 1998.

————. "Scallywags of the World." *Daily Telegraph*, September 19, 1992.

————. "The Science of Dreams." *Chemistry & Industry*, September 2, 1963.

————. "Scheming with a Smile." *Guardian*, April 22, 1988.

————. "Second Growth Coca-Cola." *Daily Telegraph*, November 23, 1991.

————. "Secrets of the Emperor's Bunker." *Guardian*, September 13, 2005.

————. "The See-Through Brain." *Guardian*, February 12, 1970.

————. "Senses of an Ending." *Guardian*, October 28, 1982.

————. "Sermons from the Mount." *Sunday Times*, November 10, 1991.

————. "Sex without the Hollywood Rule Book." *Guardian*, May 30, 1991.

————. "Shrine to the Bear of Little Brain." *Daily Telegraph*, October 10, 1992.

————. "Sinister Spider?" *Daily Telegraph*, June 27, 1992.

————. "Small Man as Victim of Mob Psychology." *Guardian*, October 10, 1991.

————. "Spaced Out." *New Society*, April 18, 1974.

————. "A Staircase of Corpses." *New Statesman*, March 26, 2001.

———. "Stars and Their Lives." *Observer*, February 20, 2005.

———. "Stepping Beyond the Silver Screen." *Guardian Weekly/Observer*, April 19, 1998.

———. "Sticking to His Guns." *Guardian*, August 24, 1993.

———. "Still Life on a Virgin Canvas." *Guardian*, May 23, 1991.

———. "Strange Seas of Thought." *Guardian*, June 3, 1966.

———. "Survival Instincts." *Sunday Times*, March 1, 1992.

———. "The Sweet Smell of Excess on Sunset Boulevard." *Independent on Sunday*, June 10, 1990.

———. "Technical Market Research." *Chemistry & Industry*, March 11, 1962.

———. "They're Falling Out of the Sky." *Daily Telegraph*, August 1, 1998.

———. "Think Like a Swarm." *Daily Telegraph*, October 6, 2001.

———. "The Third Man." *Times*, October 3, 2002.

———. "This Boy Does Talk. Who Is He?" *Guardian*, June 1, 2002.

———. "The Transistorised Brain." *Guardian*, January 28, 1966.

———. "A Truly Modern Monster." *Guardian*, October 24, 1986.

———. "The Ultimate Sacrifice." *New Statesman*, September 9, 2002.

———. "The Unlimited Dream Company." *New Statesman*, July 8, 2002.

———. "Unlocking the Past." *Daily Telegraph*, September 21, 1991.

———. "Up with the Celestial Helmsmen." *Guardian*, May 7, 2005.

———. "Urchin in Pursuit of the Parade." *Guardian*, January 17, 1991.

———. "Use of the Chemical Literature." *Chemistry & Industry*, April 5, 1963.

———. "Walt Disney on Dope." *Guardian*, June 23, 1989.

———. "Was the Holocaust Scripted by This Man?" *Daily Telegraph*, September 25, 1993.

———. "Waste of Beauty." *Guardian*, October 7, 1966.

———. "Weirdly Wise." *Observer*, August 17, 1997.

———. "What Japan Did Next." *Sunday Times*, August 29, 1999.

———. "What to Do Till the Analyst Comes." *Guardian*, March 31, 1966.

———. "When Flying Was Fun." *Guardian*, June 3, 2005.

———. "Where Have All the Space Ships Gone?" *Times*, June 29, 1968.

———. "A Wilder West." *Guardian*, April 26, 1984.

———. "A World of Endless Summer." *Evening Standard*, March 15, 2004.

———. "Writing a Technical Paper." *Chemistry & Industry*, June 16, 1962.

———. "The Year's Science Fiction." *Guardian*, December 29, 1967.

———. "Zap Code." *New Statesman*, March 25, 1977.

7   NEW STATESMAN

Ballard, J. G. "Diary." *New Statesman*, December 20, 1999.

———. "Diary." *New Statesman*, May 28, 2001.

———. "Diary: A Fascist's Guide to the Premiership." *New Statesman*, September 4, 2006.

———. "Now Parliament Is Just Another Hypermarket." *New Statesman*, May 9, 2005.

8   FORUM DISCUSSIONS

Ballard, J. G. "A Response to the Invitation to Respond." *Science Fiction Studies* 18, no. 3 (November 1991): 329.

———. "Science Fiction Cannot Be Immune from Change." In *SF Symposium*, 157–159. Rio de Janeiro: Instituto Nacional do Cinema, 1969.

Ballard, J. G., and Anne Atkins. "Nurse, the Screens." *Guardian*, March 28, 1998, sec. The Week.

Ballard, J. G., et al. "Cyberpunk Forum/Symposium." *Mississippi Review* 47/48 (1988): 16.

———. "The House That Jencks Built." *Modern Review*, no. 20 (April-May 1995): 31.

———. "Public Lending Rights: A Symposium." *New Review* 2, no. 21 (December 1975): 17–18.

———. "The State of Fiction: A Symposium." *New Review* 5, no. 1 (Summer 1978): 19–20.

———. "Tunnel Visionaries." *Modern Review*, no. 15 (July 1994): 31.

9   CAPSULE COMMENTARIES

Ballard, J. G. "First Buy, Next Buy." *Sunday Telegraph*, November 13, 2005.

———. "Franz Kafka: The Outsider." *Sunday Times*, June 20, 1993.

———. "I Wish I'd Written . . ." *Guardian*, September 16, 1994.

———. "The Last Book I Bought." *Daily Telegraph*, October 7, 2000.

———. "The Perfect Beach." *Observer*, January 13, 2002.

———. "Sunday Times/Gollancz SF Story Competition." *Sunday Times*, December 15, 1985.

———. "True Confessions." *Daily Telegraph*, May 7, 1994.

———. "The Westway." In *City Secrets: London*, edited by Tim Adams. London: Little Bookroom, 2001.

———. "Writer's Rooms." *Guardian*, March 9, 2007.

Ballard, J. G., et al. "Books of the Year." *Daily Telegraph*, November 27, 1993.

———. "Apocalypse How?" *Spin*, November 1, 1995.

———. "The Author's Author." *Guardian*, October 26, 1998.

———. "The Best of Tomes." *Guardian*, December 8, 1995.

———. "The Best Reading of 1994." *Times*, November 26, 1994.

———. "Book of the Century." *Daily Telegraph*, January 17, 1998.

———. "Books of Christmas." *Guardian*, November 24, 2007.

———. "Books of the Year." *Daily Telegraph*, November 27, 1993.

———. "Books of the Year." *Daily Telegraph*, November 26, 1994.

———. "Books of the Year." *Daily Telegraph*, November 23, 2002.

———. "Books of the Year." *New Statesman*. London: New Statesman, December 3, 2001.

———. "Books of the Year." *New Statesman*. London: New Statesman, December 1, 2003.

———. "Books of the Year." *New Statesman*. London: New Statesman, November 29, 2004.

———. "Books of the Year." *Observer*, November 26, 1995.

———. "Books of the Year." *Sunday Times*, November 29, 1992.

———. "Britain's Changing Places." *Guardian*, November 2, 1994.

———. "Christmas Books." *Sunday Times*, December 9, 1984.

———. "Green Lights." *Guardian*, October 6, 1989.

———. "Just What They've Always Wanted." *Guardian*, December 24, 1993.

———. "The Magnificent Seven." *Esquire*, May 1994.

———. "Pick of the Books of 1986." *Guardian*, December 5, 1986.

———. "Pieces of Hate." *Time Out*, June 29, 1994.

———. "Should the 'Friendly Fire' Pilots Be Blamed?" *Independent on Sunday*, May 24, 1992.

———. "Signs of the Times." *Observer*, December 31, 1995.

———. "Style-Setters on Style." *Sunday Times*, March 21, 1993.

———. "Summer Choices." *Daily Telegraph*, July 8, 2000.

———. "Summer Reading." *Guardian*, June 29, 2002.

———. "What Would Make You Move Back to London?" *New Statesman*, June 4, 2001.

———. "Where Did You Get That?" *Independent*, January 29, 1994.

———. "Writers' Reading in 1987." *Guardian*, December 11, 1987.

10 MEMOIR AND TRIBUTES

Ballard, J. G. "'The CIA Are Watching Me' He Confided." *Guardian*, August 4, 1997.

———. "The End of My War." *Sunday Times*, August 20, 1995.

———. "J. G. Ballard." In *A Is for Brian: A 65th Birthday Present for Brian W. Aldiss*, edited by Frank Hatherley, Margaret Aldiss, and Malcolm Edwards, 13. Brighton: Avernus, 1990.

———. "J. G. Ballard." In *The Pleasure of Reading*, edited by Antonia Fraser, 90–95. London: Bloomsbury, 1992.

———. "J. G. Ballard." *Time Out*, October 13, 1993.

———. "Junkyard Dreams." *Times*, May 12, 1987.

———. "Look Back at Empire." *Guardian*, March 4, 2006.

———. "Michael Dempsey and Friends." *Guardian*, December 8, 1990.

———. "Smashing Days on the Road." *Independent*, May 19, 1990.

———. "The Widest Windows onto the New." *Aloud* (October 1992).

SUGGESTED FURTHER READING

BOOKS

Baxter, Jeannette, ed. *Contemporary Critical Perspectives: J. G. Ballard*. London: Bloomsbury, 2008.

———. *J. G. Ballard's Surrealist Imagination: Spectacular Authorship*. Farnham: Ashgate, 2009.

Baxter, Jeannette, and Rowland Wymer, eds. *J. G. Ballard: Visions and Revisions*. Basingstoke and New York: Palgrave Macmillan, 2011.

Brown, Richard, Christopher Duffy, and Elizabeth Stainforth, eds. *J. G. Ballard: Landscapes of Tomorrow*. Leiden: Brill, 2016.

Deep Ends. Toronto: The Terminal Press, 2014.

Deep Ends. Toronto: The Terminal Press, 2015.

Deep Ends. Toronto: The Terminal Press, 2016.

Deep Ends. Powell River: The Terminal Press, 2018.

Deep Ends. Powell River: The Terminal Press, 2019.

Deep Ends. Powell River: The Terminal Press, 2020.

Deep Ends. Powell River: The Terminal Press, 2021.

Francis, Mark, and Kay Pallister, eds. *Crash: Homage to J. G. Ballard*. London: Gagosian, 2010.

Francis, Samuel. *The Psychological Fictions of J. G. Ballard*. London and New York: Continuum, 2011.

Gasiorek, Andrzej, *J. G. Ballard*. Manchester: Manchester University Press, 2005.

Luckhurst, Roger. *The Angle between Two Walls*. Liverpool: Liverpool University Press, 1997.

Moynihan, Thomas, and Iain Hamilton Grant, eds. *Spinal Catastrophism: A Secret History*. Falmouth: Urbanomic, 2019.

Paddy, David Ian. *The Empires of J. G. Ballard: An Imagined Geography*. Canterbury: Gylphi, 2015.

Sellars, Simon, and Dan O'Hara, eds. *Extreme Metaphors: Selected Interviews with J. G. Ballard, 1967–2008*. London: Fourth Estate, 2012.

Vale, V., ed. *J. G. Ballard: Quotes*. San Francisco: RE/Search Publications, 2004.

Vale, V., and Andrea Juno, eds. *RE/Search: J. G. Ballard*. San Francisco: RE/Search Publications, 1984.

Wilson, D. Harlan. *J. G. Ballard*. Urbana: Illinois University Press, 2017.

ESSAYS

Baudrillard, Jean, and Arthur B. Evans. "Ballard's 'Crash' ('Crash' de Ballard)." *Science Fiction Studies* 18, no. 3 (1991): 313–320.

Baxter, Jeannette. "Encountering the Holocaust in J. G. Ballard's Post-War Science Fictions." *Textual Practice* 26, no. 3 (2012): 379–398.

Beckett, Chris. "J. G. Ballard's '*Crash!* A Science Theatre Presentation for the ICA': The Context of a Document Newly Discovered." *Electronic British Library Journal* (2019): 1–43.

———. "J. G. Ballard's 'Elaborately Signalled Landscape': The Drafting of Concrete Island." *Electronic British Library Journal* (2015): 1–21.

———. "Near Vermilion Sands: The Context and Date of Composition of an Abandoned Literary Draft by J. G. Ballard." *Electronic British Library Journal* (2014): 1–28.

———. "The Progress of the Text: The Papers of J. G. Ballard at the British Library." *Electronic British Library Journal* 12 (2011): 1–24.

Bell, Duncan. "J. G. Ballard's Surrealist Liberalism." *Political Theory* 49, no. 6 (2021): 934–967.

Brown, Richard. "Ballard, Sexual Landscapes and Nature." *Green Letters* 22, no. 4 (2018): 426–437.

Clarke, Jim. "Reading Climate Change in J. G. Ballard." *Critical Survey* 25, no. 2 (2013): 7–21.

Duncan, Pansy. "Taking the Smooth with the Rough: Texture, Emotion, and the Other Postmodernism." *PMLA* 129, no. 2 (2014): 204–222.

Evans, Joel. "The Mob: J. G. Ballard's Turn to the Collective." *Novel* 53, no. 3 (2020): 436–451.

Hayles, N. Katherine. "The Borders of Madness." *Science Fiction Studies* 18, no. 3 (1991): 321–323.

I. C. R. "Editorial Introduction: Postmodernism's SF/SF's Postmodernism." *Science Fiction Studies* 18, no. 3 (1991): 305–308.

Knowles, Thomas. "J. G. Ballard and the 'Natural' World." *Green Letters* 22, no. 4 (October 2, 2018): 341–353.

Kraitsowits, Stephan. "Elemental Ballard." *Critique: Studies in Contemporary Fiction* 55, no. 4 (2014): 422–436.

Landon, Brooks. "Responding to the Killer B's." *Science Fiction Studies* 18, no. 3 (1991): 326–327.

Lehman, Robert S. "Back to the Future: Late Modernism in J. G. Ballard's *The Drowned World*." *Journal of Modern Literature* 41, no. 4 (2018): 161–178.

Luckhurst, Roger. "J. G. Ballard: *Crash*." In *Companion to Science Fiction*, edited by David Seed, 512–521. London: Wiley Blackwell, 2005.

Matthews, Graham. "Consumerism's Endgame: Violence and Community in J. G. Ballard's Late Fiction." *Journal of Modern Literature* 36, no. 2 (2013): 122–139.

McCarthy, Tom. "Writing Machines." *London Review of Books* 36, no. 24 (2014): 21–22.

Nichols, Peter. "Jerry Cornelius at the Atrocity Exhibition: Anarchy and Entropy in New Worlds Science Fiction." *Foundation*, no. 9 (1975): 28, 31.

Oramus, Dominika. "Against the Anthropocene? Epidemics in J. G. Ballard's Short Stories." *English Studies* 101, no. 8 (2020): 998–1008.

Porush, David. "The Architextuality of Transcendence." *Science Fiction Studies* 18, no. 3 (1991): 323–325.

Smith, Zadie. "On 'Crash.'" *New York Review of Books* 61, no. 12 (2014): 12–14.

Sobchack, Vivian. "Baudrillard's Obscenity." *Science Fiction Studies* 18, no. 3 (1991): 327–329.

Stanley, Rachael. "'The Scientist on Safari': J. G. Ballard and the Naturalist Gaze." *Textual Practice* 29, no. 6 (2015): 1165–1185.

Tew, Philip. "Acts of Reconsideration: J. G. Ballard (1930–2009) Annotating and Revising Editions of *The Atrocity Exhibition*." *Textual Practice* 26, no. 3 (2012): 399–420.

Tomberg, Jaak. "Morality and Amorality in Ba(Udri)Llard's Crash: A Poetic Perspective." *Science-Fiction Studies* 47, no. 1 (2020): 47–72.

Trexler, Adam, and Adeline Johns-Putra. "Climate Change in Literature and Literary Criticism." *WIREs Climate Change* 2, no. 2 (March 1, 2011): 185–200.

SPECIAL ISSUES OF JOURNALS AND MAGAZINES

Critical Quarterly, "Ben Wheatley, J. G. Ballard, and High-Rise," volume 58, no. 1 (2016), 1, E1–E6, 3–128.

Green Letters, "J. G. Ballard and the 'Natural' World," volume 22, no. 4 (2018), 341–456.

Interzone (April 1996).

Literary Geographies, "Ballard's Island: Histories, Modernities and Materialities," volume 2, no. 1 (2016), 1–121.

INDEX